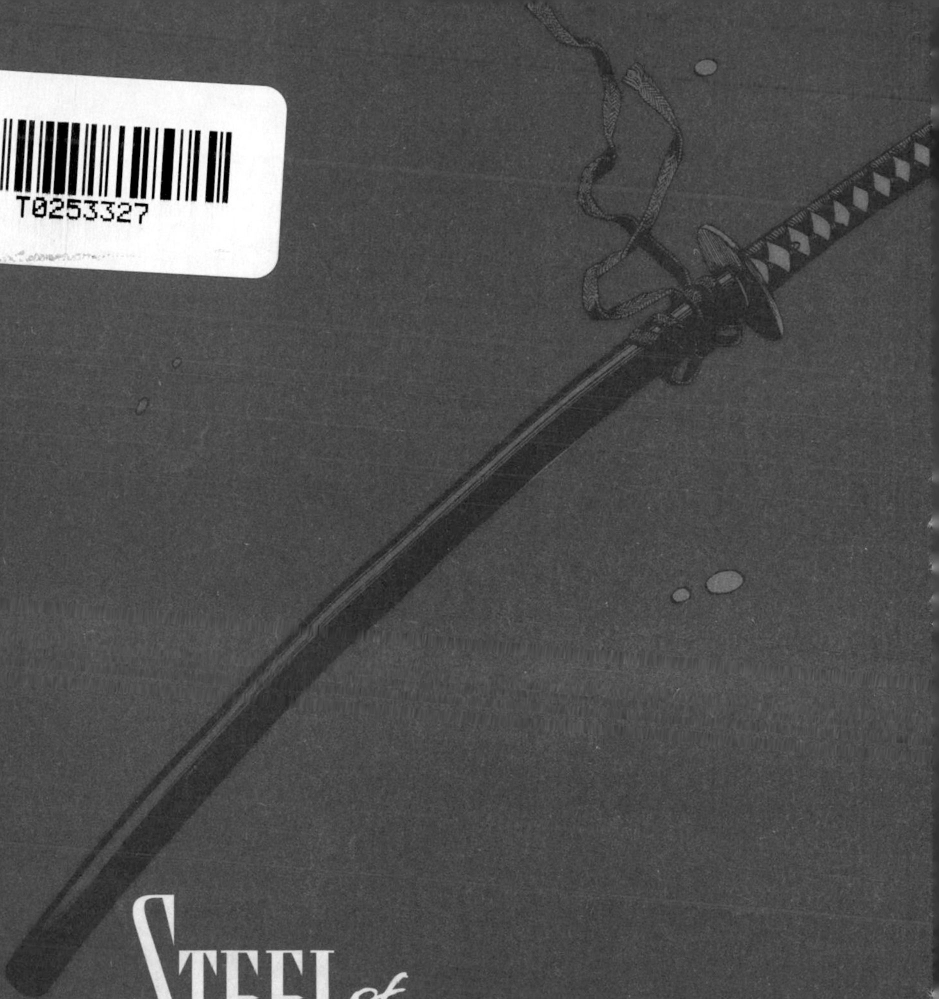

STEEL of the CELESTIAL SHADOWS 3

STORY & ART

DARUMA MATSUURA

SUPERVISION BY

TOSHIKI MIZUTANI
NOBORU HISAYAMA

〘 CHARACTERS 〙

MADARA

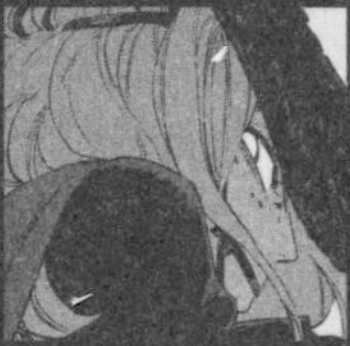

A woman shunned by society for her ability. She stands in the way of Konosuke and Aki.

AKI

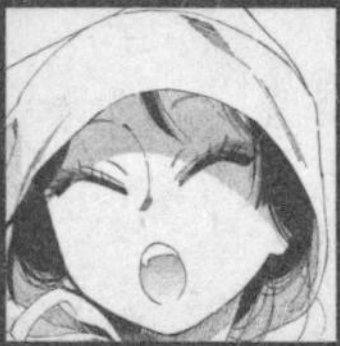

A bright and cheery traveling *ichiko* medium. She's arrived in Edo for reasons of her own.

TSUKI

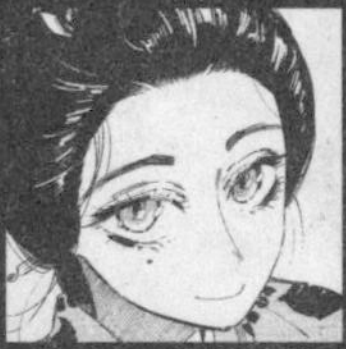

An otherworldly beauty who mysteriously appeared from nowhere to wed Konosuke. Why does she adore him so?

RYUDO KONOSUKE

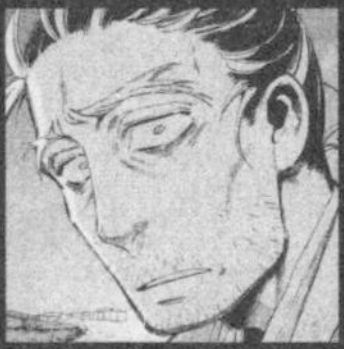

A low-ranking samurai who can't seem to catch a break. Metal warps when he touches it or it gets near his body, so he can't wield a blade.

Ryudo Konosuke is a low-ranking samurai struggling to survive abject poverty. He owes his destitution to his seemingly cursed ability to warp any metal that comes near him. One day, a beautiful woman named Tsuki shows up at Konosuke's door and marries him. Their happiness is short-lived, however, as Tsuki is whisked away by a strange man with supernatural powers. When Aki—a blind medium with the ability to view a person's future—finds her way to Konosuke, he is determined to use his new friend's power to save Tsuki. But there are dark forces conspiring against him...

[CONTENTS]

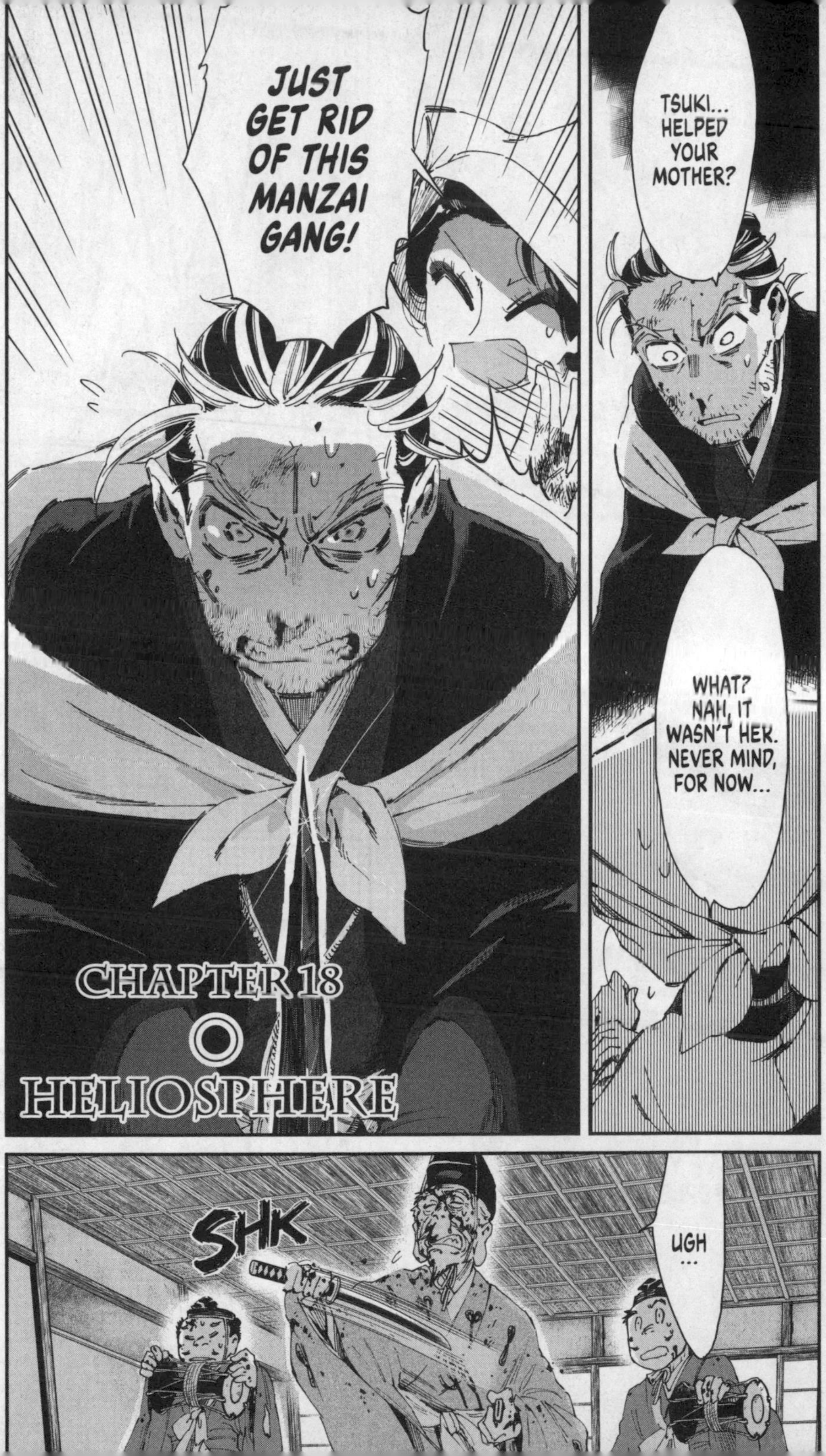
TSUKI... HELPED YOUR MOTHER?
WHAT? NAH, IT WASN'T HER. NEVER MIND, FOR NOW...
JUST GET RID OF THIS MANZAI GANG!
CHAPTER 18
O HELIOSPHERE
UGH ...
SHK

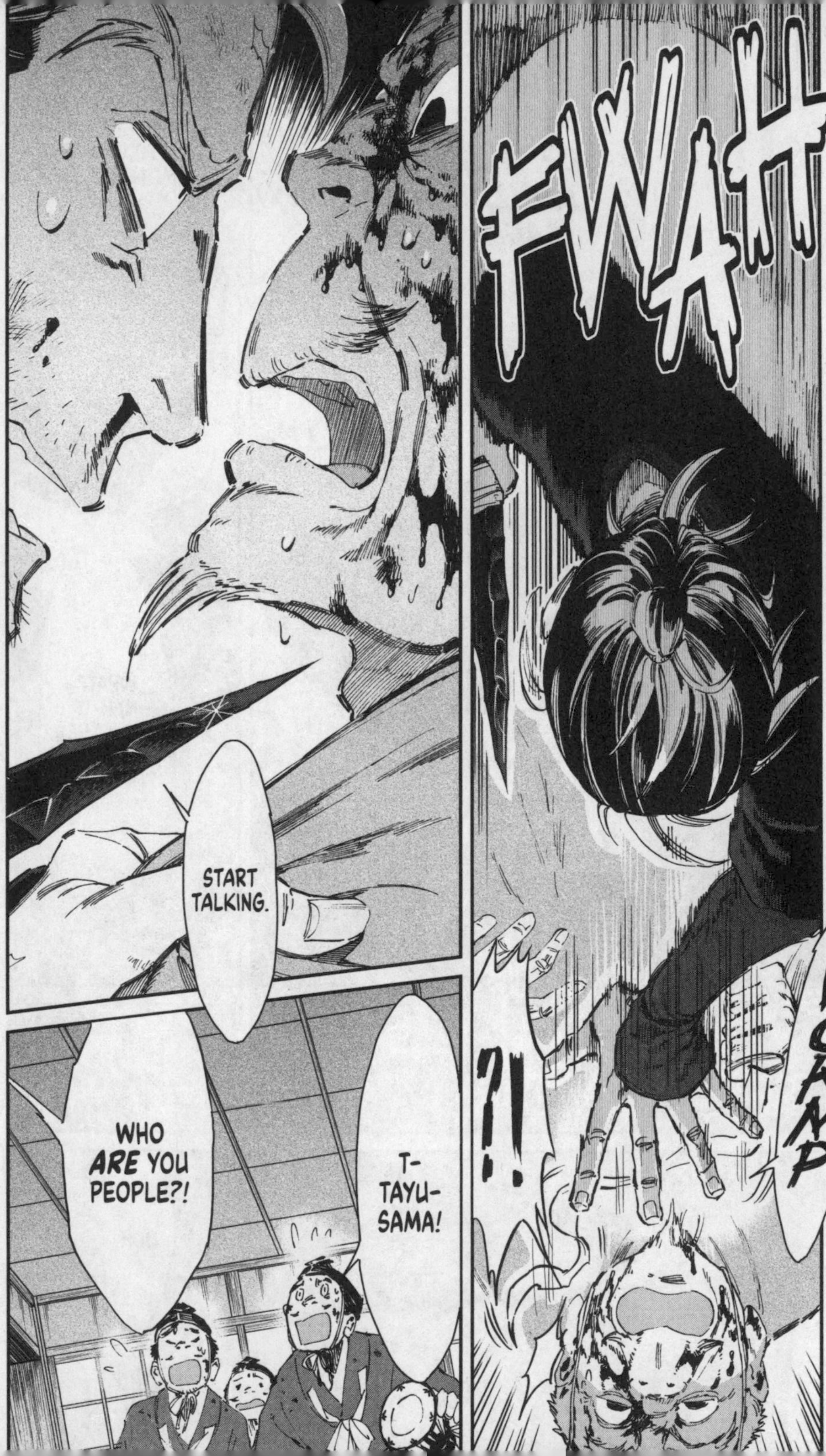
FWAH
WORMP
?!
START TALKING.
T-TAYU-SAMA!
WHO *ARE* YOU PEOPLE?!

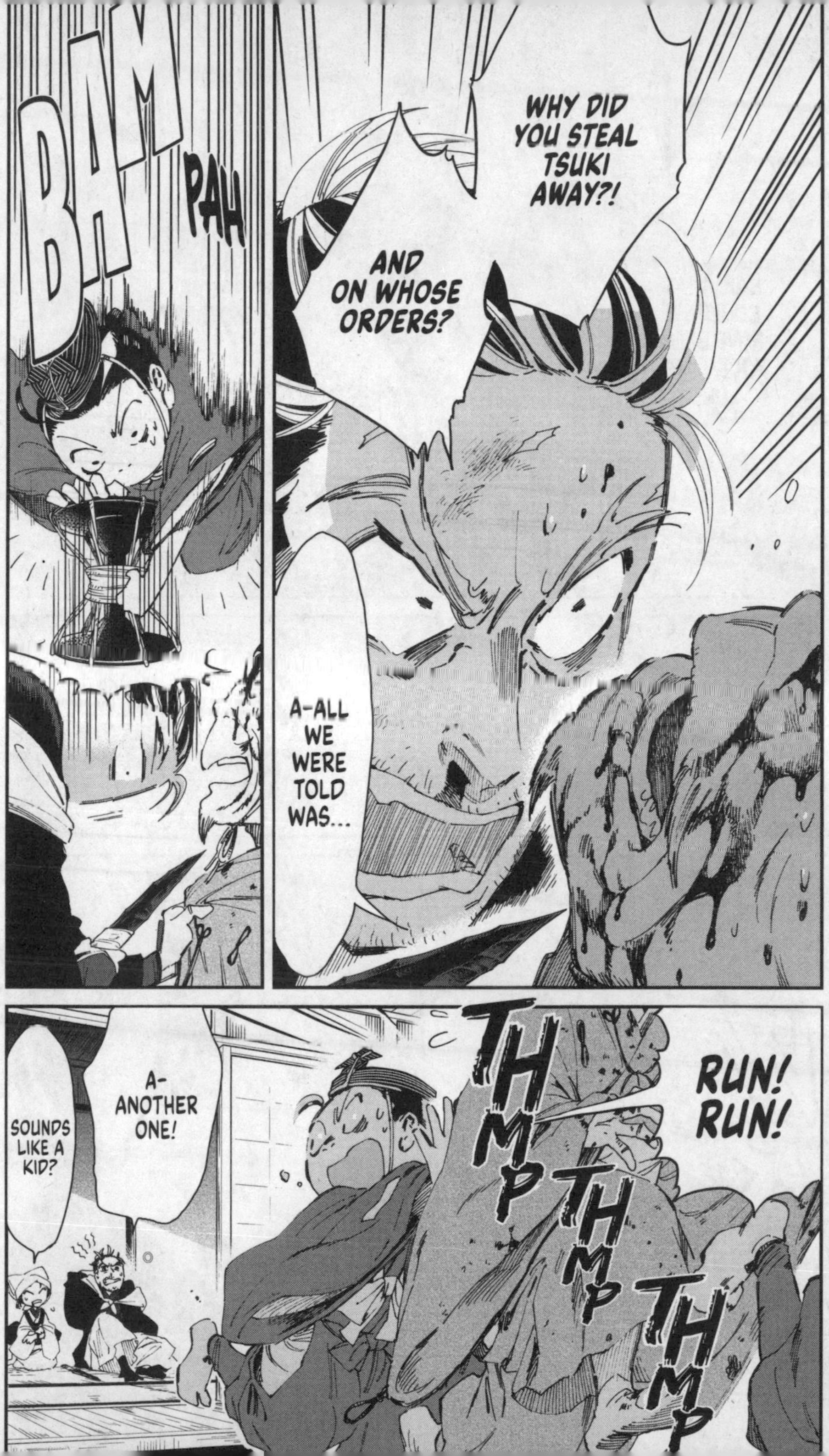
WHY DID YOU STEAL TSUKI AWAY?!
AND ON WHOSE ORDERS?
A-ALL WE WERE TOLD WAS...
BAM
PAH
RUN! RUN!
THMP THMP THMP
A- ANOTHER ONE!
SOUNDS LIKE A KID?

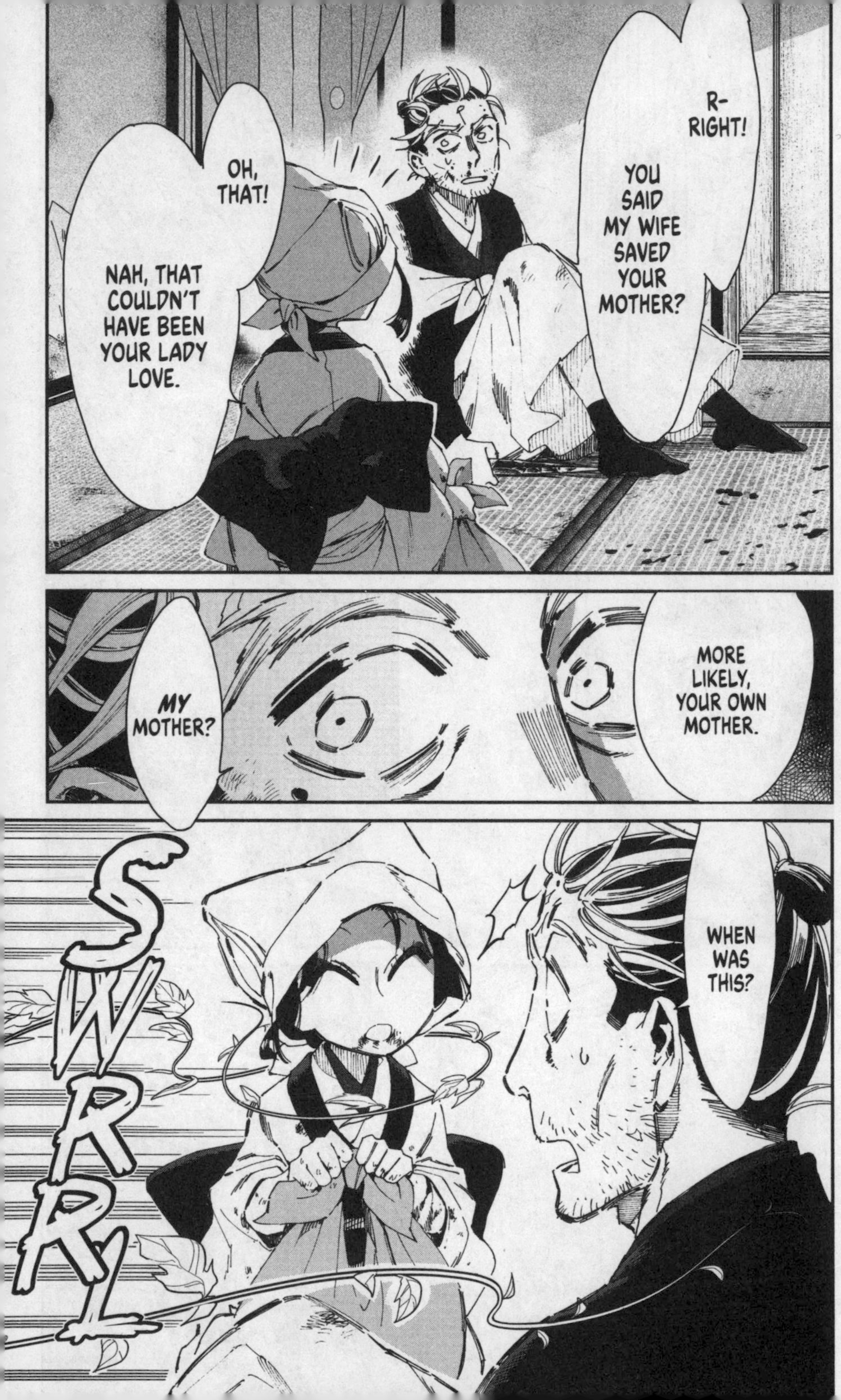
R-
RIGHT!
YOU SAID MY WIFE SAVED YOUR MOTHER?
OH, THAT!
NAH, THAT COULDN'T HAVE BEEN YOUR LADY LOVE.
MORE LIKELY, YOUR OWN MOTHER.
MY MOTHER?
WHEN WAS THIS?
SWRRL

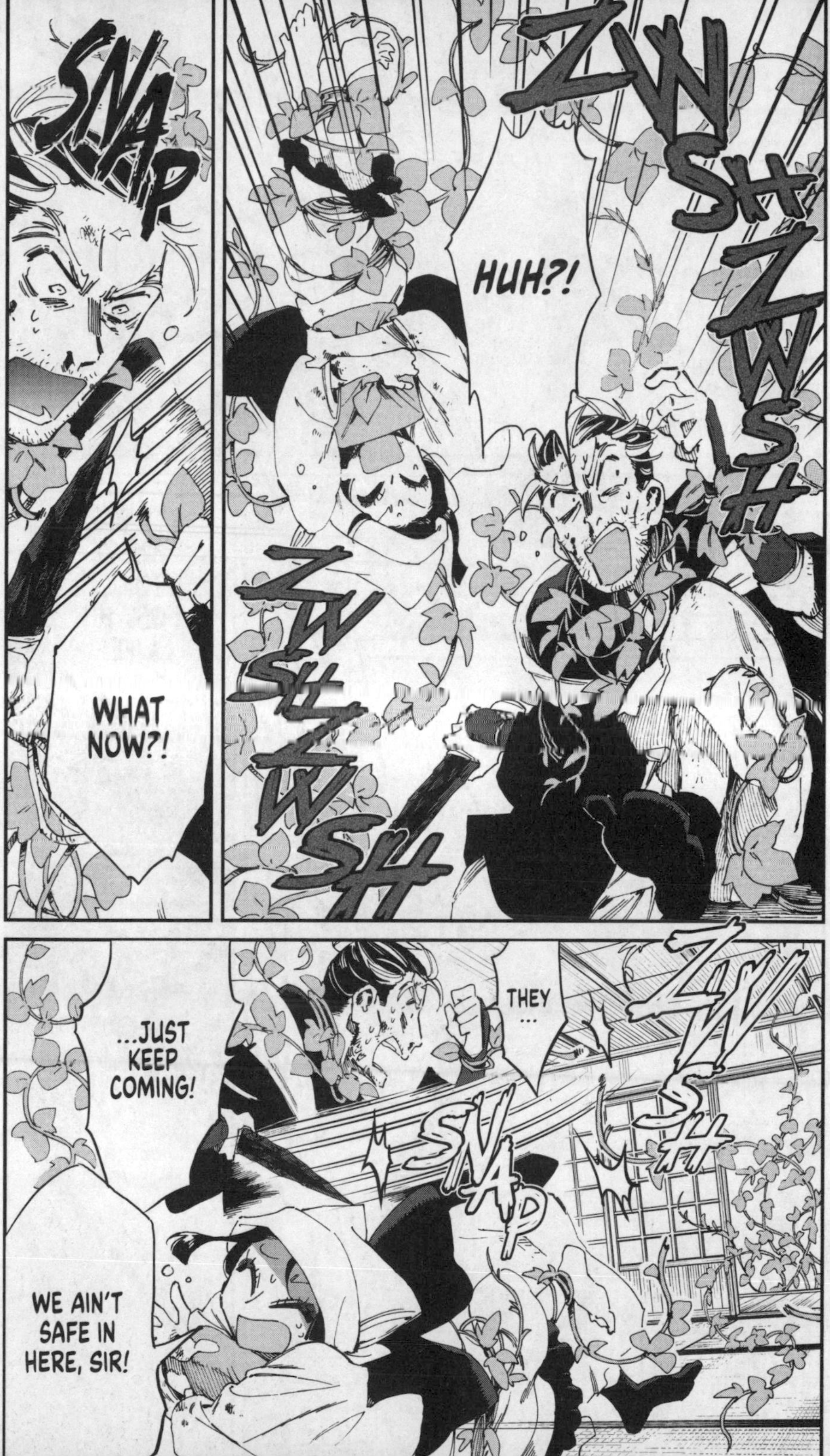
ZWSH
ZWSH
HUH?!
ZWSH
ZWSH
SNAP
WHAT NOW?!
ZWSH
THEY...
...JUST KEEP COMING!
SNAP
WE AIN'T SAFE IN HERE, SIR!

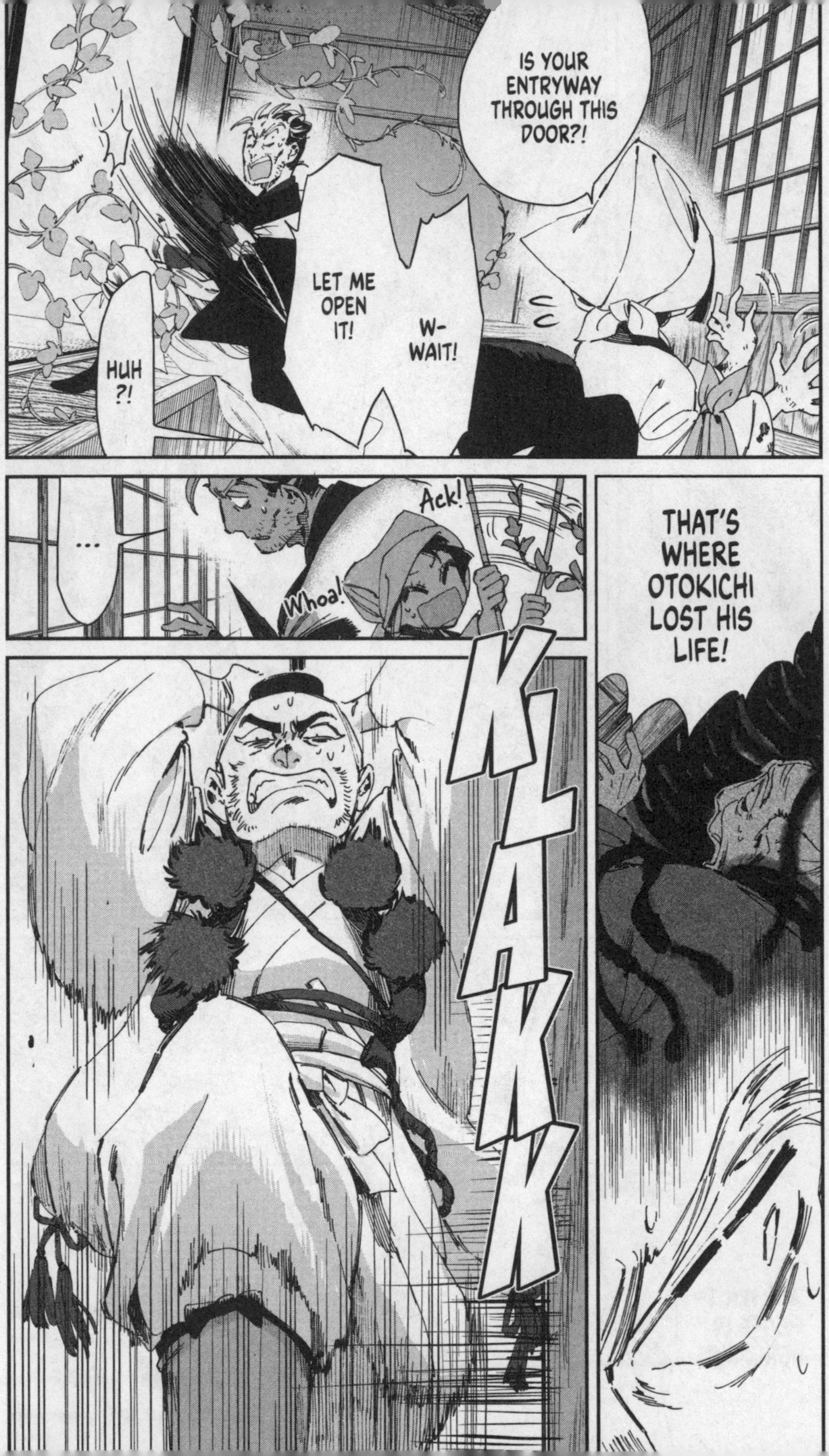
IS YOUR ENTRYWAY THROUGH THIS DOOR?!
LET ME OPEN IT!
W-WAIT!
HUH?!
THAT'S WHERE OTOKICHI LOST HIS LIFE!
Ack!
...
Whoa!
KLAK

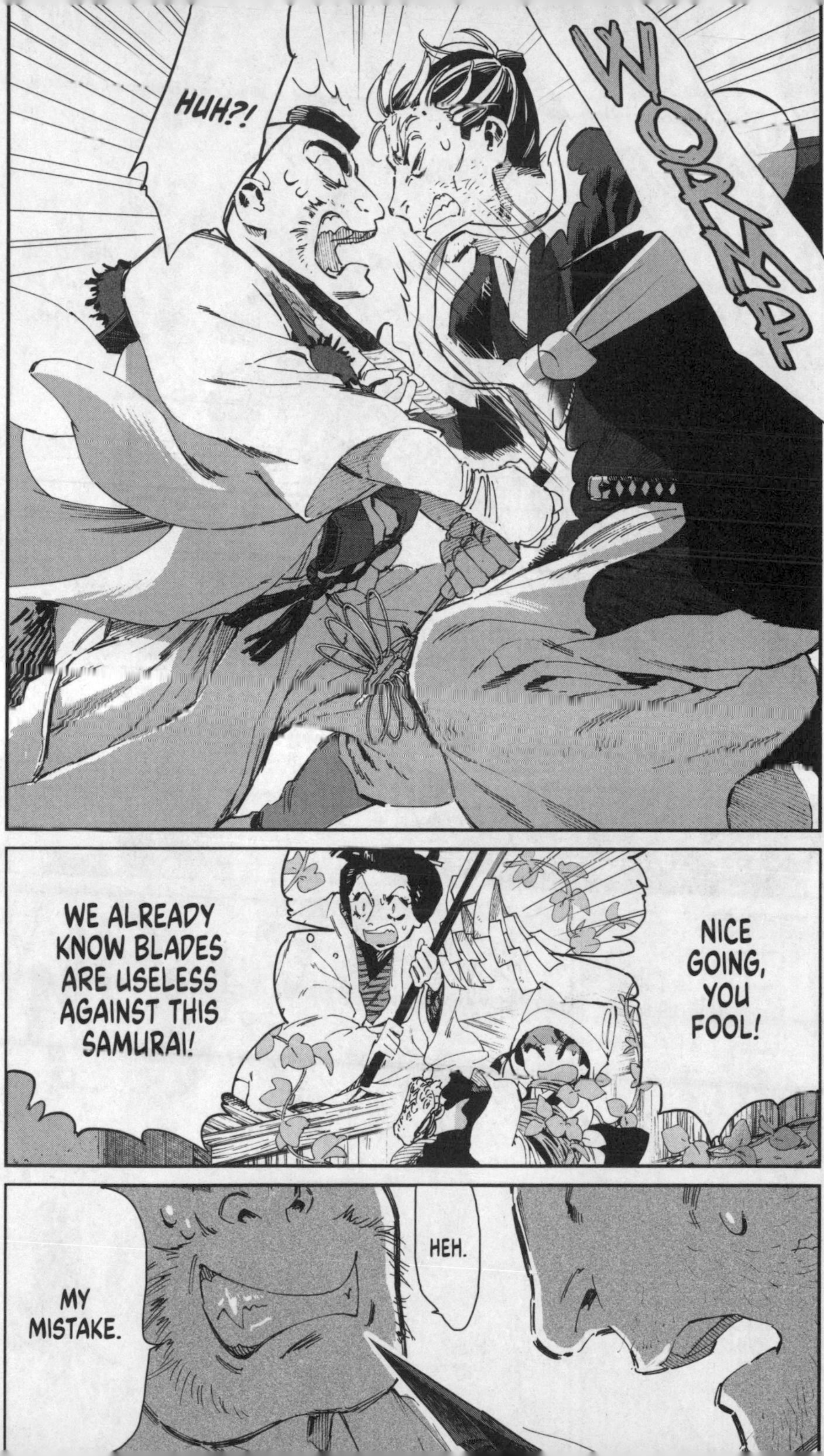
WOMP
HUH?!
NICE GOING, YOU FOOL!
WE ALREADY KNOW BLADES ARE USELESS AGAINST THIS SAMURAI!
HEH.
MY MISTAKE.

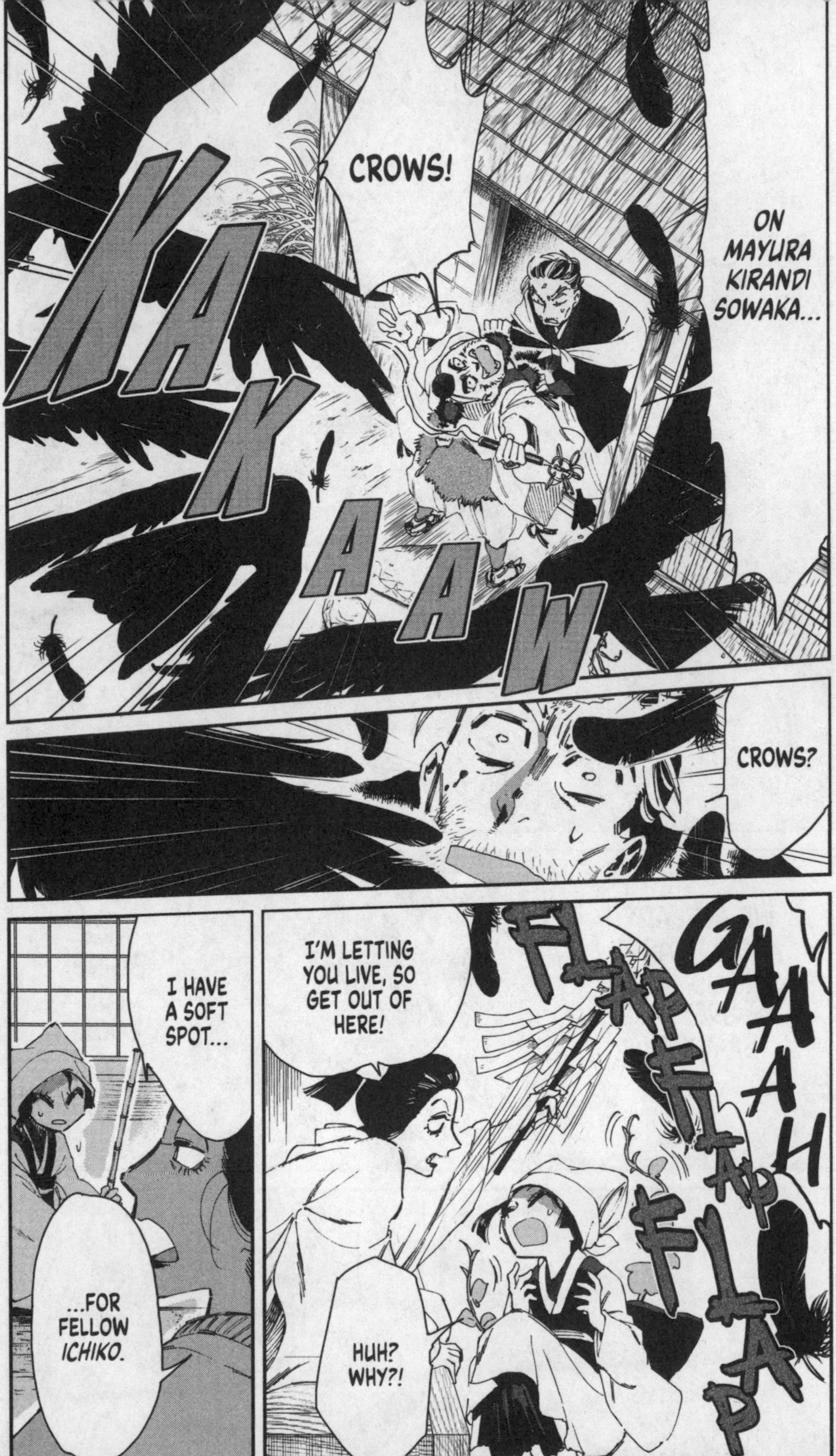
ON MAYURA KIRANDI SOWAKA...
CROWS!
KAKAAAW
CROWS?
GAAAAH
FLAP FLAP FLAP FLAP
I'M LETTING YOU LIVE, SO GET OUT OF HERE!
HUH? WHY?!
I HAVE A SOFT SPOT...
...FOR FELLOW ICHIKO.

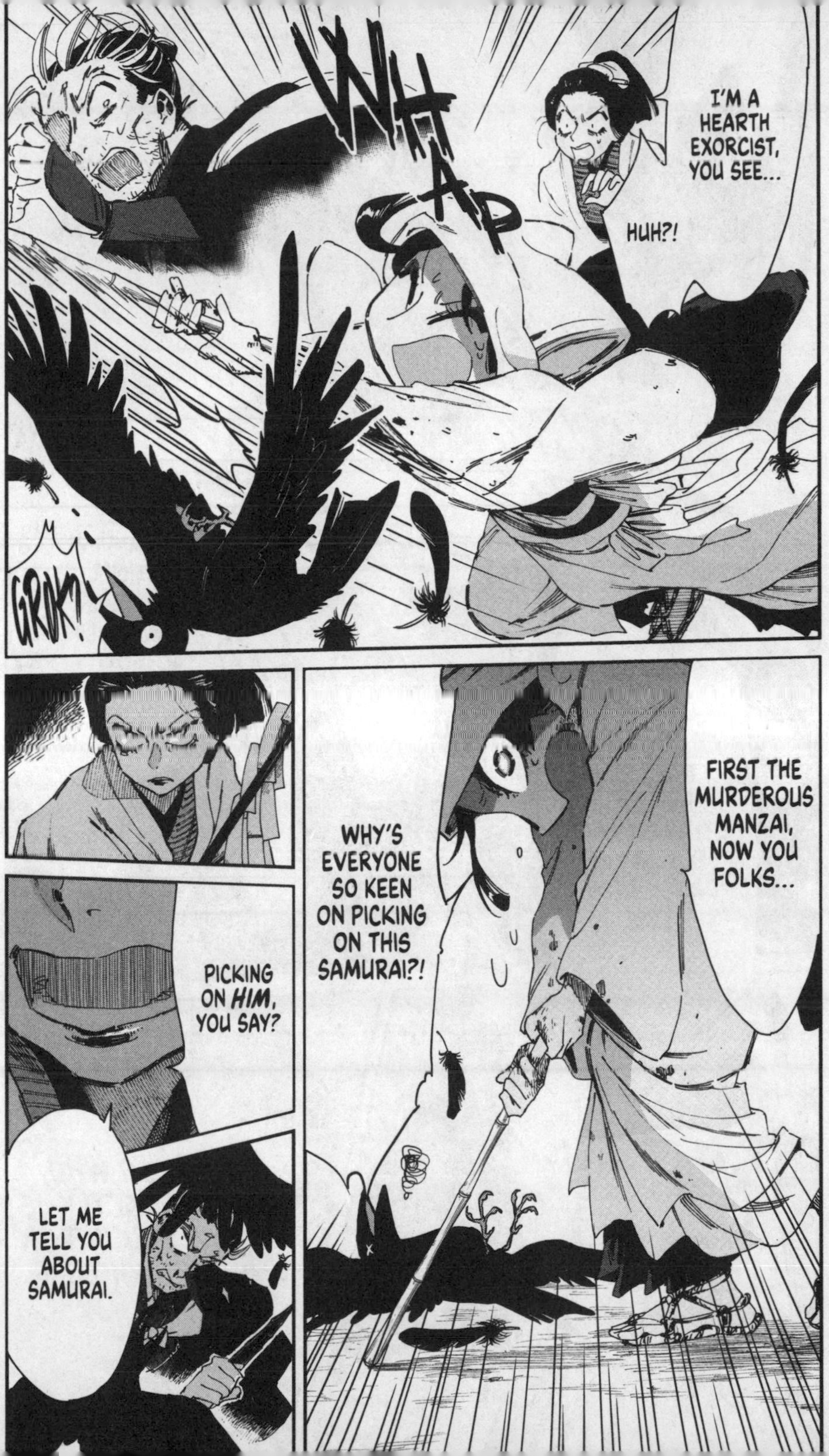
I'M A HEARTH EXORCIST, YOU SEE...
HUH?!
WHAP
GROK?!
FIRST THE MURDEROUS MANZAI, NOW YOU FOLKS...
WHY'S EVERYONE SO KEEN ON PICKING ON THIS SAMURAI?!
PICKING ON *HIM*, YOU SAY?
LET ME TELL YOU ABOUT SAMURAI.

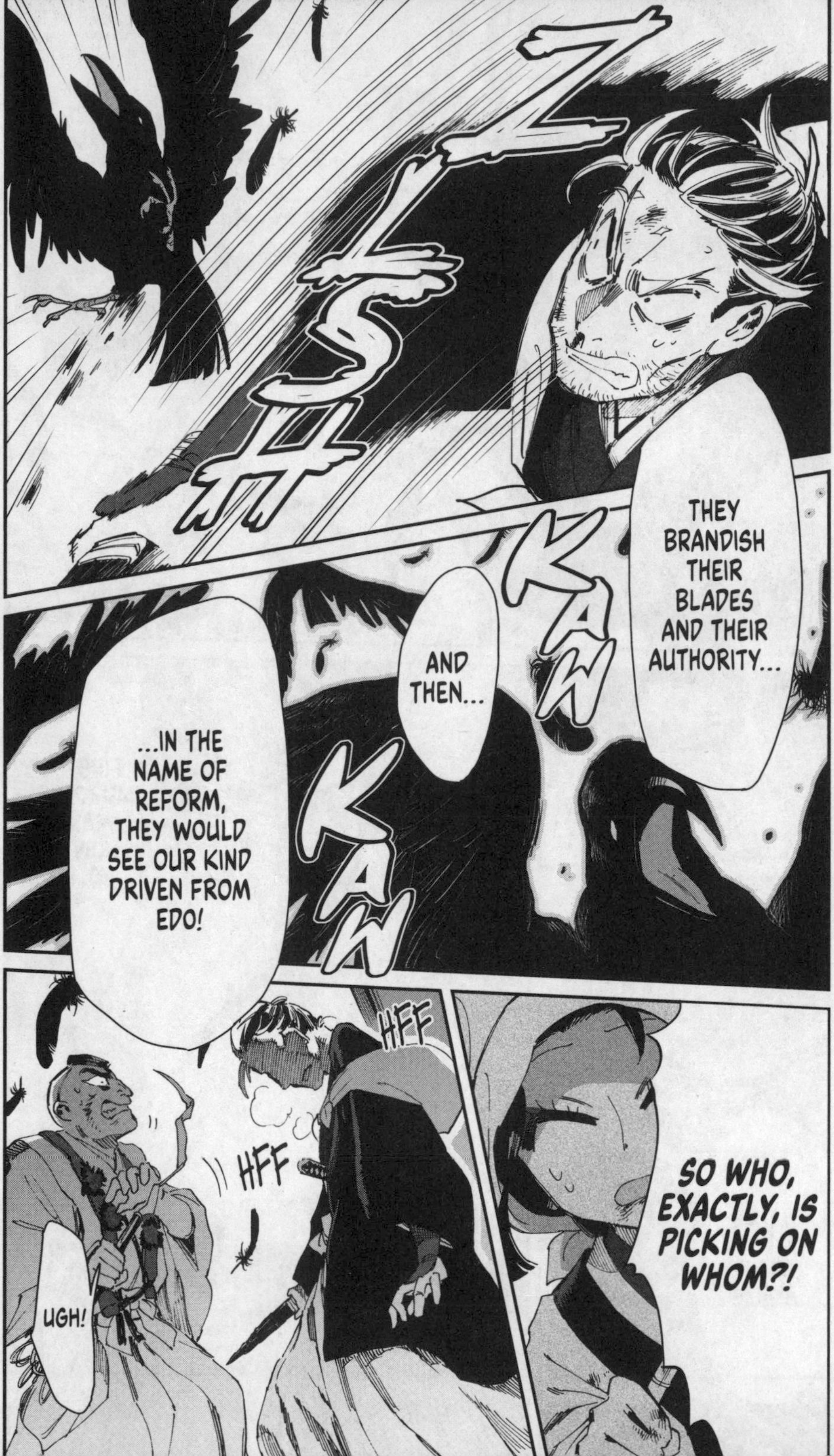
THEY BRANDISH THEIR BLADES AND THEIR AUTHORITY...
KAW
AND THEN...
KAW
...IN THE NAME OF REFORM, THEY WOULD SEE OUR KIND DRIVEN FROM EDO!
SO WHO, EXACTLY, IS PICKING ON WHOM?!
HFF
HFF
UGH!

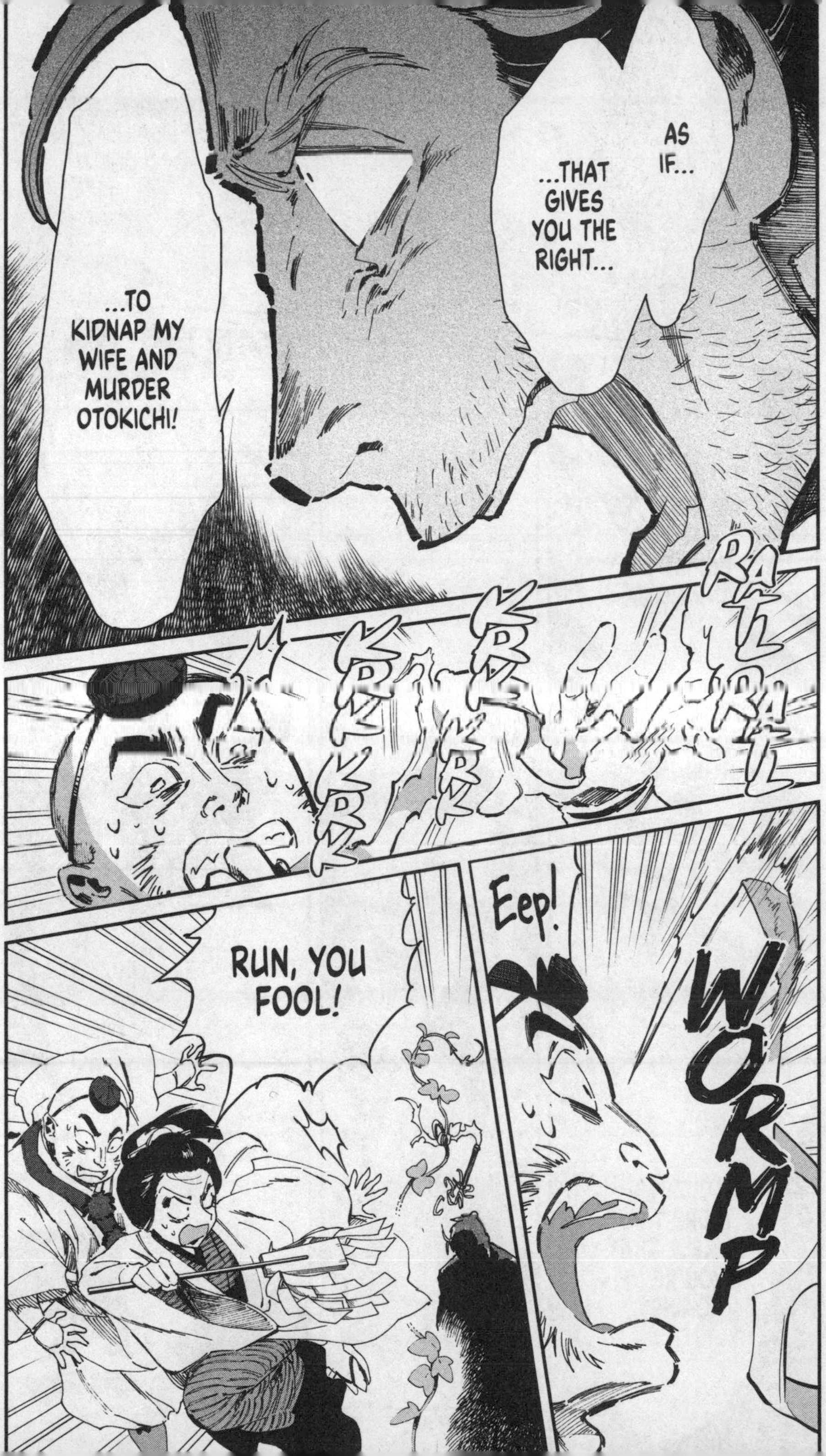
AS IF...
...THAT GIVES YOU THE RIGHT...
...TO KIDNAP MY WIFE AND MURDER OTOKICHI!
Eep!
WORMP
RUN, YOU FOOL!

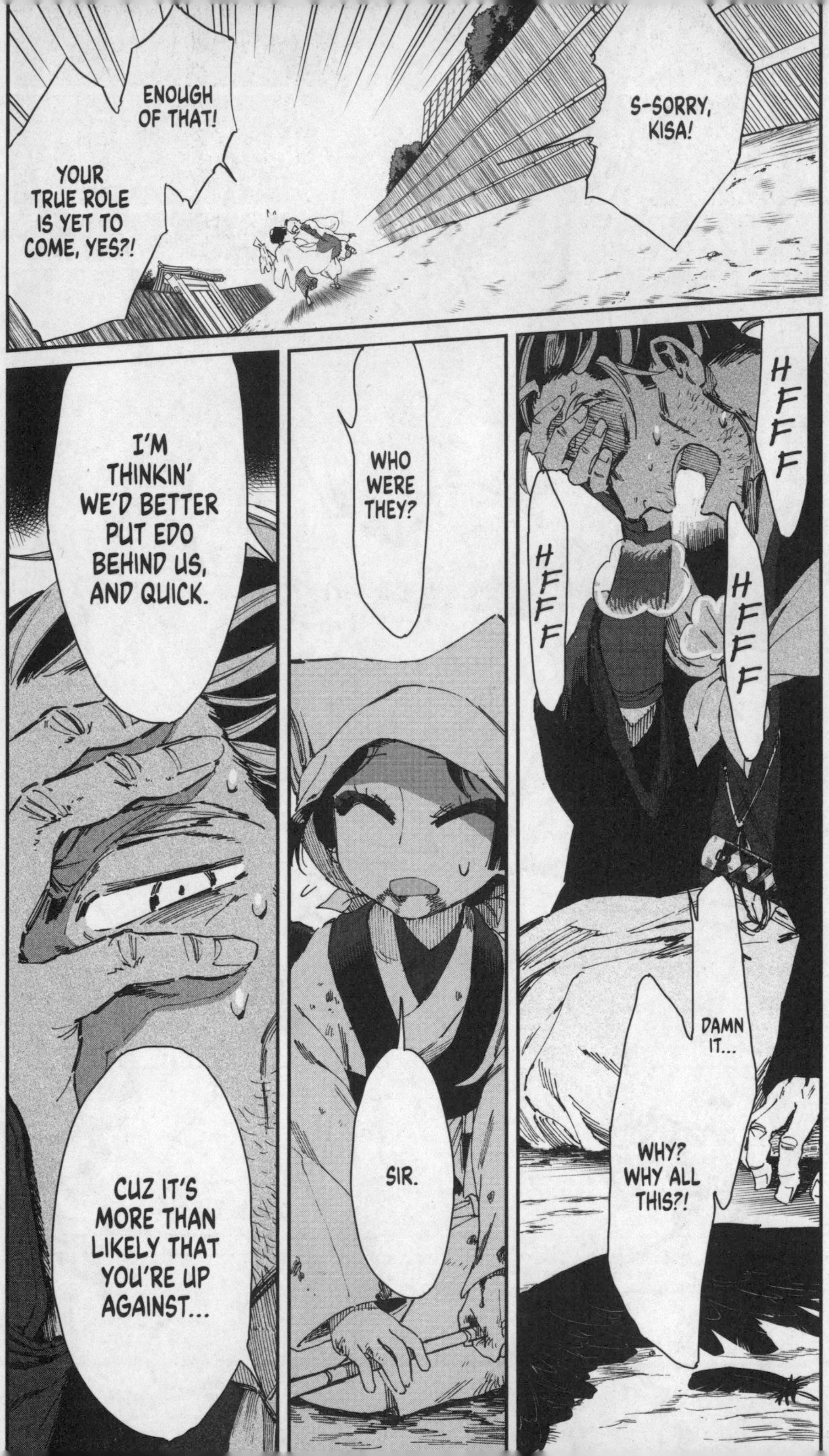
S-SORRY, KISA!
ENOUGH OF THAT!
YOUR TRUE ROLE IS YET TO COME, YES?!
HFFF
HFFF
HFFF
DAMN IT...
WHY? WHY ALL THIS?!
WHO WERE THEY?
SIR.
I'M THINKIN' WE'D BETTER PUT EDO BEHIND US, AND QUICK.
CUZ IT'S MORE THAN LIKELY THAT YOU'RE UP AGAINST...

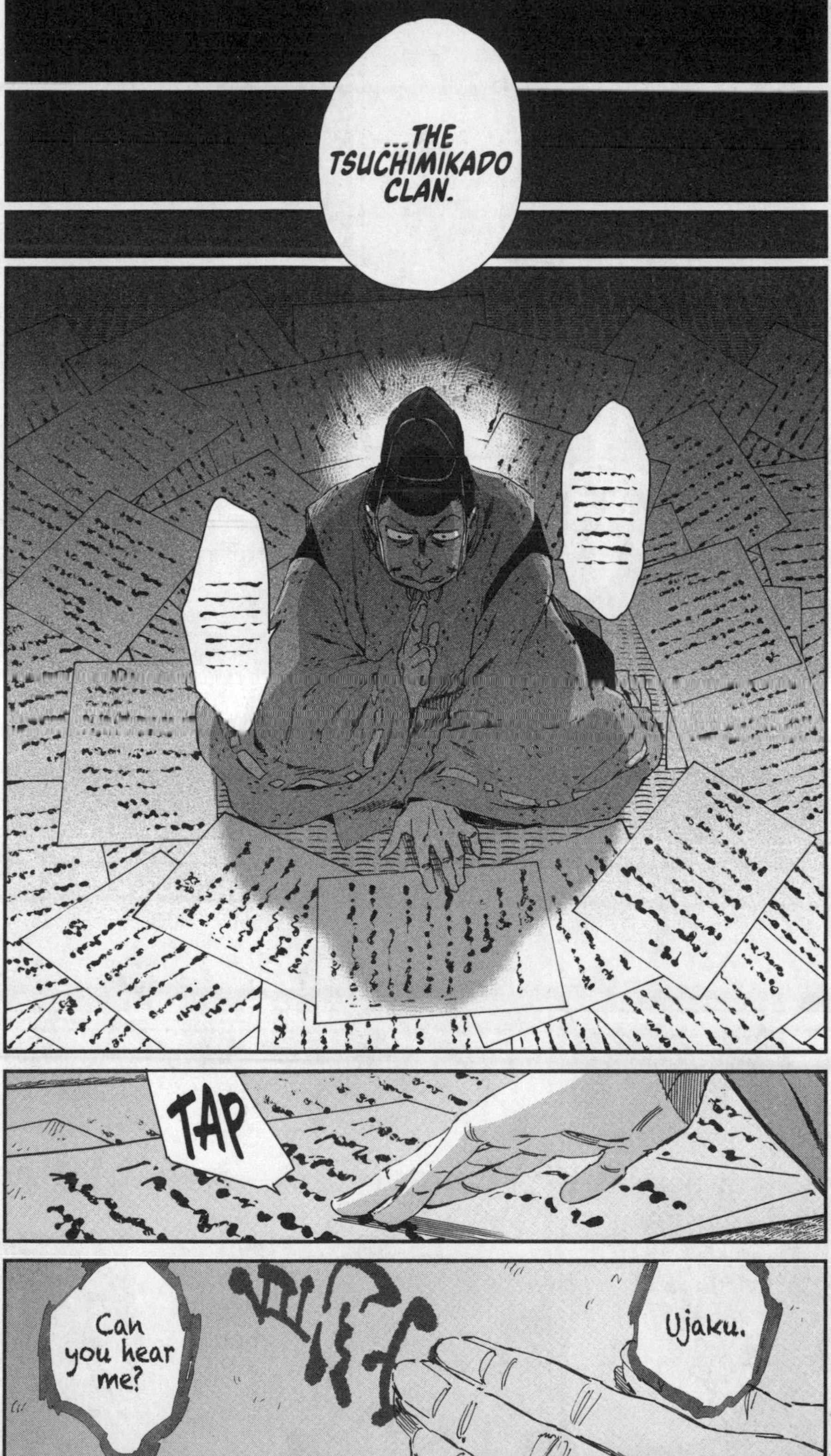
...THE TSUCHIMIKADO CLAN.
TAP
Ujaku.
Can you hear me?

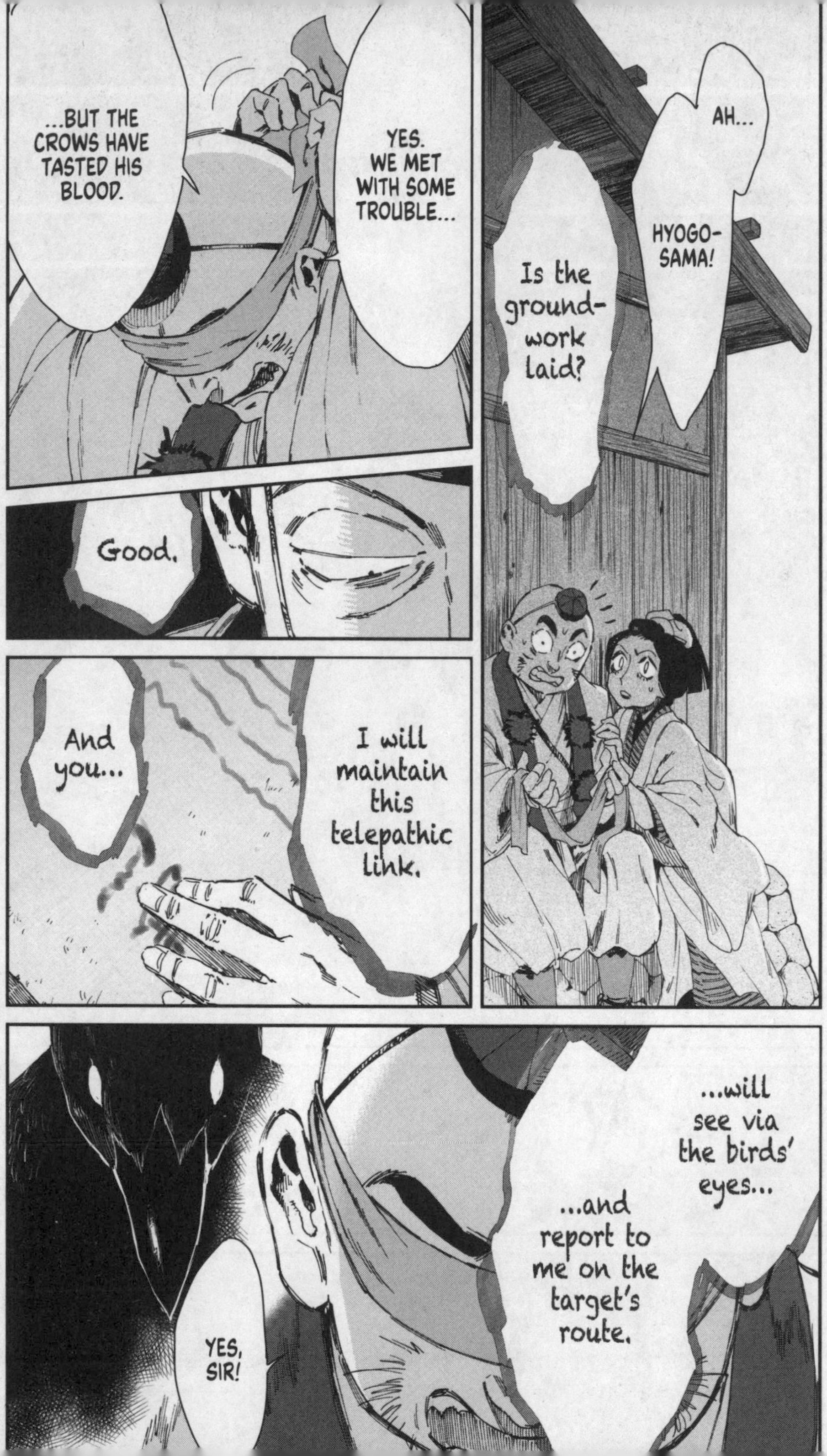
AH...
HYOGO-SAMA!
Is the ground-work laid?
YES. WE MET WITH SOME TROUBLE...
...BUT THE CROWS HAVE TASTED HIS BLOOD.
Good.
I will maintain this telepathic link.
And you...
...will see via the birds' eyes...
...and report to me on the target's route.
YES, SIR!

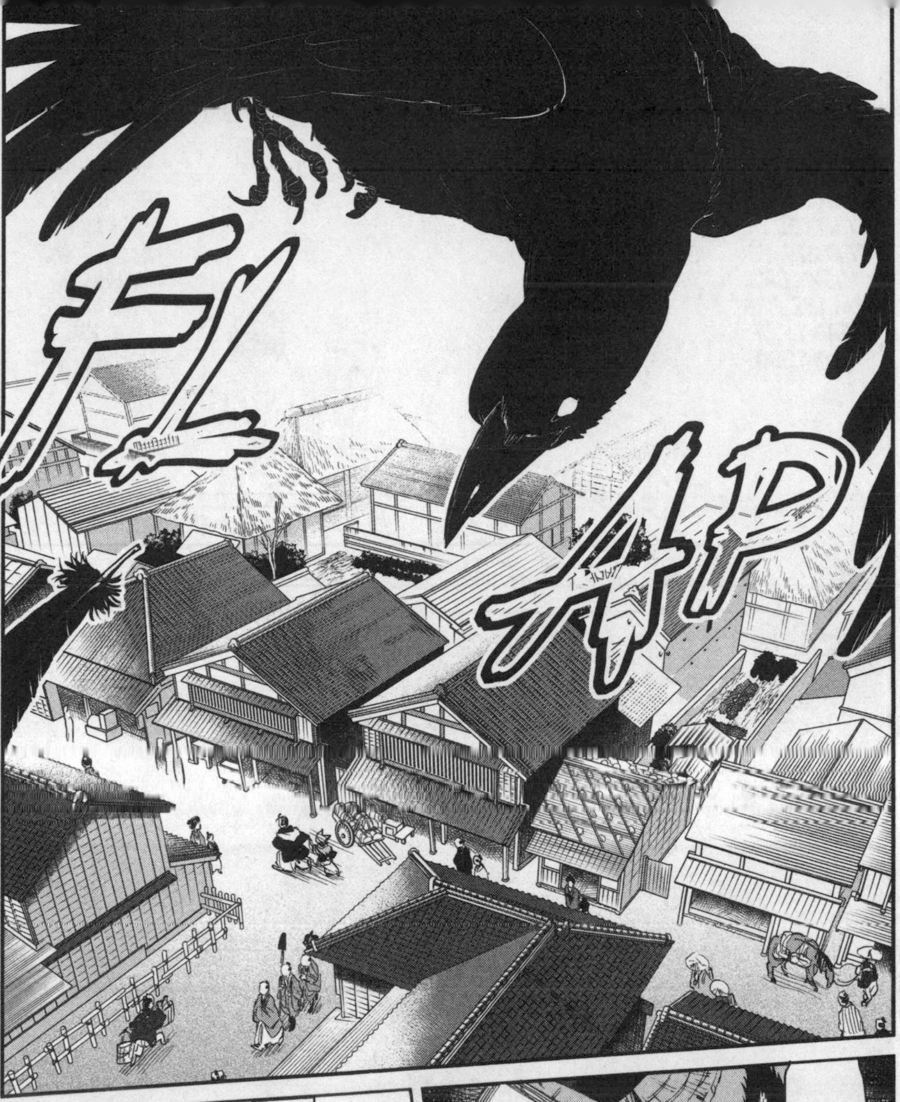
FLAP

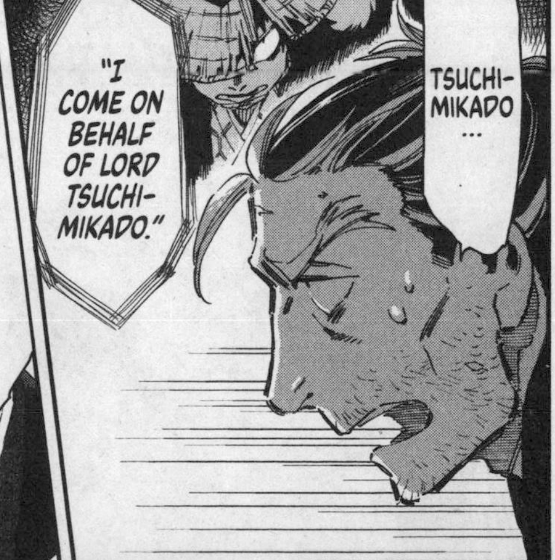
TSUCHI-MIKADO...
"I COME ON BEHALF OF LORD TSUCHI-MIKADO."

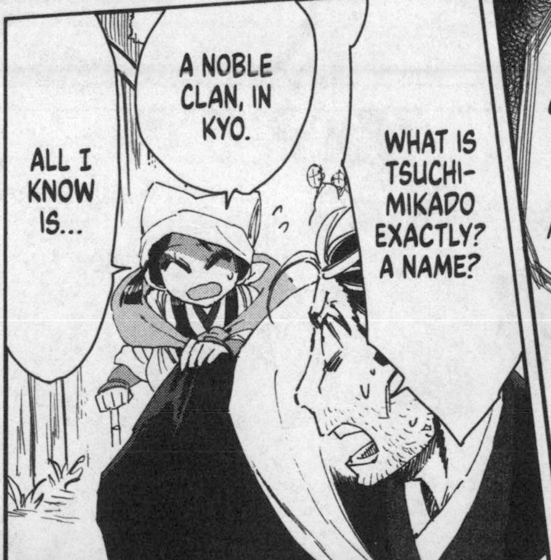
WHAT IS TSUCHI-MIKADO EXACTLY? A NAME?
ALL I KNOW IS...
A NOBLE CLAN, IN KYO.

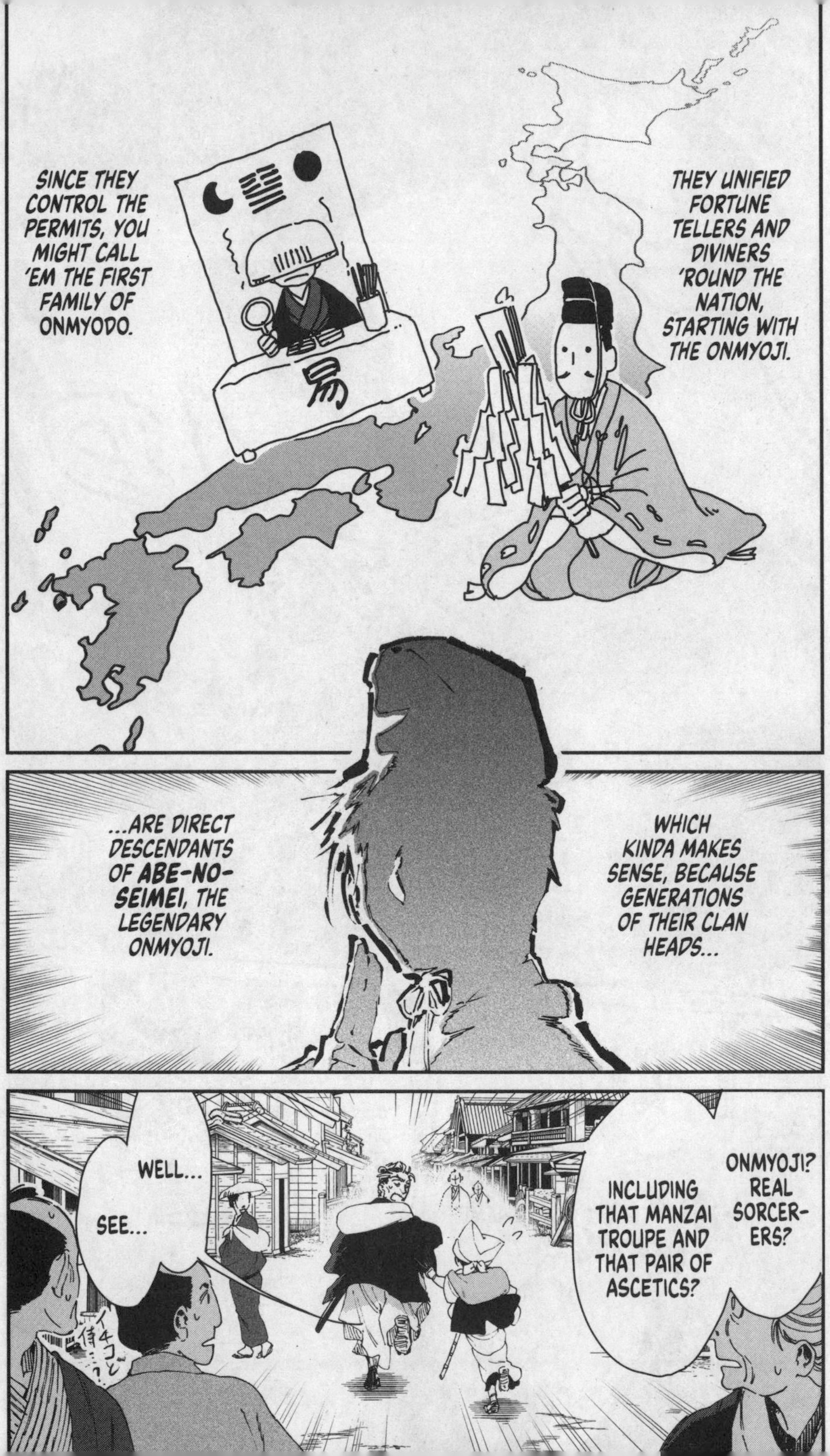
THEY UNIFIED FORTUNE TELLERS AND DIVINERS 'ROUND THE NATION, STARTING WITH THE ONMYOJI.
SINCE THEY CONTROL THE PERMITS, YOU MIGHT CALL 'EM THE FIRST FAMILY OF ONMYODO.
易
WHICH KINDA MAKES SENSE, BECAUSE GENERATIONS OF THEIR CLAN HEADS...
...ARE DIRECT DESCENDANTS OF **ABE-NO-SEIMEI**, THE LEGENDARY ONMYOJI.
ONMYOJI? REAL SORCERERS?
INCLUDING THAT MANZAI TROUPE AND THAT PAIR OF ASCETICS?
WELL...
SEE...

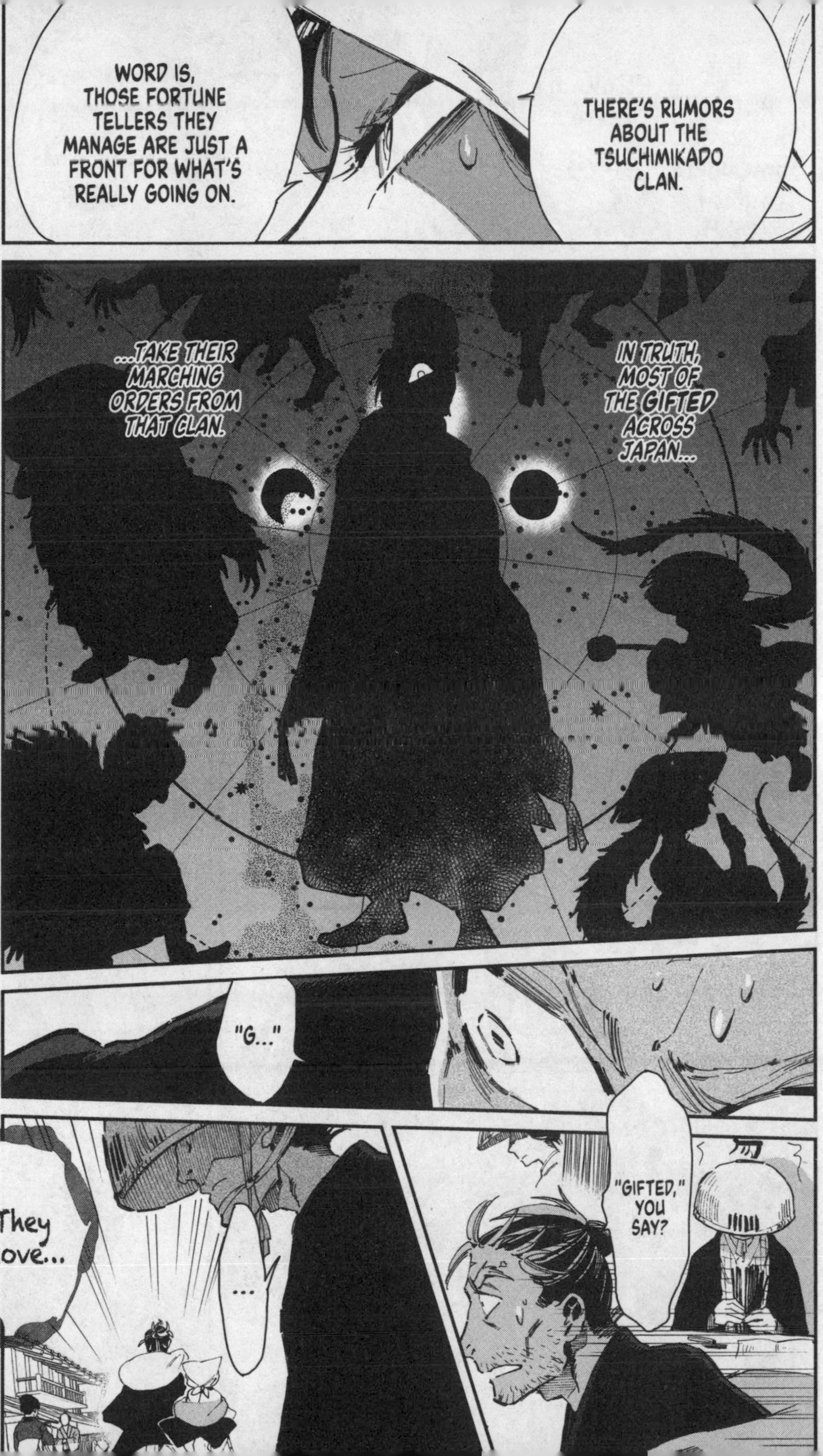
THERE'S RUMORS ABOUT THE TSUCHIMIKADO CLAN.
WORD IS, THOSE FORTUNE TELLERS THEY MANAGE ARE JUST A FRONT FOR WHAT'S REALLY GOING ON.
IN TRUTH, MOST OF THE GIFTED ACROSS JAPAN...
...TAKE THEIR MARCHING ORDERS FROM THAT CLAN.
"G..."
"GIFTED," YOU SAY?
...
They move...

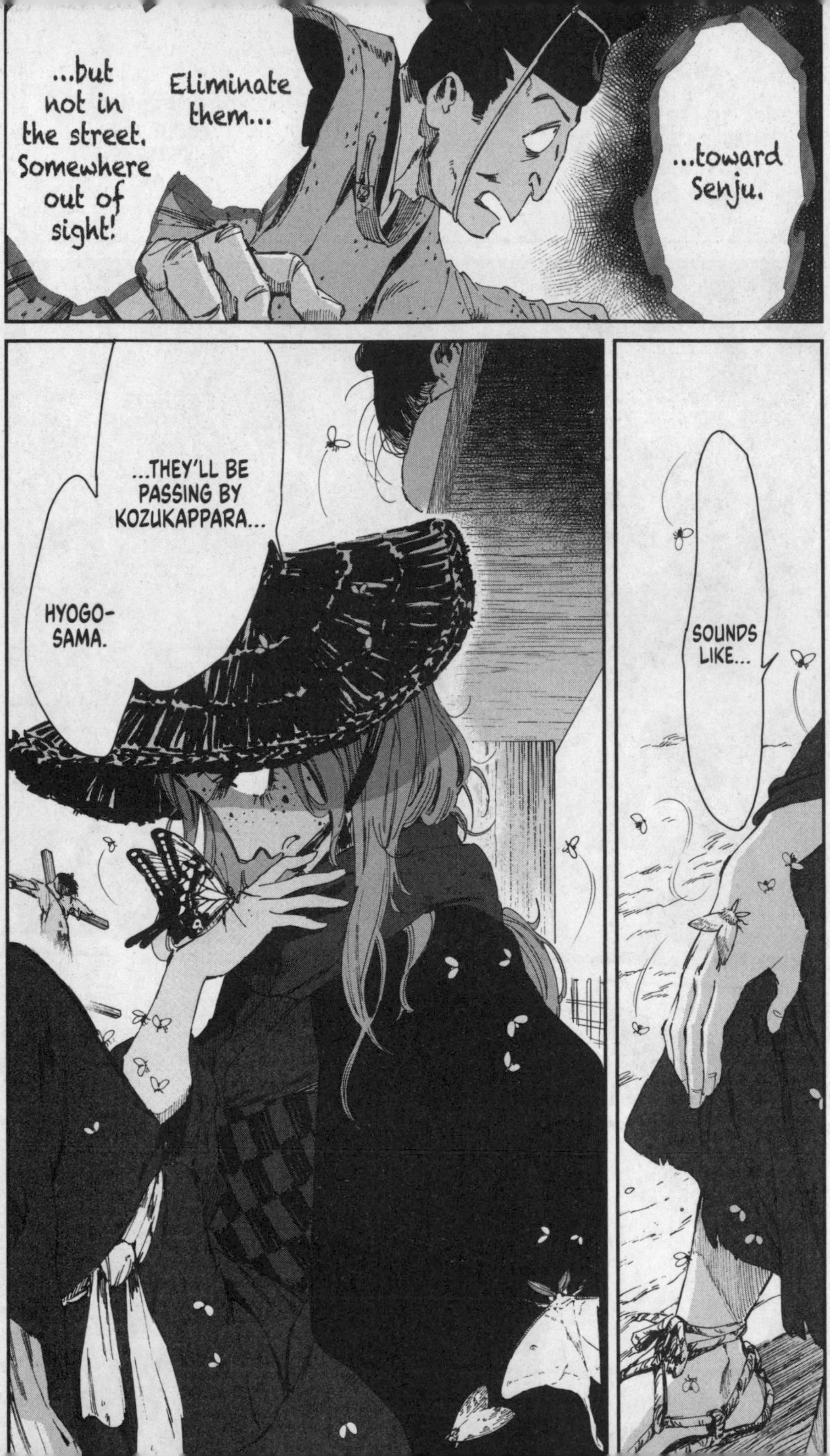
...toward Senju.
Eliminate them...
...but not in the street. Somewhere out of sight!
SOUNDS LIKE...
...THEY'LL BE PASSING BY KOZUKAPPARA...
HYOGO-SAMA.

STEEL of the CELESTIAL SHADOWS

Trivia of the Celestial Shadows #①

Samurai Family's Hokonin Man-servants

- Divided into *wakado* (footman), *chugen* (attendant), and *komono* (lowliest servant).
- When a samurai reported to the castle for work, he would be accompanied by several such servants.
- The number of servants varied depending on family status and wealth. One might have two servants for every 100 *koku* of rice produced in a year (the koku being the standard measure of wealth at the time).
- However, many examples of *ukiyo-e* art portray a single samurai walking about with a single servant.
- A samurai unaccompanied by any servants while out and about would raise suspicions (at worst, the authorities might be alerted).
- Some servants worked for the same family for decades, while others might have been temps hired through an employment agency (Otokichi was the former type).

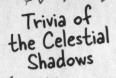

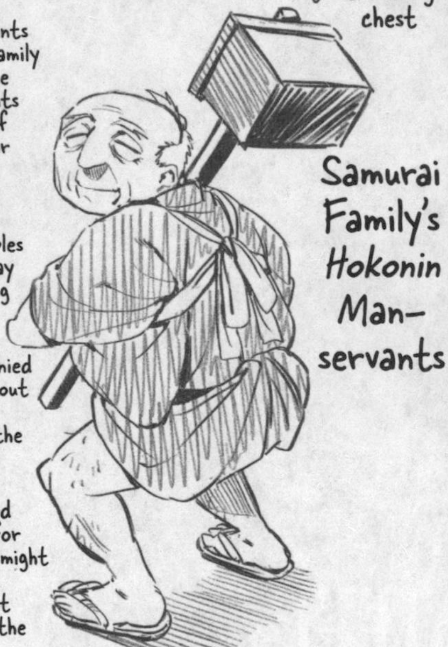

Hasami-bako traveling chest

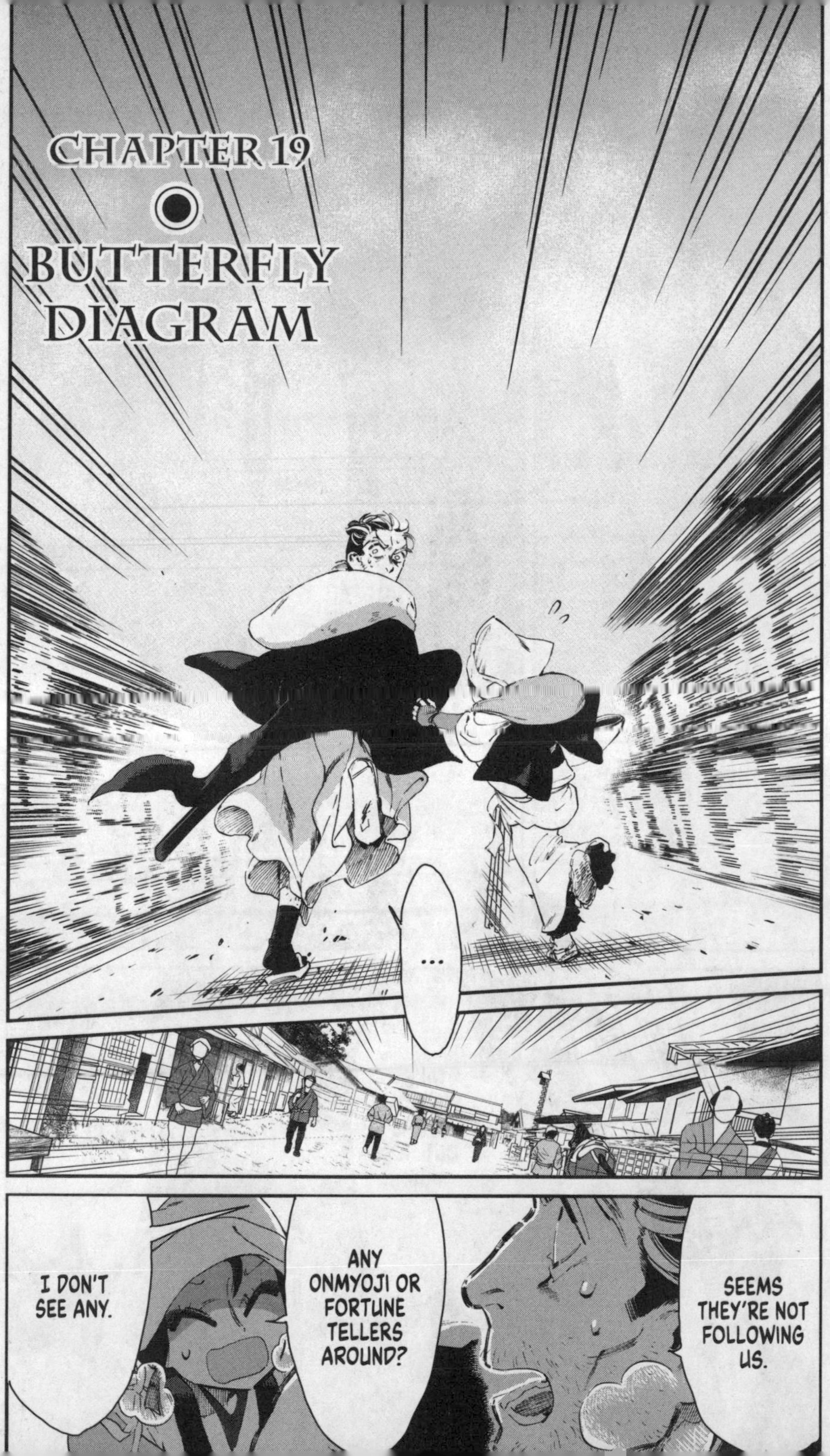
CHAPTER 19
BUTTERFLY DIAGRAM
...
SEEMS THEY'RE NOT FOLLOWING US.
ANY ONMYOJI OR FORTUNE TELLERS AROUND?
I DON'T SEE ANY.

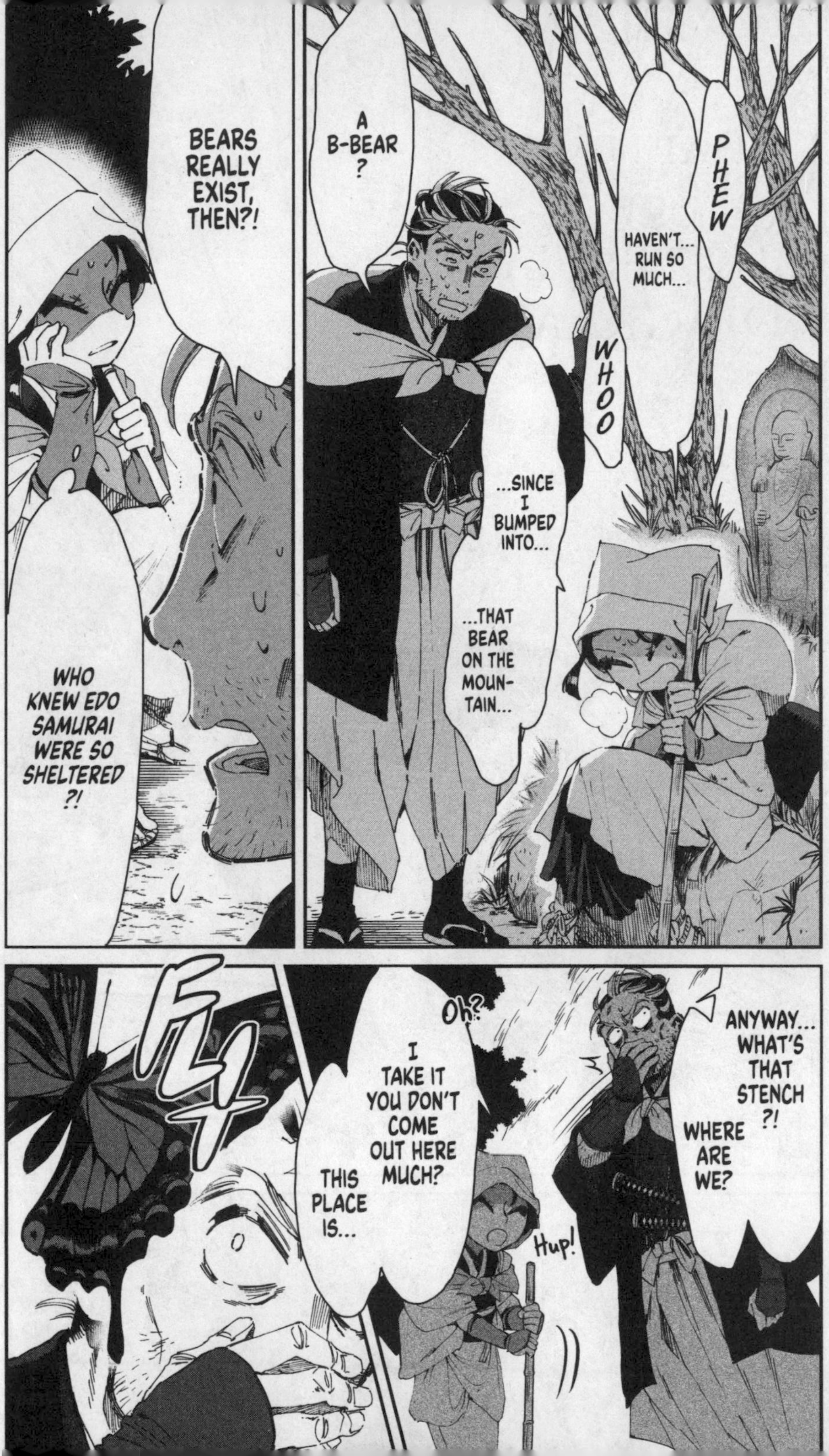
PHEW
WHOO
HAVEN'T... RUN SO MUCH...
...SINCE I BUMPED INTO...
...THAT BEAR ON THE MOUN-TAIN...
A B-BEAR?
BEARS REALLY EXIST, THEN?!
WHO KNEW EDO SAMURAI WERE SO SHELTERED?!
ANYWAY... WHAT'S THAT STENCH?!
WHERE ARE WE?
Hup!
Oh?
I TAKE IT YOU DON'T COME OUT HERE MUCH?
THIS PLACE IS...
FLY

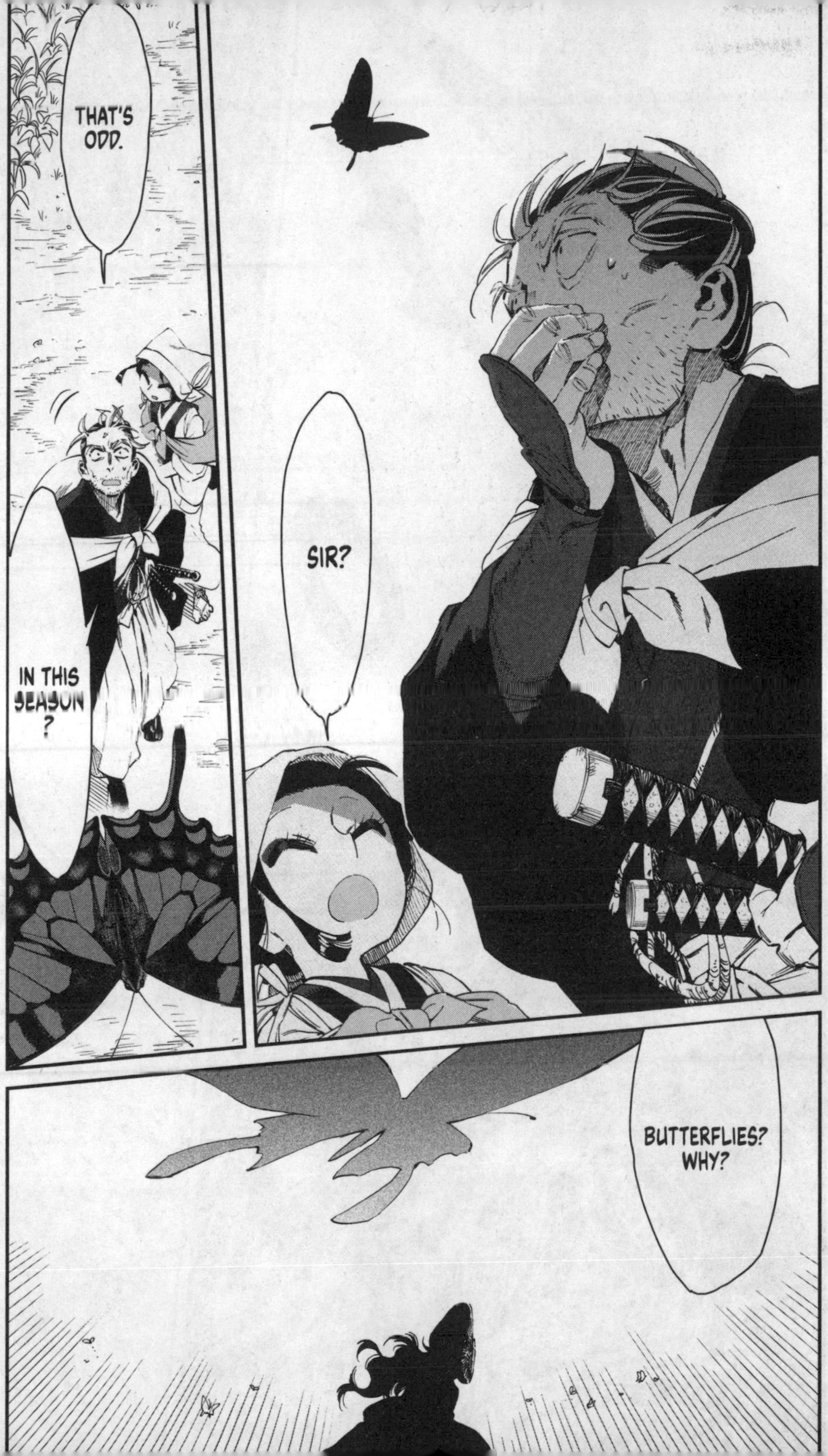
SIR?
THAT'S ODD.
IN THIS SEASON?
BUTTERFLIES? WHY?

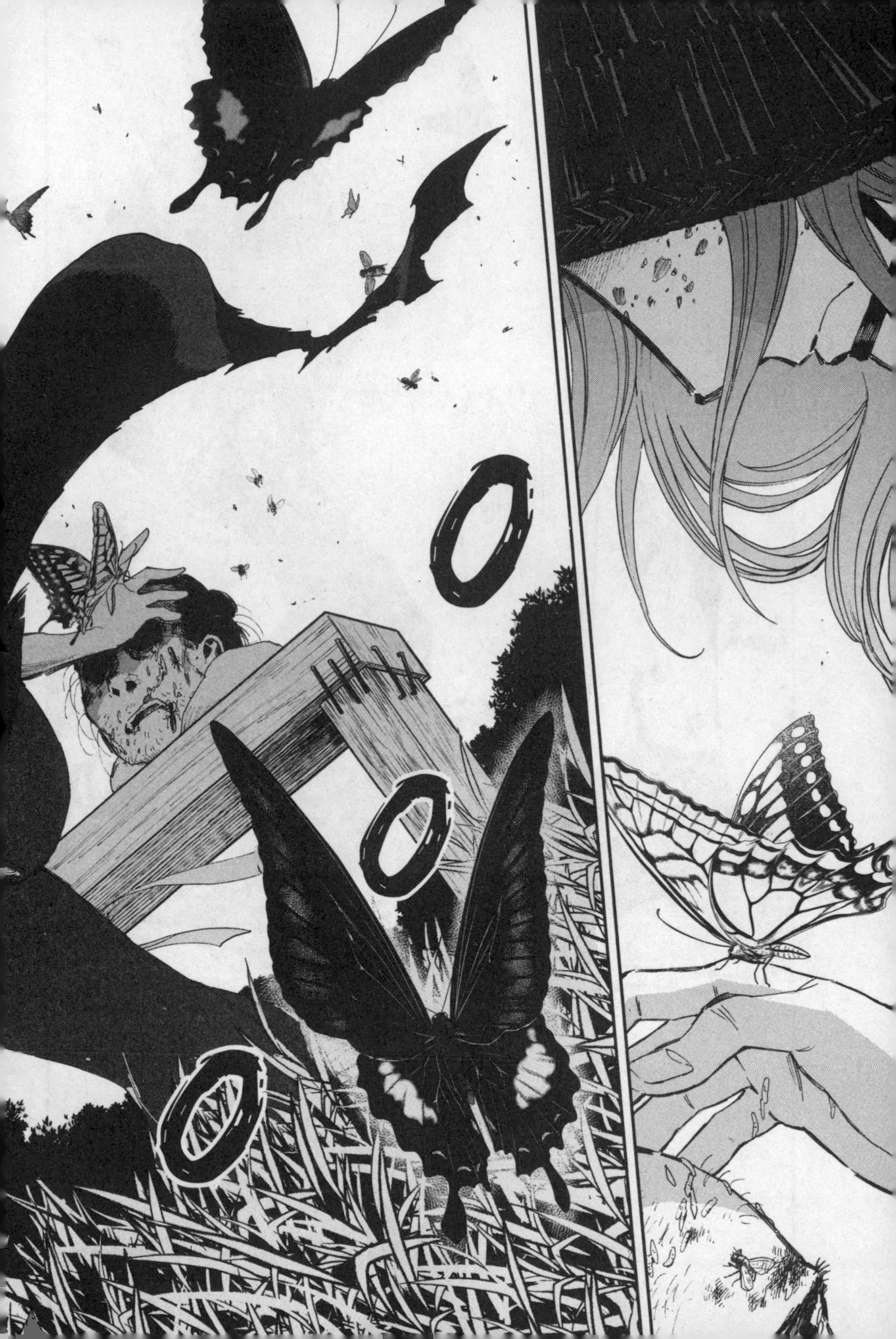

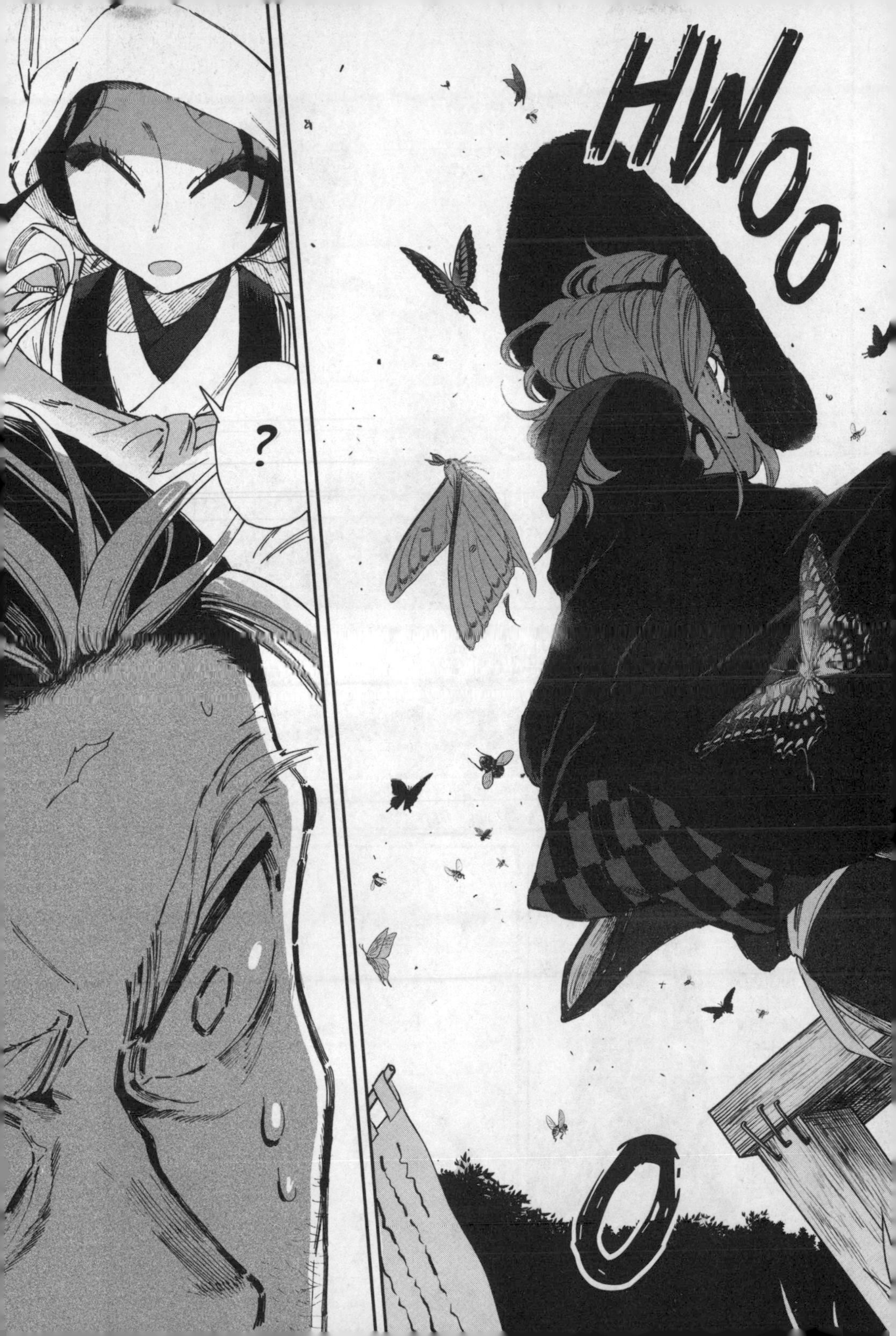
HWOO
O
?

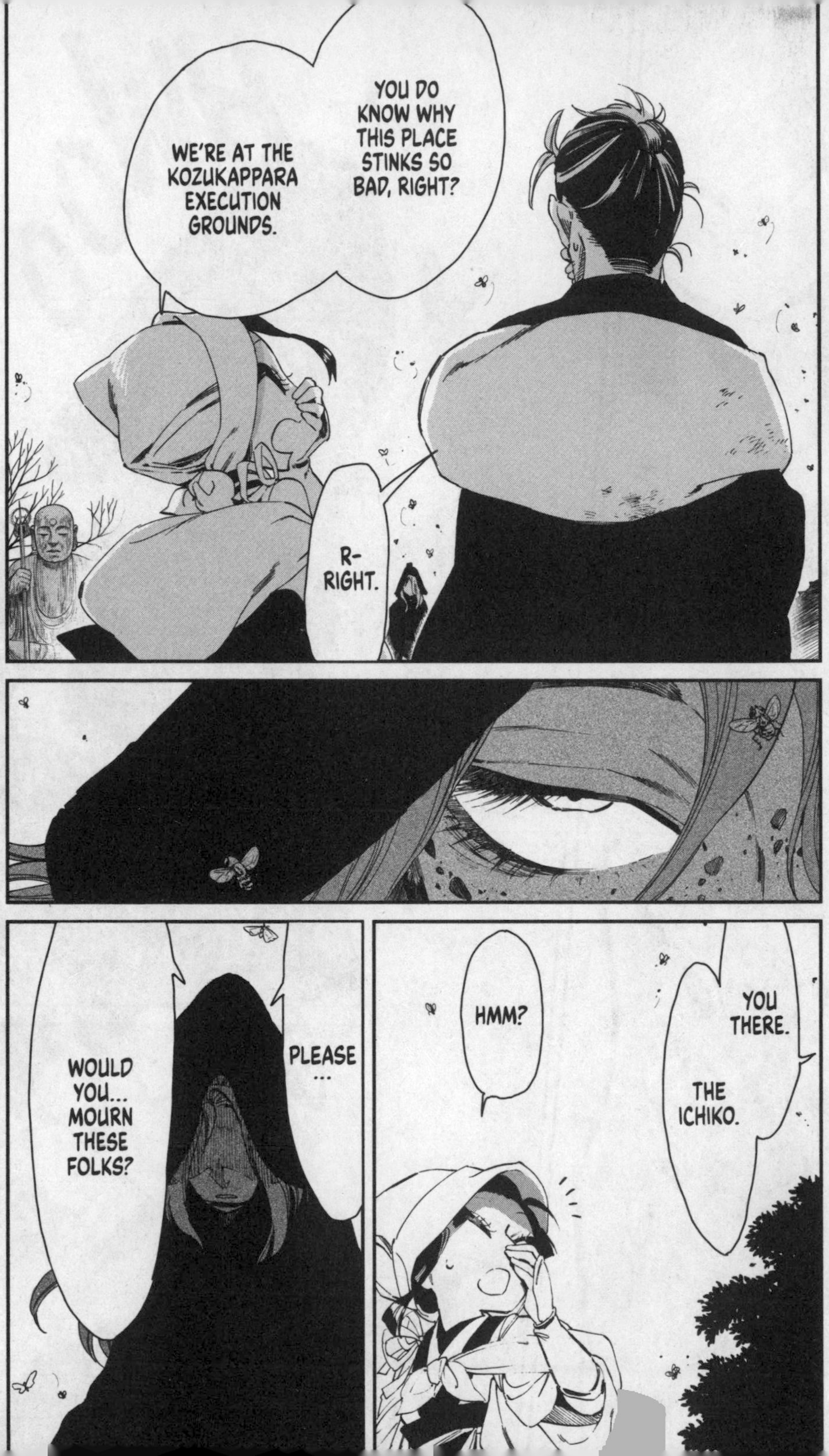
YOU DO KNOW WHY THIS PLACE STINKS SO BAD, RIGHT?
WE'RE AT THE KOZUKAPPARA EXECUTION GROUNDS.
R-RIGHT.
YOU THERE.
THE ICHIKO.
HMM?
PLEASE...
WOULD YOU... MOURN THESE FOLKS?

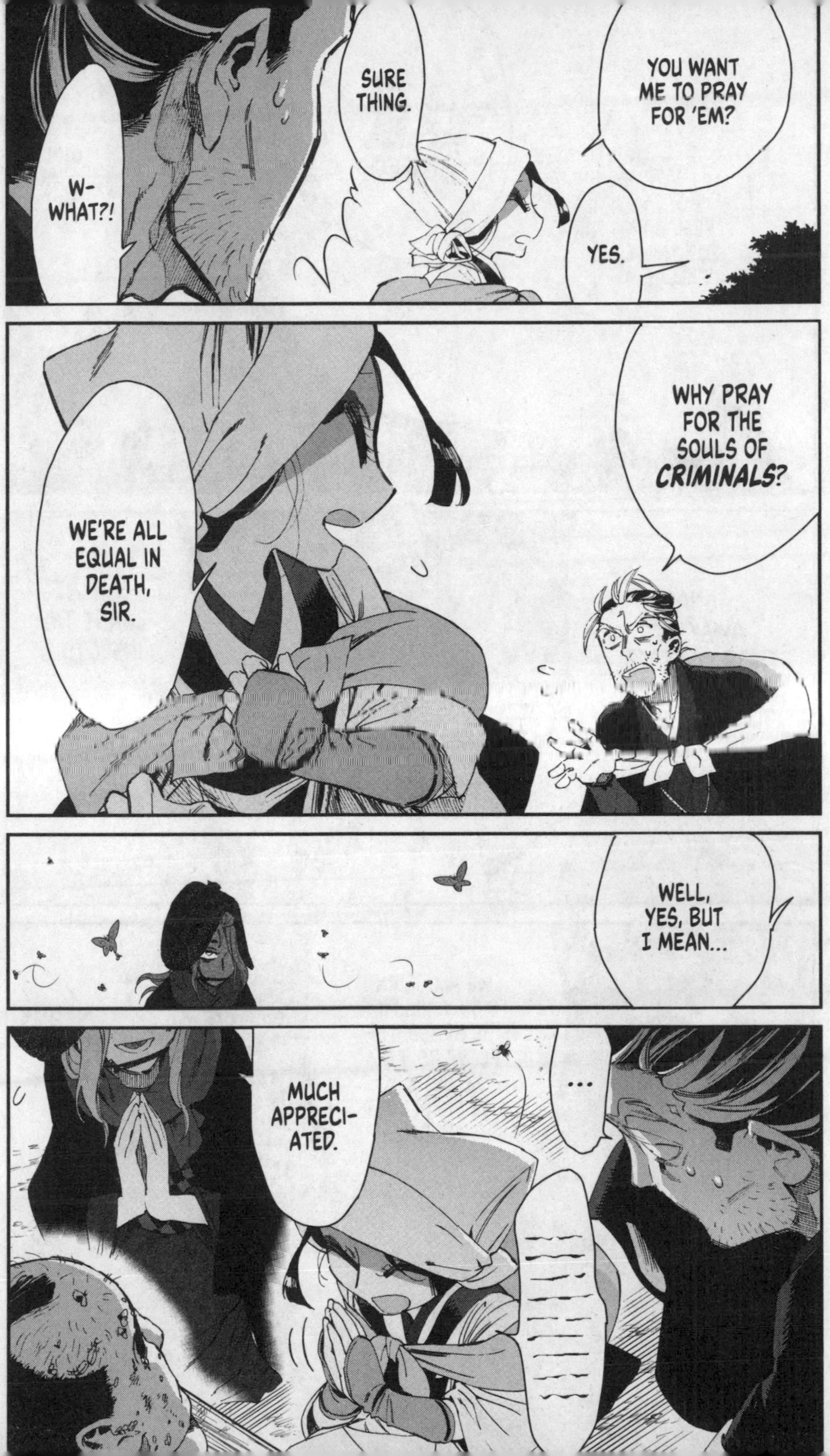
YOU WANT ME TO PRAY FOR 'EM?
YES.
SURE THING.
W-WHAT?!
WHY PRAY FOR THE SOULS OF *CRIMINALS?*
WE'RE ALL EQUAL IN DEATH, SIR.
WELL, YES, BUT I MEAN...
...
MUCH APPRECIATED.

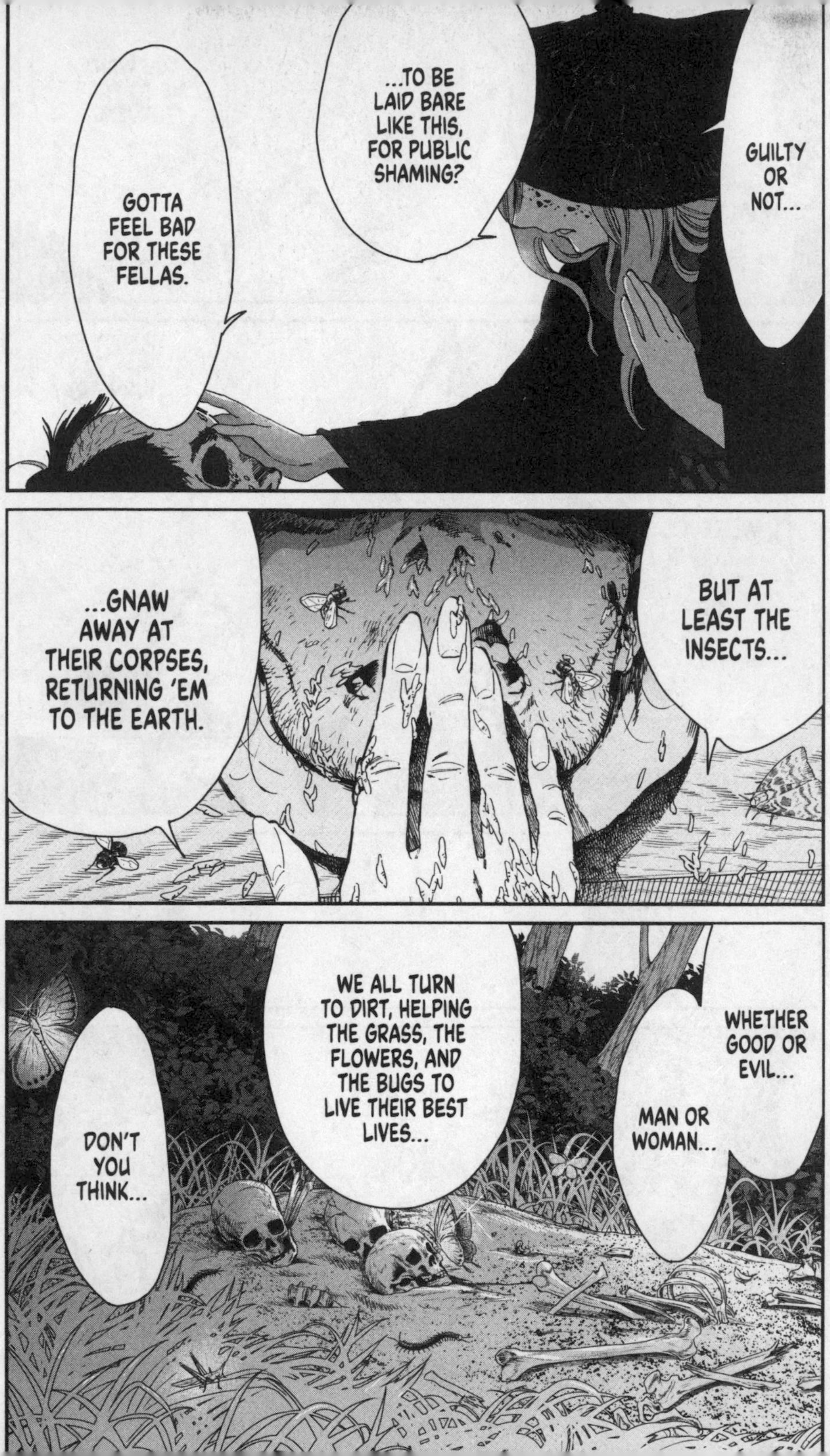
GUILTY OR NOT...
...TO BE LAID BARE LIKE THIS, FOR PUBLIC SHAMING?
GOTTA FEEL BAD FOR THESE FELLAS.
BUT AT LEAST THE INSECTS...
...GNAW AWAY AT THEIR CORPSES, RETURNING 'EM TO THE EARTH.
WHETHER GOOD OR EVIL...
MAN OR WOMAN...
WE ALL TURN TO DIRT, HELPING THE GRASS, THE FLOWERS, AND THE BUGS TO LIVE THEIR BEST LIVES...
DON'T YOU THINK...

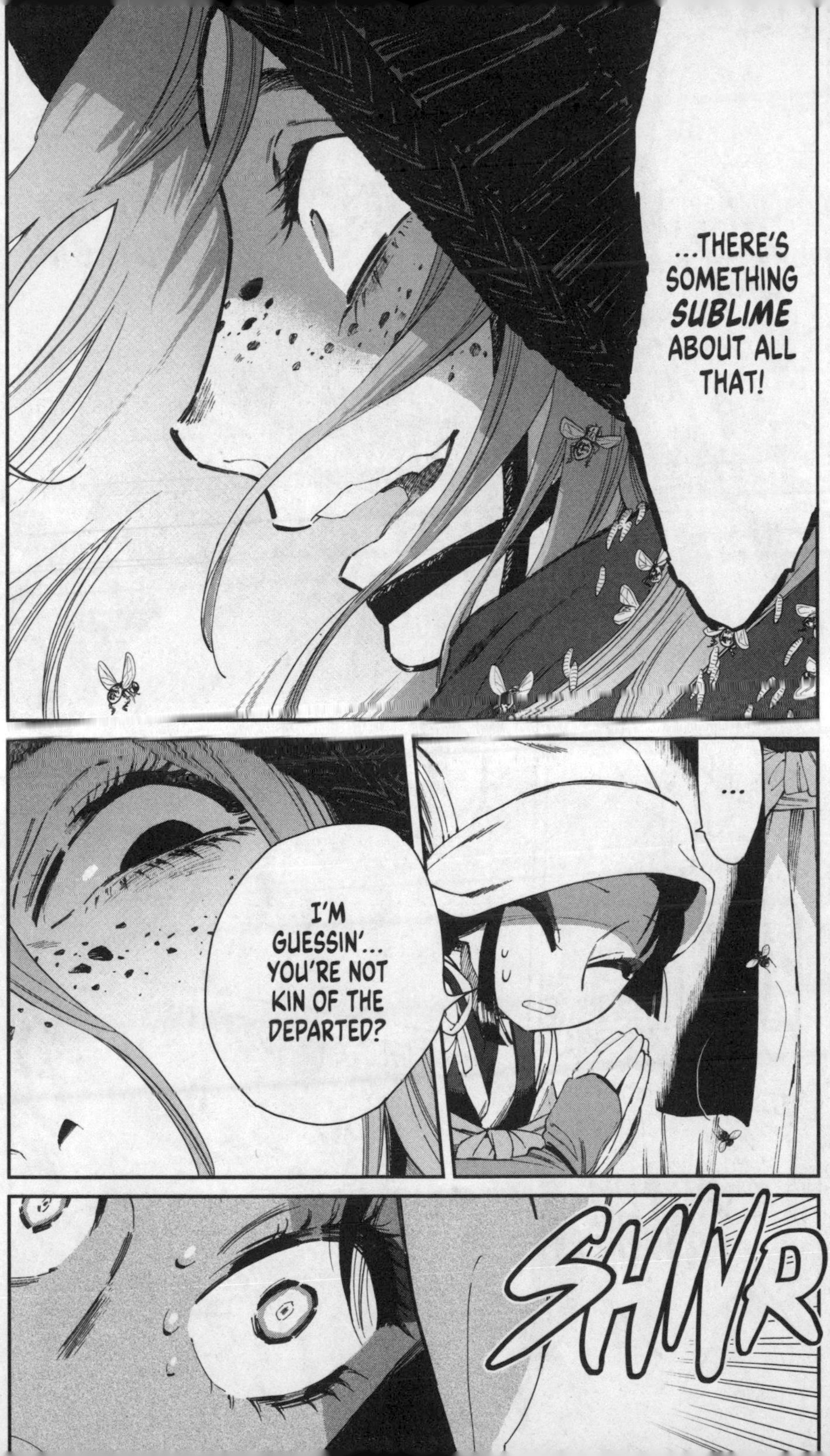
...THERE'S SOMETHING *SUBLIME* ABOUT ALL THAT!
...
I'M GUESSIN'... YOU'RE NOT KIN OF THE DEPARTED?
SHNR

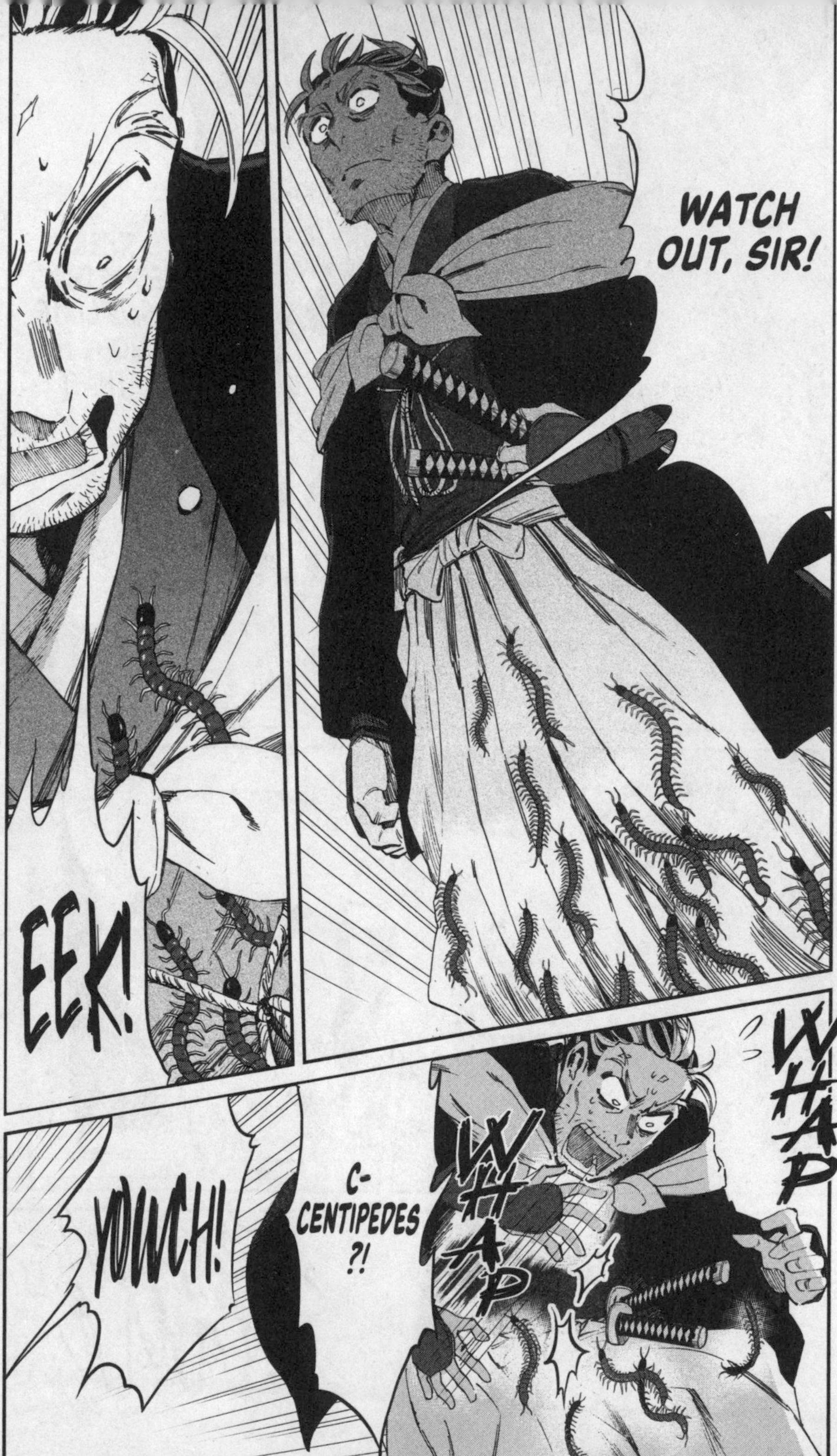
WATCH OUT, SIR!
EEK!
WHAP
WHAP
C-CENTIPEDES?!
YOUCH!

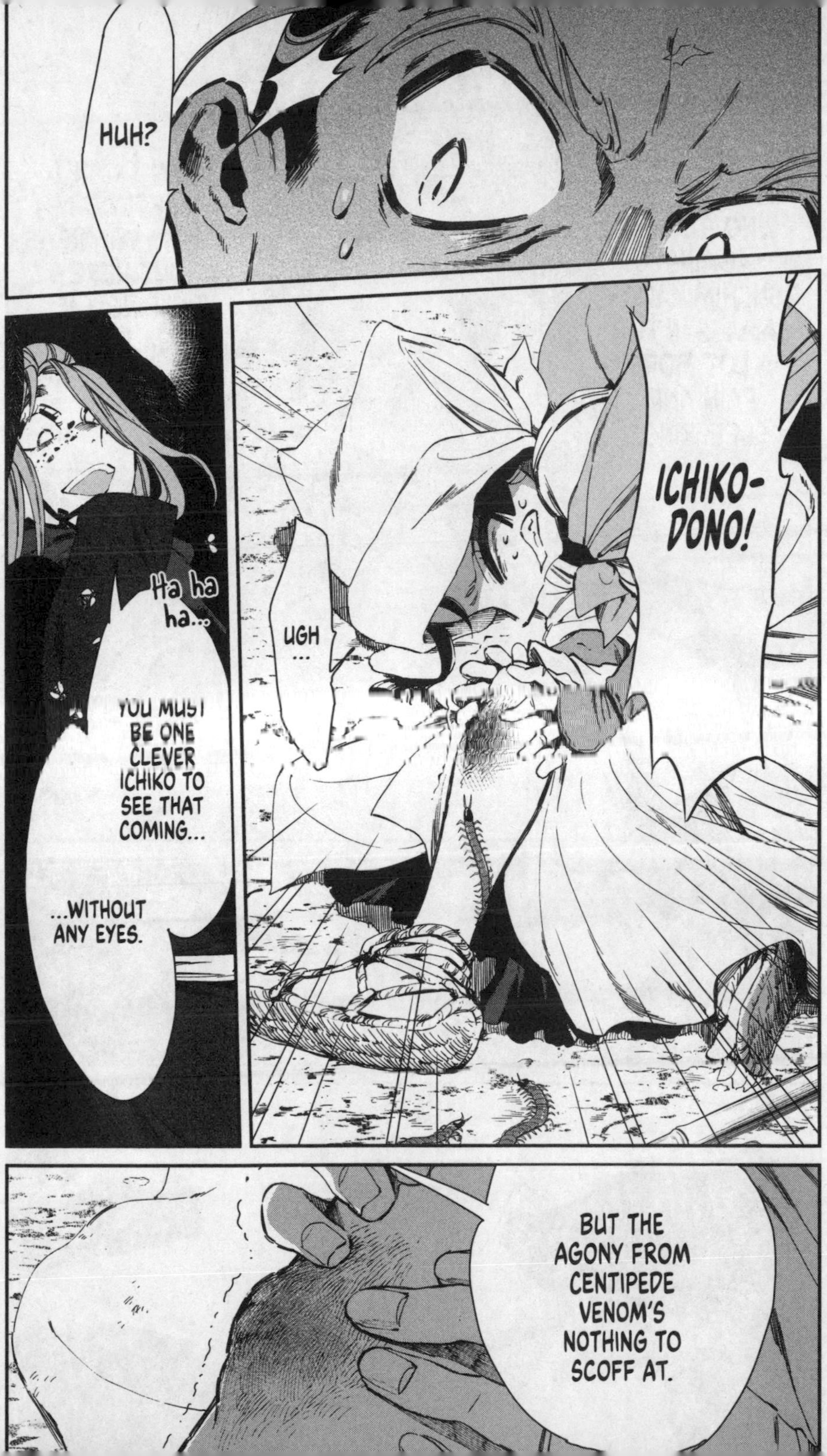
HUH?
ICHIKO-DONO!
UGH ...
Ha ha ha...
YOU MUST BE ONE CLEVER ICHIKO TO SEE THAT COMING...
...WITHOUT ANY EYES.
BUT THE AGONY FROM CENTIPEDE VENOM'S NOTHING TO SCOFF AT.

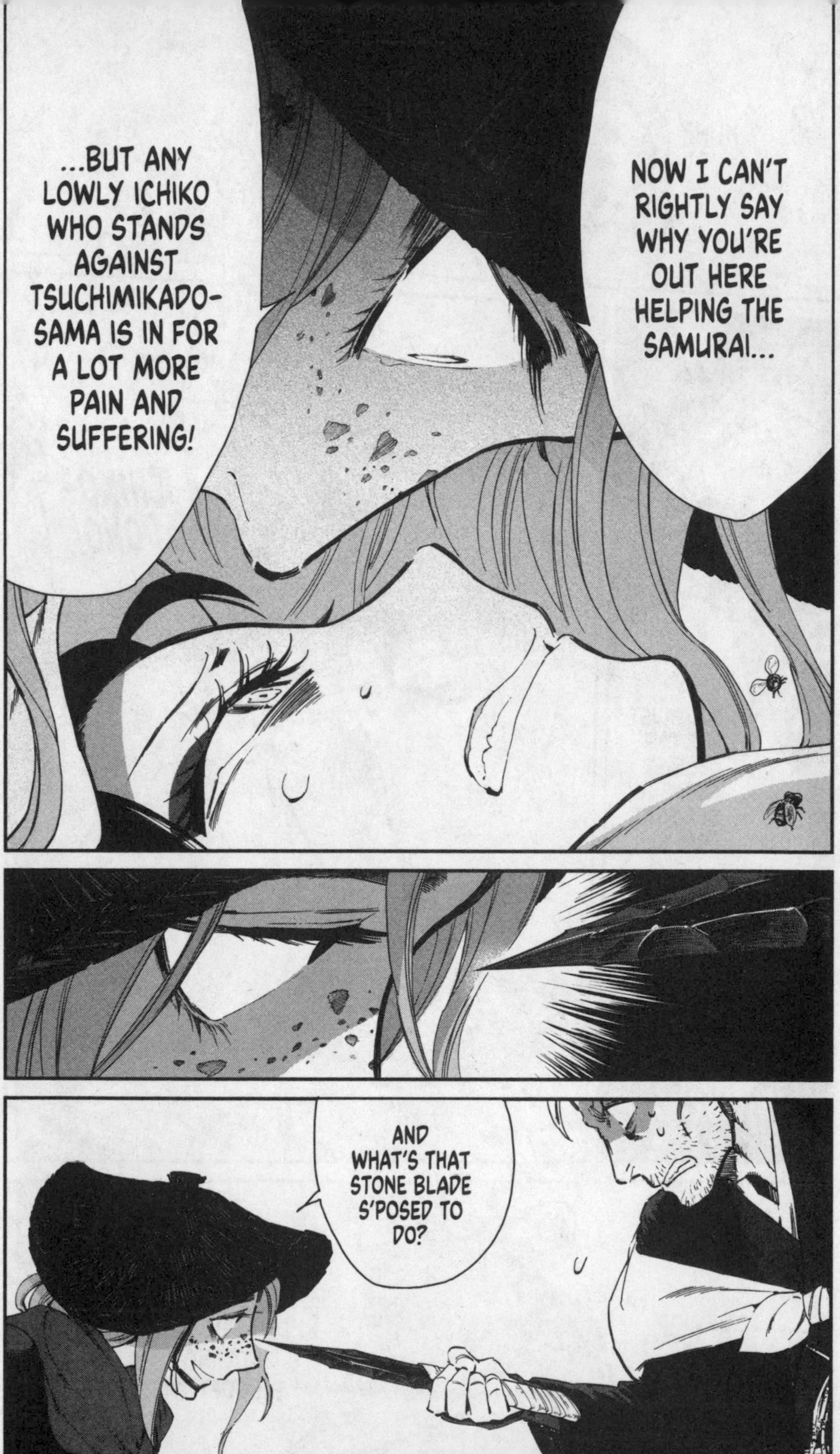
NOW I CAN'T RIGHTLY SAY WHY YOU'RE OUT HERE HELPING THE SAMURAI...
...BUT ANY LOWLY ICHIKO WHO STANDS AGAINST TSUCHIMIKADO-SAMA IS IN FOR A LOT MORE PAIN AND SUFFERING!
AND WHAT'S THAT STONE BLADE S'POSED TO DO?

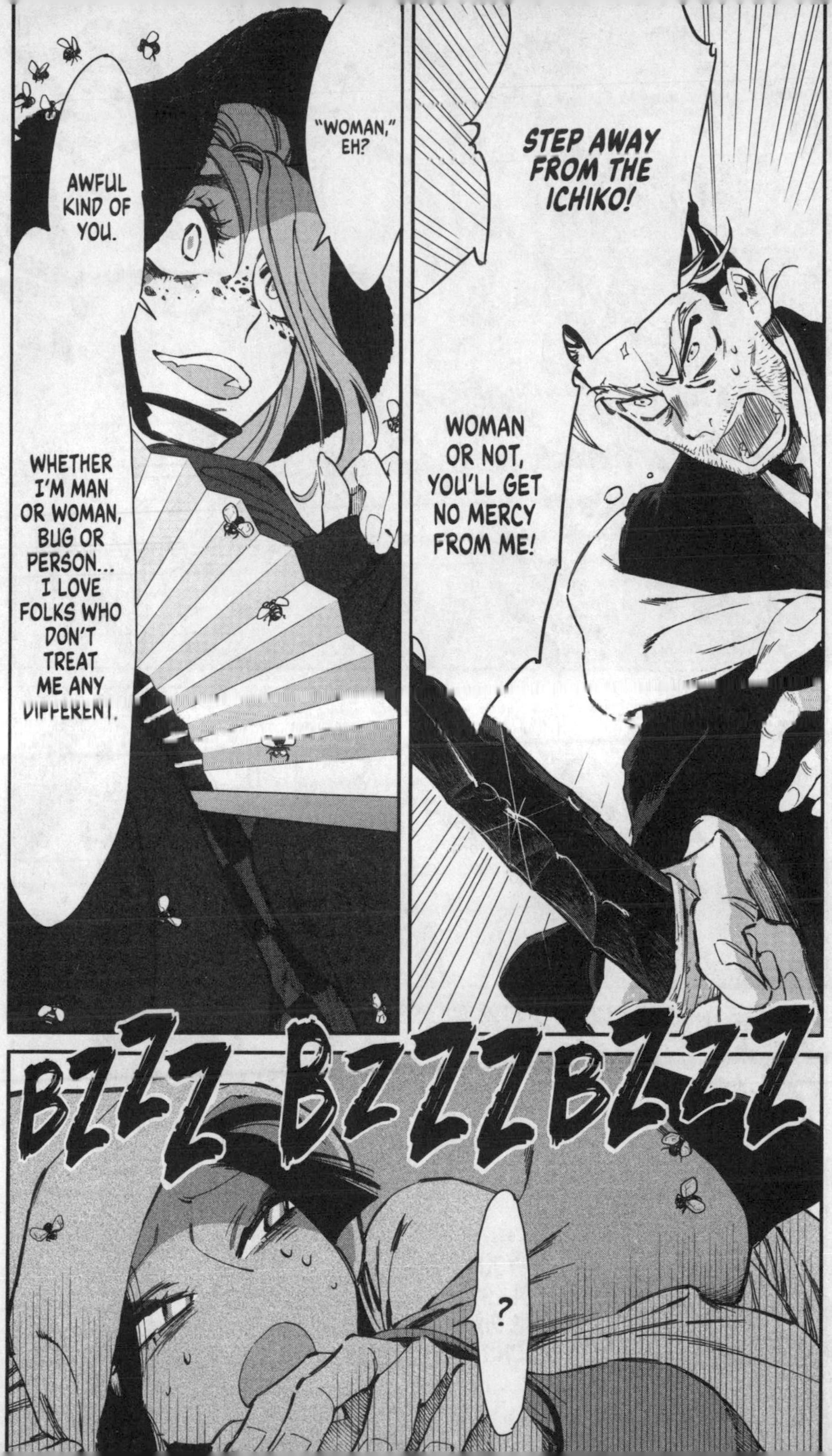
STEP AWAY FROM THE ICHIKO!
WOMAN OR NOT, YOU'LL GET NO MERCY FROM ME!
"WOMAN," EH?
AWFUL KIND OF YOU.
WHETHER I'M MAN OR WOMAN, BUG OR PERSON... I LOVE FOLKS WHO DON'T TREAT ME ANY DIFFERENT.
BZZZ BZZZBZZZ
?

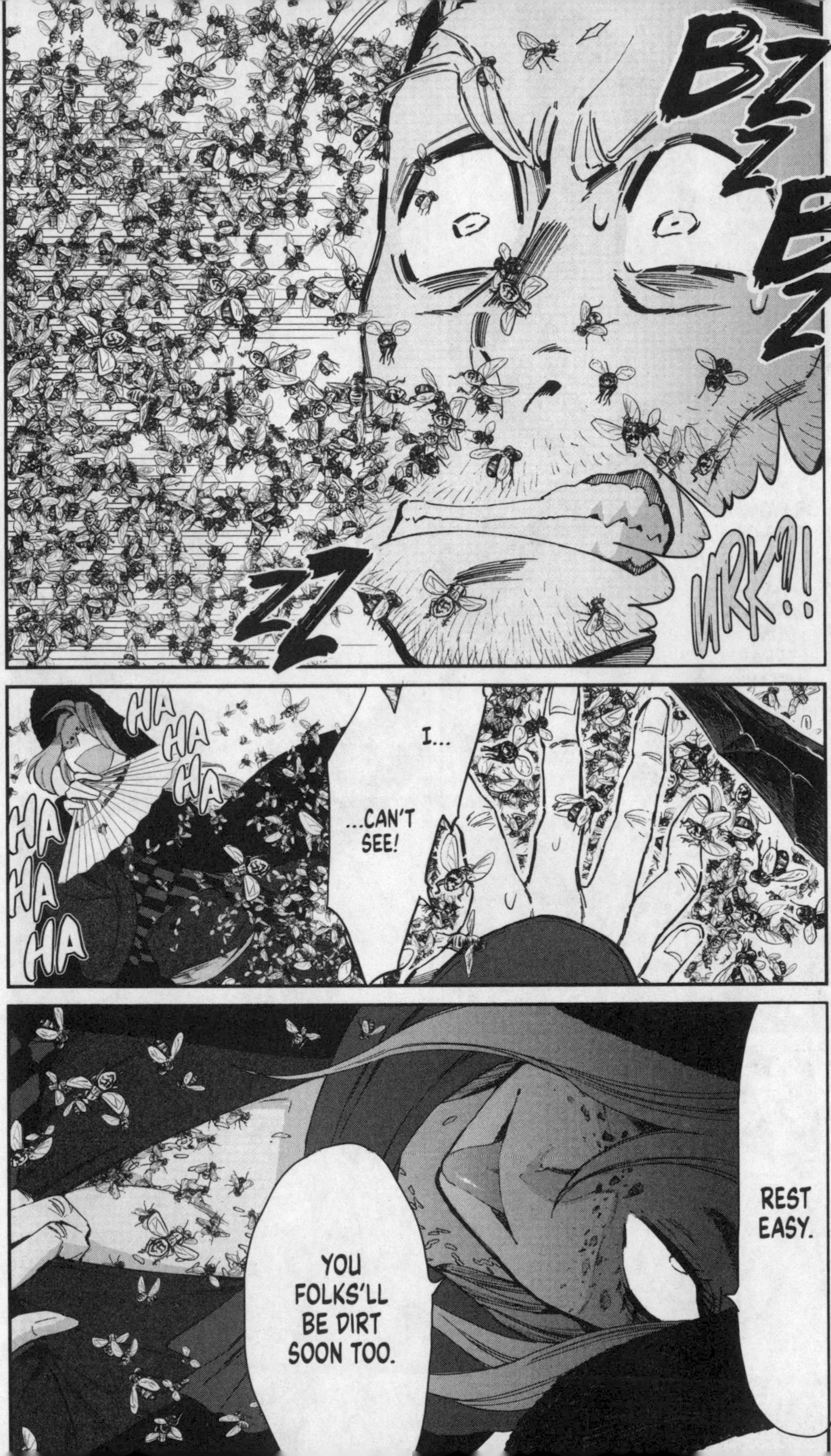
BZZBZZ
URK?!
ZZ
I...
...CAN'T SEE!
HA HA HA
HA HA HA
REST EASY.
YOU FOLKS'LL BE DIRT SOON TOO.

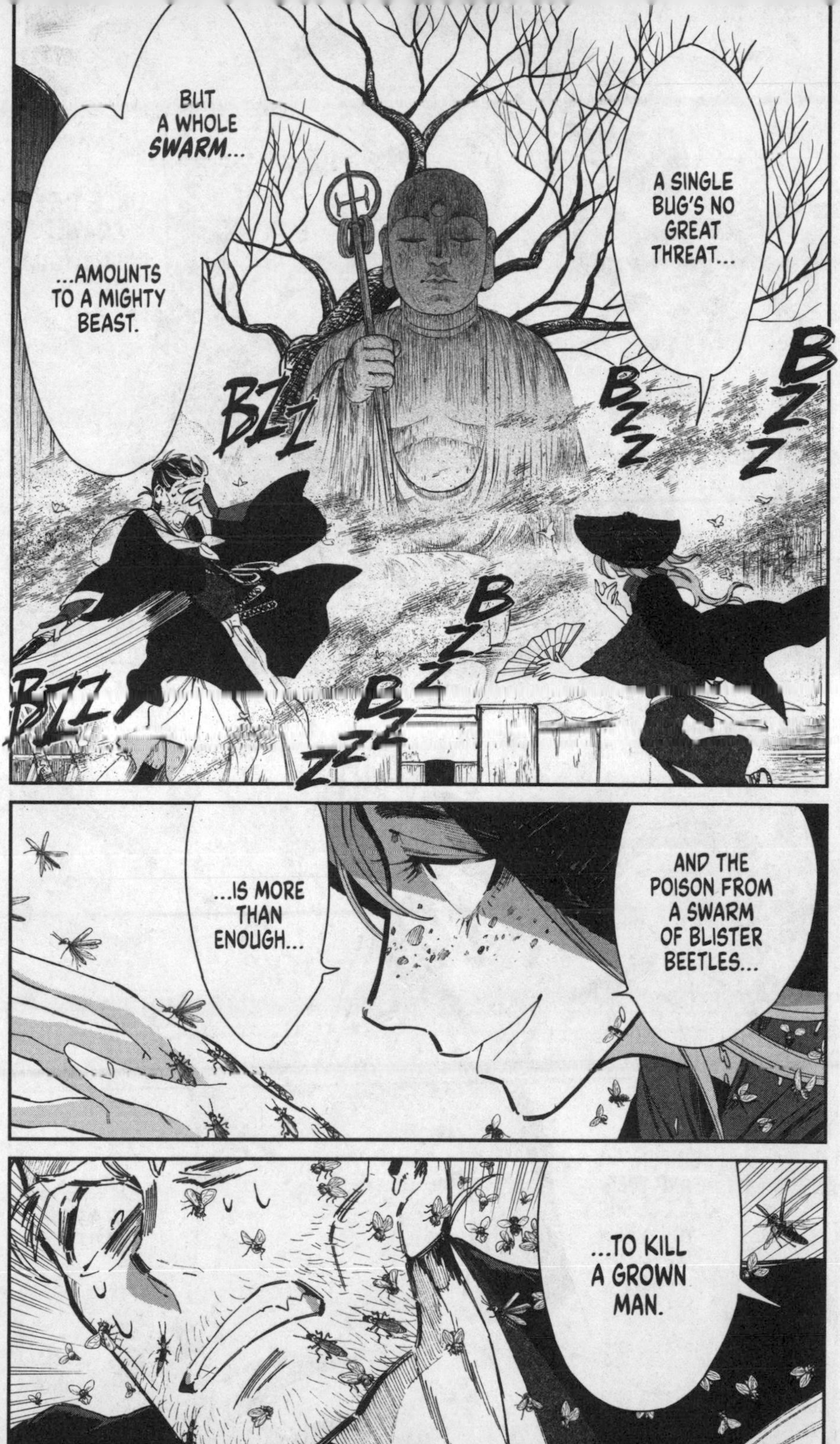
A SINGLE BUG'S NO GREAT THREAT...
BZZ
BZZ
BUT A WHOLE SWARM...
...AMOUNTS TO A MIGHTY BEAST.
BZZ
BZZ
BZZ
BZZ
AND THE POISON FROM A SWARM OF BLISTER BEETLES...
...IS MORE THAN ENOUGH...
...TO KILL A GROWN MAN.

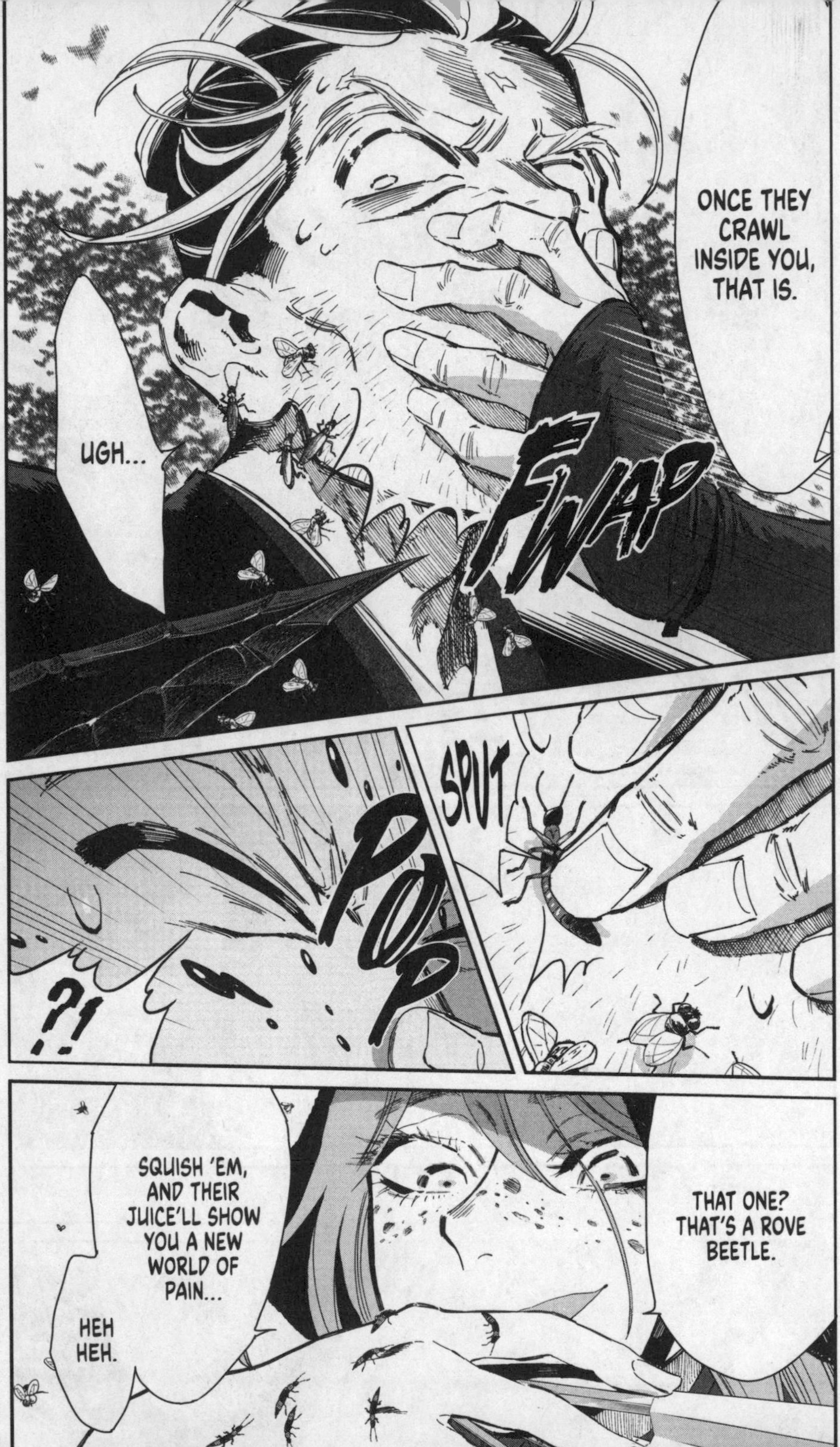
ONCE THEY CRAWL INSIDE YOU, THAT IS.
FWAP
UGH...
SPUT
POP
?!
THAT ONE? THAT'S A ROVE BEETLE.
SQUISH 'EM, AND THEIR JUICE'LL SHOW YOU A NEW WORLD OF PAIN...
HEH HEH.

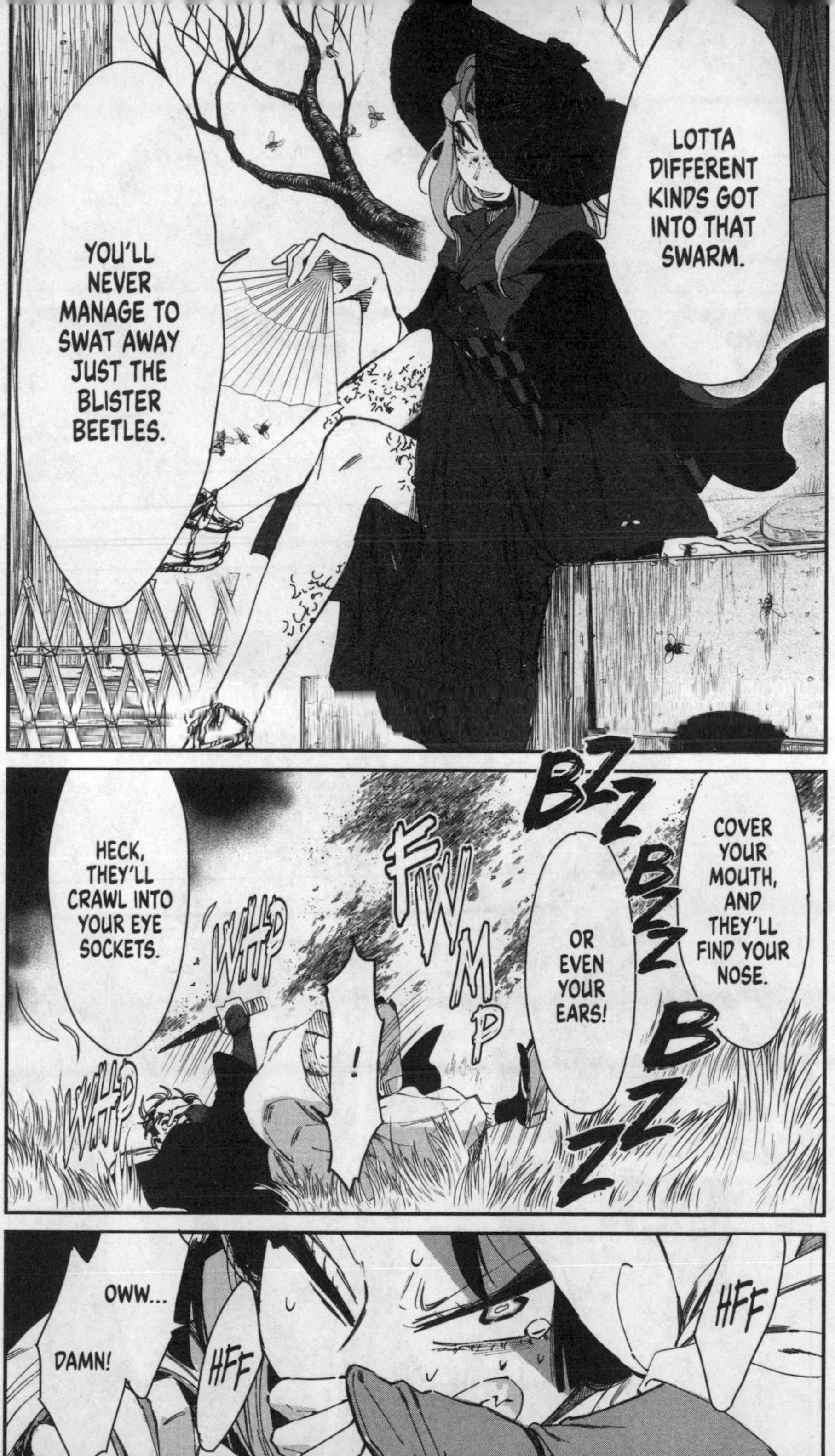
LOTTA DIFFERENT KINDS GOT INTO THAT SWARM.
YOU'LL NEVER MANAGE TO SWAT AWAY JUST THE BLISTER BEETLES.
BZZ BZZ BZZ
COVER YOUR MOUTH, AND THEY'LL FIND YOUR NOSE.
OR EVEN YOUR EARS!
FWMP
!
HECK, THEY'LL CRAWL INTO YOUR EYE SOCKETS.
WHIP
WHIP
HFF
HFF
OWW...
DAMN!

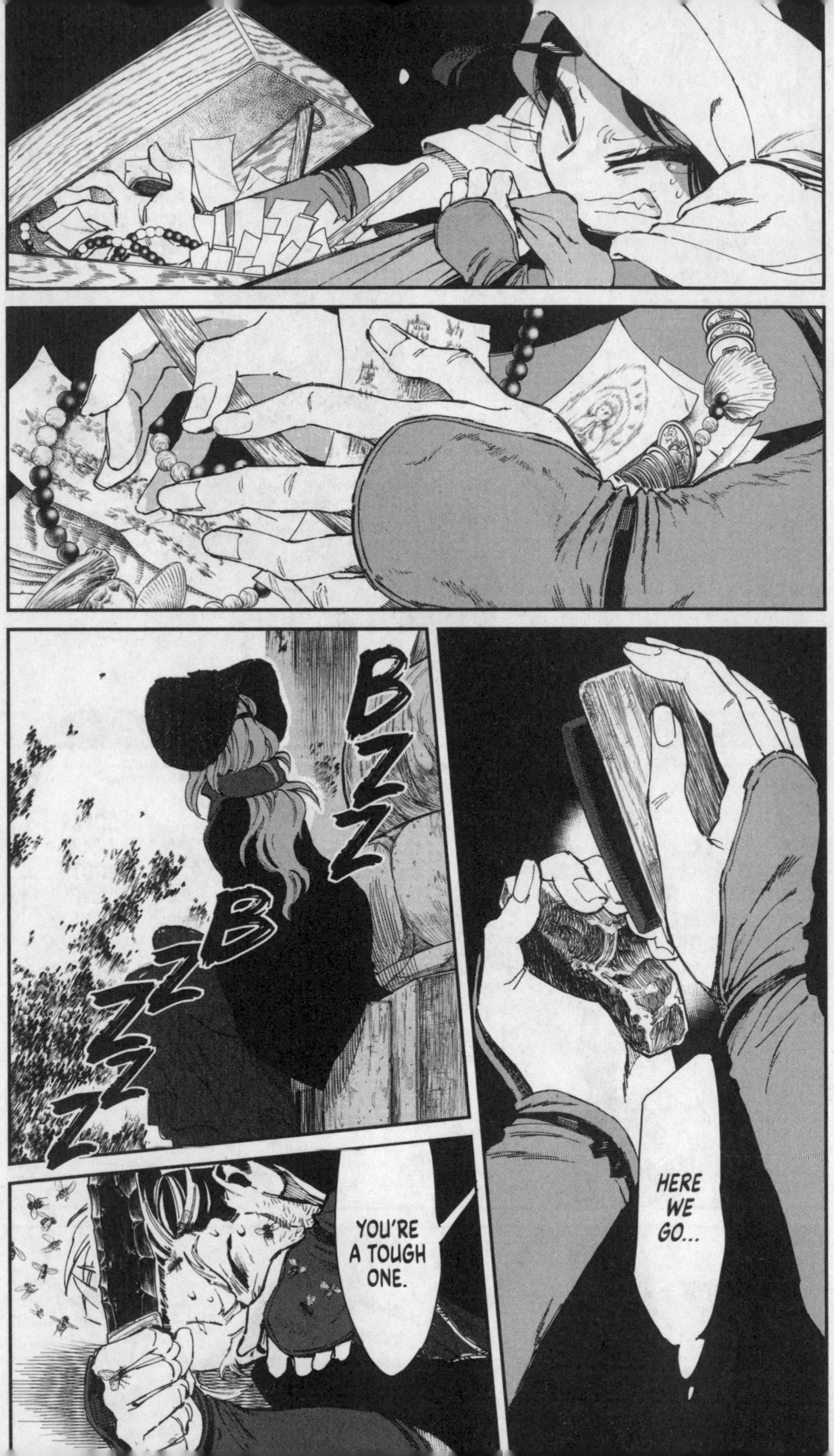
HERE WE GO...
BZZ
BZZZZ
YOU'RE A TOUGH ONE.

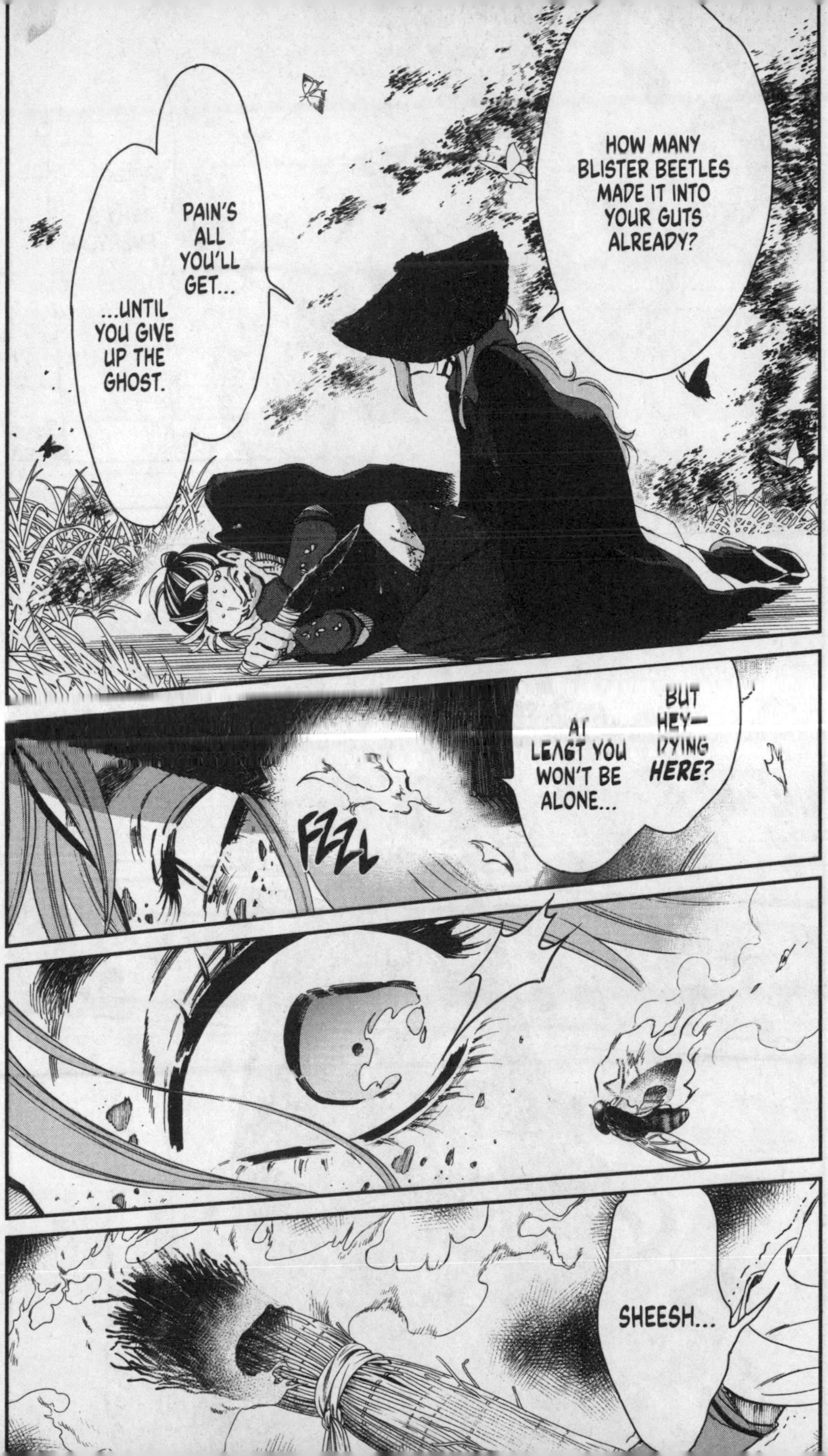
HOW MANY BLISTER BEETLES MADE IT INTO YOUR GUTS ALREADY?
PAIN'S ALL YOU'LL GET...
...UNTIL YOU GIVE UP THE GHOST.
BUT HEY— DYING HERE?
AT LEAST YOU WON'T BE ALONE...
FZZZL
SHEESH...

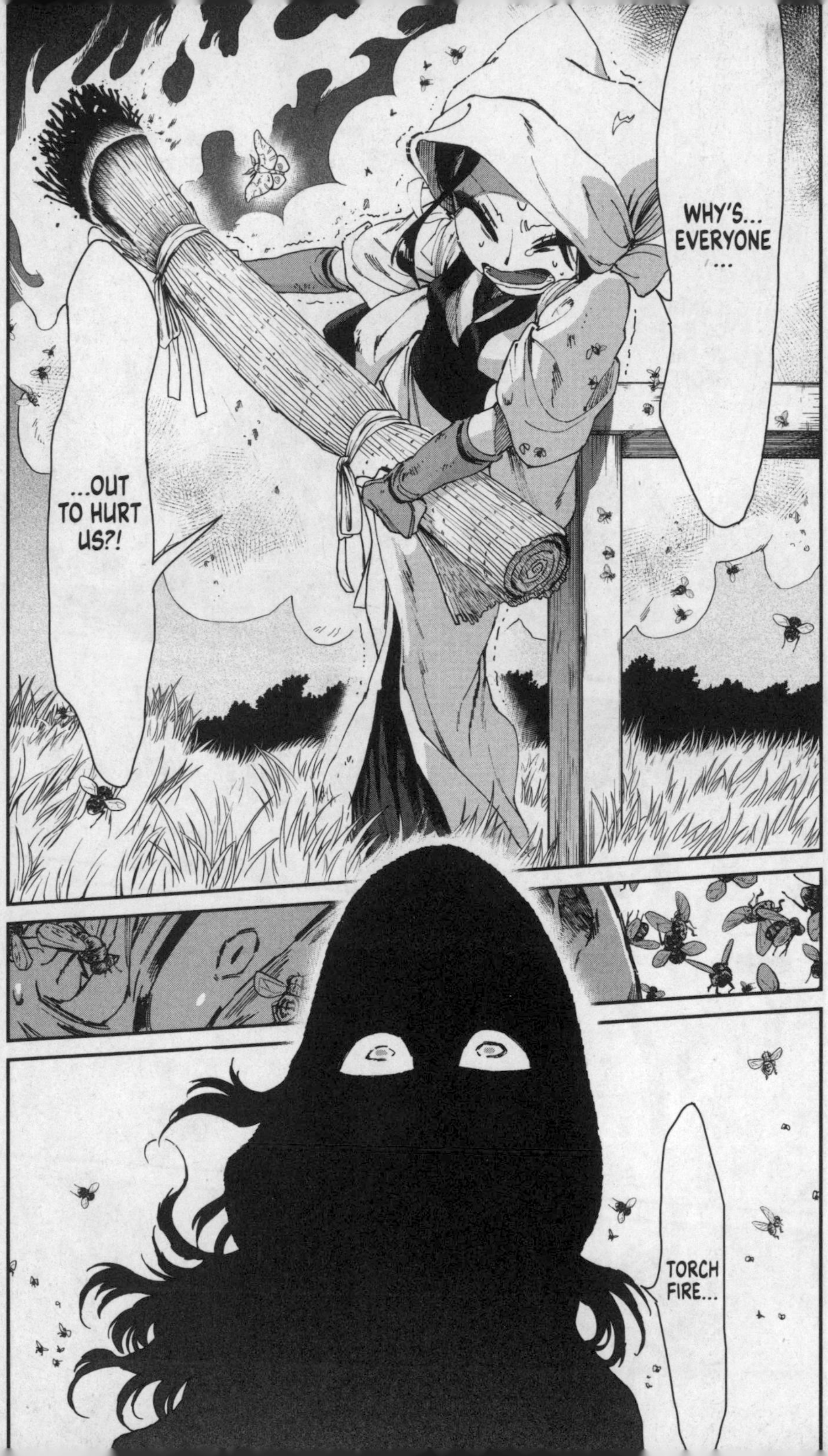
WHY'S... EVERYONE ...
...OUT TO HURT US?!
TORCH FIRE...

STEEL of the CELESTIAL SHADOWS

Trivia of the Celestial Shadows #②

Goze Buskers

° Blind female performers who roam the land, singing gozeuta songs.

◦ They usually traveled in groups, with a sighted goze leading the way.

◦ They returned home annually, at the end of the year. Those who came from snowy regions had a hard time getting home if their return trip was delayed.

◦ To hone their craft, they endured strict training from a young age.

I can't elaborate too much on this, but there was more I wanted to do with these characters. I'd like to have them appear again.

You can find Showa-era goze songs on YouTube, if you're interested.

Those strong voices really hit you deep down.

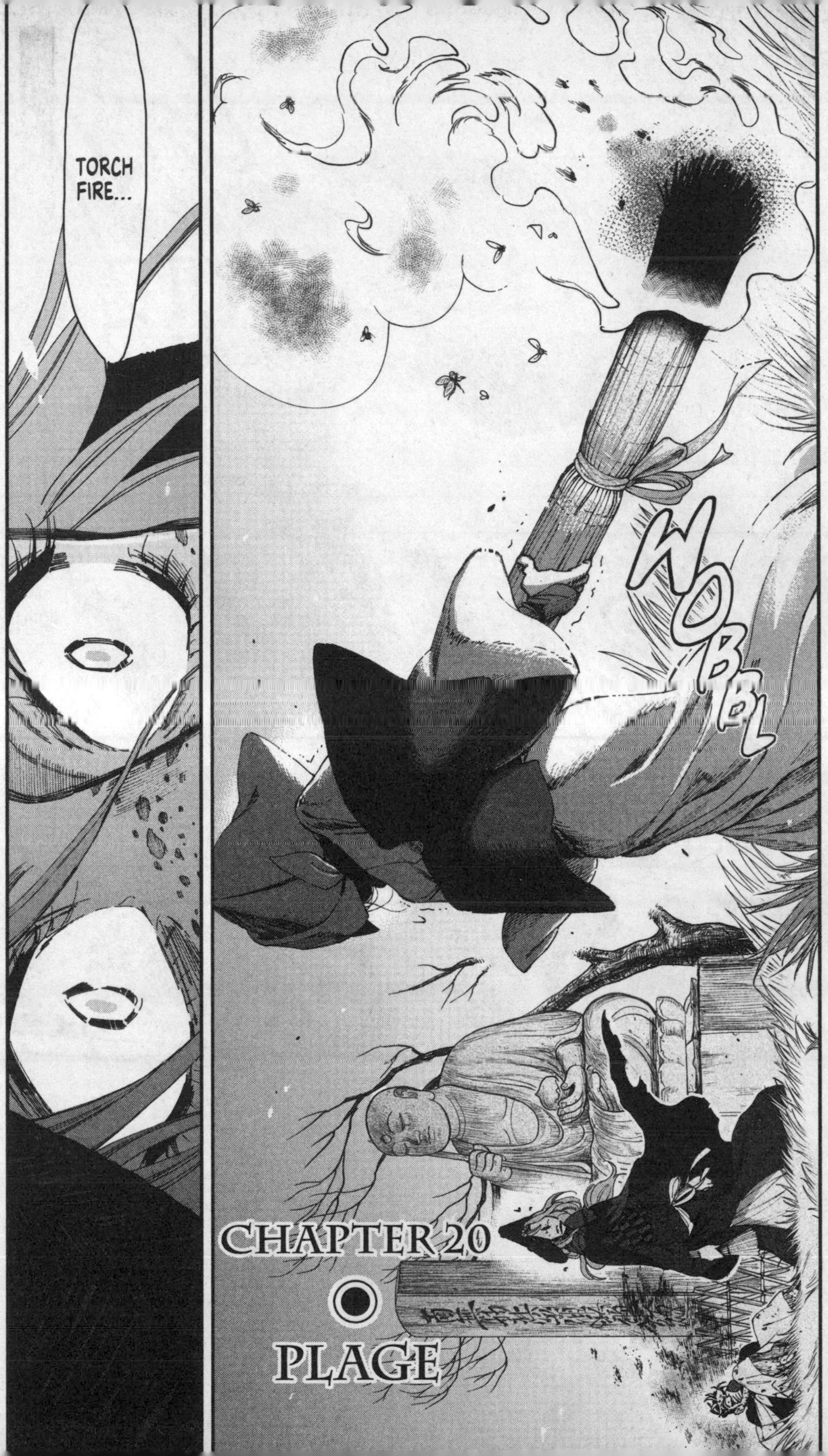
WOBBL
CHAPTER 20
PLAGE
TORCH FIRE...

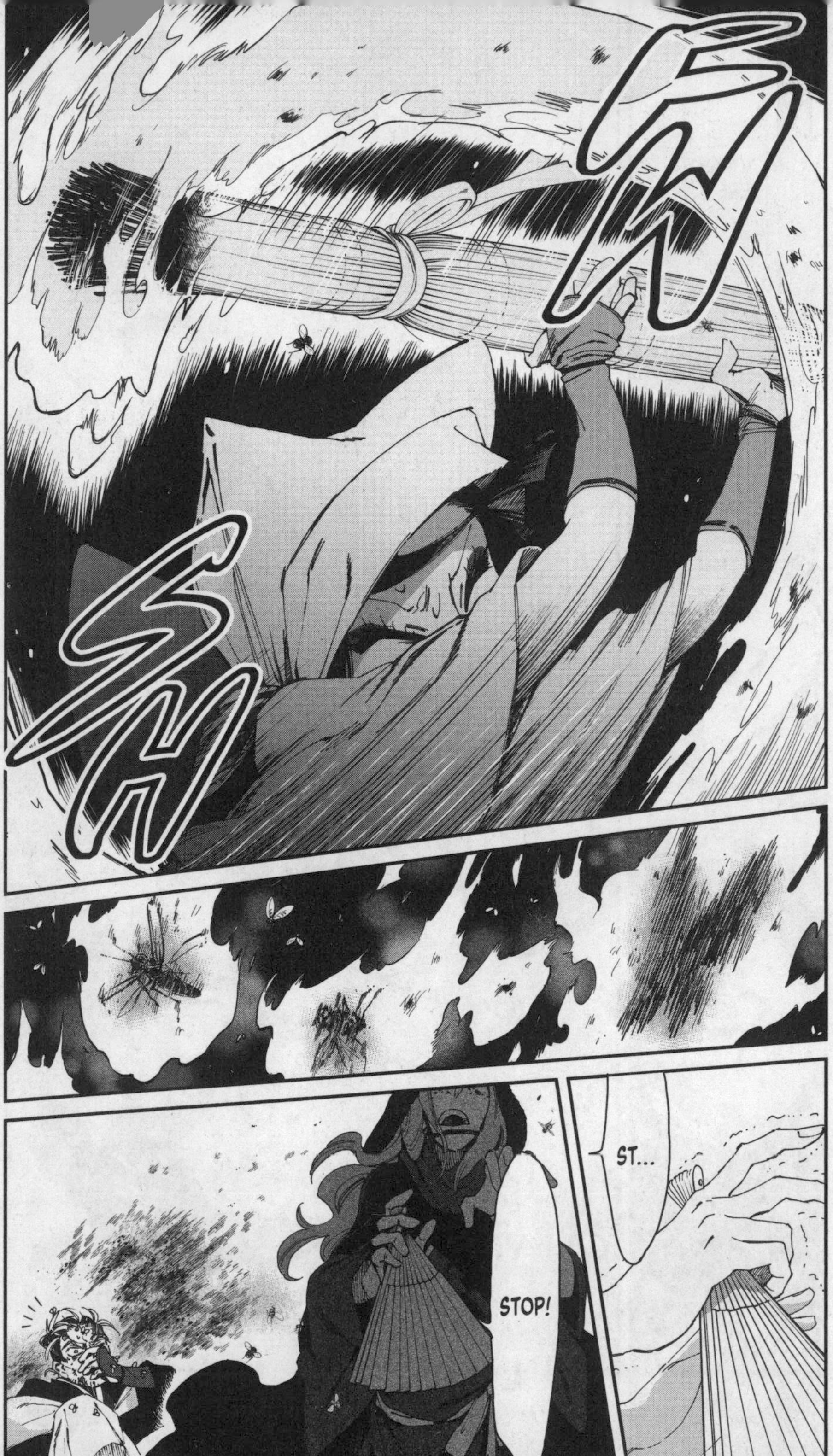
ST...
STOP!

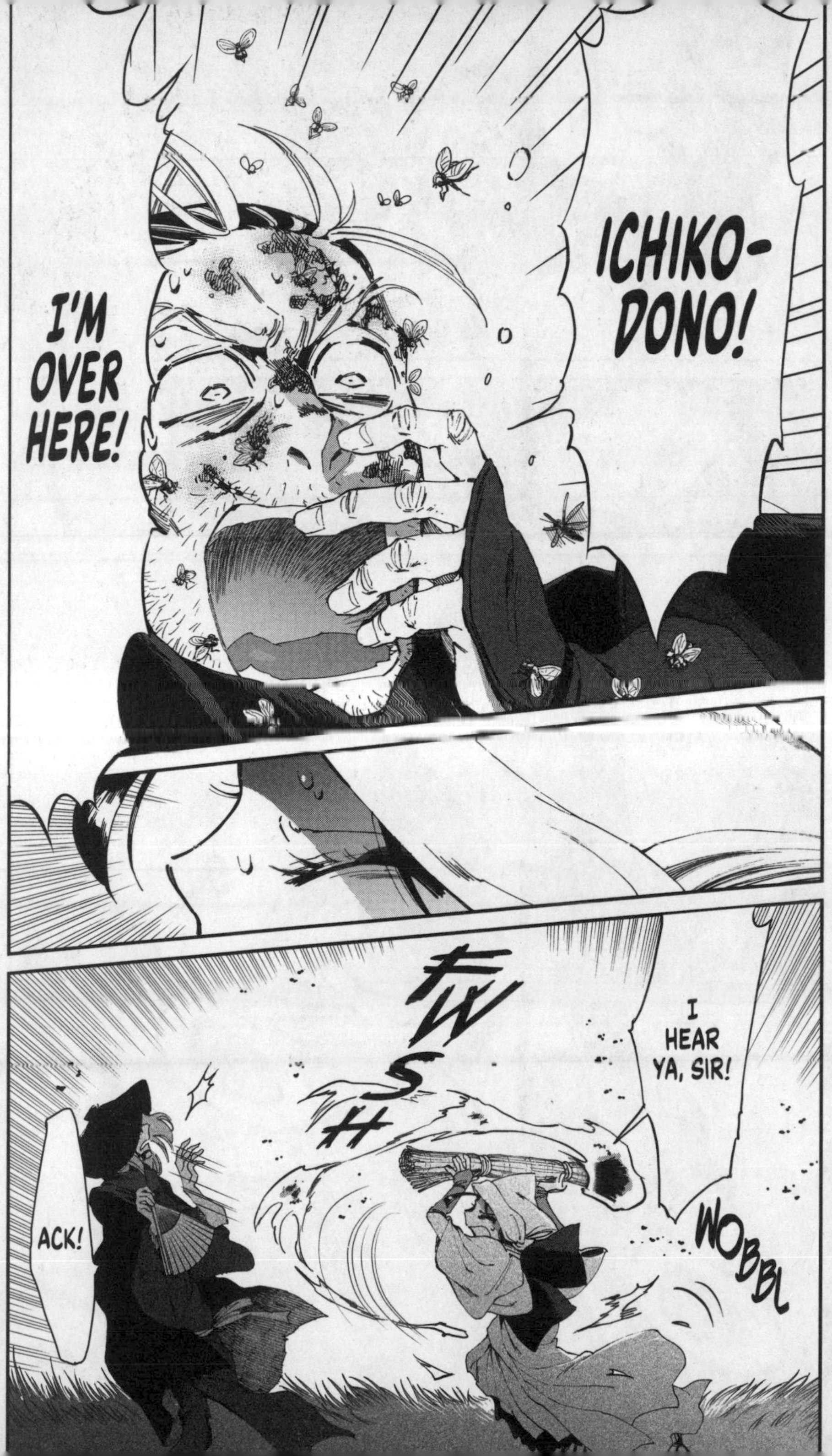
ICHIKO-DONO!
I'M OVER HERE!
I HEAR YA, SIR!
FWSH
WOBBL
ACK!

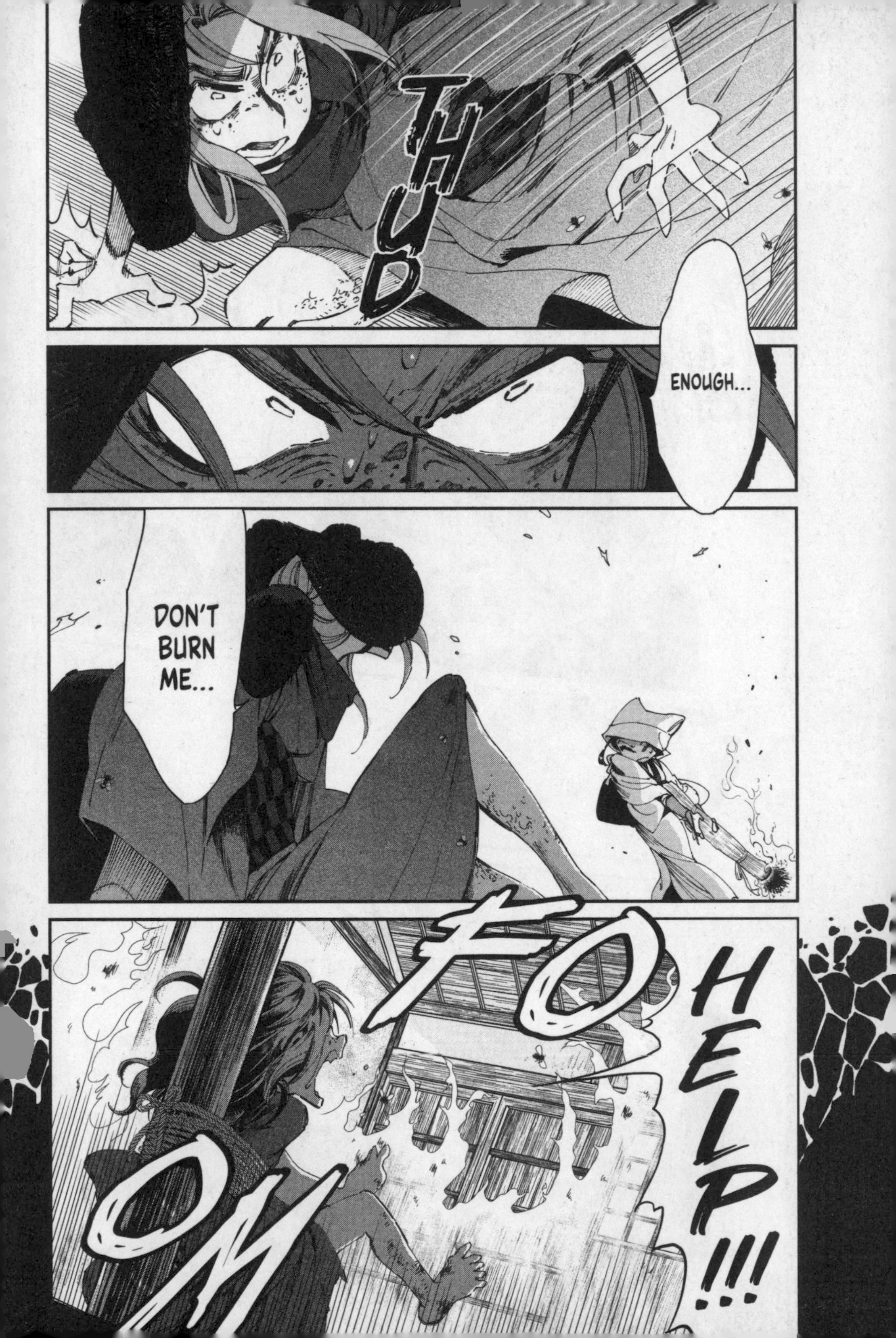
THUD
ENOUGH...
DON'T BURN ME...
HELP!!!
FOOM

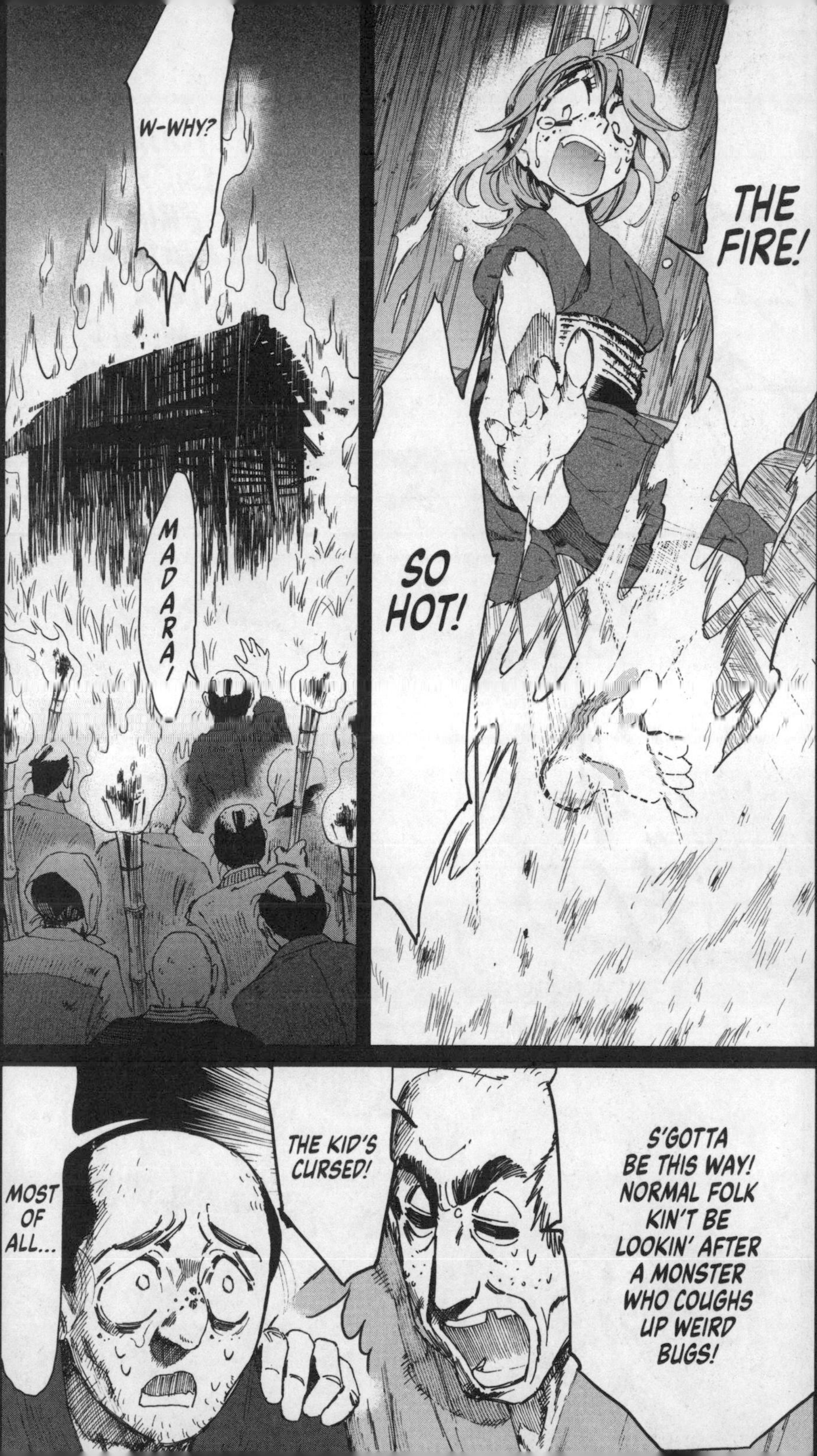
THE FIRE!
SO HOT!
W-WHY?
MADARA!
S'GOTTA BE THIS WAY! NORMAL FOLK KIN'T BE LOOKIN' AFTER A MONSTER WHO COUGHS UP WEIRD BUGS!
THE KID'S CURSED!
MOST OF ALL...

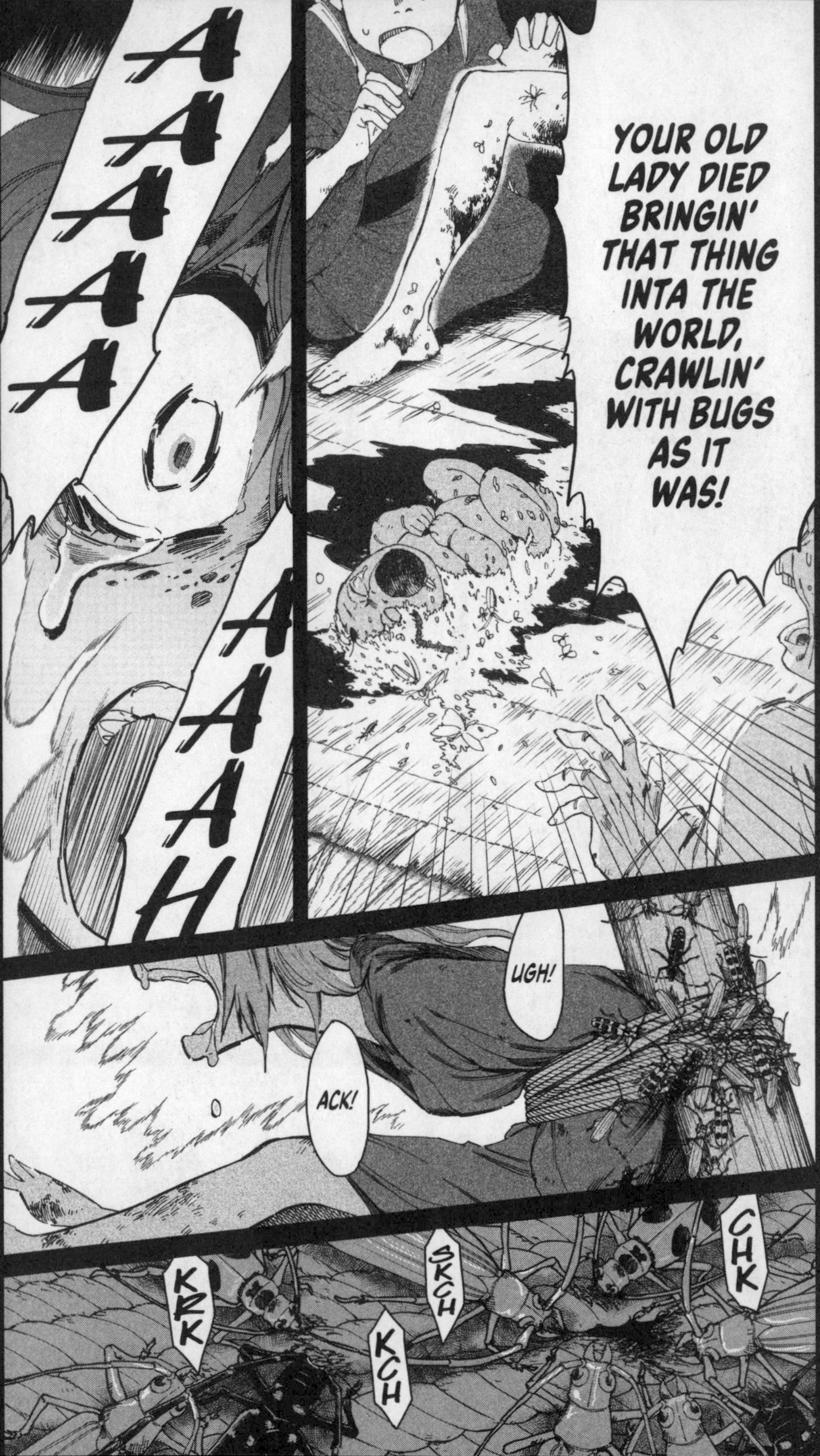
YOUR OLD LADY DIED BRINGIN' THAT THING INTA THE WORLD, CRAWLIN' WITH BUGS AS IT WAS!
AAAAA
AAAH
UGH!
ACK!
CHK
SKCH
KCH
KRK

DAMNED
BUGS.

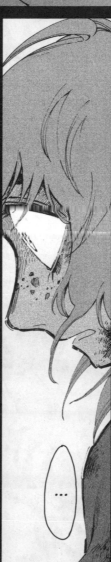

HFF

HFF

HFF

IF
ONLY...

...

...THEY
DIDN'T
SPRING
OUTTA ME
LIKE THAT.

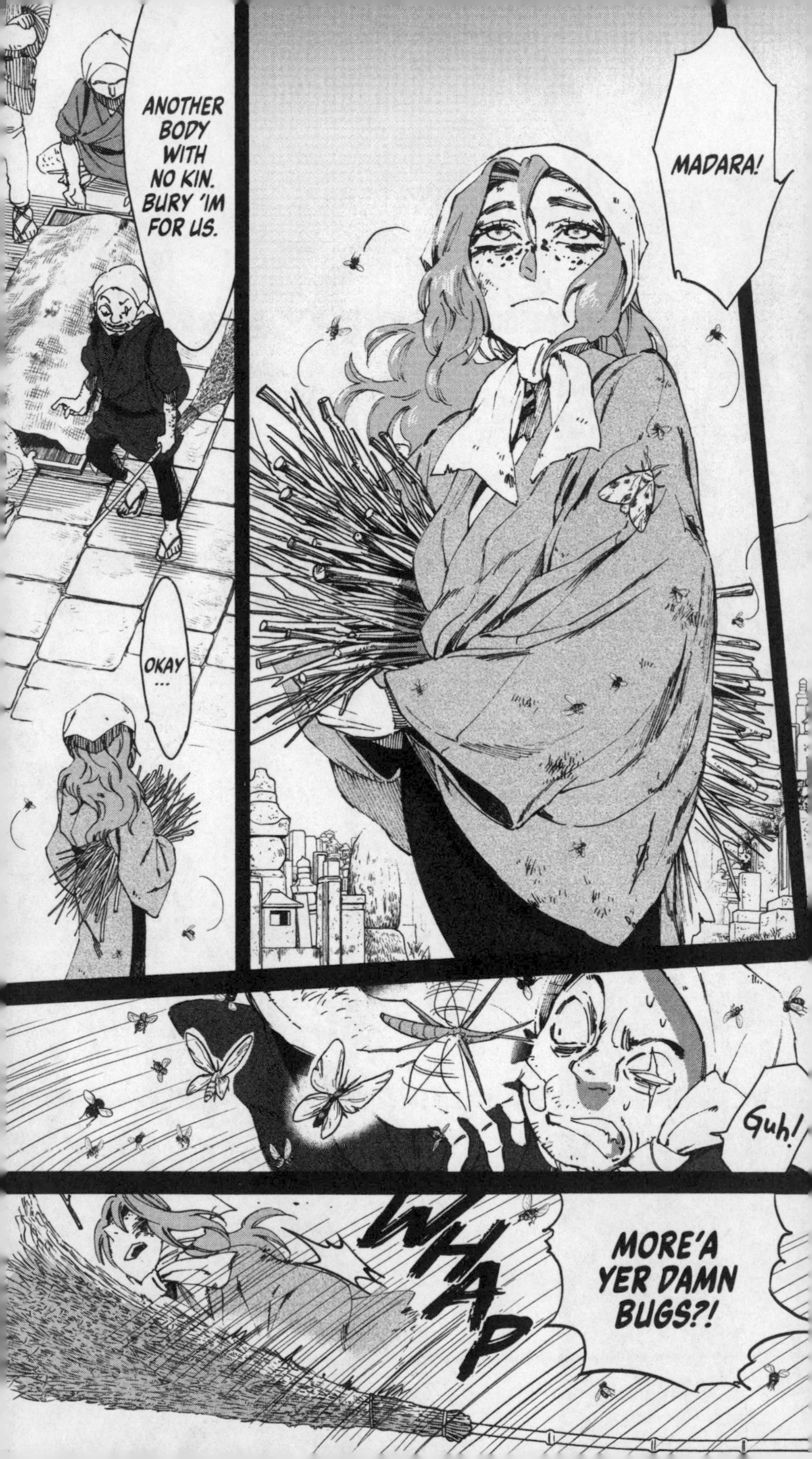
MADARA!
ANOTHER BODY WITH NO KIN. BURY 'IM FOR US.
OKAY ...
Guh!
MORE'A YER DAMN BUGS?!
WHAP

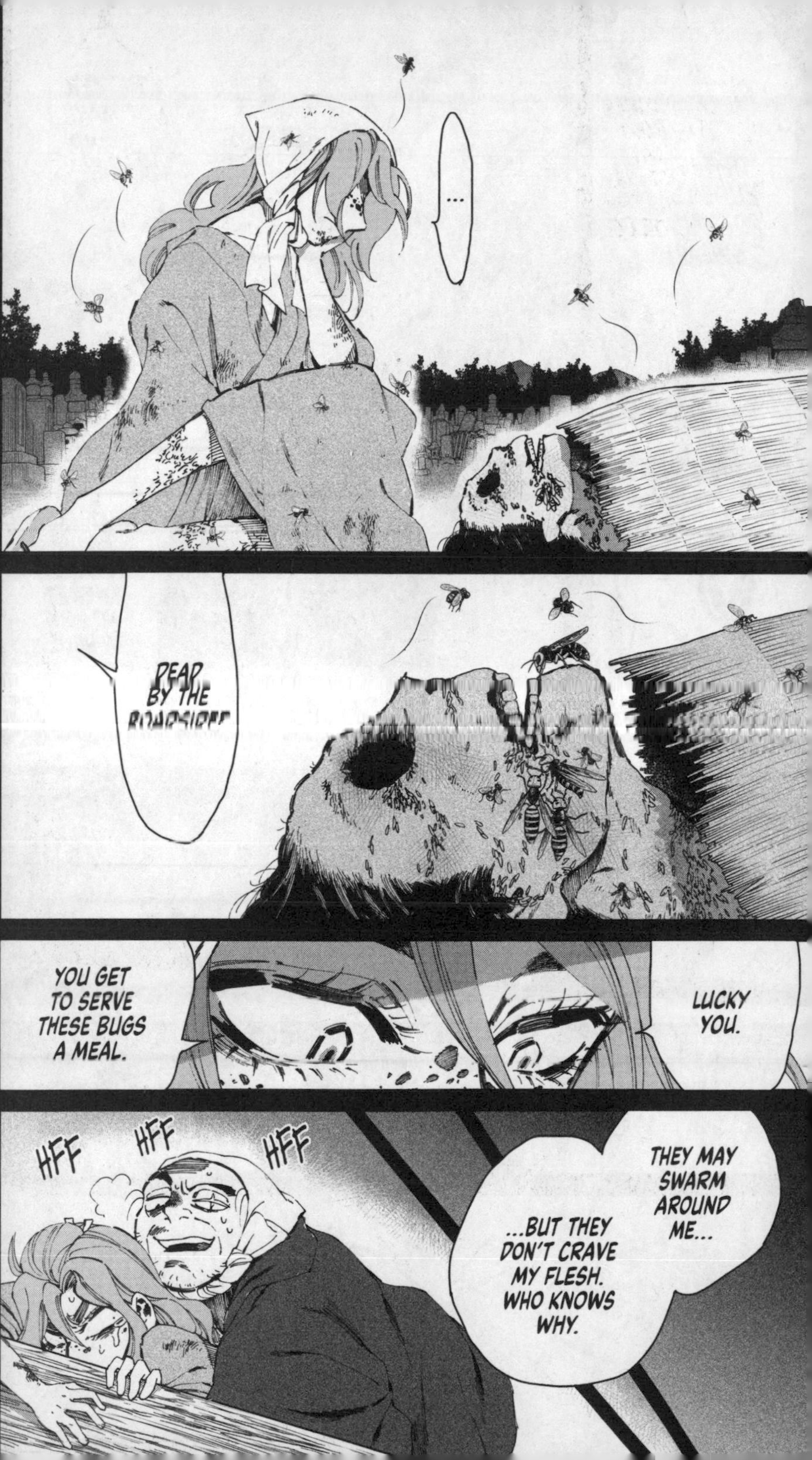
...
DEAD BY THE
LUCKY YOU.
YOU GET TO SERVE THESE BUGS A MEAL.
THEY MAY SWARM AROUND ME...
...BUT THEY DON'T CRAVE MY FLESH. WHO KNOWS WHY.
HFF
HFF
HFF

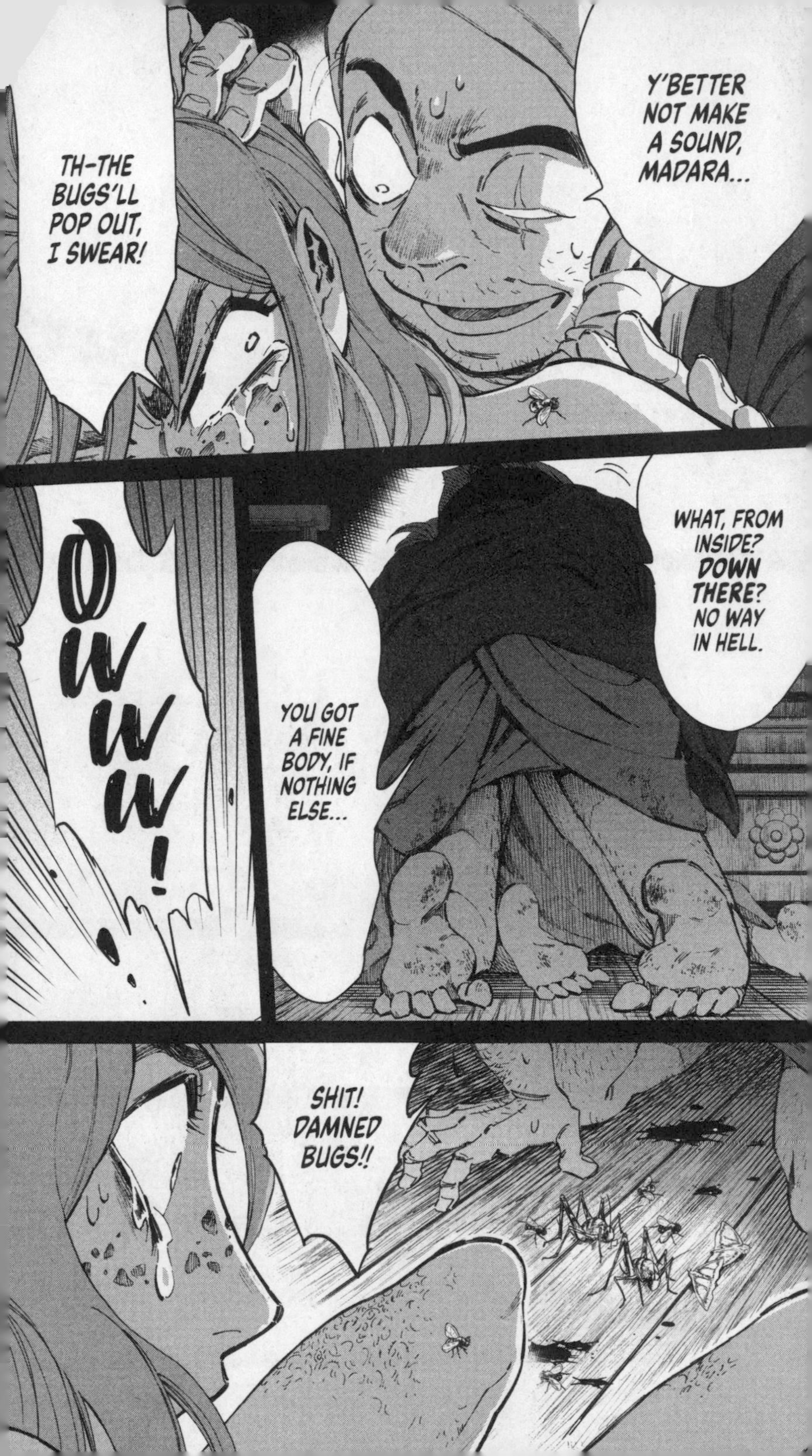
Y'BETTER NOT MAKE A SOUND, MADARA...
TH-THE BUGS'LL POP OUT, I SWEAR!
WHAT, FROM INSIDE? DOWN THERE? NO WAY IN HELL.
YOU GOT A FINE BODY, IF NOTHING ELSE...
OWWW!
SHIT! DAMNED BUGS!!

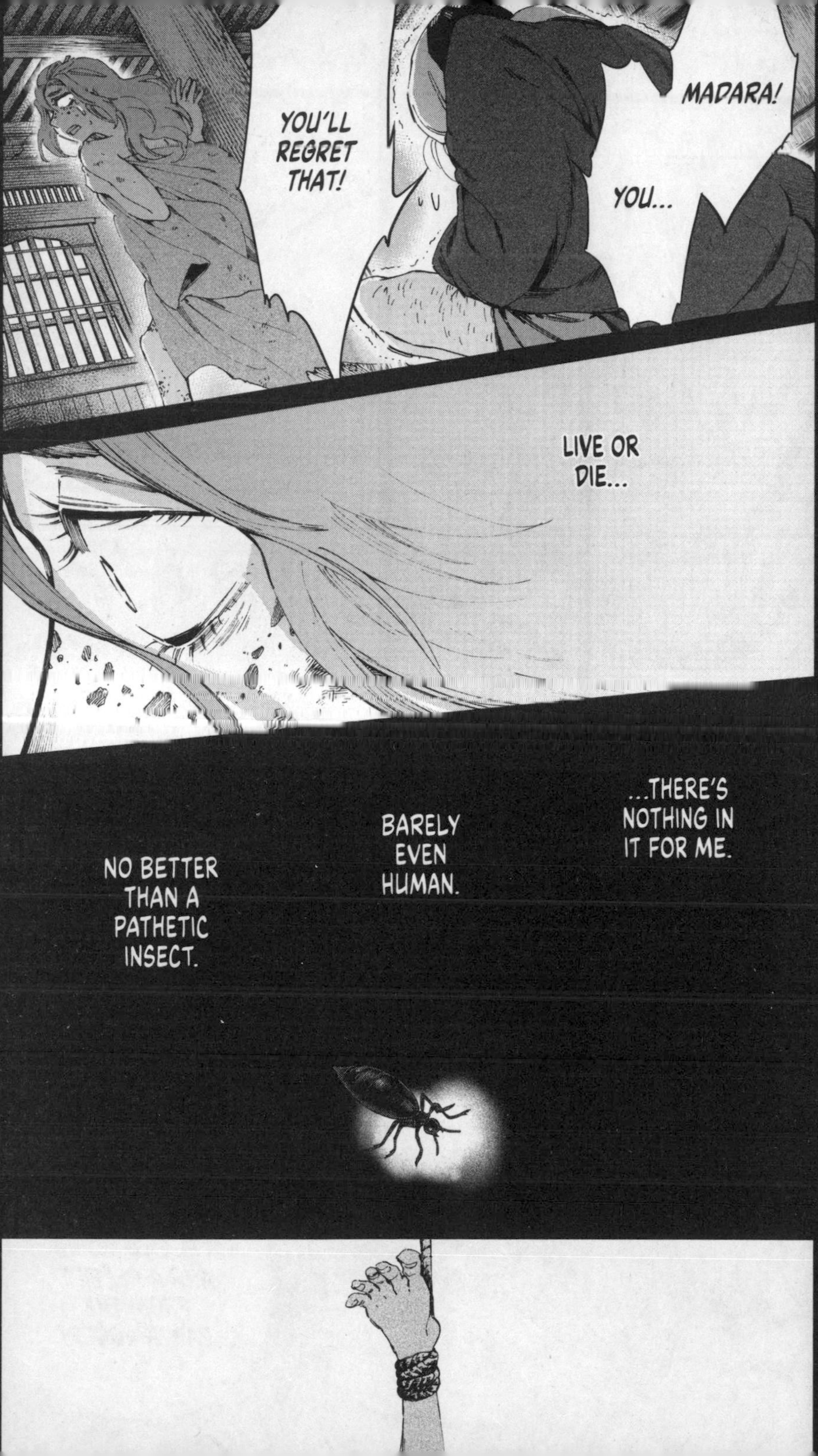
MADARA!
YOU...
YOU'LL REGRET THAT!
LIVE OR DIE...
...THERE'S NOTHING IN IT FOR ME.
BARELY EVEN HUMAN.
NO BETTER THAN A PATHETIC INSECT.

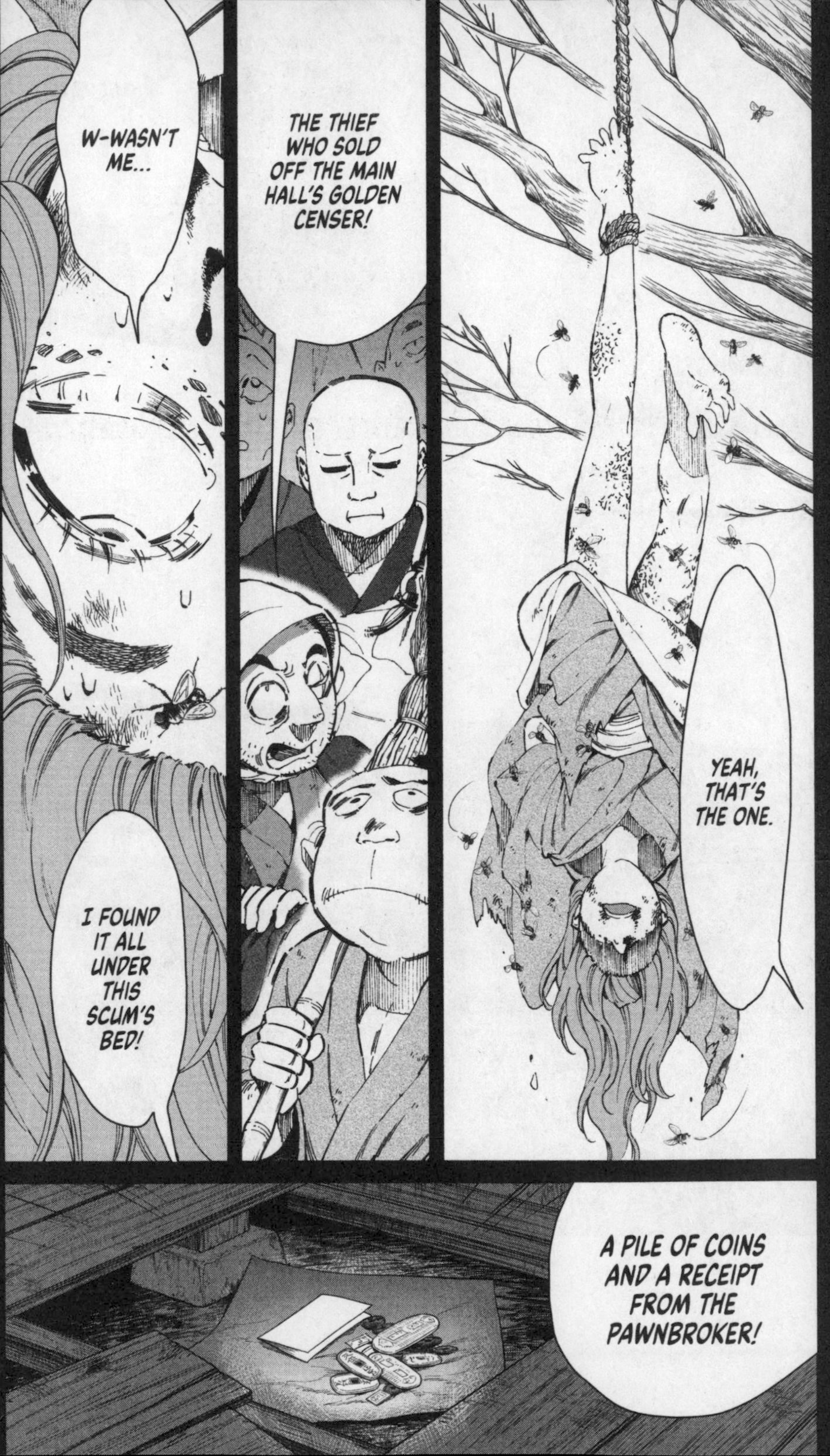
YEAH, THAT'S THE ONE.
THE THIEF WHO SOLD OFF THE MAIN HALL'S GOLDEN CENSER!
W-WASN'T ME...
I FOUND IT ALL UNDER THIS SCUM'S BED!
A PILE OF COINS AND A RECEIPT FROM THE PAWNBROKER!

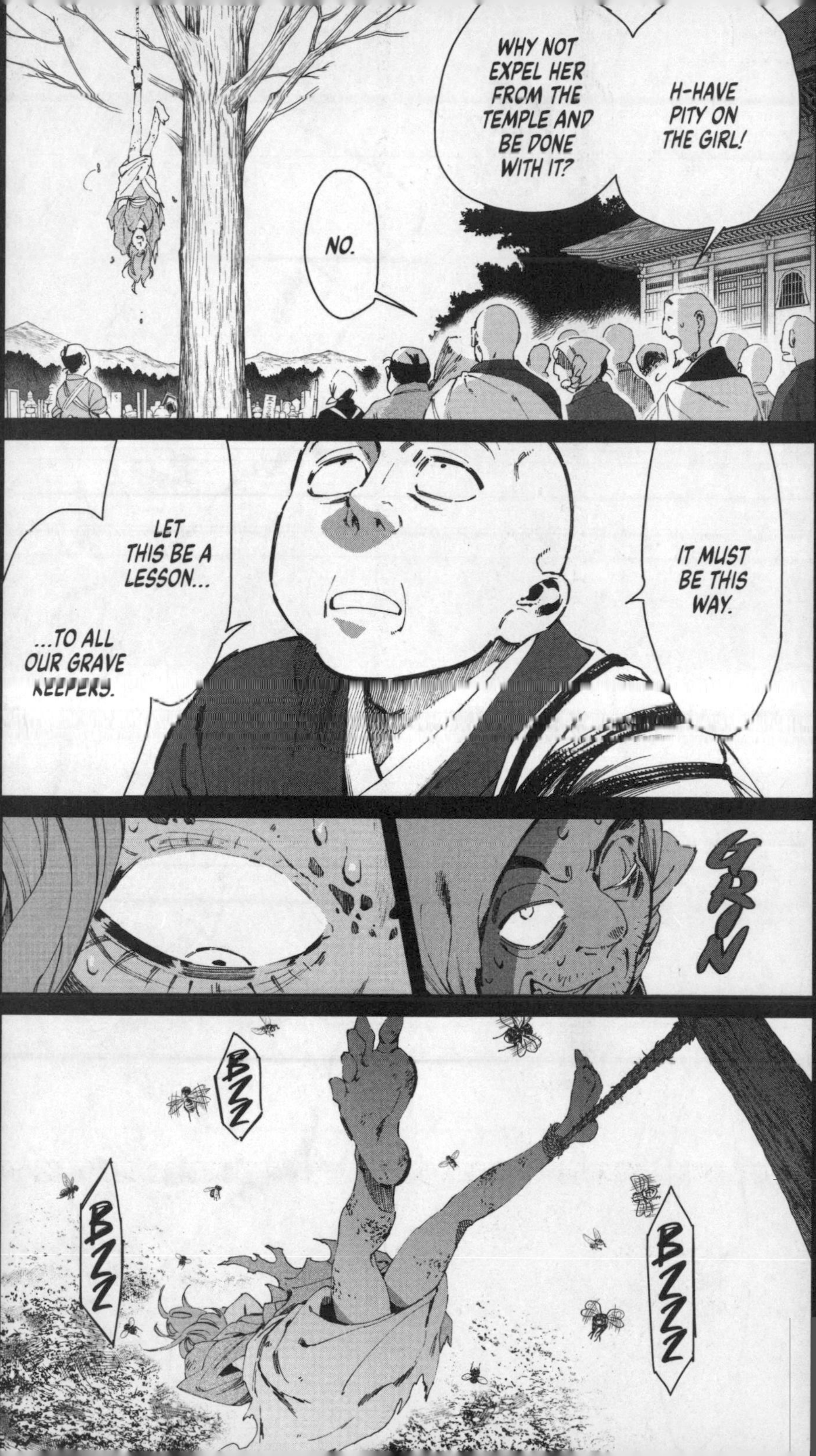
H-HAVE PITY ON THE GIRL!
WHY NOT EXPEL HER FROM THE TEMPLE AND BE DONE WITH IT?
NO.
IT MUST BE THIS WAY.
LET THIS BE A LESSON...
...TO ALL OUR GRAVE KEEPERS.
GRIN
BZZZ
BZZ
BZZ

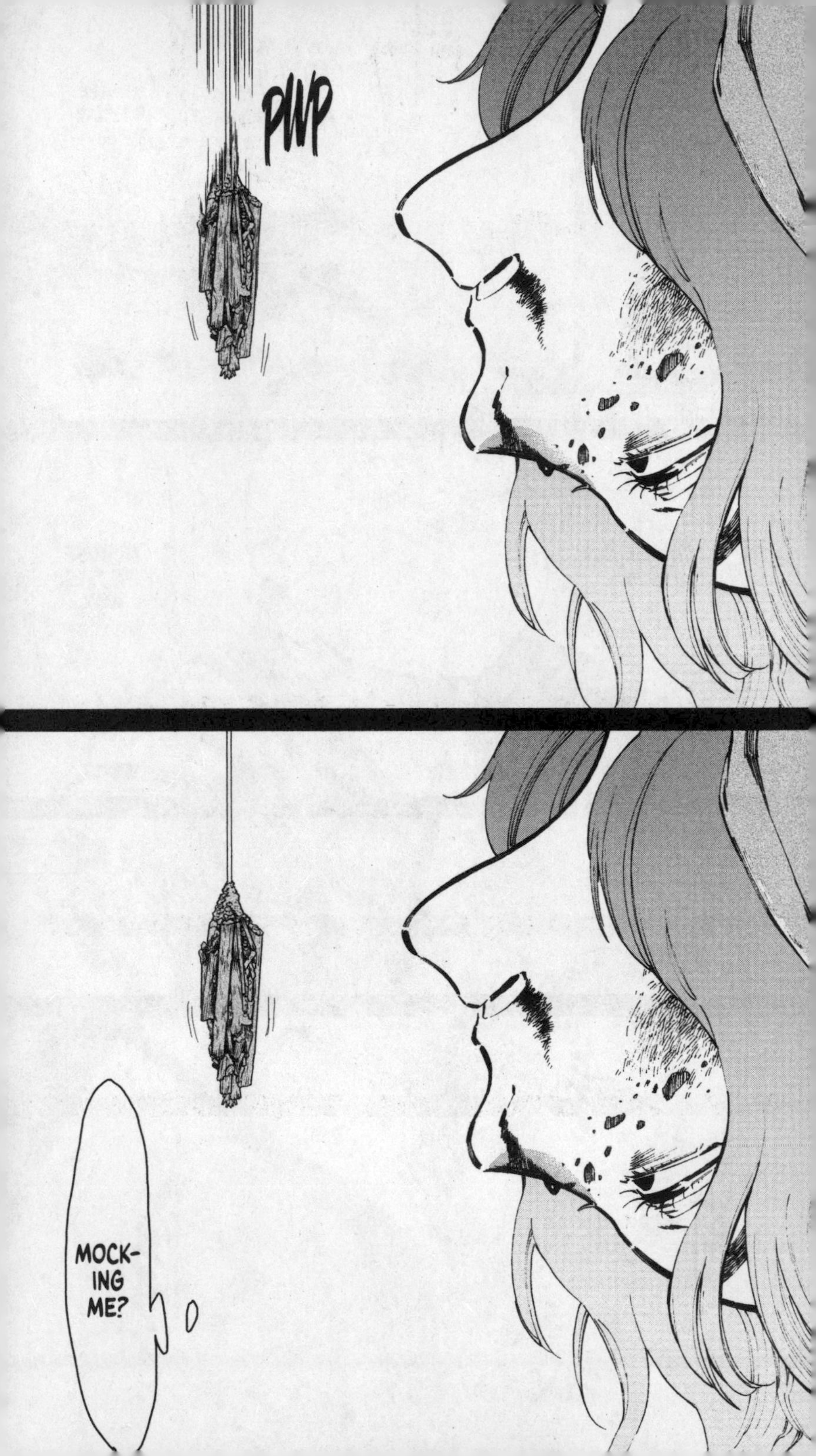
PWP
MOCK-ING ME?

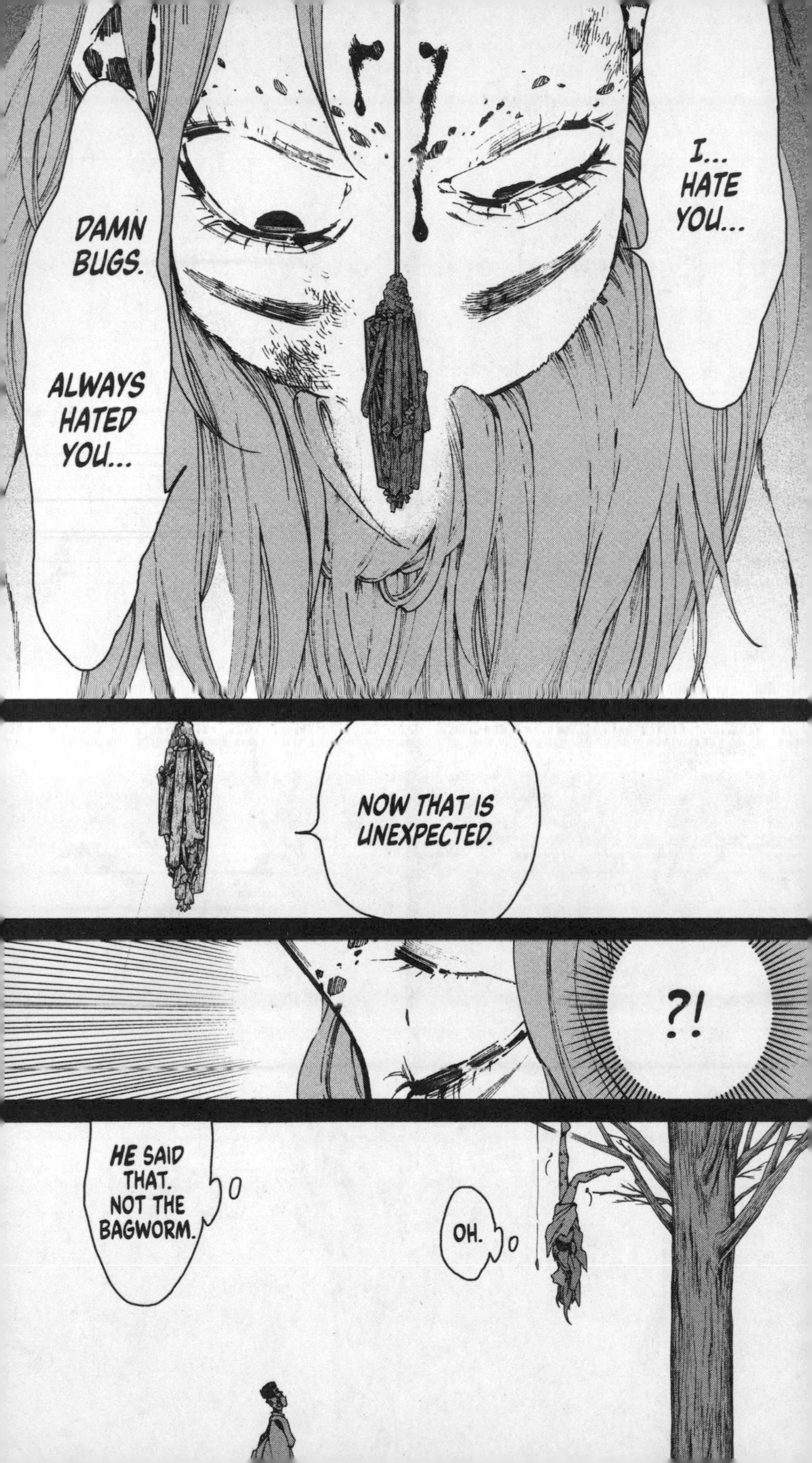
I... HATE YOU...
DAMN BUGS.
ALWAYS HATED YOU...
NOW THAT IS UNEXPECTED.
?!
HE SAID THAT. NOT THE BAGWORM.
OH.

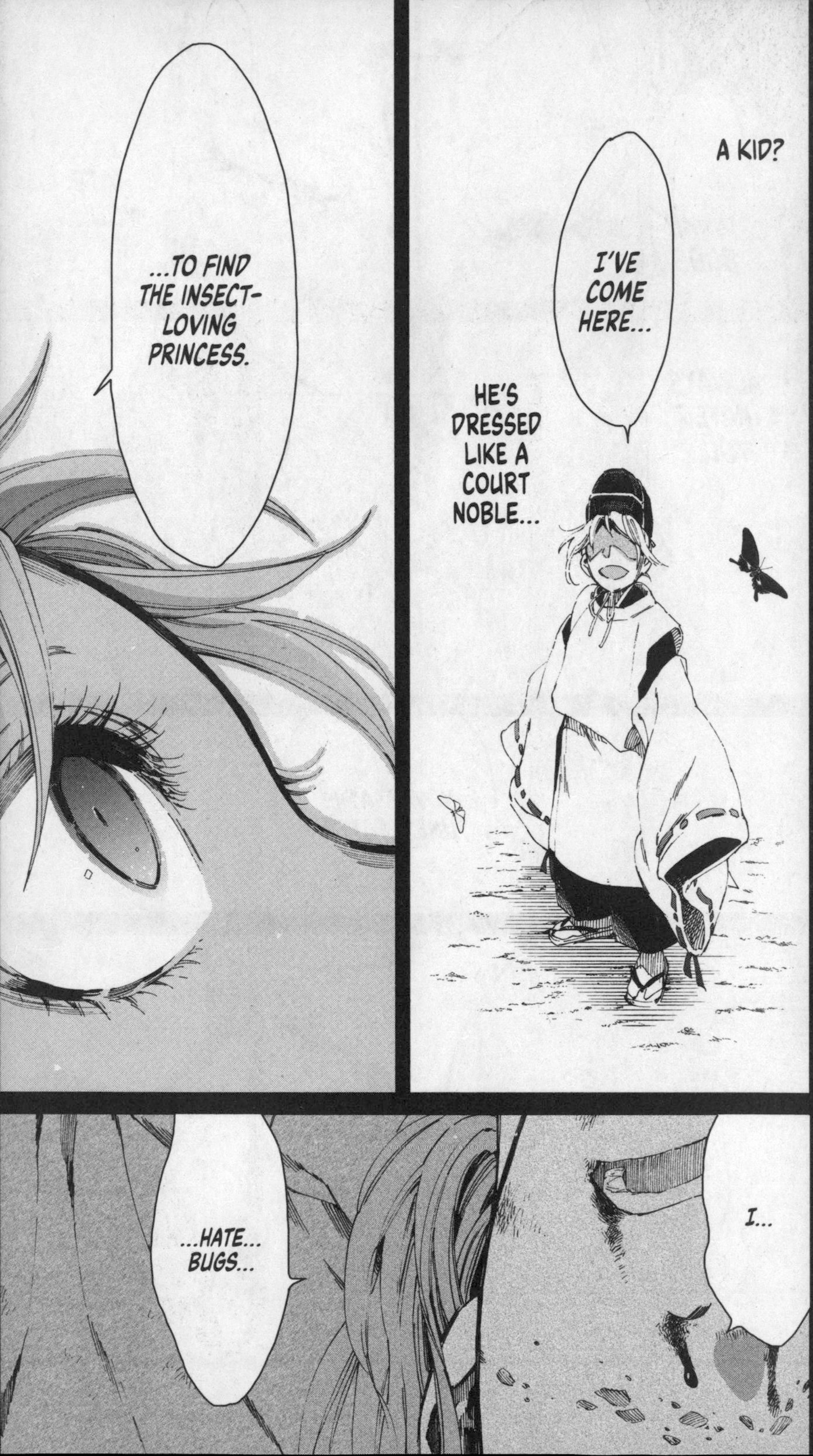
A KID?
I'VE COME HERE...
HE'S DRESSED LIKE A COURT NOBLE...
...TO FIND THE INSECT-LOVING PRINCESS.
I...
...HATE... BUGS...

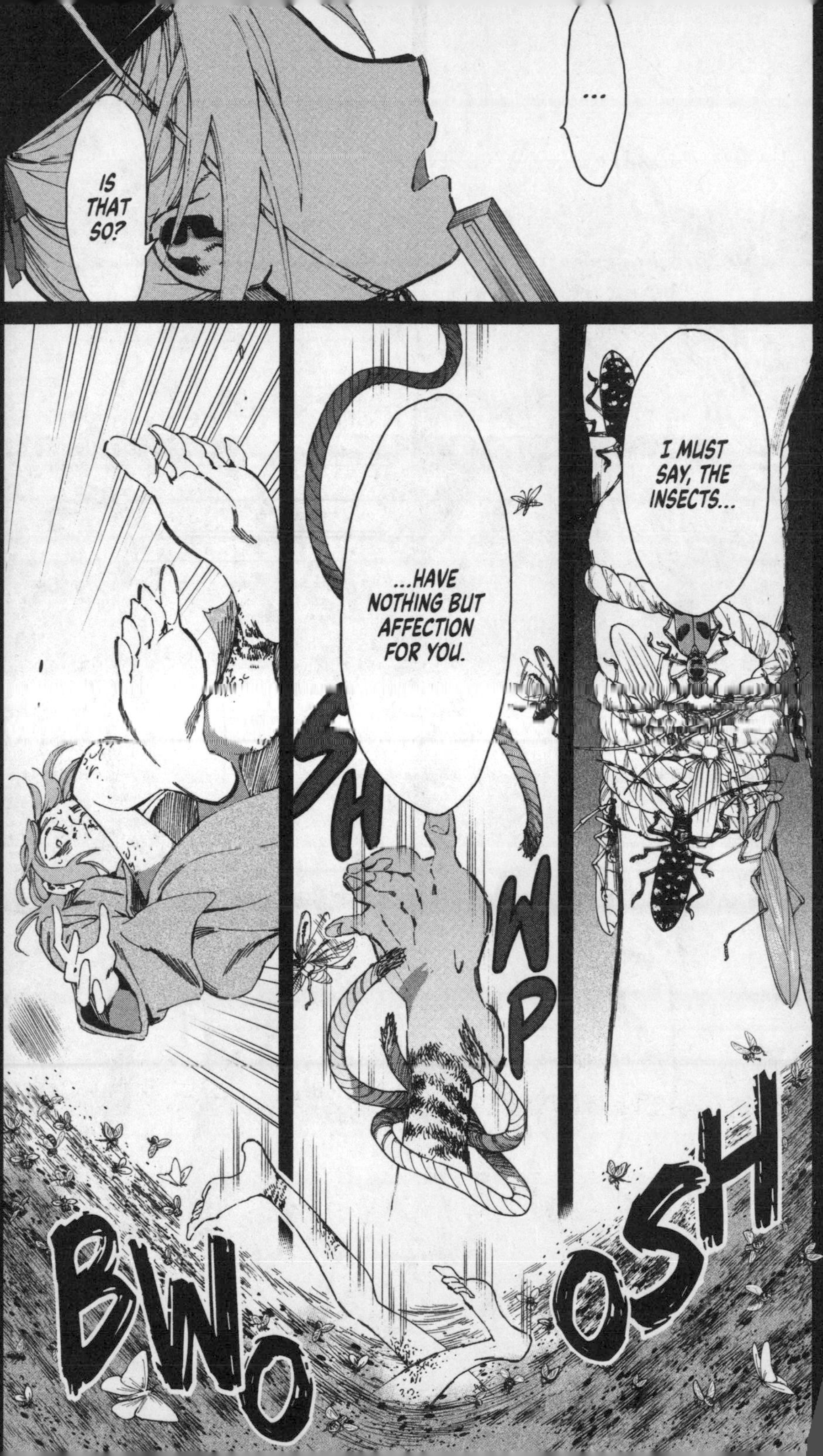
...
IS THAT SO?
I MUST SAY, THE INSECTS...
...HAVE NOTHING BUT AFFECTION FOR YOU.
SHWP
BWOOSH

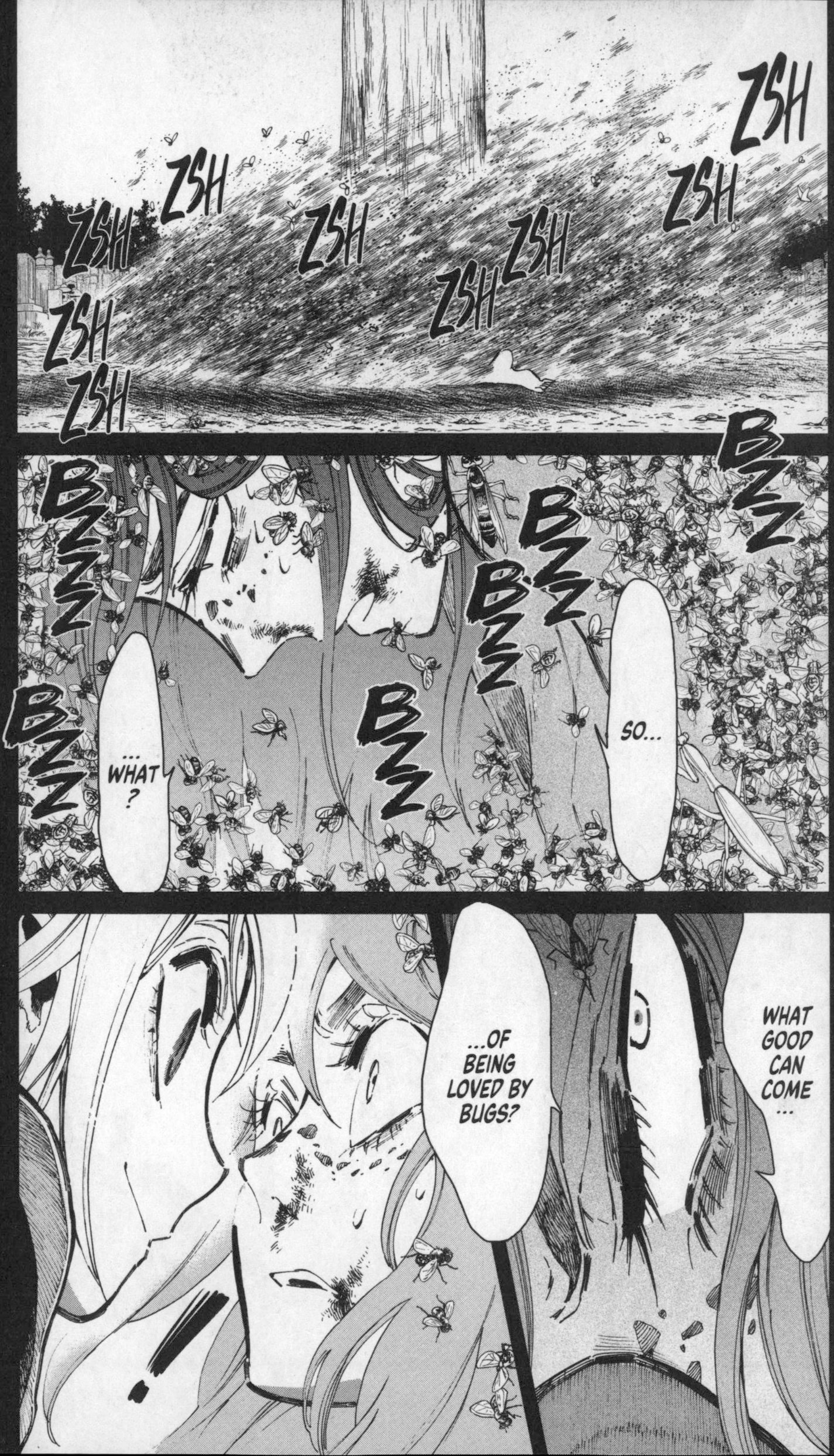
ZSH
ZSH
ZSH
ZSH
ZSH
ZSH
ZSH
ZSH
ZSH
BZZ
BZZ
BZZ
SO...
BZZ
BZZ
...WHAT?
WHAT GOOD CAN COME ...
...OF BEING LOVED BY BUGS?

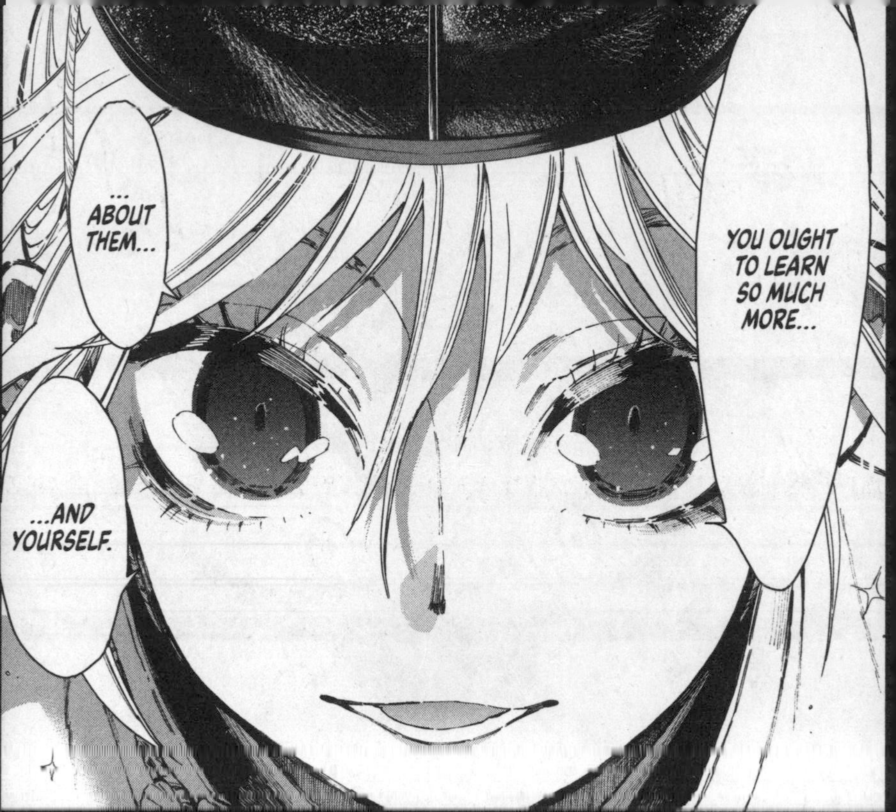
YOU OUGHT TO LEARN SO MUCH MORE...
...ABOUT THEM...
...AND YOURSELF.

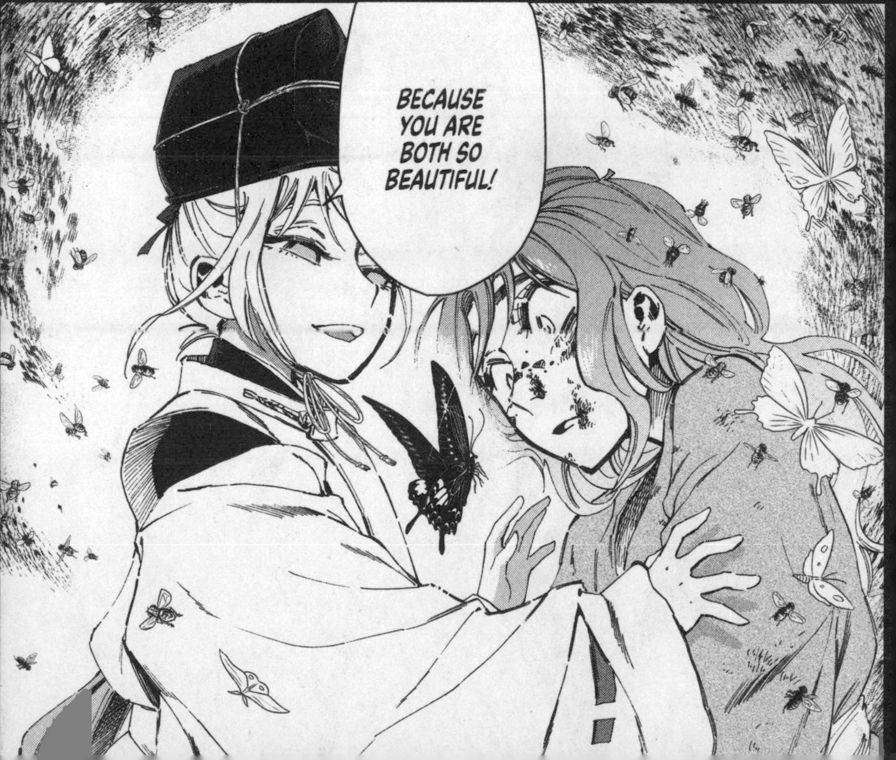
BECAUSE YOU ARE BOTH SO BEAUTIFUL!

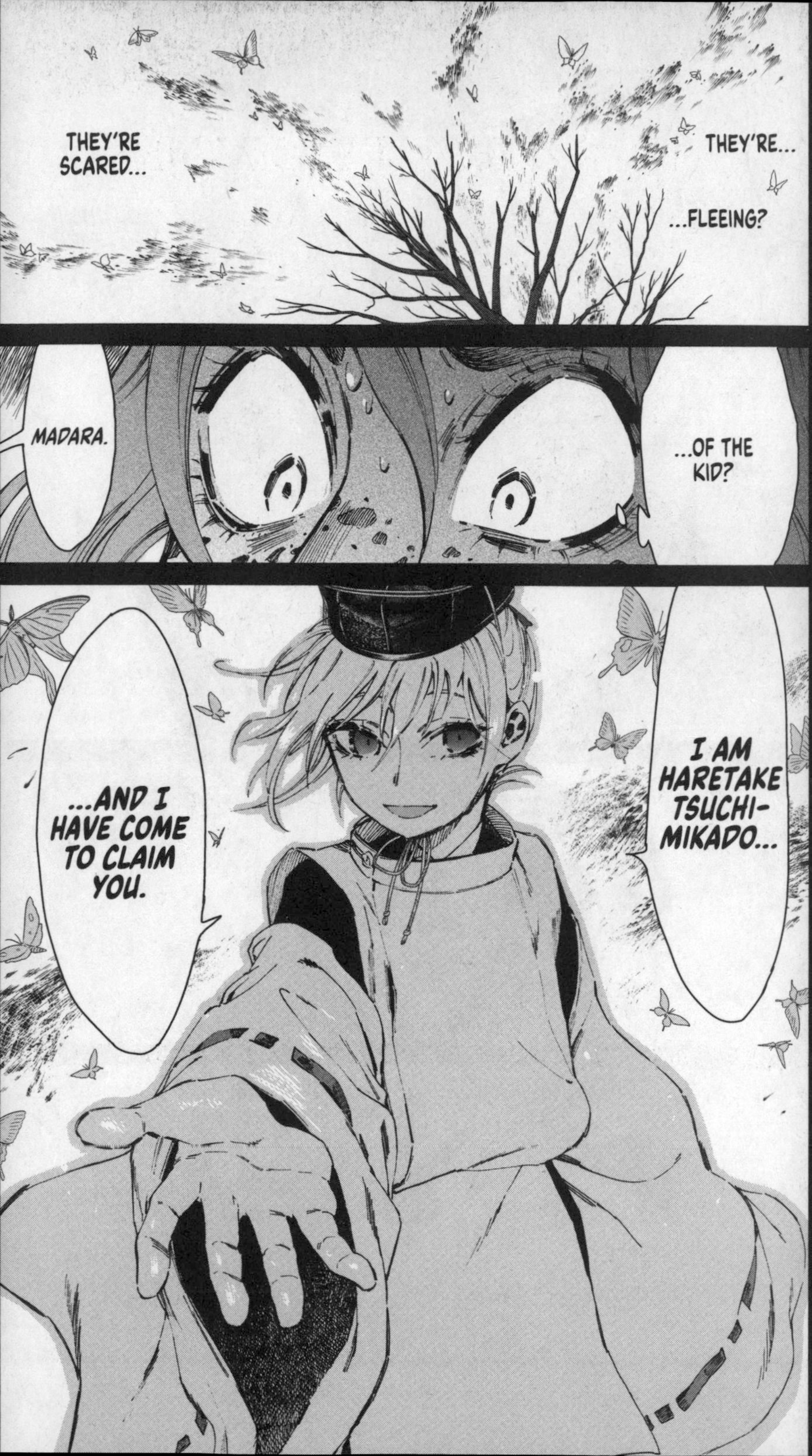
THEY'RE...
...FLEEING?
THEY'RE SCARED...
...OF THE KID?
MADARA.
I AM HARETAKE TSUCHI-MIKADO...
...AND I HAVE COME TO CLAIM YOU.

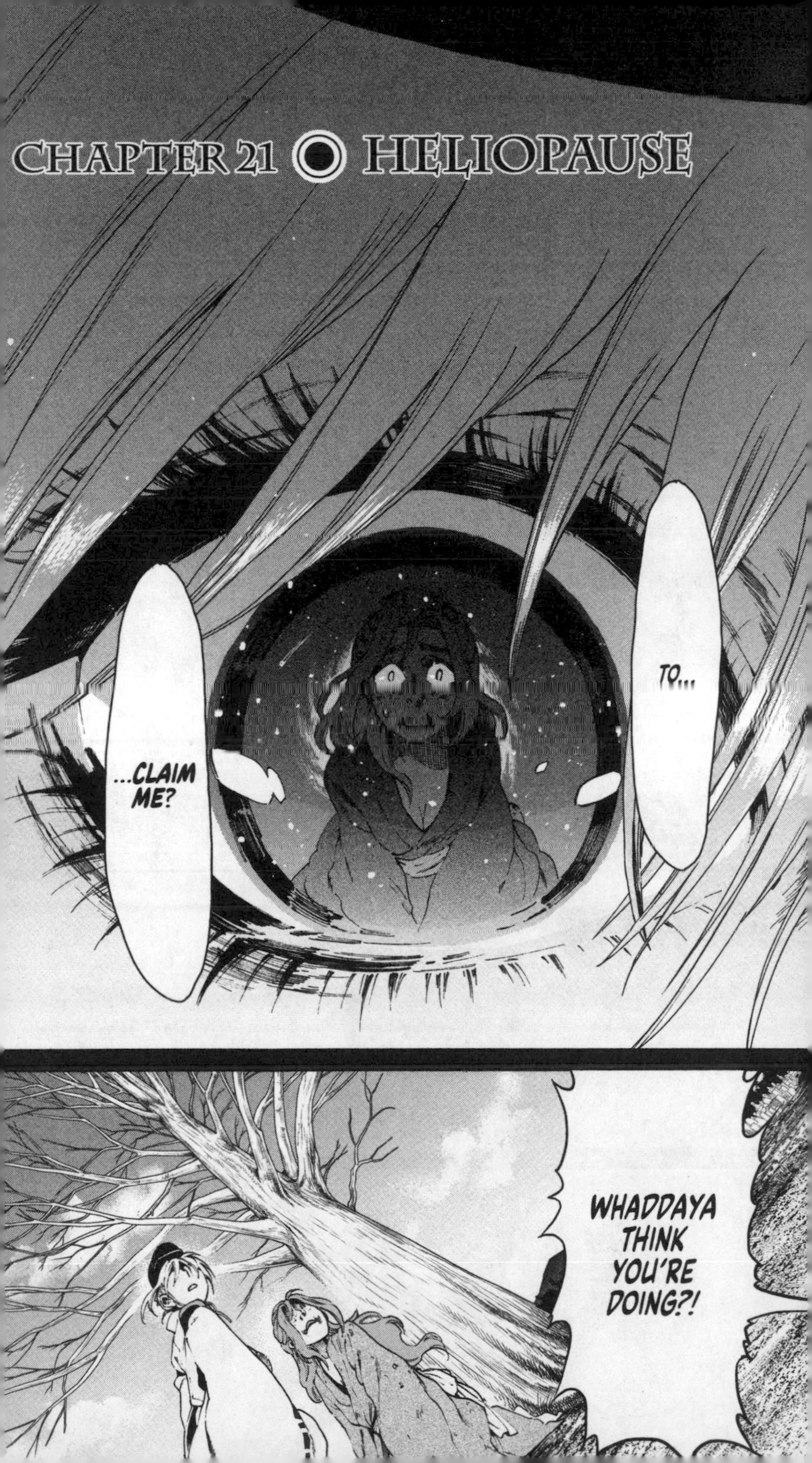
CHAPTER 21 HELIOPAUSE
TO...
...CLAIM ME?
WHADDAYA THINK YOU'RE DOING?!

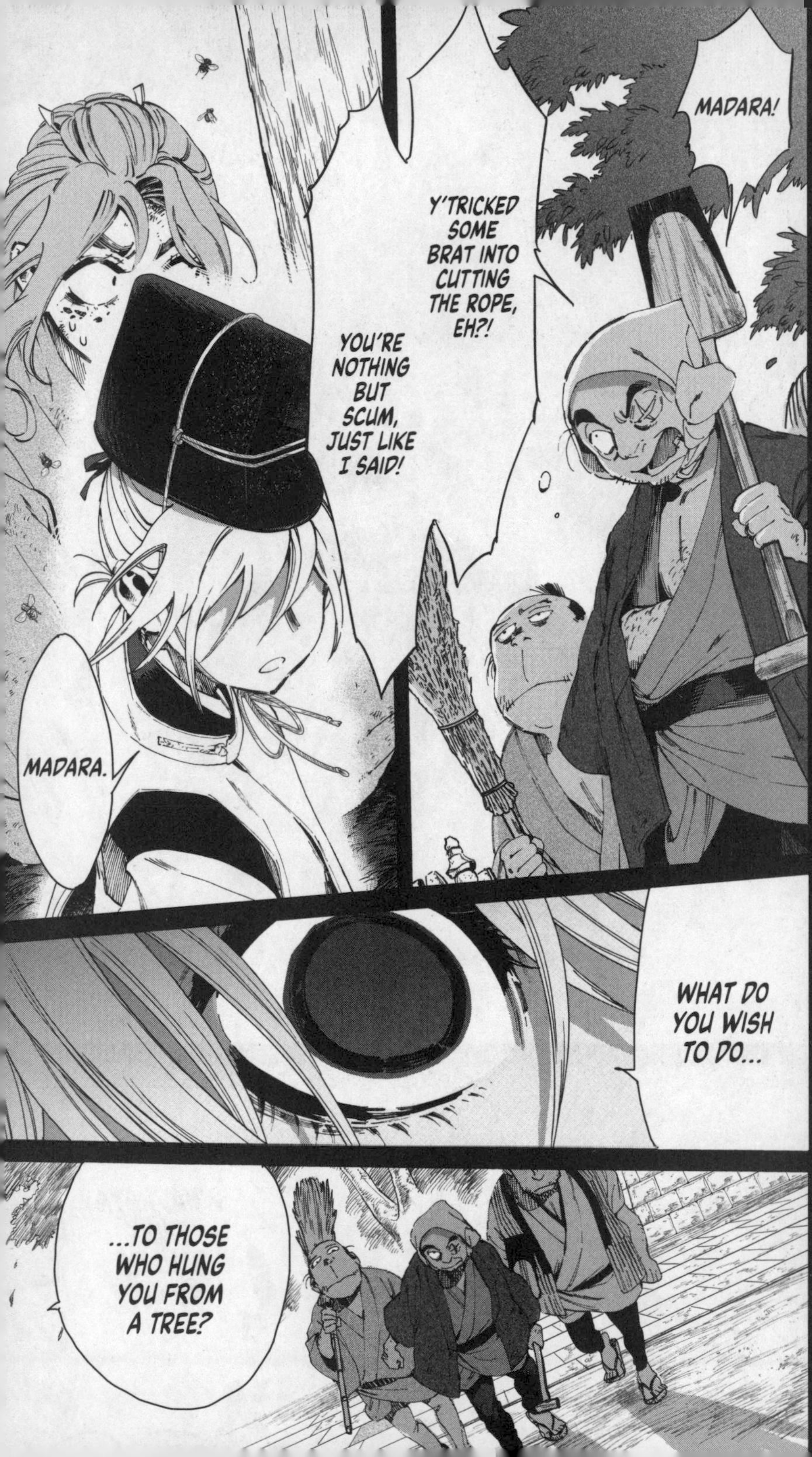
MADARA!
Y'TRICKED SOME BRAT INTO CUTTING THE ROPE, EH?!
YOU'RE NOTHING BUT SCUM, JUST LIKE I SAID!
MADARA.
WHAT DO YOU WISH TO DO...
...TO THOSE WHO HUNG YOU FROM A TREE?

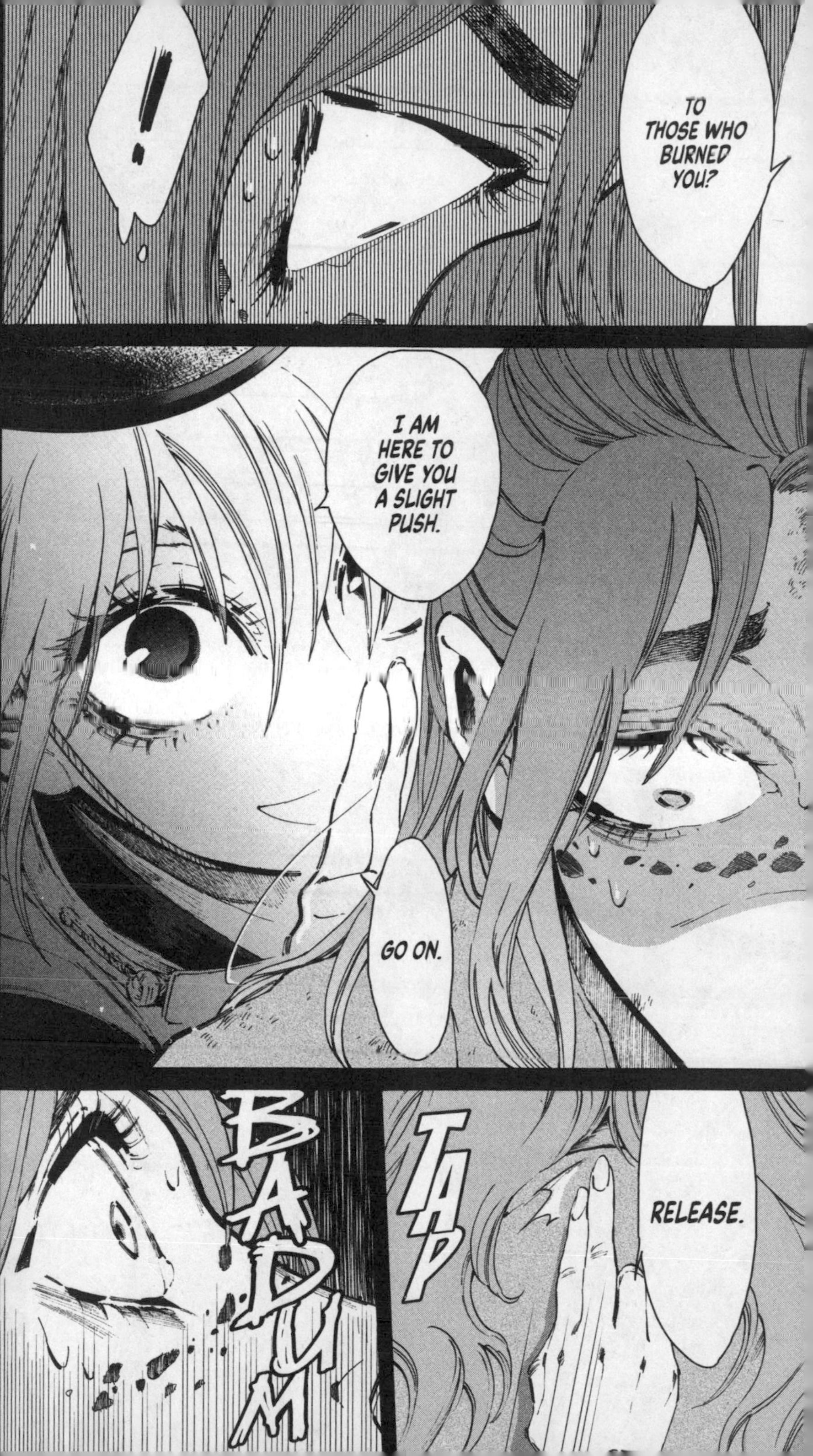
TO THOSE WHO BURNED YOU?
!
I AM HERE TO GIVE YOU A SLIGHT PUSH.
GO ON.
RELEASE.
TAP
BADUM

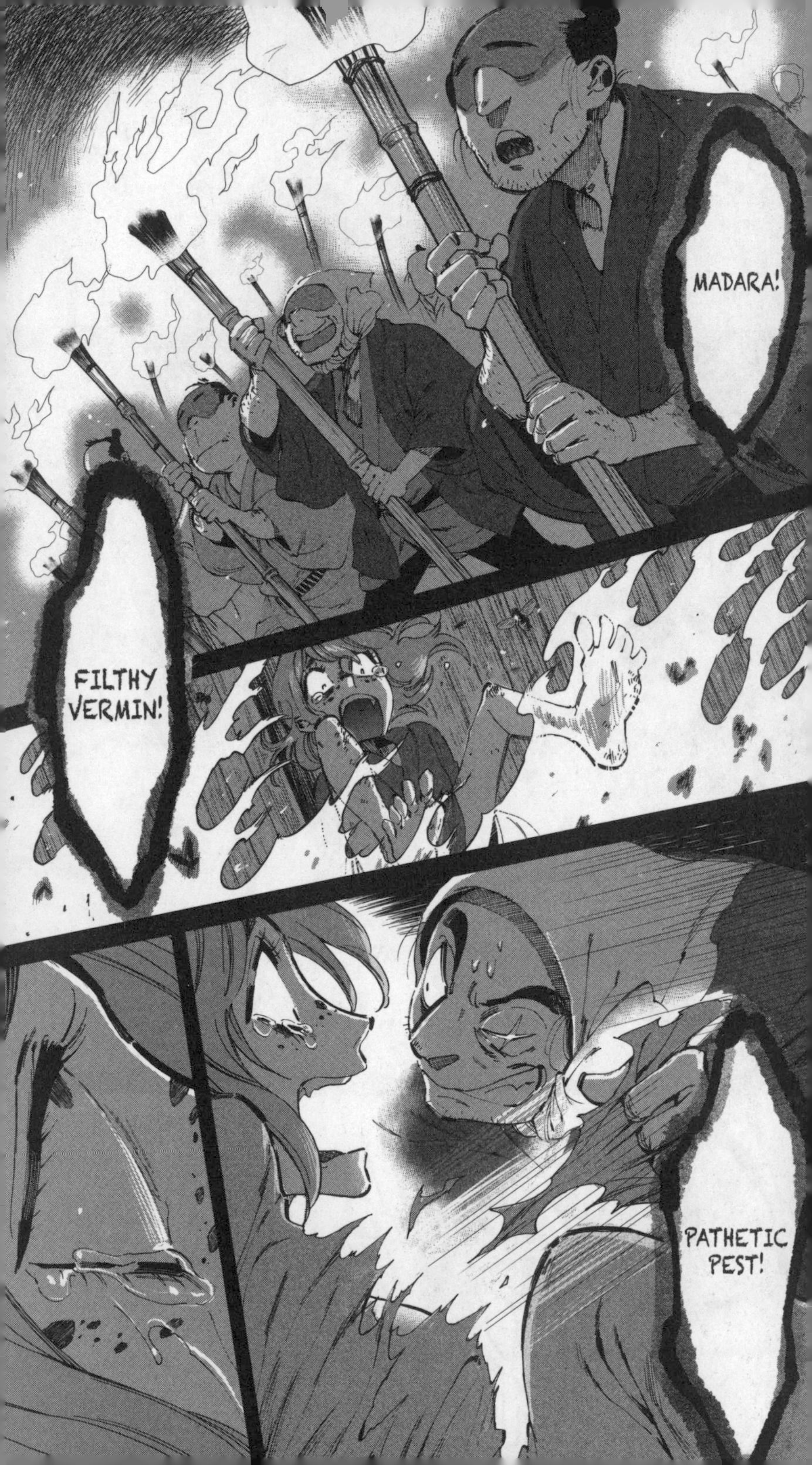
MADARA!
FILTHY VERMIN!
PATHETIC PEST!

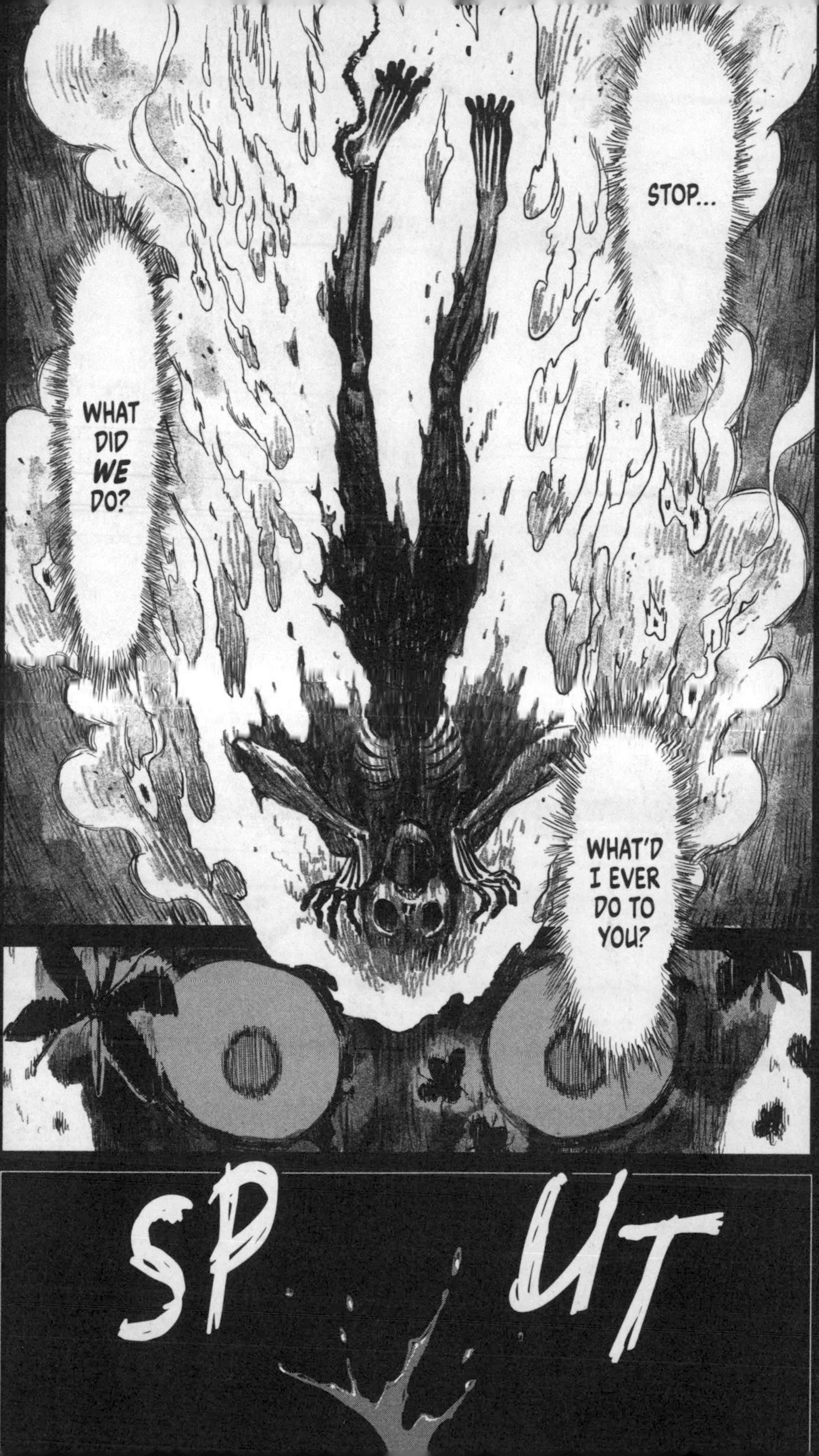
STOP...
WHAT DID **WE** DO?
WHAT'D I EVER DO TO YOU?
SP UT

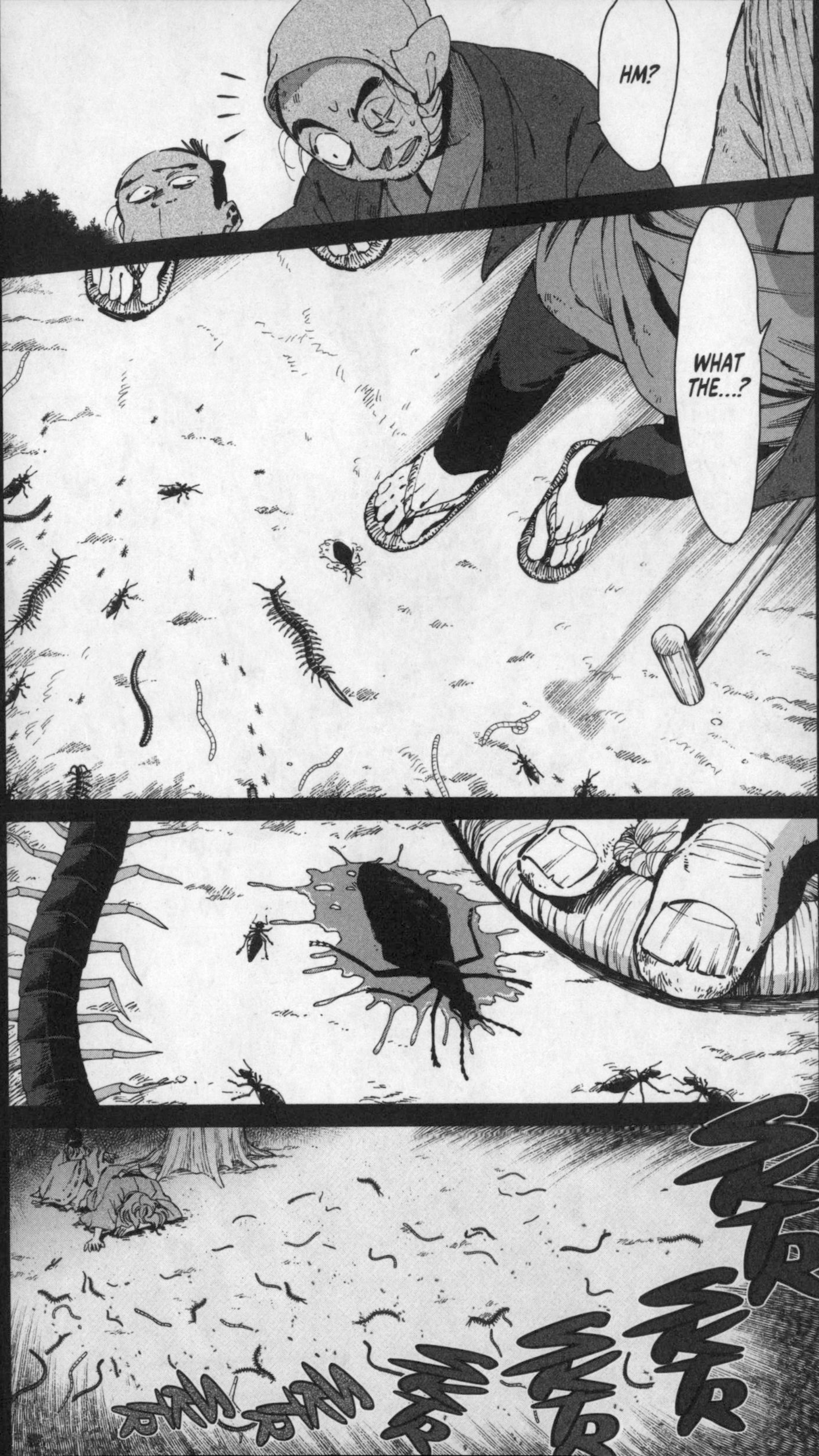
HM?
WHAT THE...?

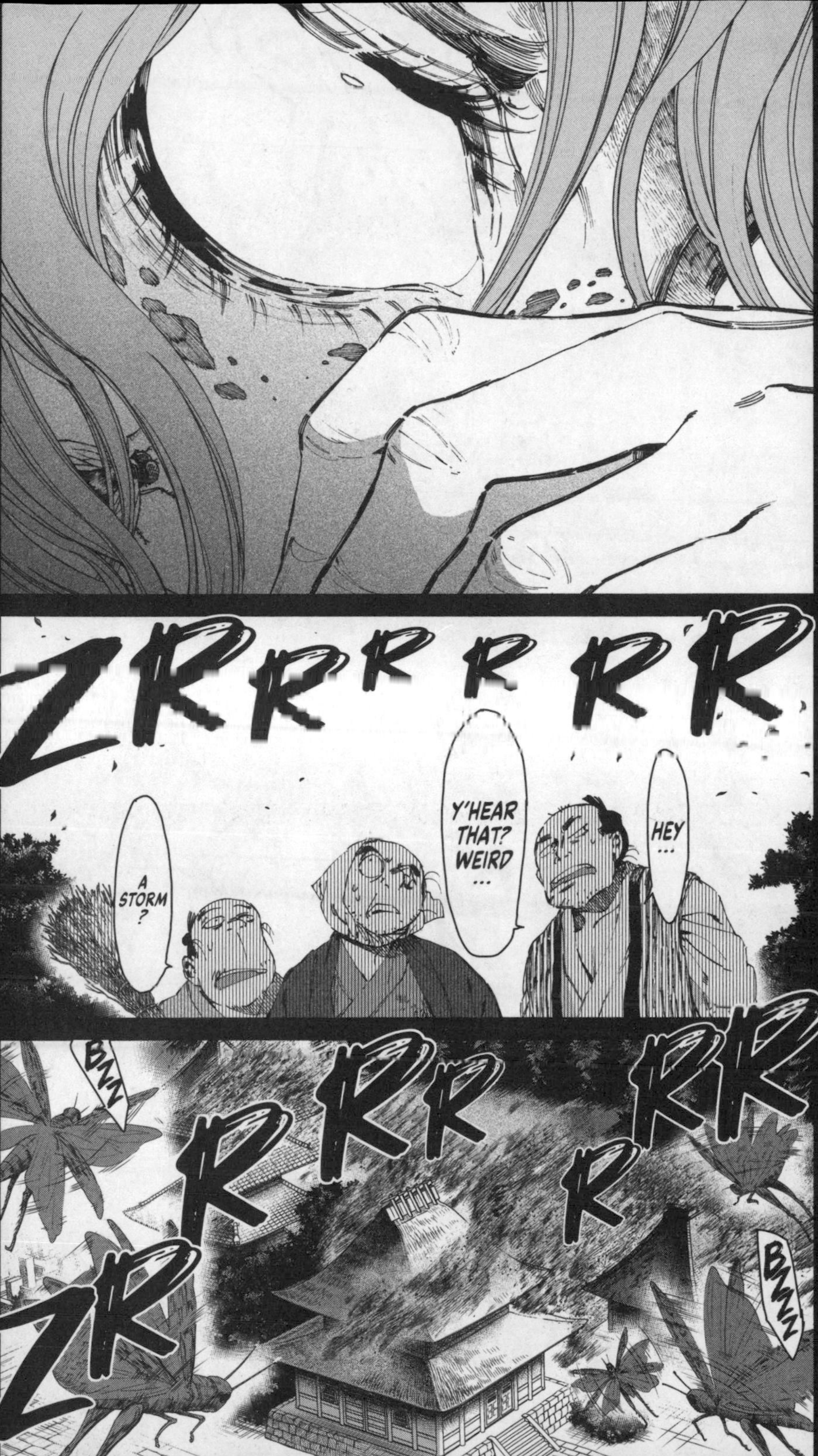
ZRRRRRR
HEY...
Y'HEAR THAT? WEIRD...
A STORM?
BZZZ
ZRRRRRR
BZZ

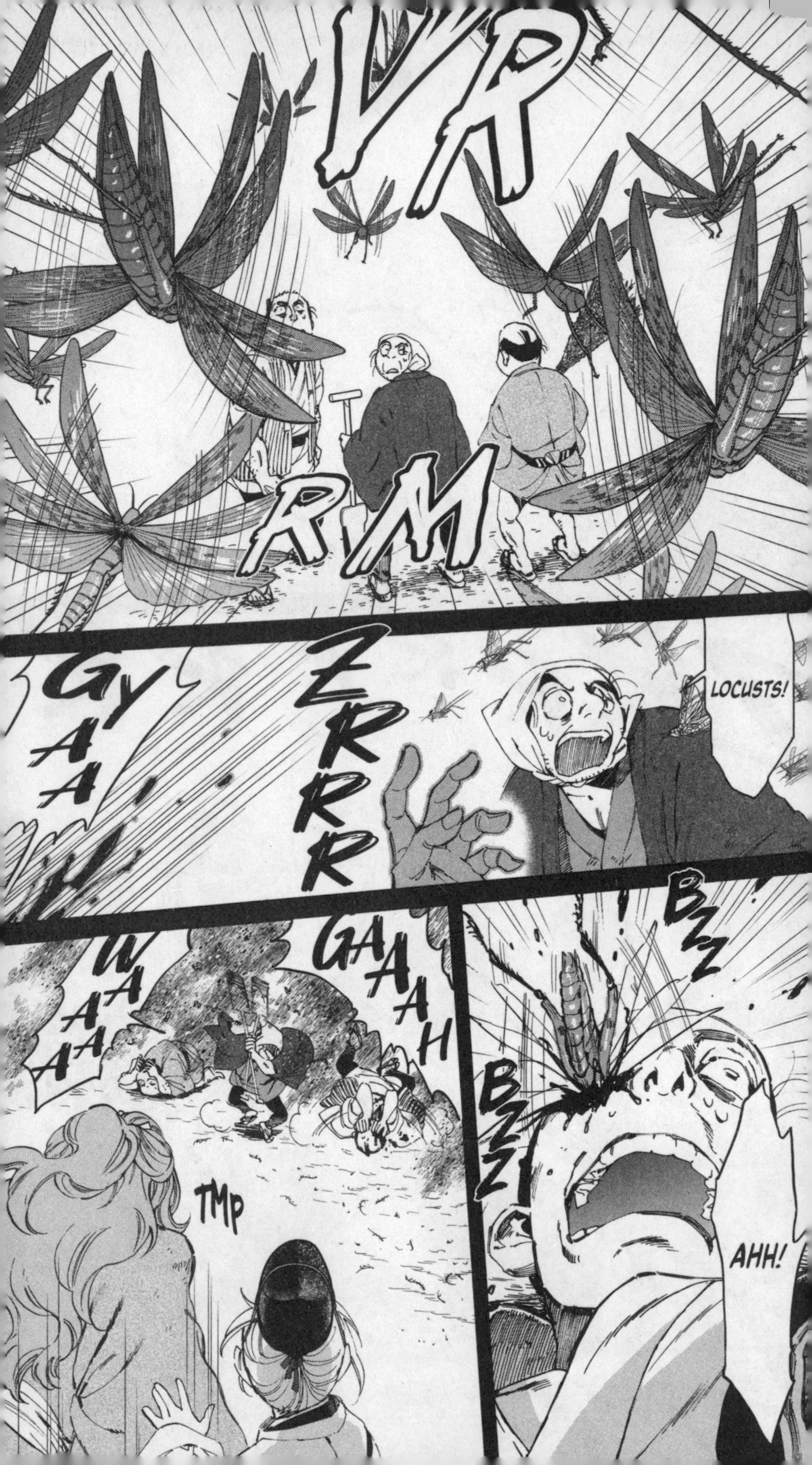

VR
RM
LOCUSTS!
ZRRRR
GYAA
BZZ
BZZZ
AHH!
GAAAAH
UAAAAA
TMP

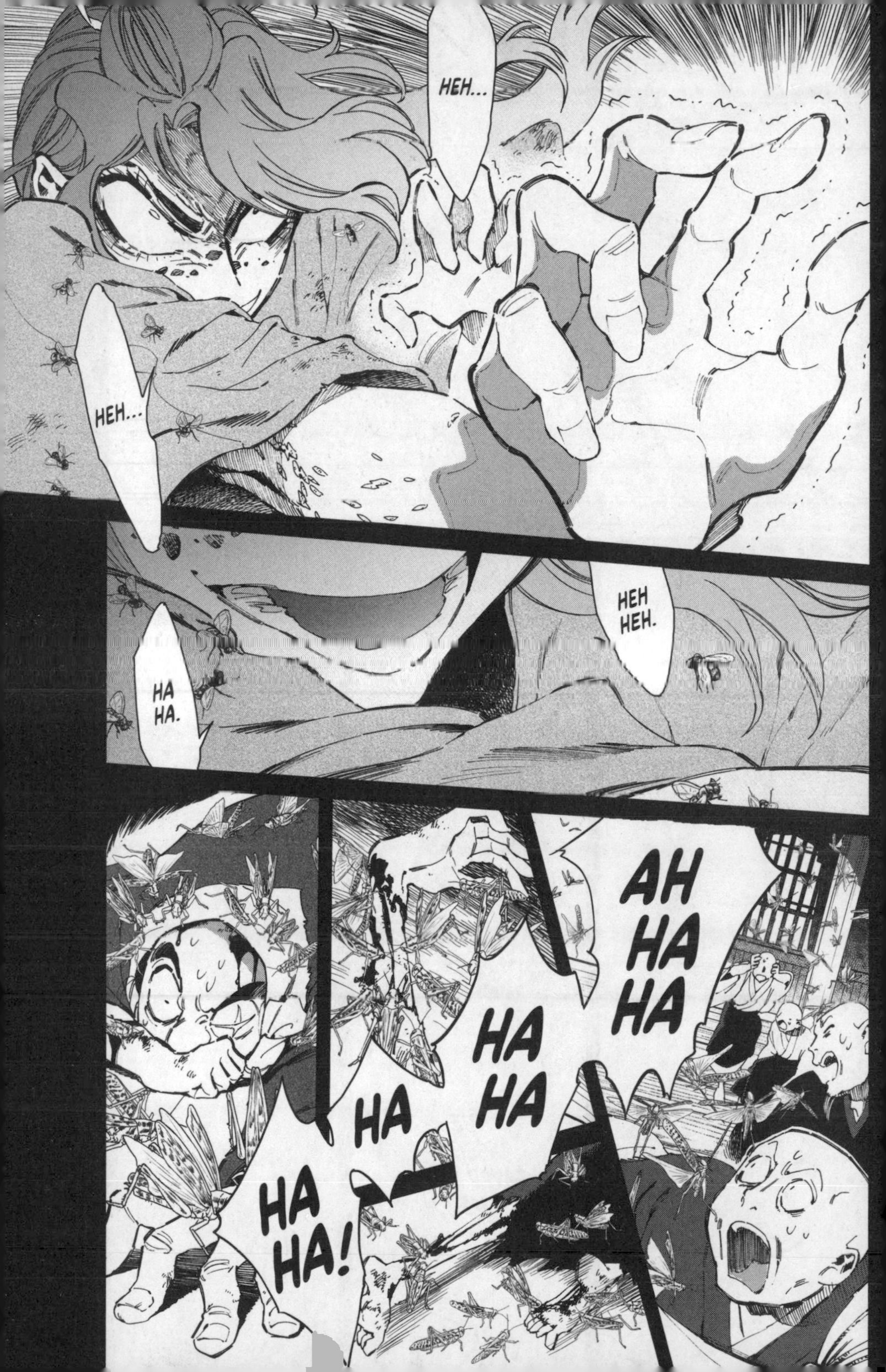
HEH...
HEH...
HEH HEH.
HA HA.
AH HA HA
HA HA
HA
HA HA!

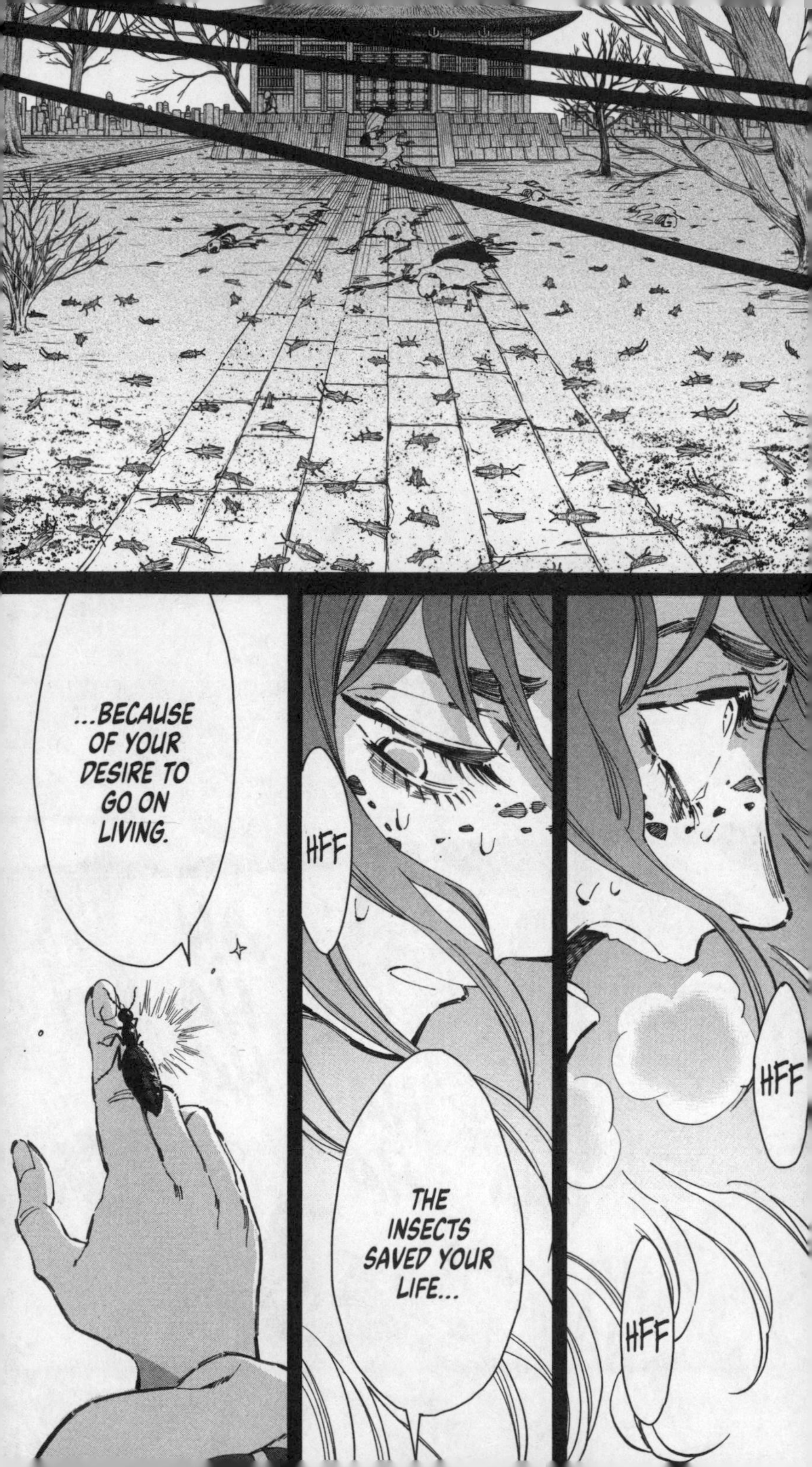
HFF
HFF
HFF
THE INSECTS SAVED YOUR LIFE...
...BECAUSE OF YOUR DESIRE TO GO ON LIVING.

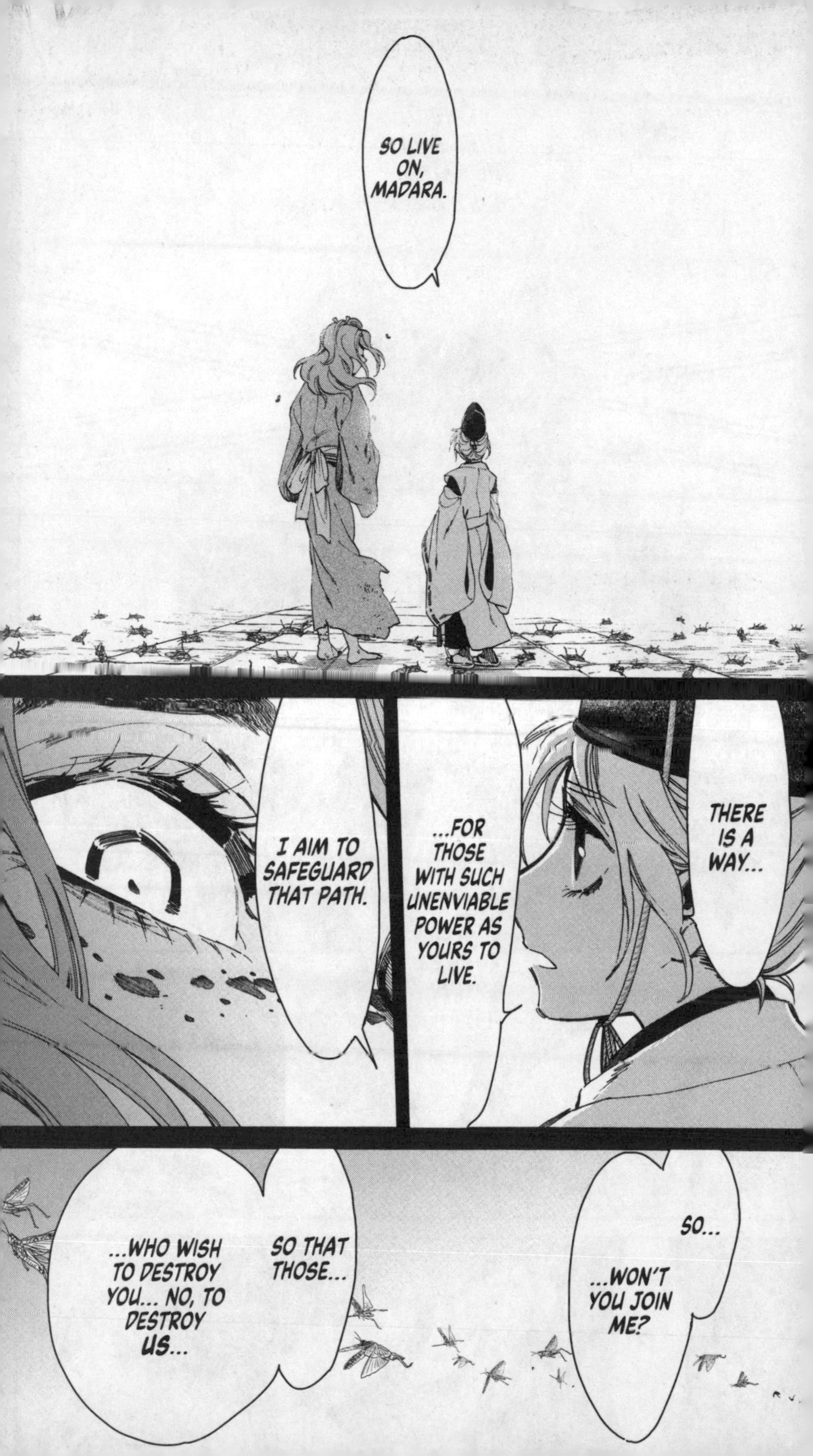
SO LIVE ON, MADARA.
THERE IS A WAY...
...FOR THOSE WITH SUCH UNENVIABLE POWER AS YOURS TO LIVE.
I AIM TO SAFEGUARD THAT PATH.
SO...
...WON'T YOU JOIN ME?
SO THAT THOSE...
...WHO WISH TO DESTROY YOU... NO, TO DESTROY US...

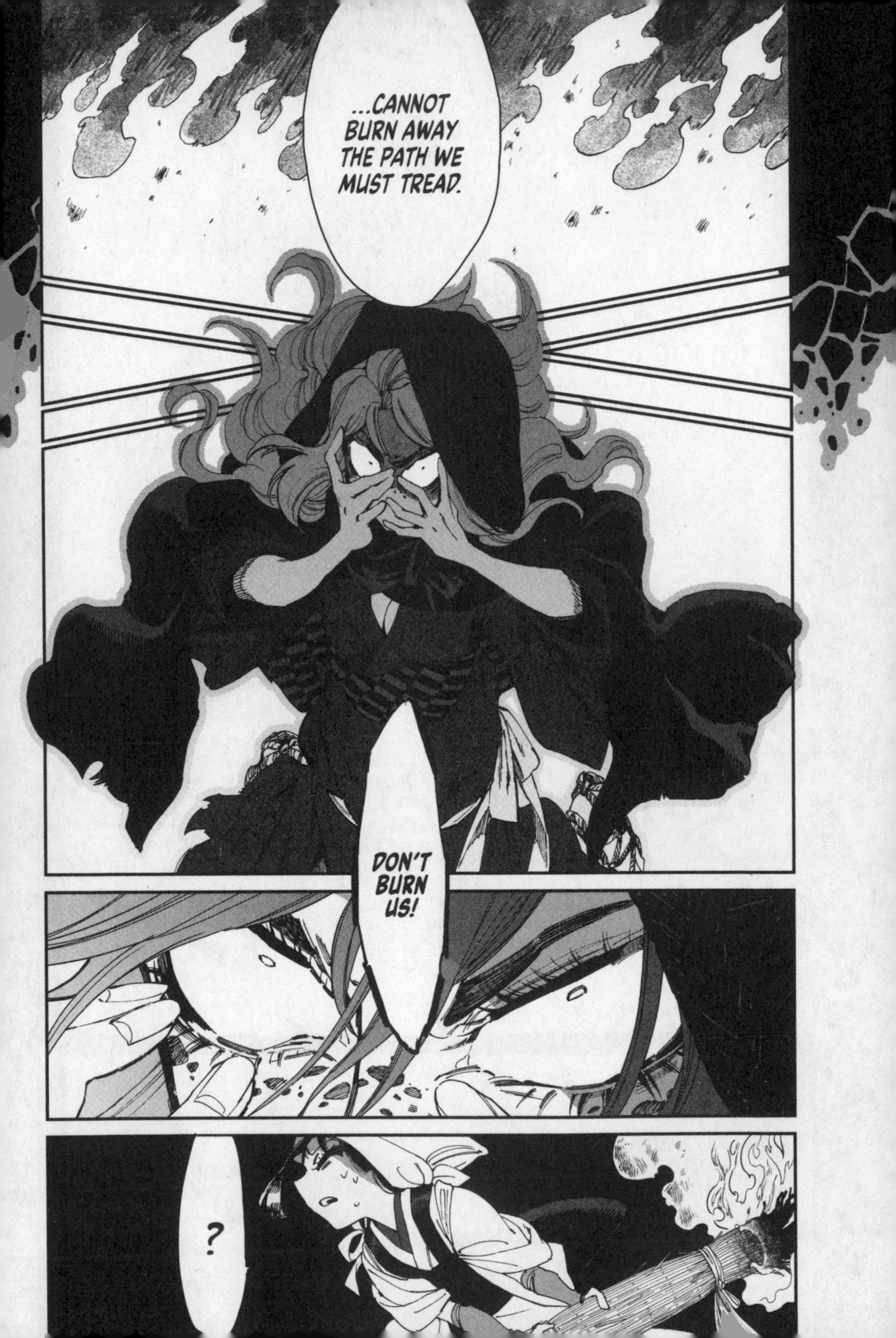
...CANNOT BURN AWAY THE PATH WE MUST TREAD.
DON'T BURN US!
?

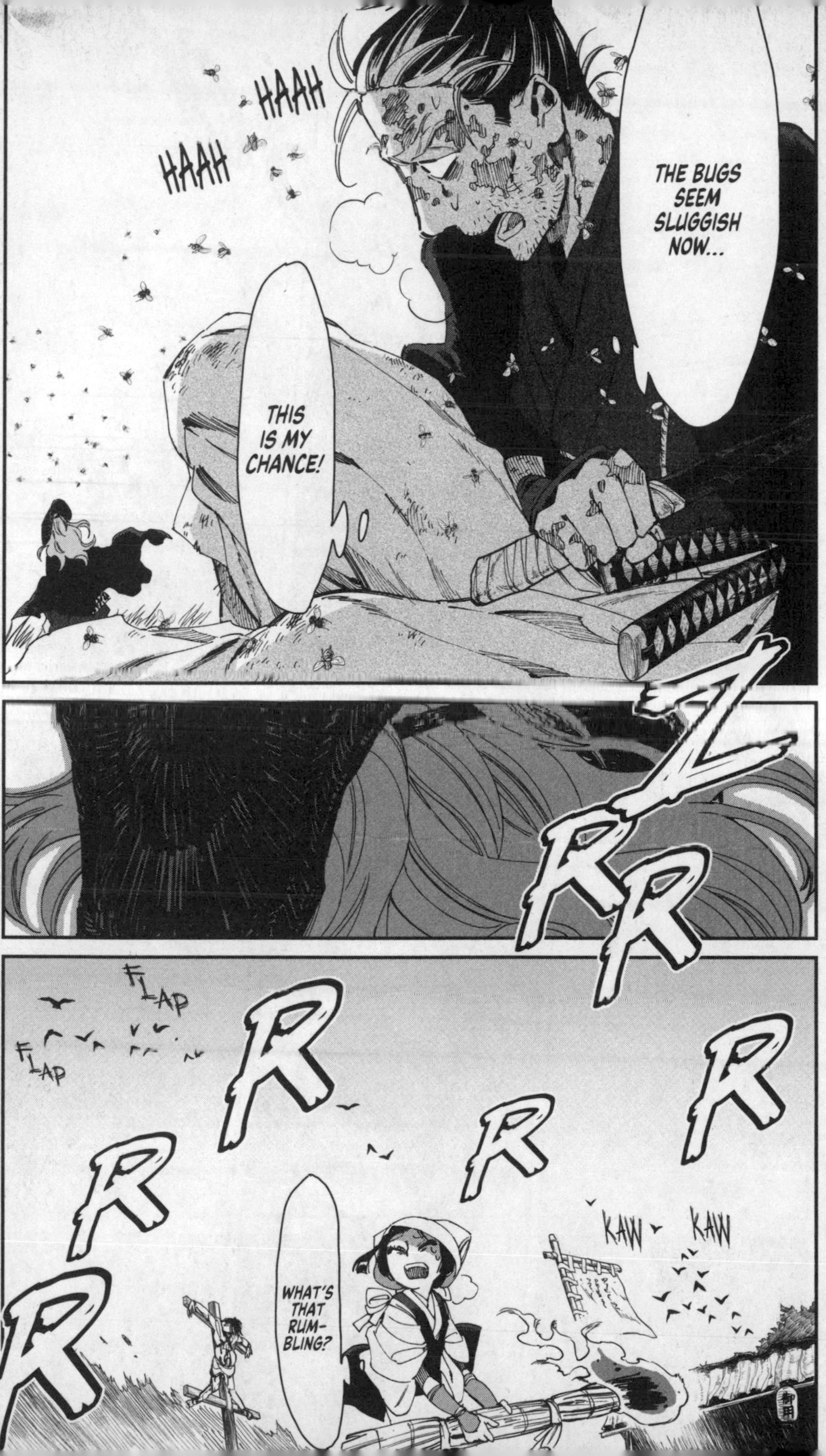
THE BUGS SEEM SLUGGISH NOW...
HAAH
HAAH
THIS IS MY CHANCE!
ZRR
RRRRRR
FLAP
FLAP
KAW KAW
WHAT'S THAT RUM-BLING?

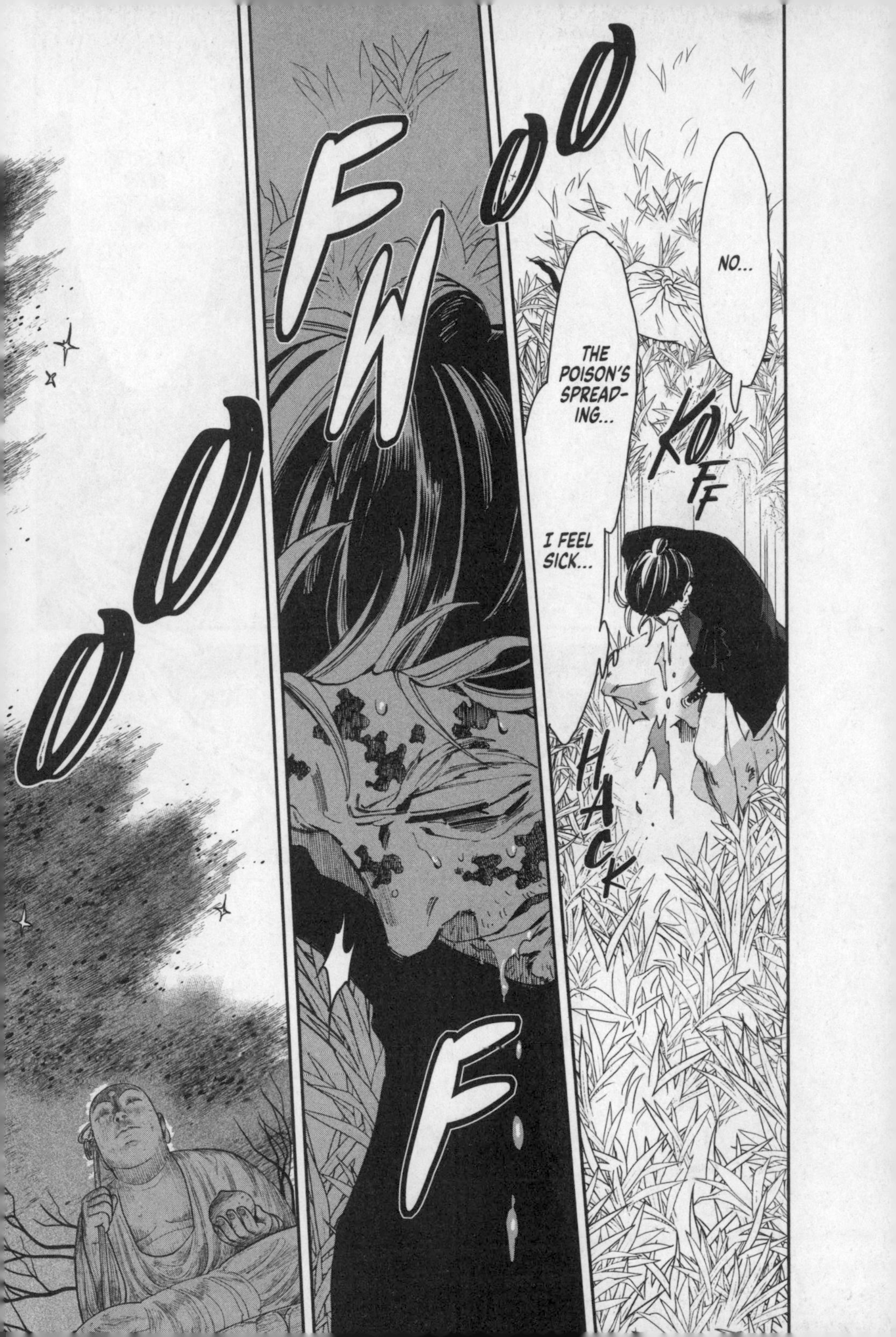
NO...
THE POISON'S SPREAD-ING...
KOFF
I FEEL SICK...
HACK
FWOOOOOOOOO
F

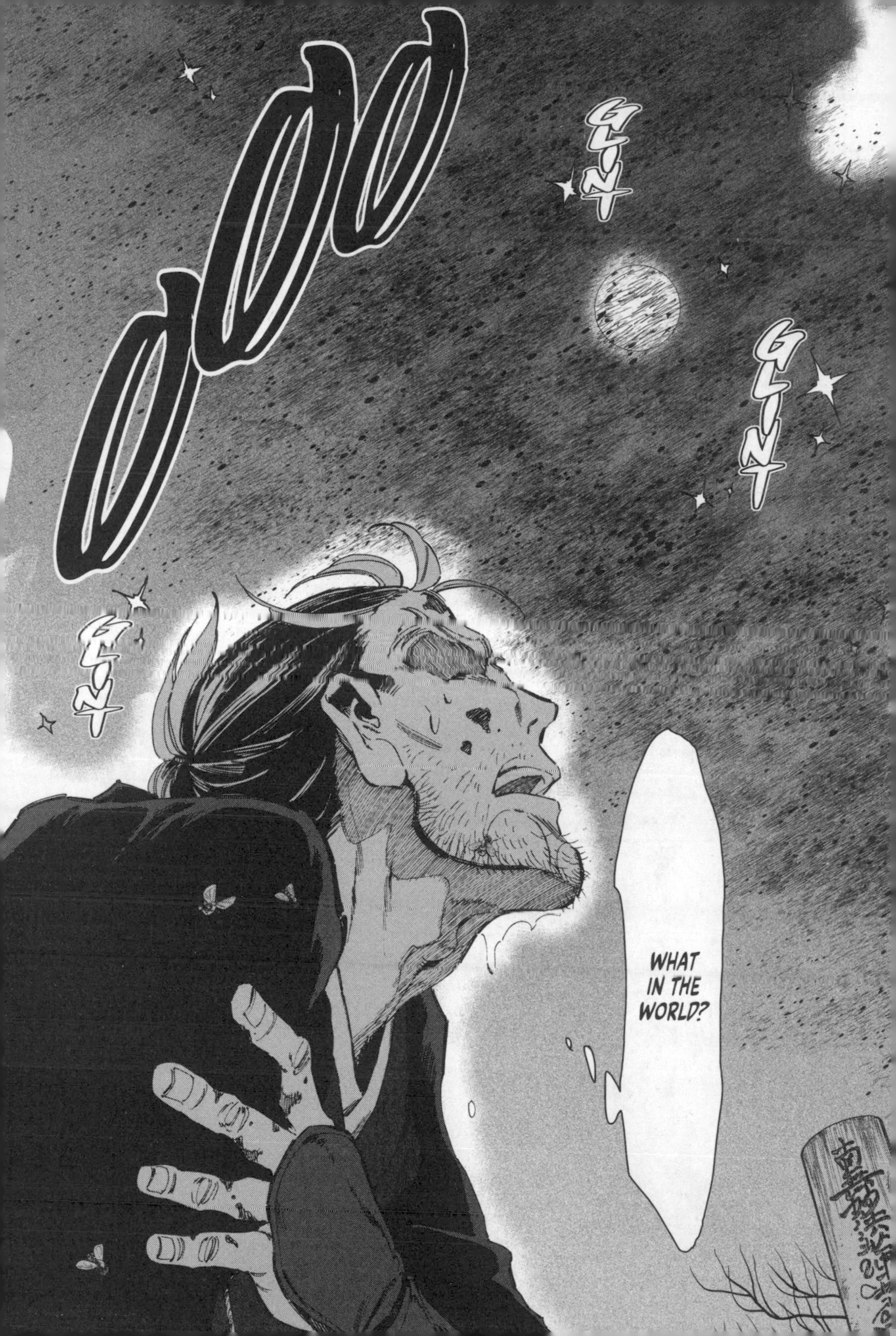
GOOO
GLINT
GLINT
GLINT
WHAT IN THE WORLD?

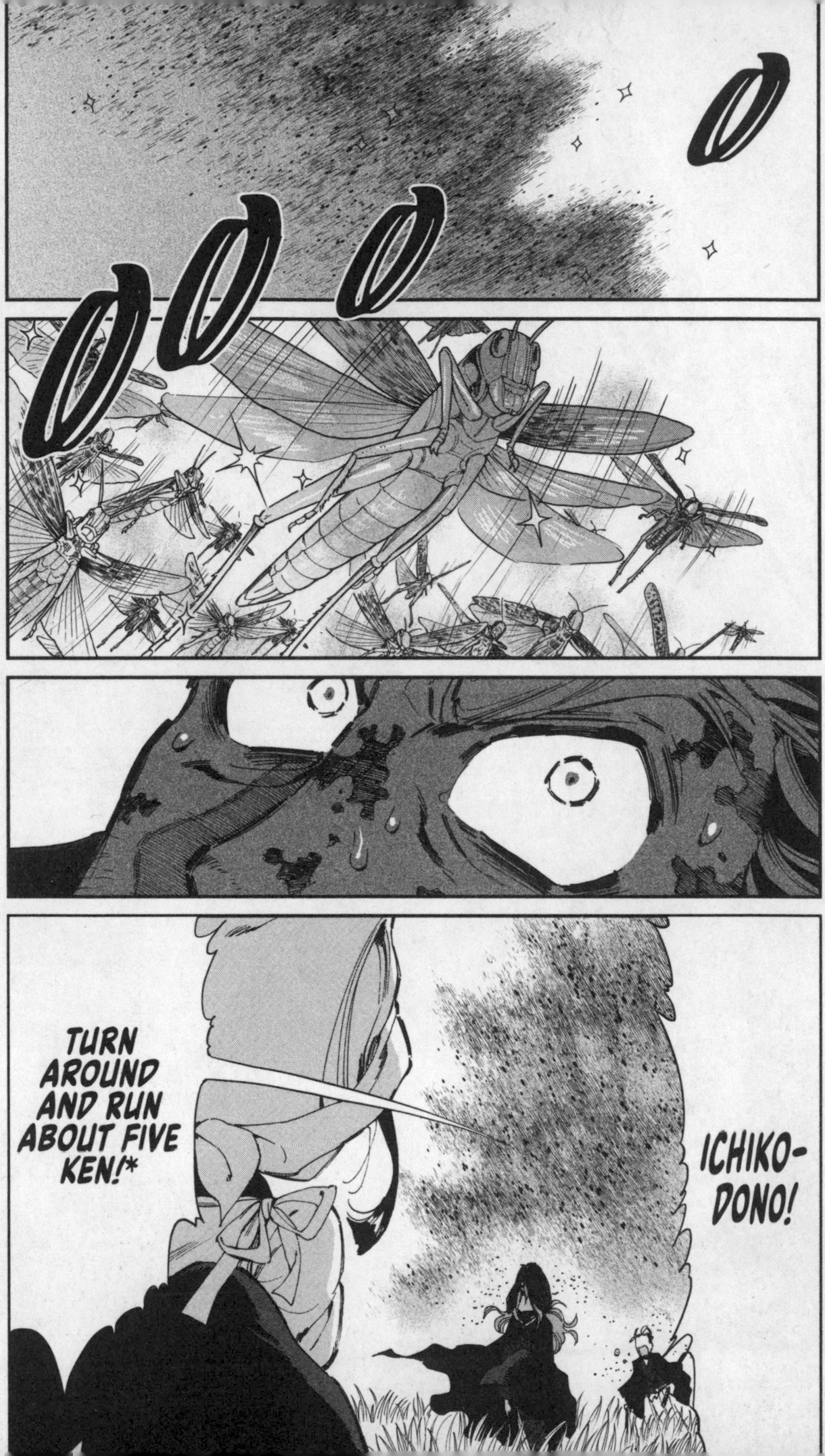
ICHIKO-DONO!
TURN AROUND AND RUN ABOUT FIVE KEN!*

*ABOUT NINE METERS

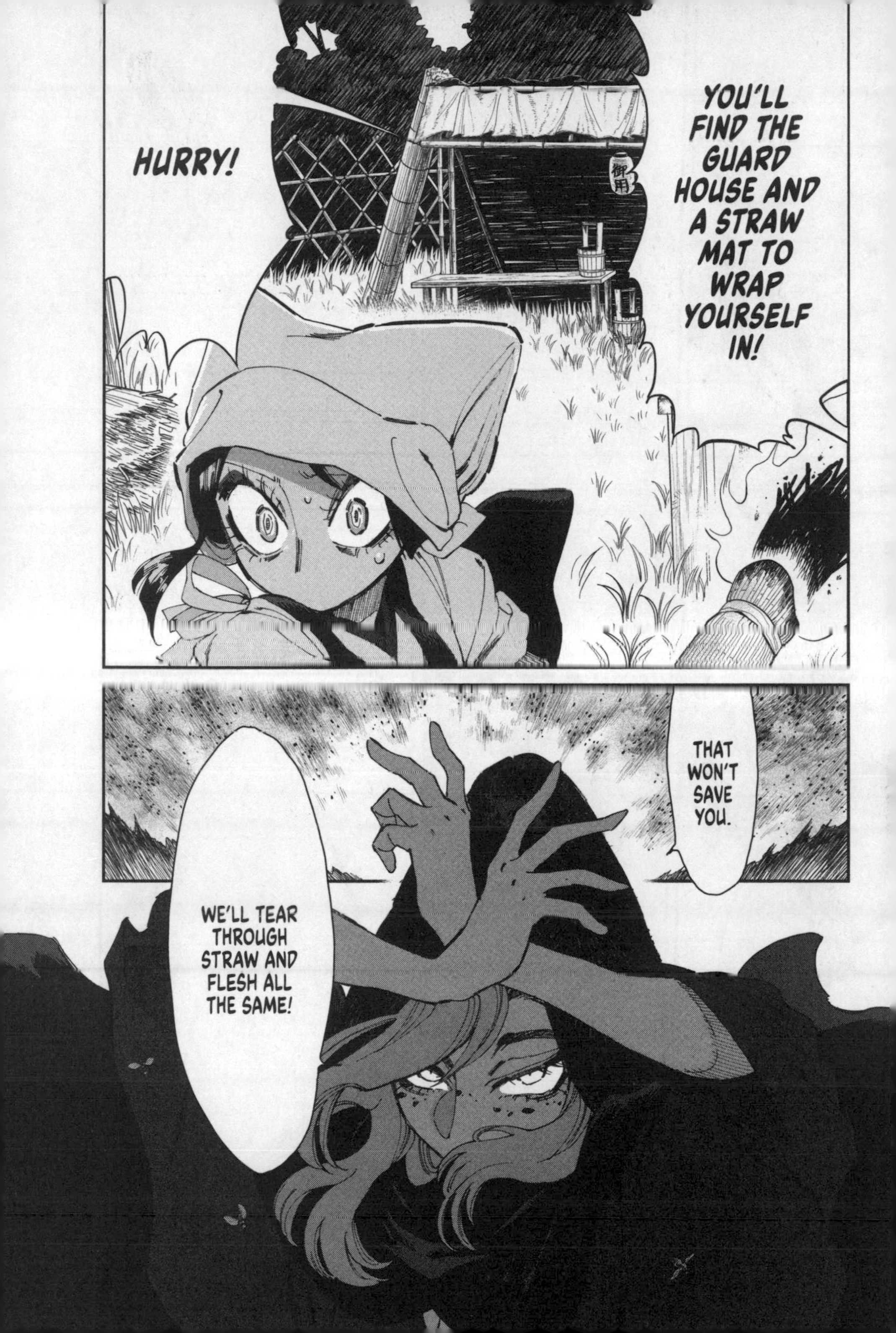
YOU'LL FIND THE GUARD HOUSE AND A STRAW MAT TO WRAP YOURSELF IN!
御用
HURRY!
THAT WON'T SAVE YOU.
WE'LL TEAR THROUGH STRAW AND FLESH ALL THE SAME!

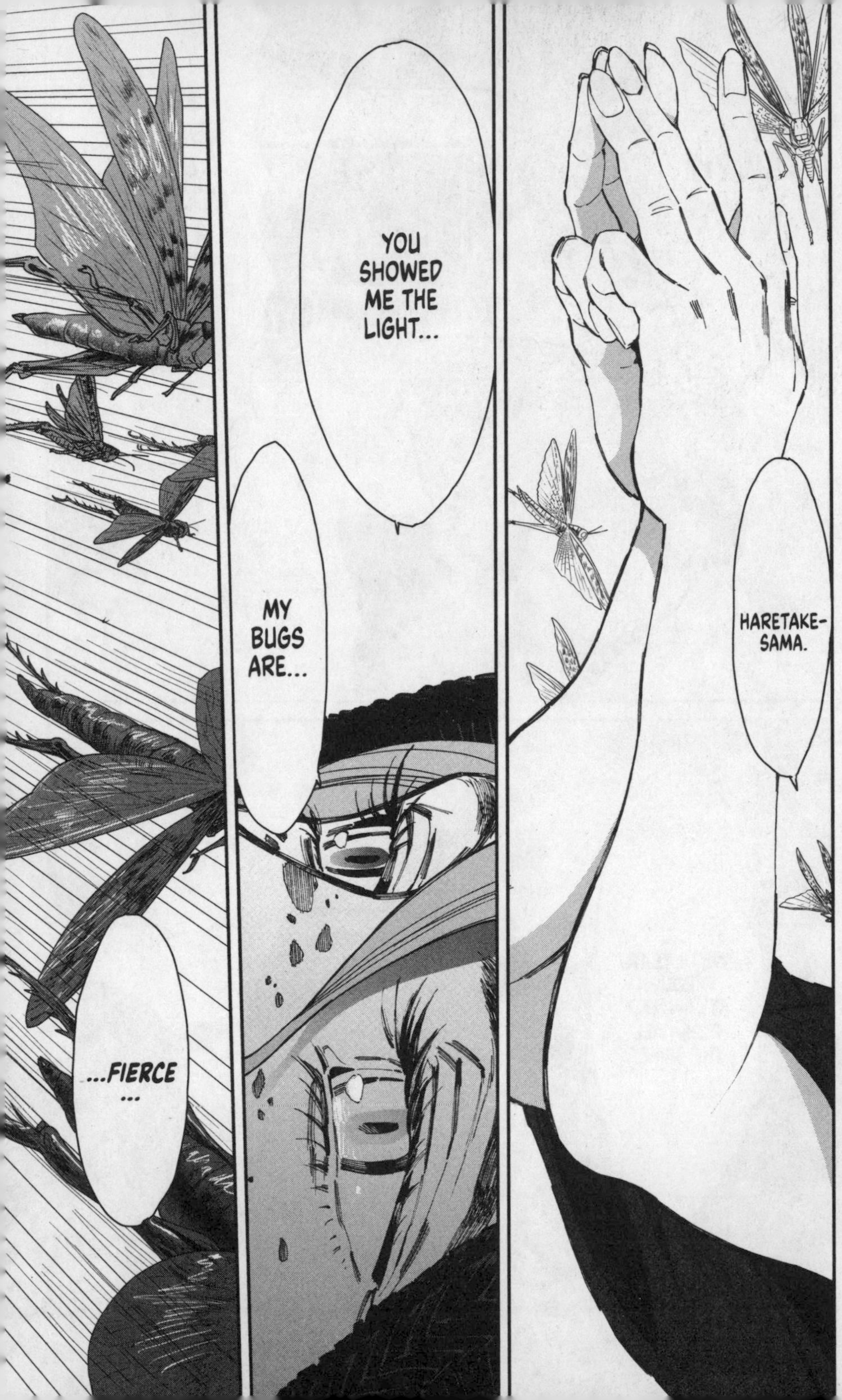
HARETAKE-SAMA.
YOU SHOWED ME THE LIGHT...
MY BUGS ARE...
...FIERCE ...

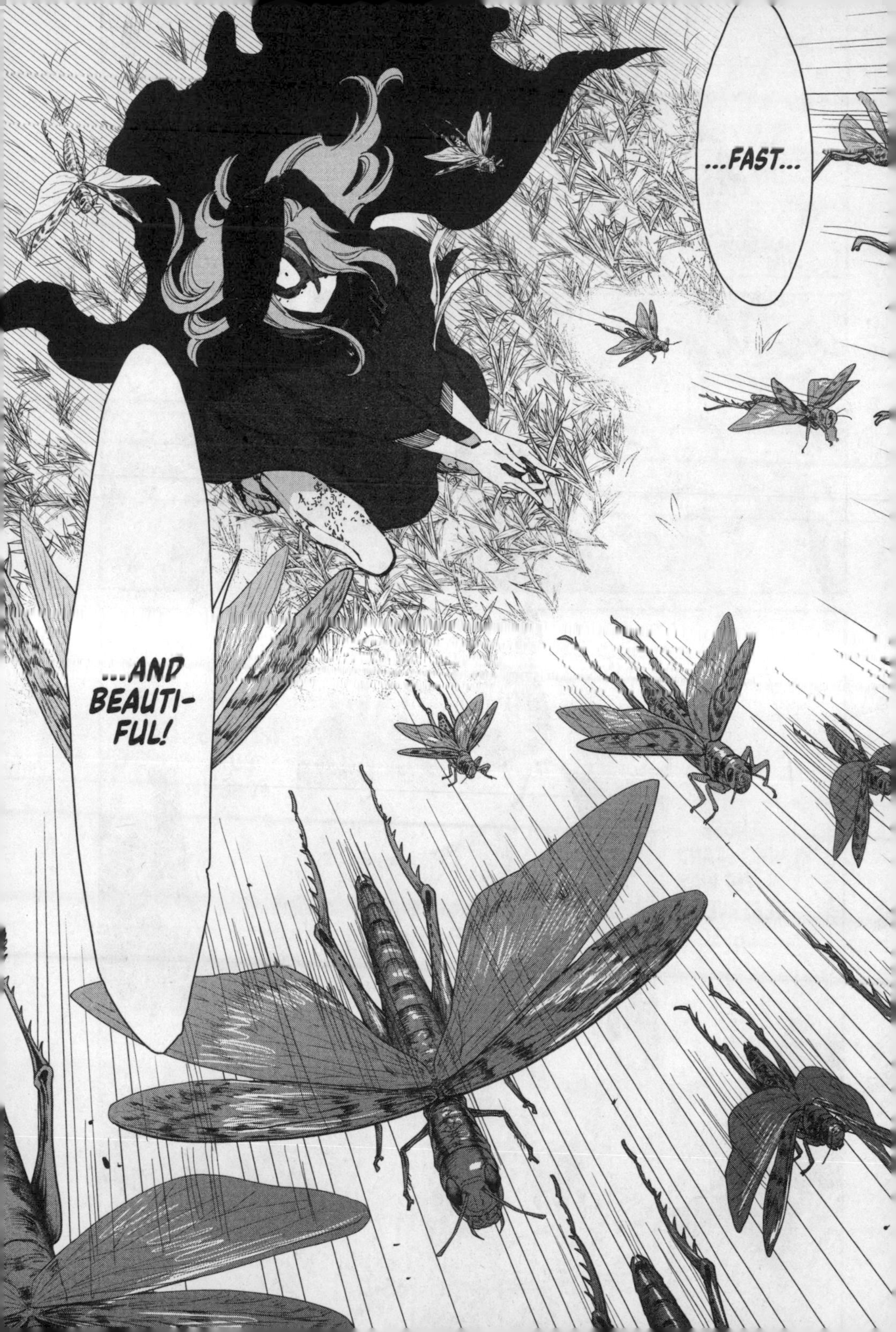
...FAST...
...AND BEAUTI-FUL!

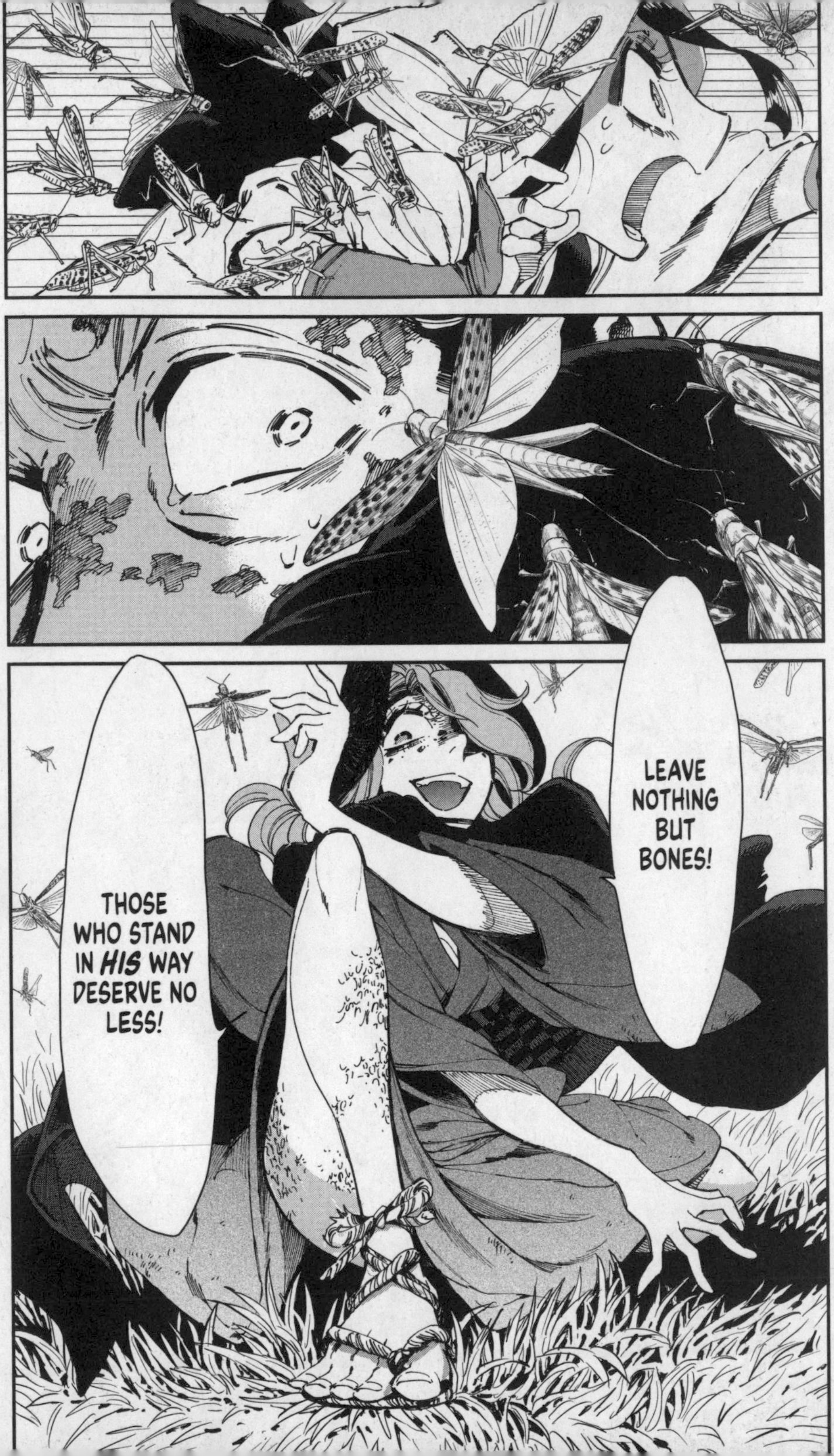
LEAVE NOTHING BUT BONES!
THOSE WHO STAND IN HIS WAY DESERVE NO LESS!

STEEL of the CELESTIAL SHADOWS

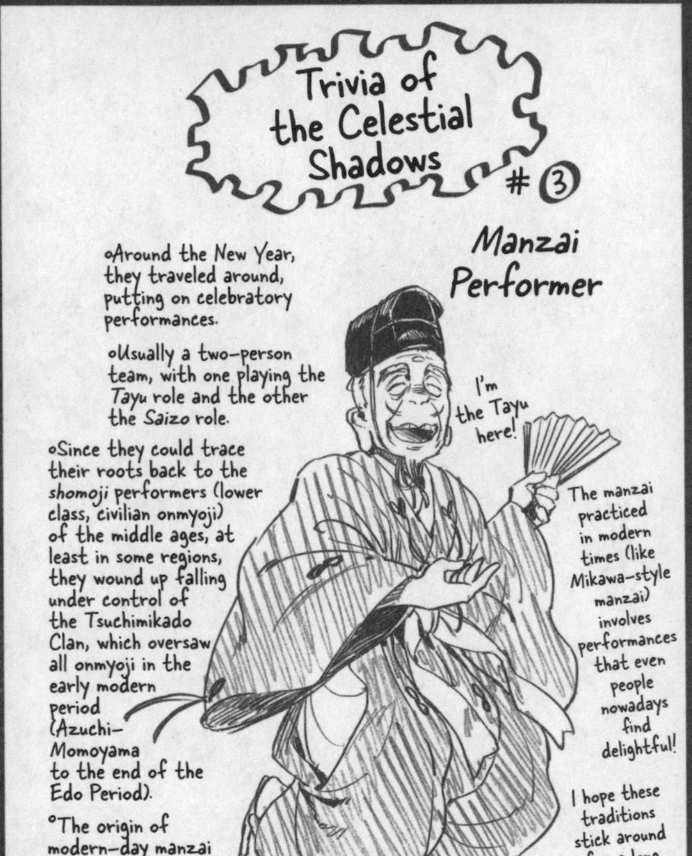

Trivia of the Celestial Shadows #③

Manzai Performer

o Around the New Year, they traveled around, putting on celebratory performances.

o Usually a two-person team, with one playing the *Tayu* role and the other the *Saizo* role.

o Since they could trace their roots back to the *shomoji* performers (lower class, civilian onmyoji) of the middle ages, at least in some regions, they wound up falling under control of the Tsuchimikado Clan, which oversaw all onmyoji in the early modern period (Azuchi–Momoyama to the end of the Edo Period).

° The origin of modern-day manzai comedy performances.

I'm the Tayu here!

The manzai practiced in modern times (like Mikawa-style manzai) involves performances that even people nowadays find delightful!

I hope these traditions stick around for a long time.

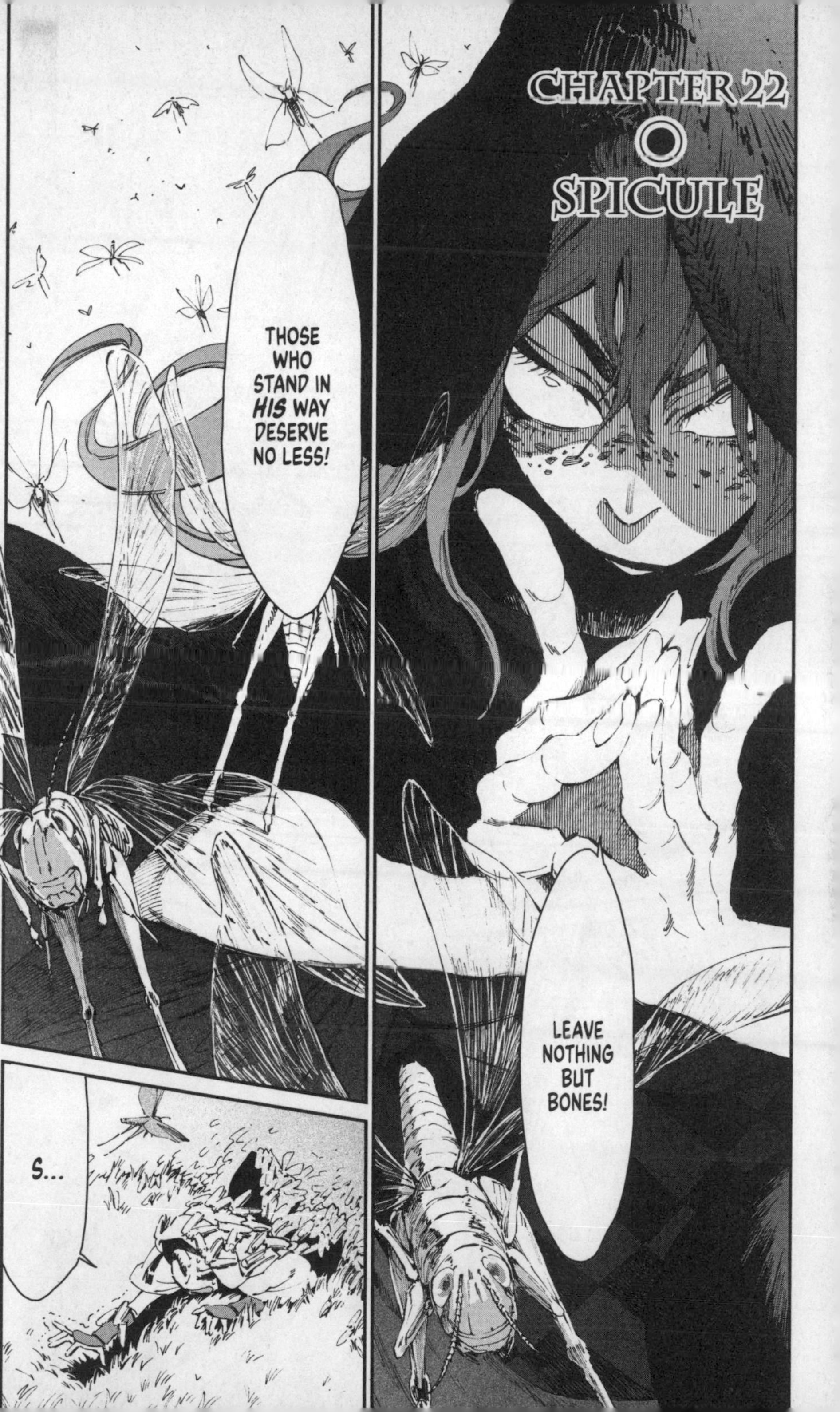
CHAPTER 22
SPICULE
LEAVE NOTHING BUT BONES!
THOSE WHO STAND IN *HIS* WAY DESERVE NO LESS!
S...

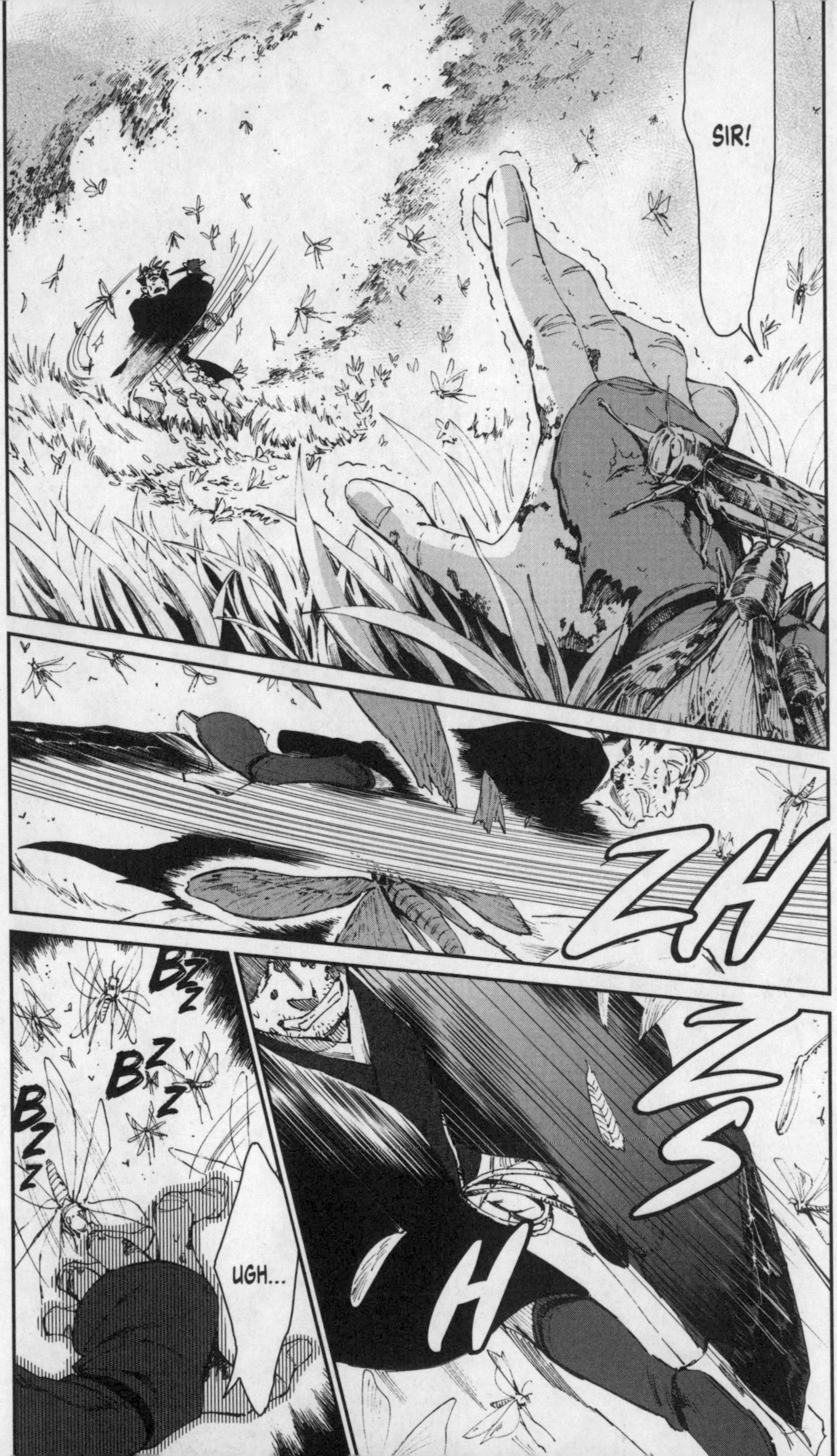
SIR!
ZH
ZZH
BZZZ
BZZ
BZZ
UGH...

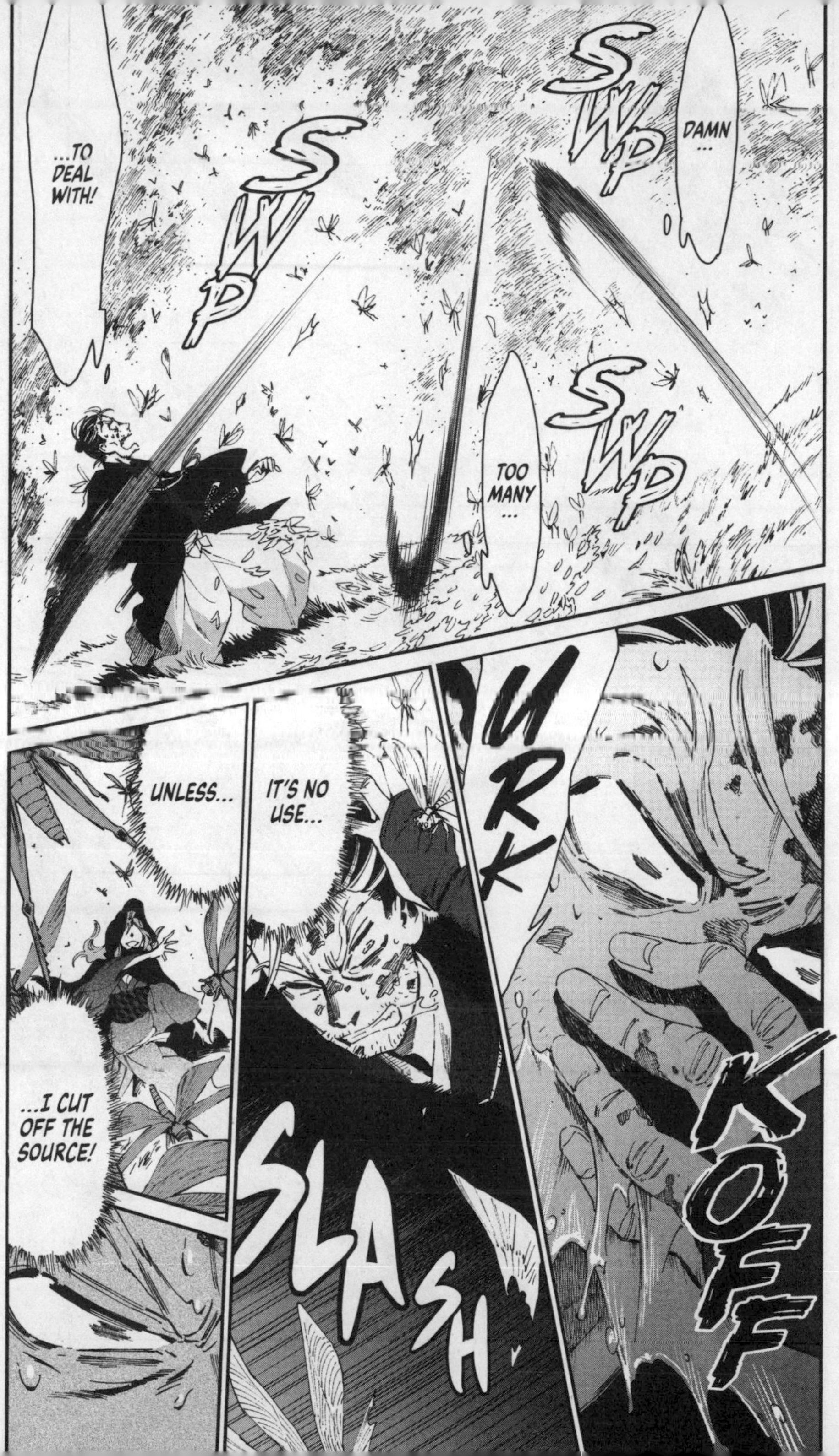
SWP
DAMN...
SWP
TOO MANY...
SWP
...TO DEAL WITH!
URK
KOFF
IT'S NO USE...
SLASH
UNLESS...
...I CUT OFF THE SOURCE!

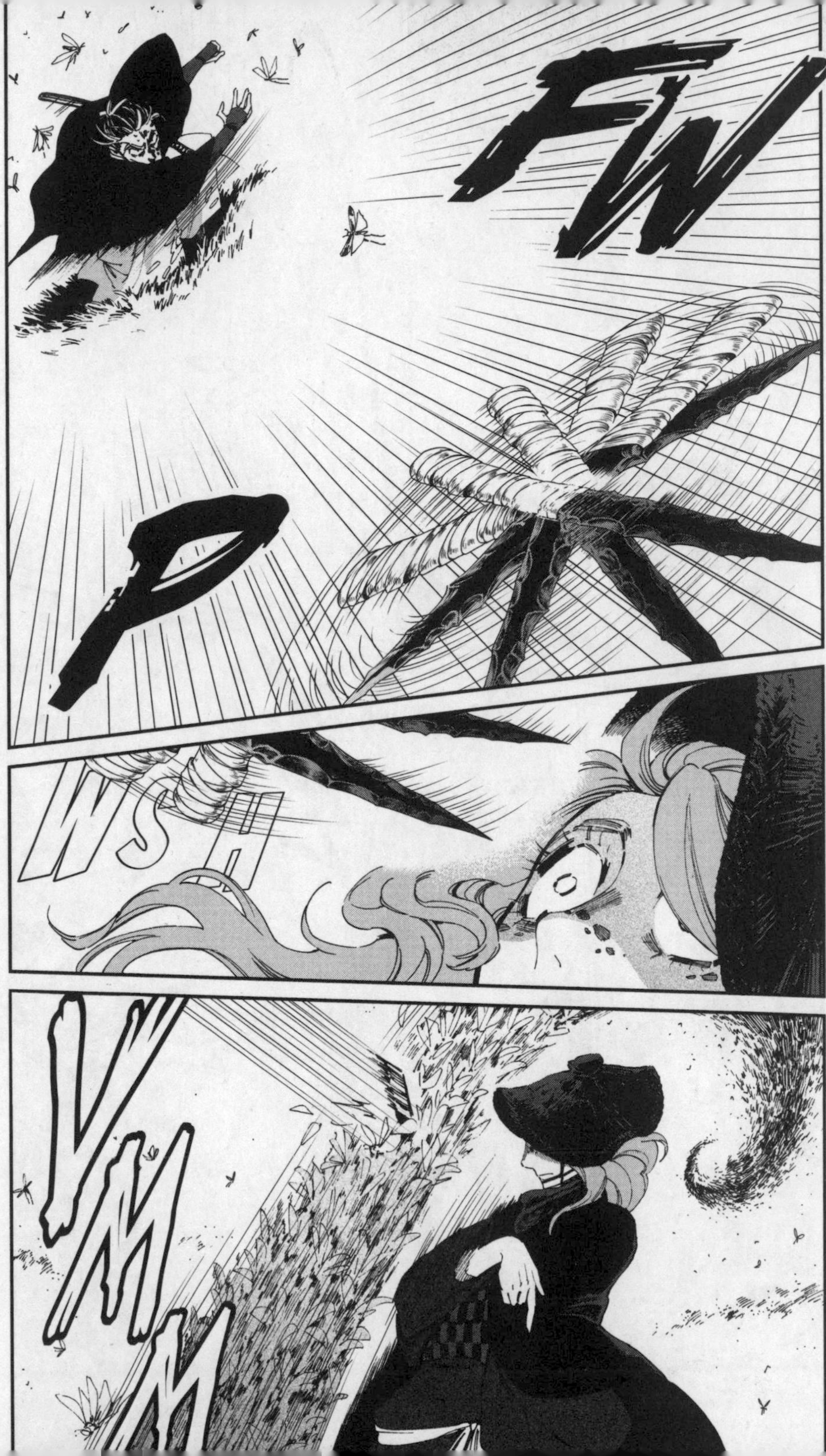
FW
WSH

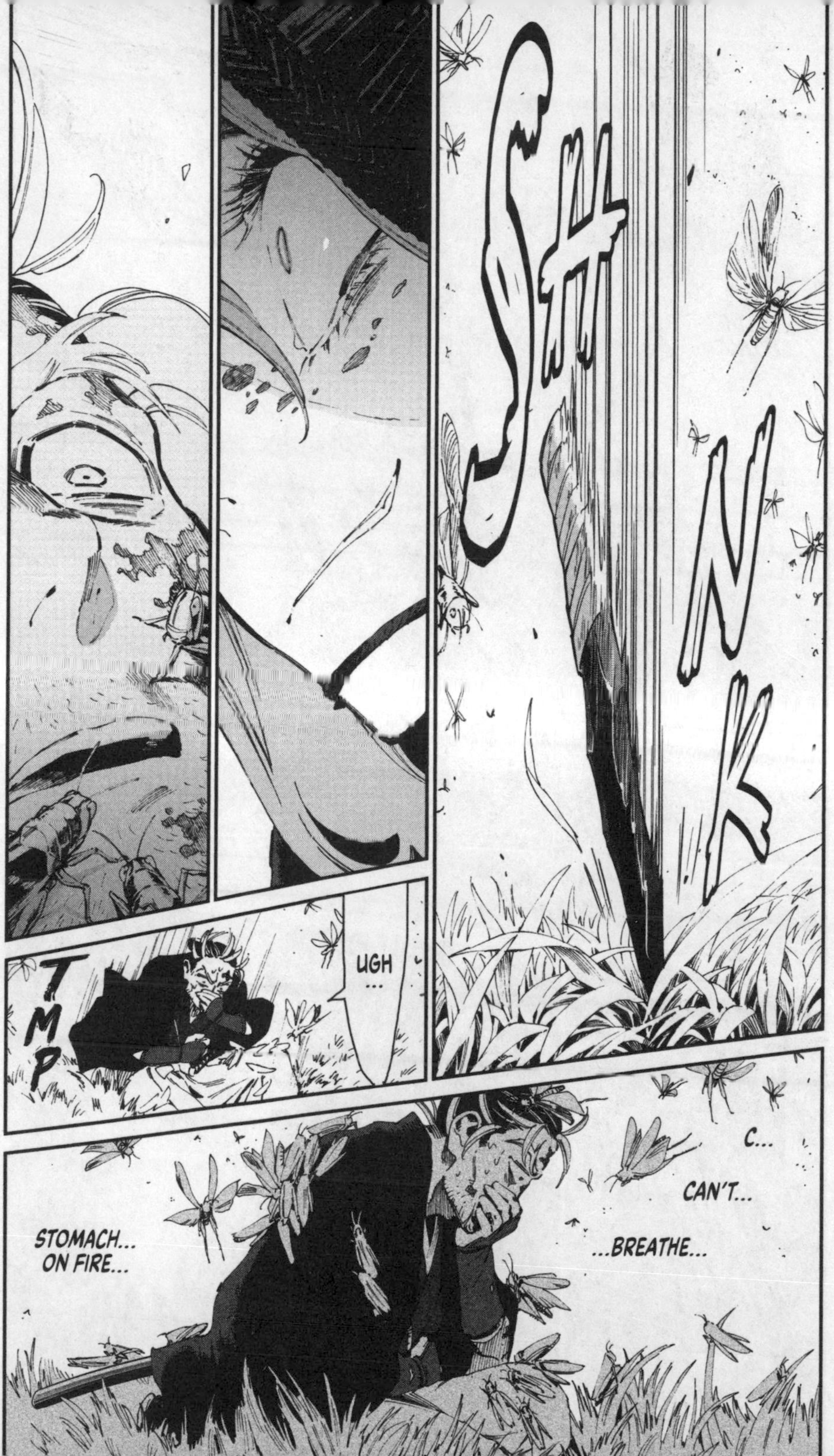
SHNK
UGH...
TMP
C...
CAN'T...
...BREATHE...
STOMACH... ON FIRE...

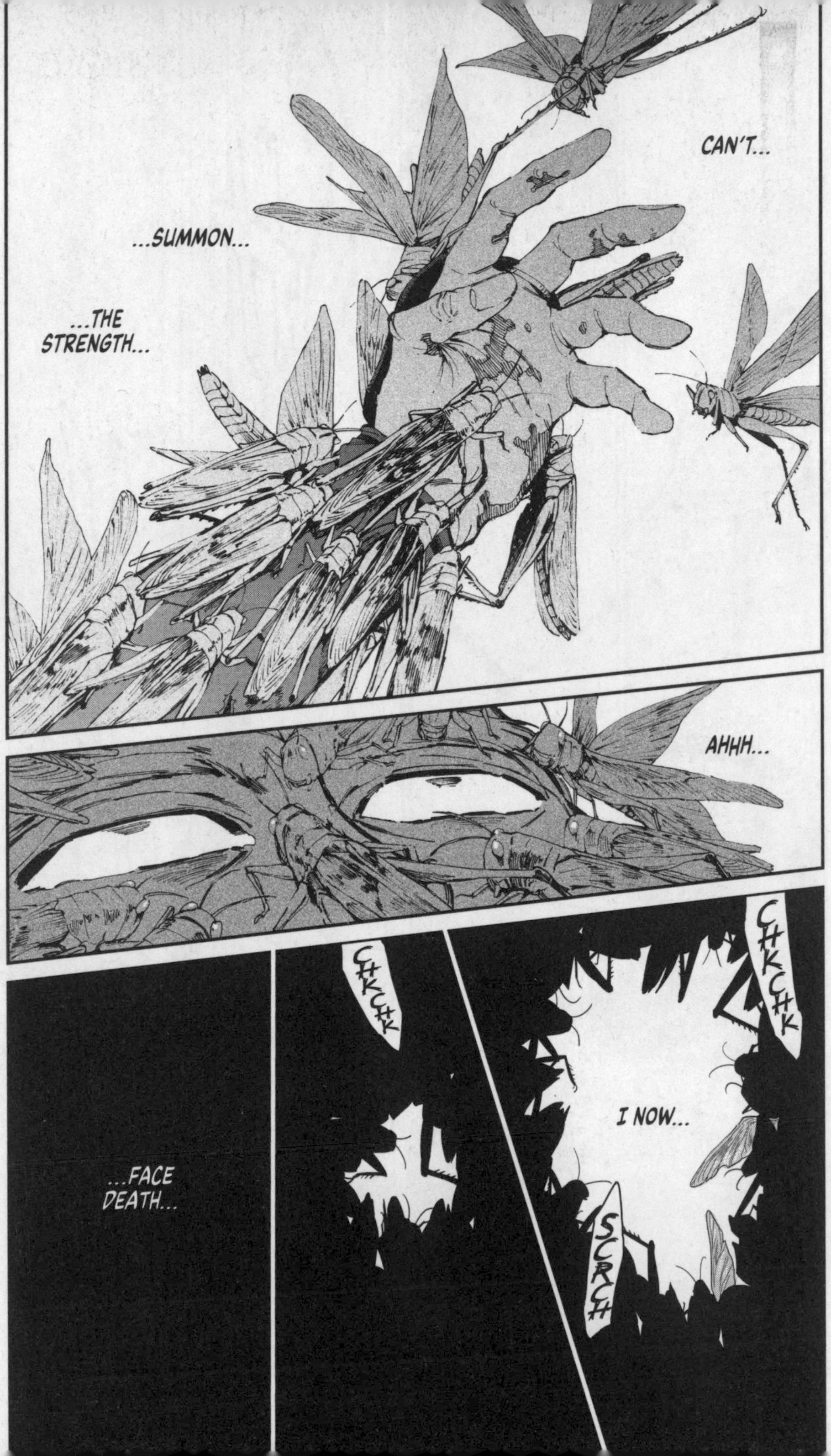
CAN'T...
...SUMMON...
...THE STRENGTH...
AHHH...
CHKCHK
I NOW...
SCRCH
CHKCHK
...FACE DEATH...

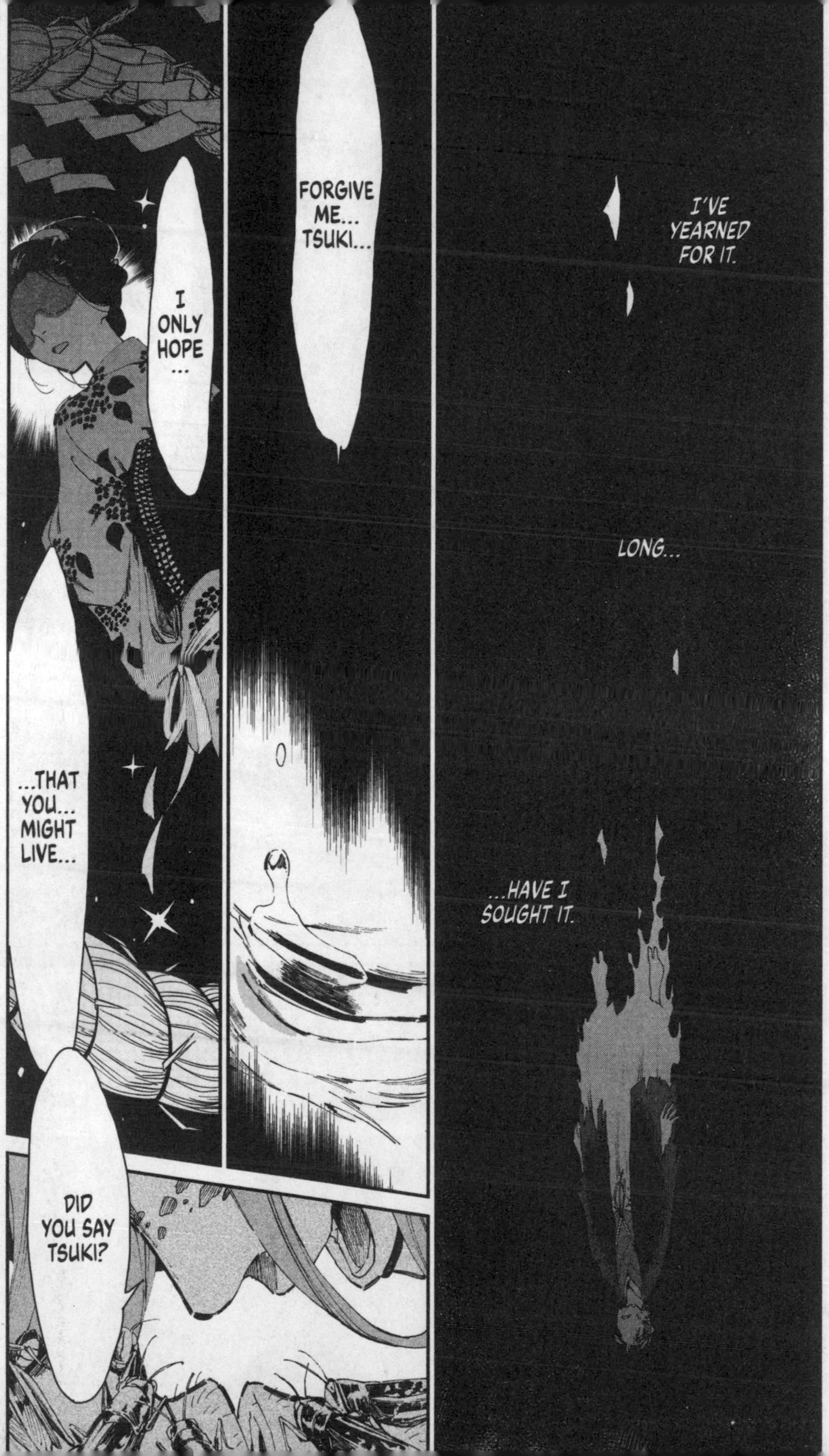
I'VE YEARNED FOR IT.
LONG...
...HAVE I SOUGHT IT.
FORGIVE ME... TSUKI...
I ONLY HOPE...
...THAT YOU... MIGHT LIVE...
DID YOU SAY TSUKI?

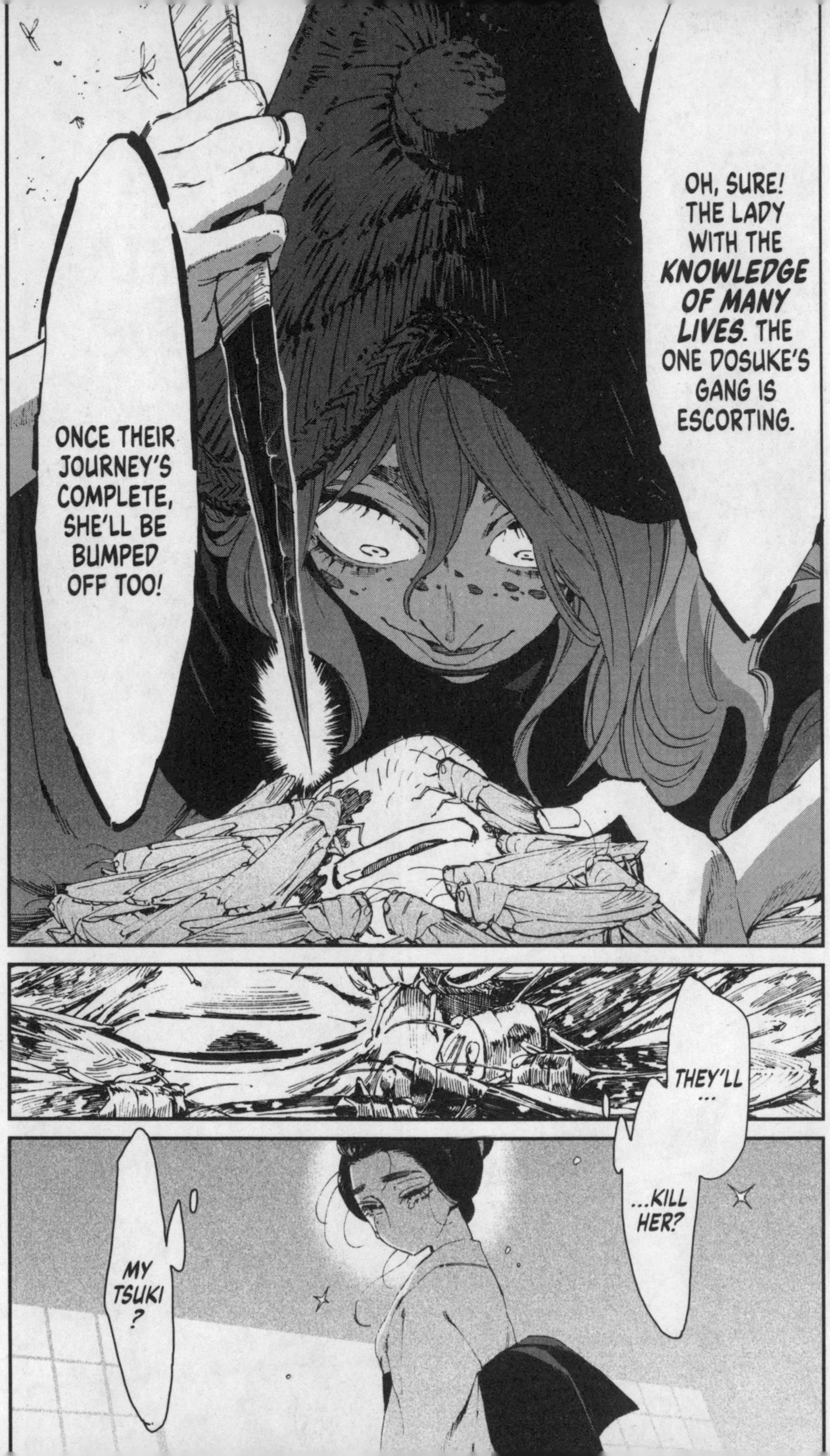
OH, SURE! THE LADY WITH THE KNOWLEDGE OF MANY LIVES. THE ONE DOSUKE'S GANG IS ESCORTING.
ONCE THEIR JOURNEY'S COMPLETE, SHE'LL BE BUMPED OFF TOO!
THEY'LL ...
...KILL HER?
MY TSUKI ?

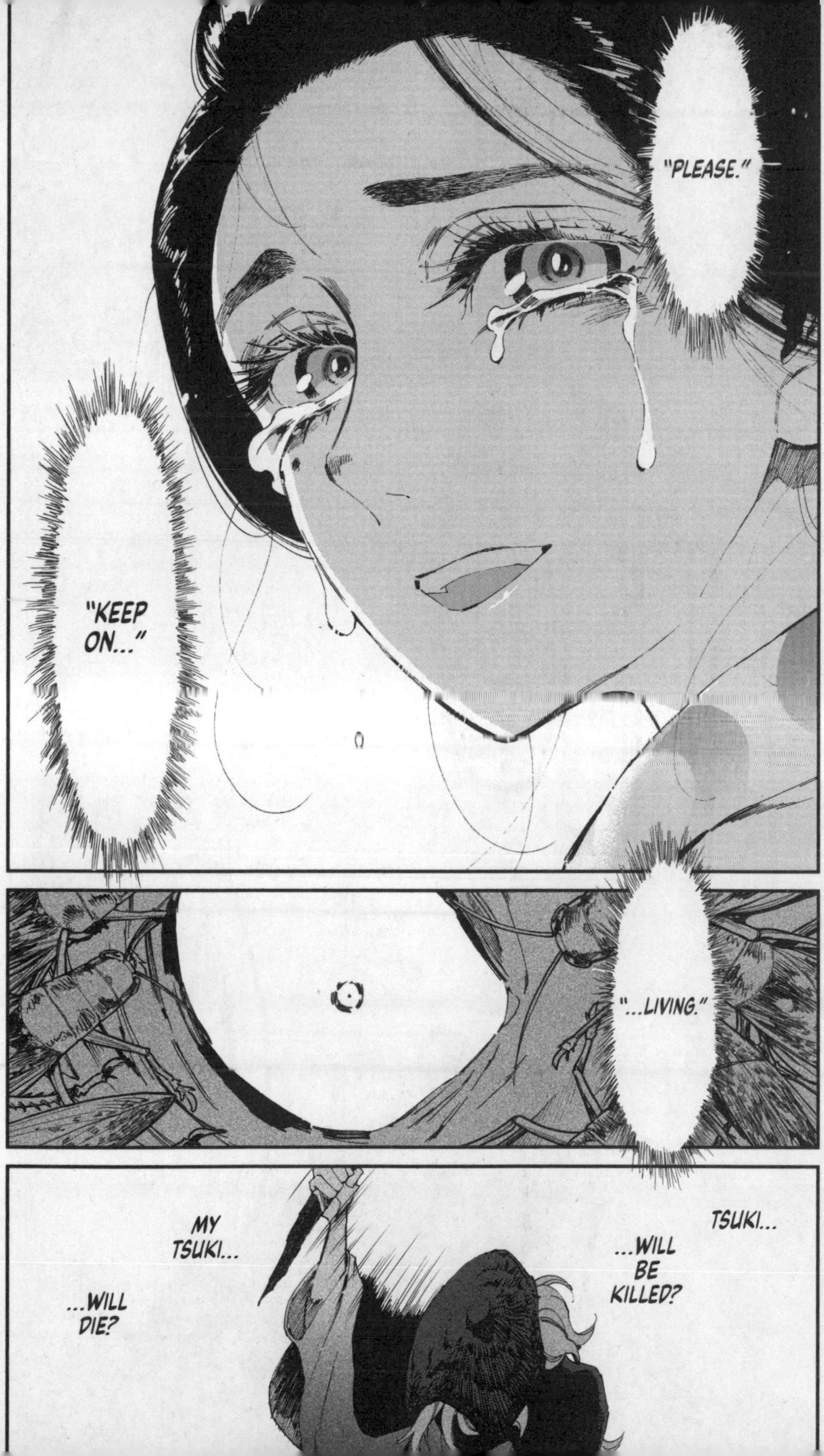
"PLEASE."
"KEEP ON..."
"...LIVING."
TSUKI...
...WILL BE KILLED?
MY TSUKI...
...WILL DIE?

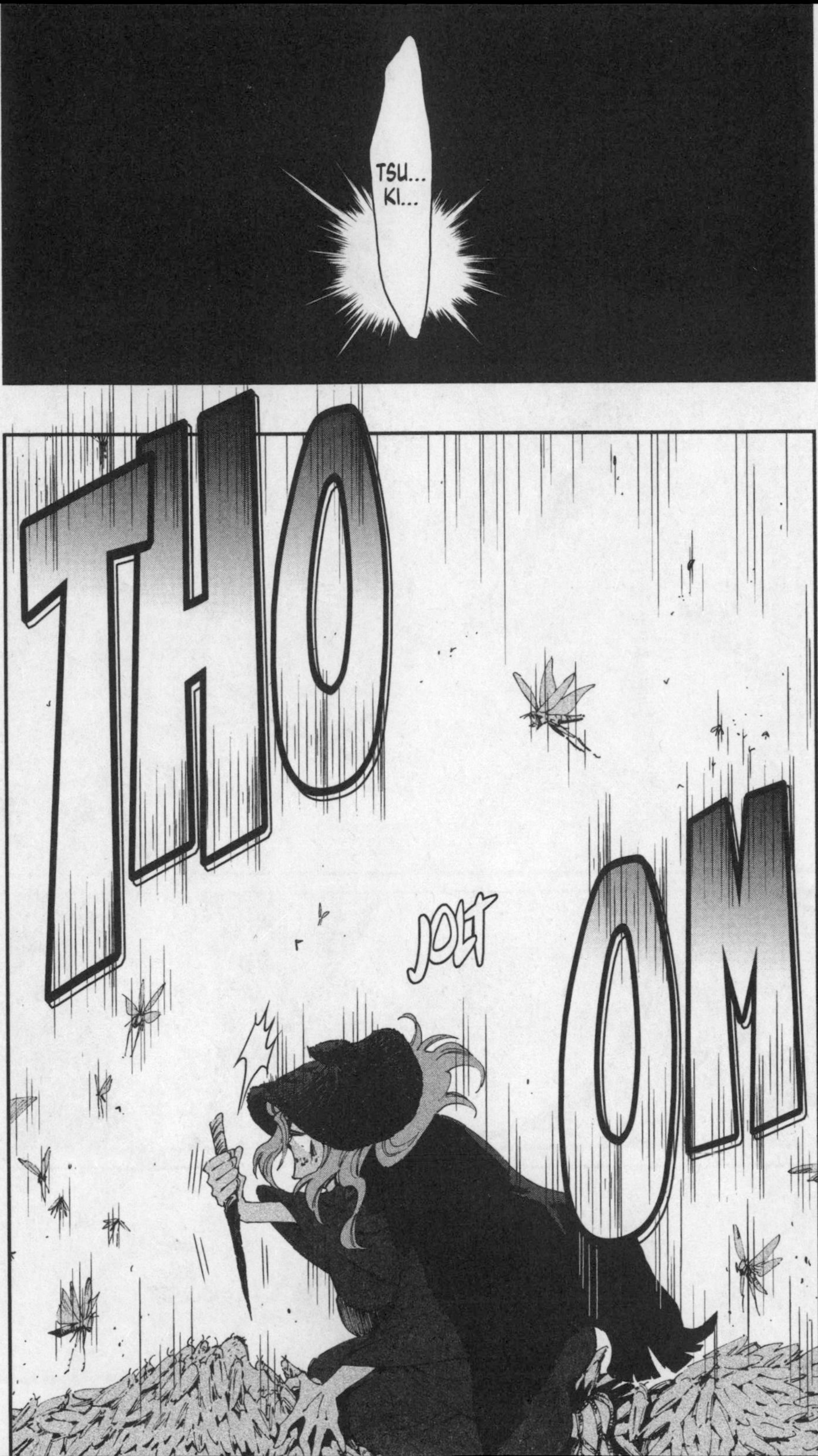
TSU...
KI...
THO
OM
JOLT

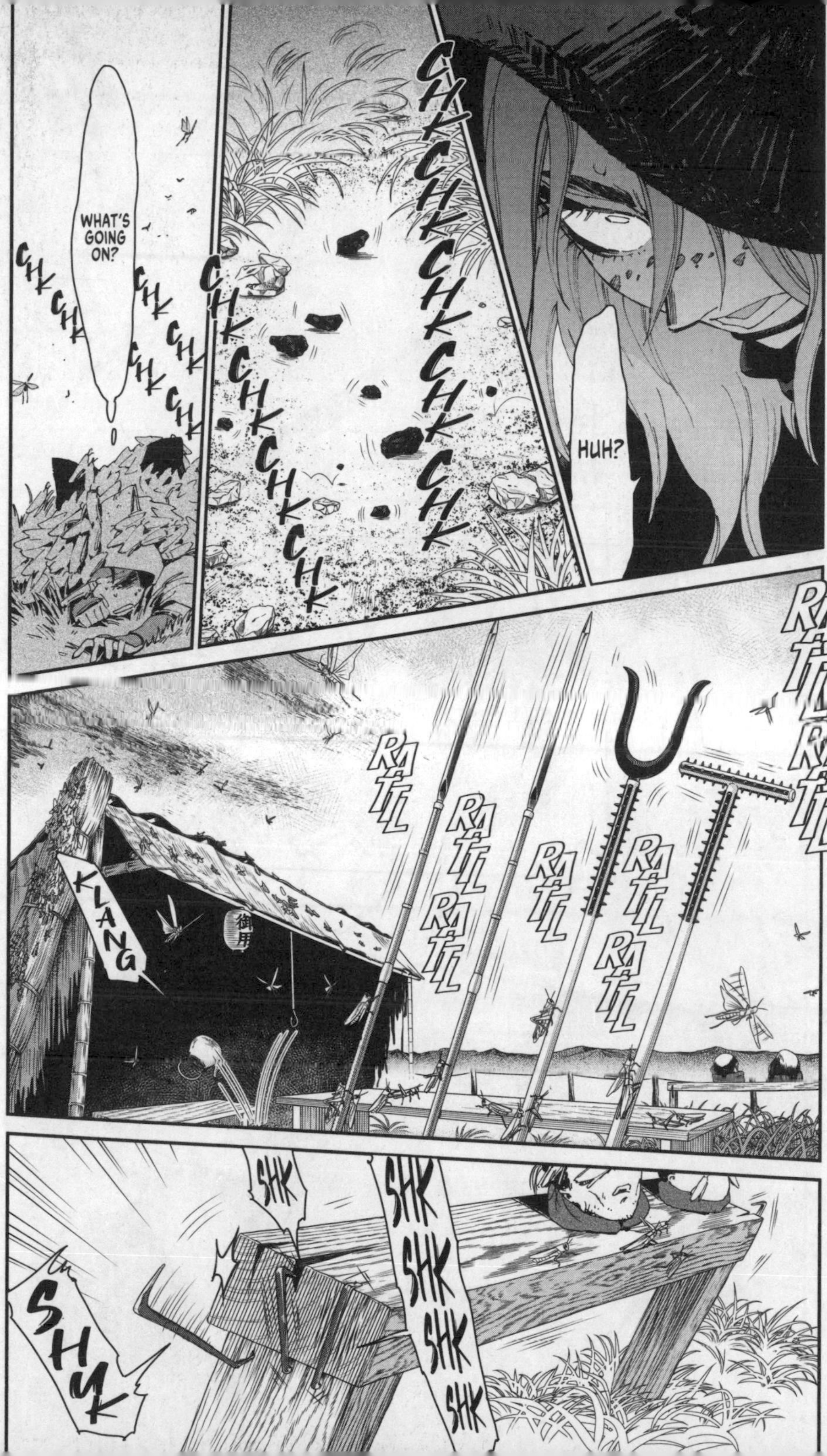
CHKCHKCHKCHKCHKCHK
HUH?
CHKCHKCHKCHKCHK
WHAT'S GOING ON?
CHKCHK
CHKCHKCHK
RATTLRATTL
RATTL
RATTLRATTL
RATTL
RATTL
RATTL
RATTL
KLANG
SHK
SHK SHK SHK SHK
SHUK

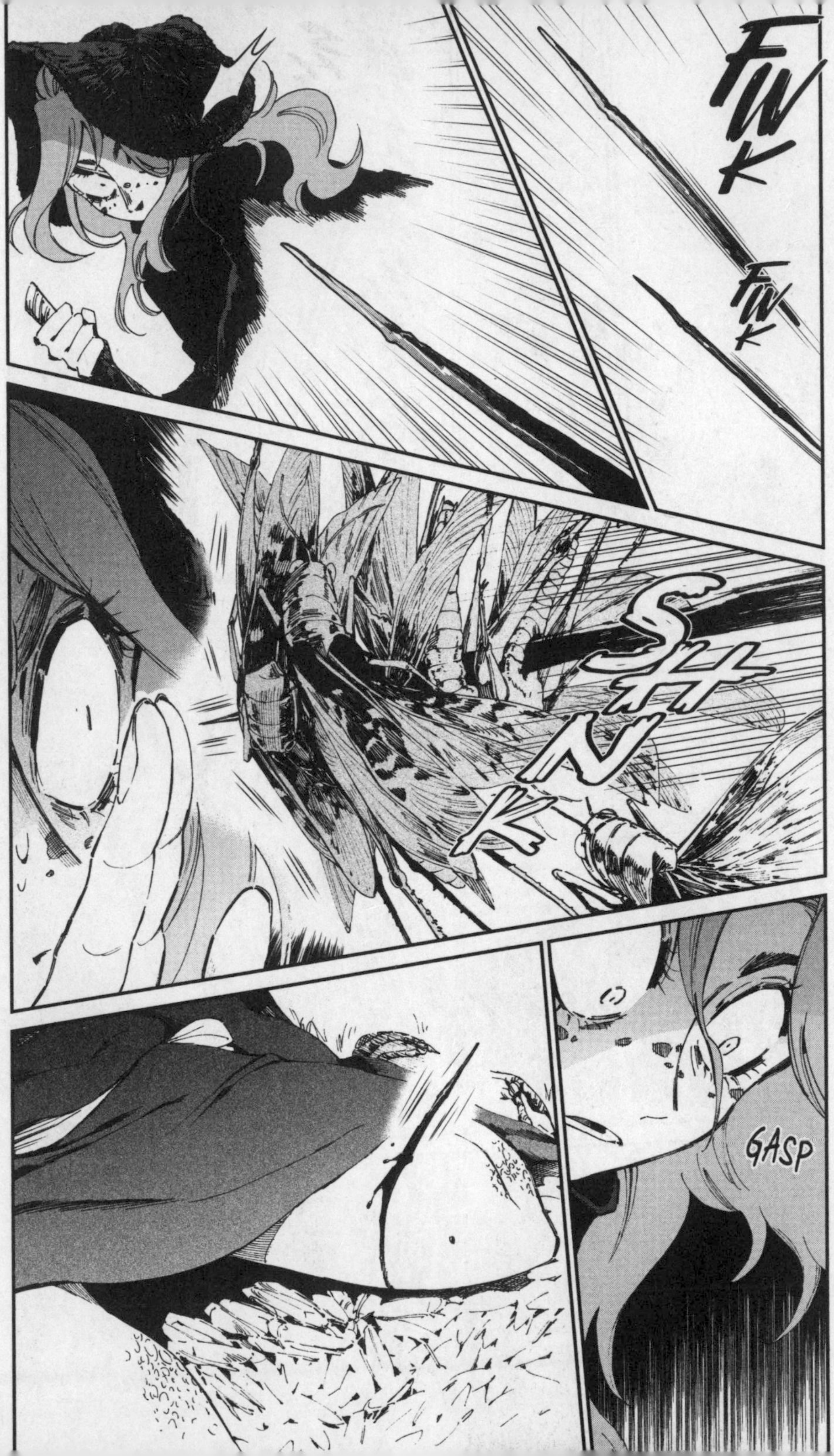
FWK
FWK
SHNK
GASP

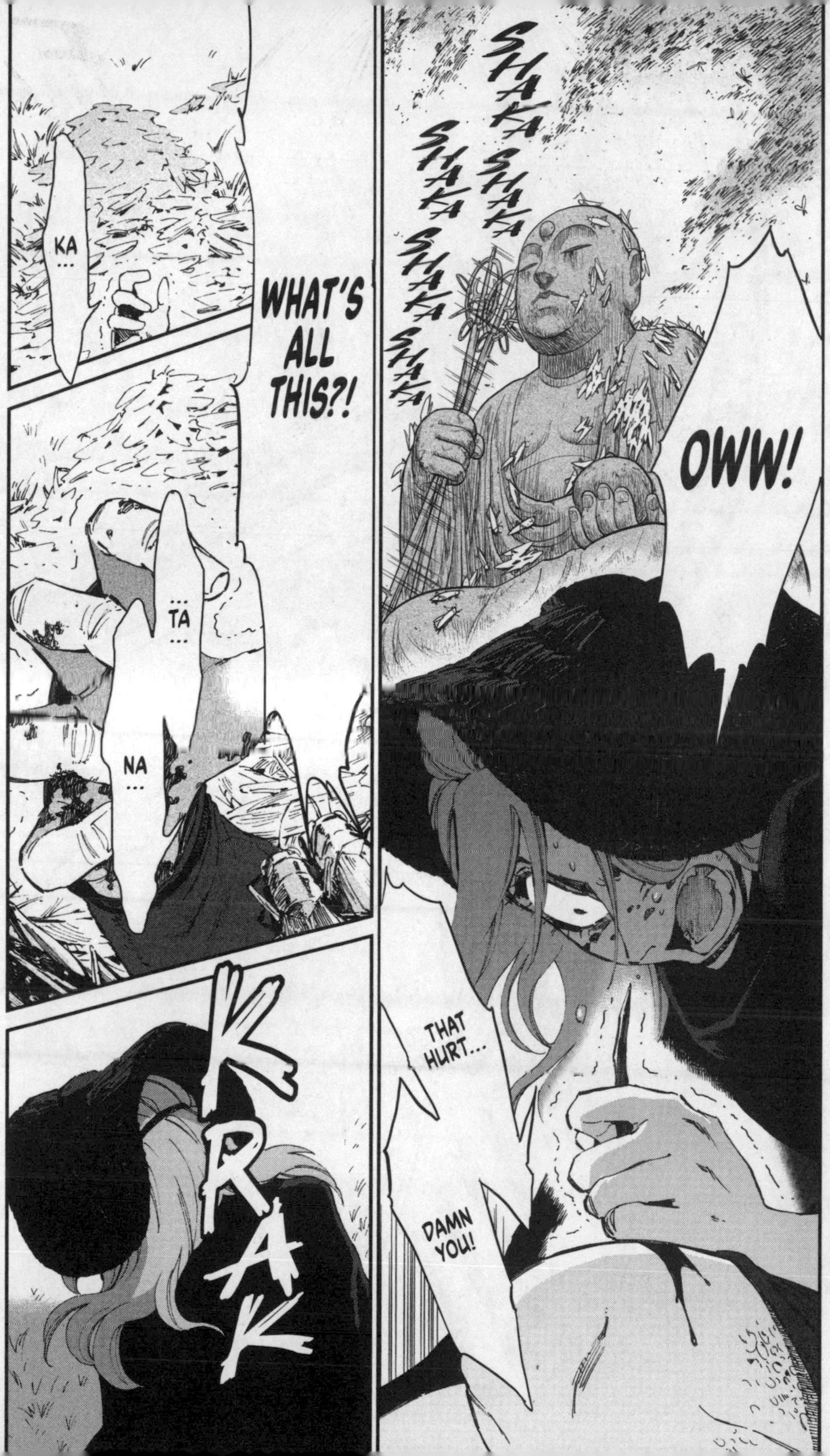
SHAKA SHAKA SHAKA SHAKA SHAKA
OWW!
THAT HURT...
DAMN YOU!
KA...
WHAT'S ALL THIS?!
...TA...
NA...
KRAK

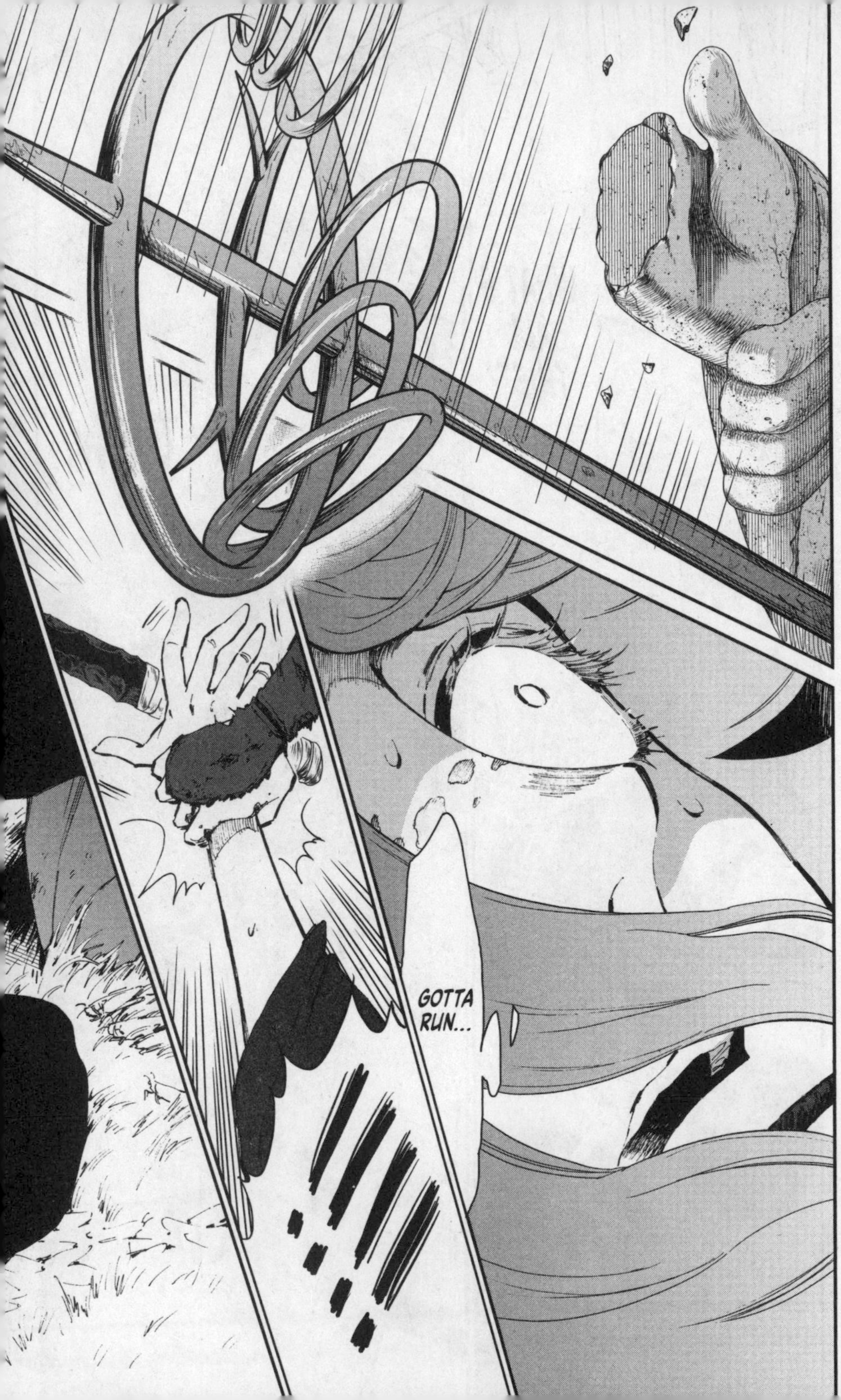
GOTTA RUN...

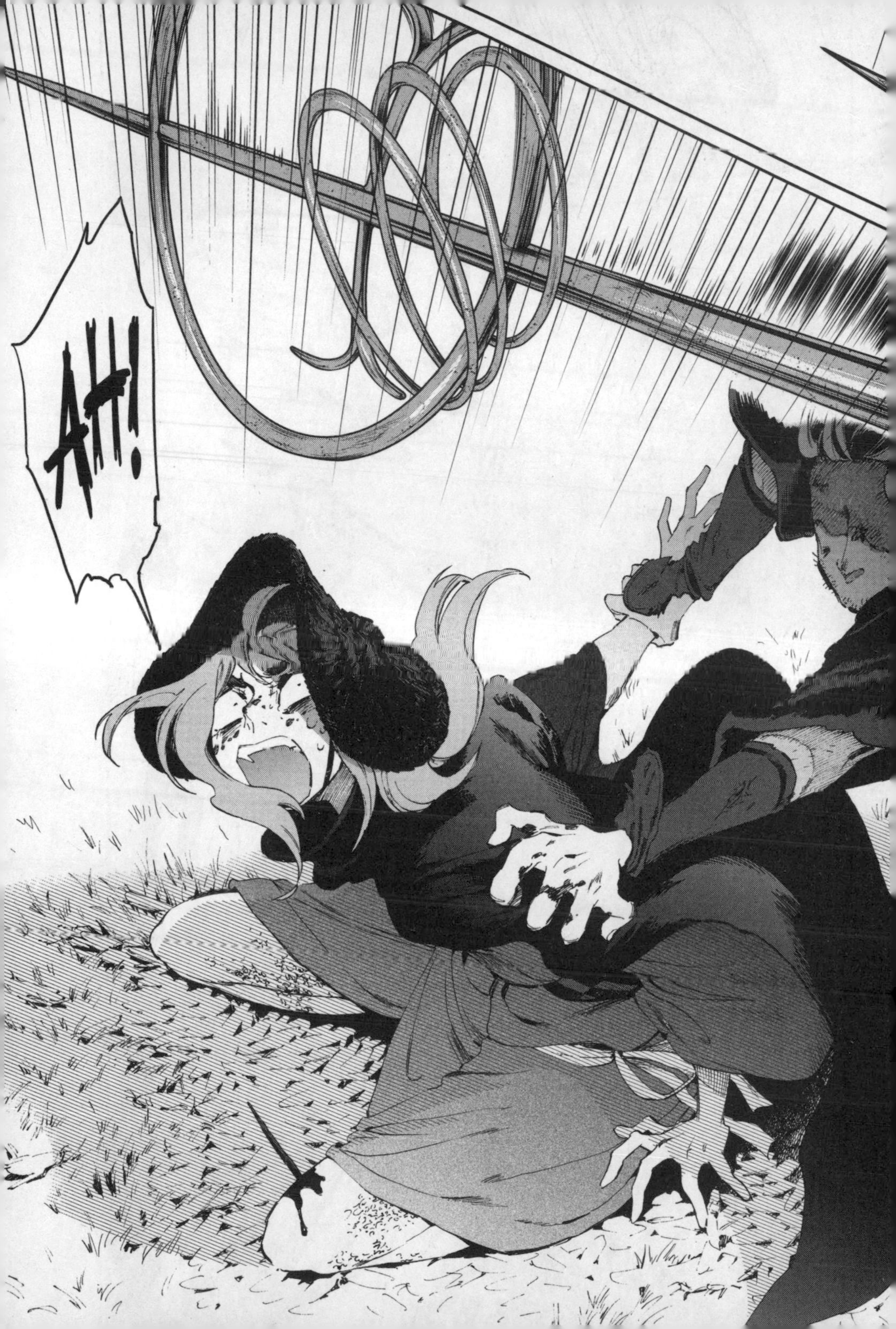
AH!

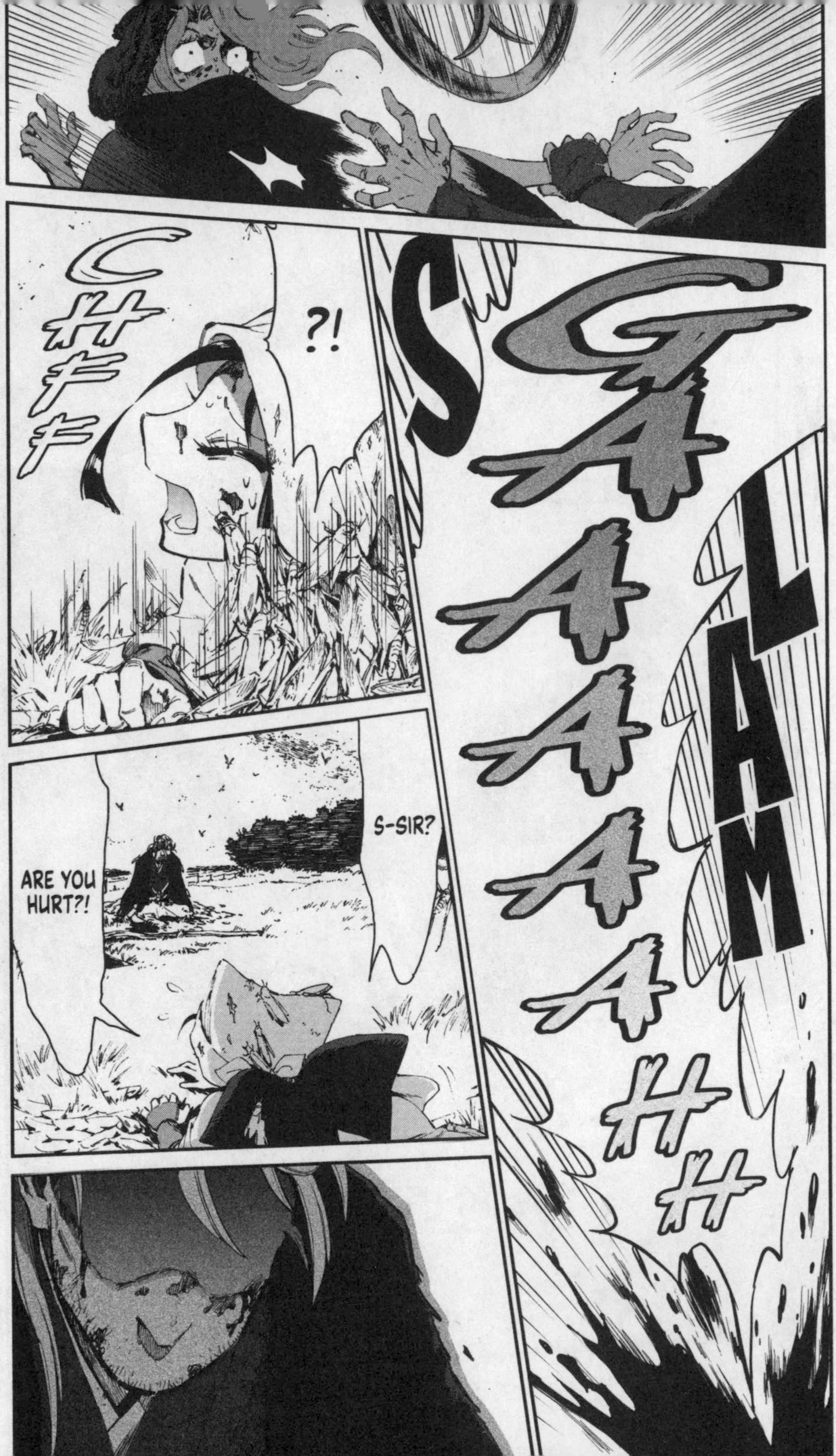
GAAAAAHH
SLAM
CHFF
?!
S-SIR?
ARE YOU HURT?!

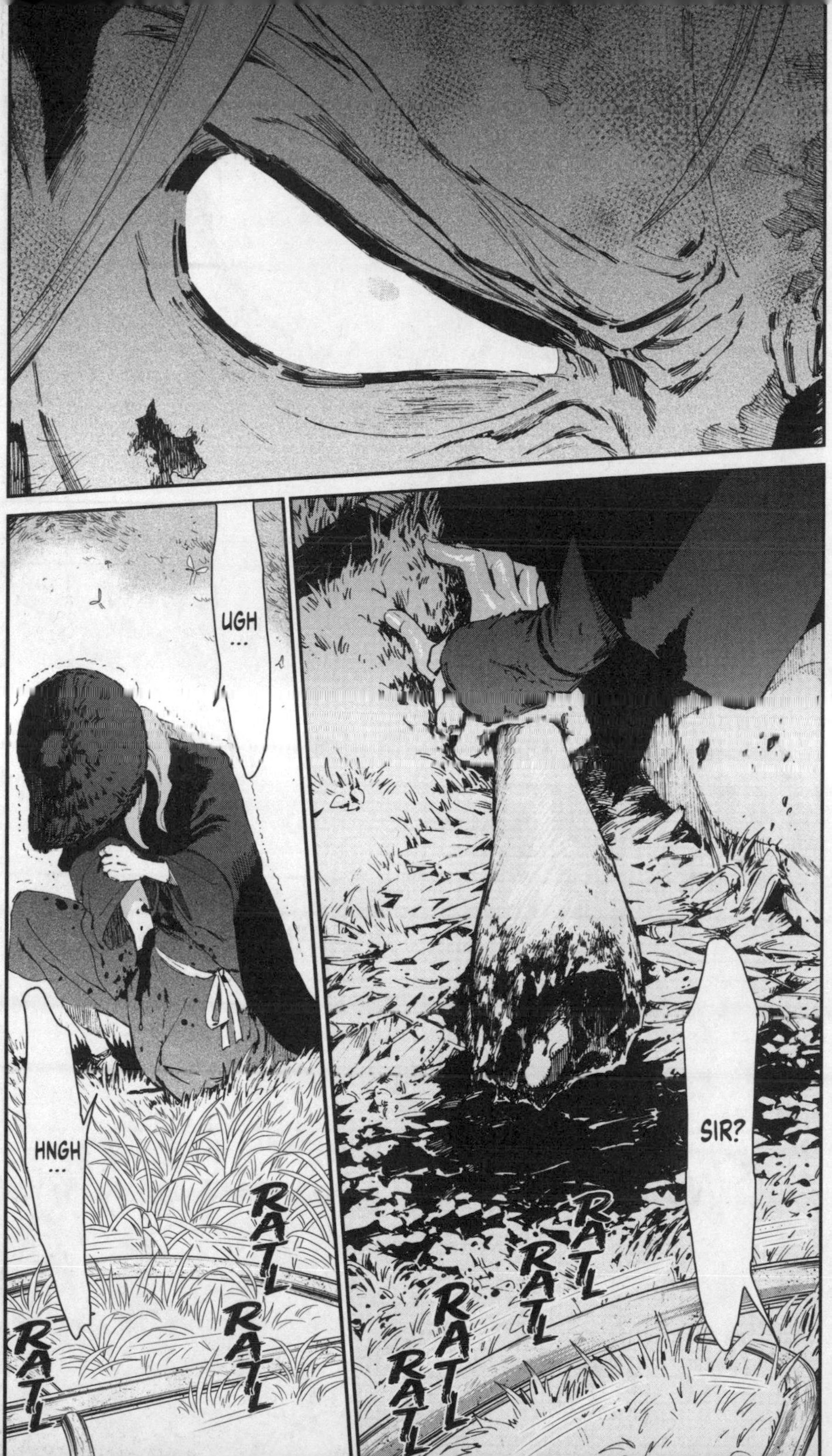
SIR?
RATL
RATL
RATL
RATL
UGH...
HNGH...
RATL
RATL
RATL

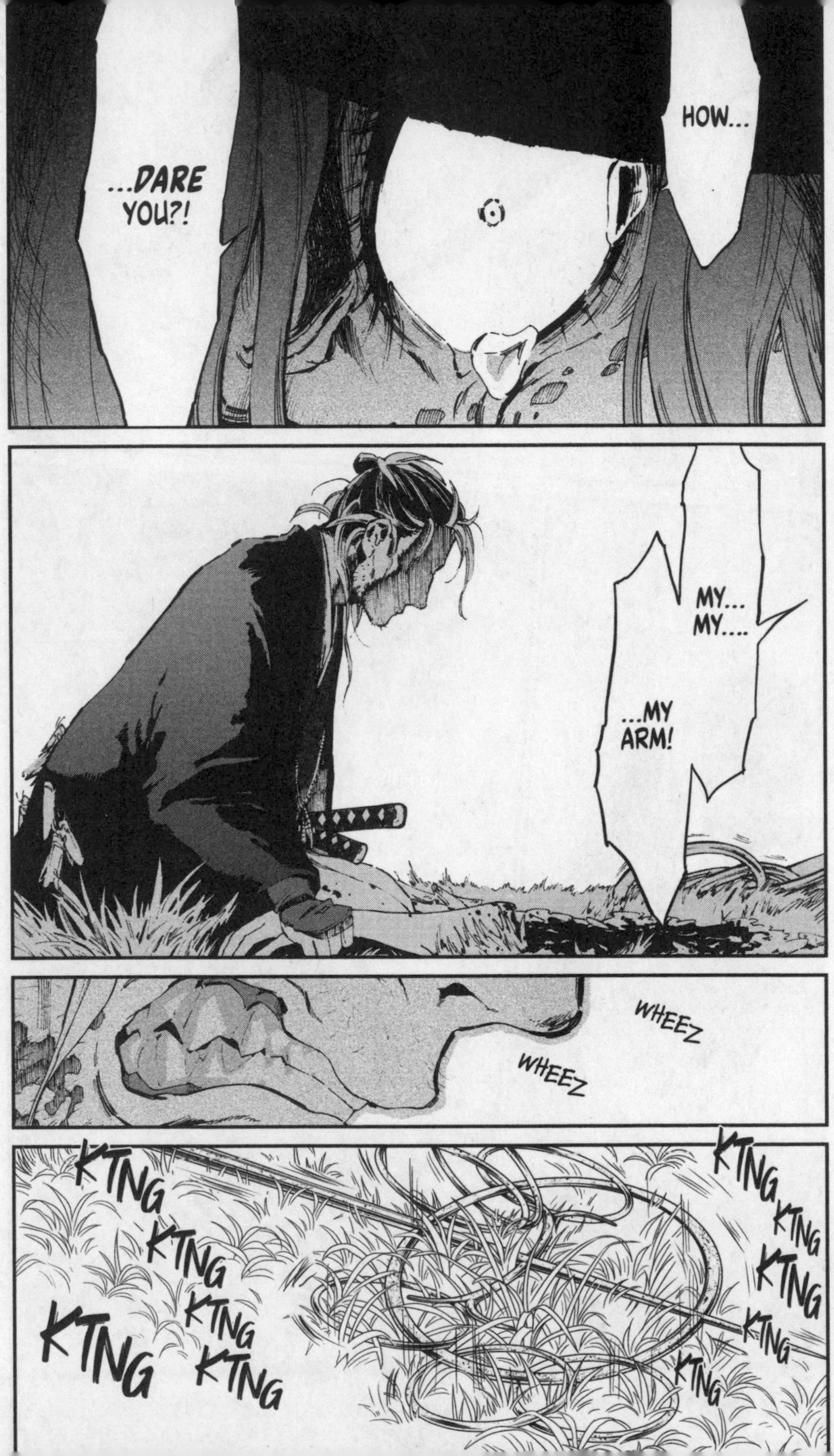
HOW...
...DARE YOU?!
MY... MY....
...MY ARM!
WHEEZ
WHEEZ
KTNG KTNG KTNG KTNG KTNG
KTNG KTNG KTNG KTNG KTNG

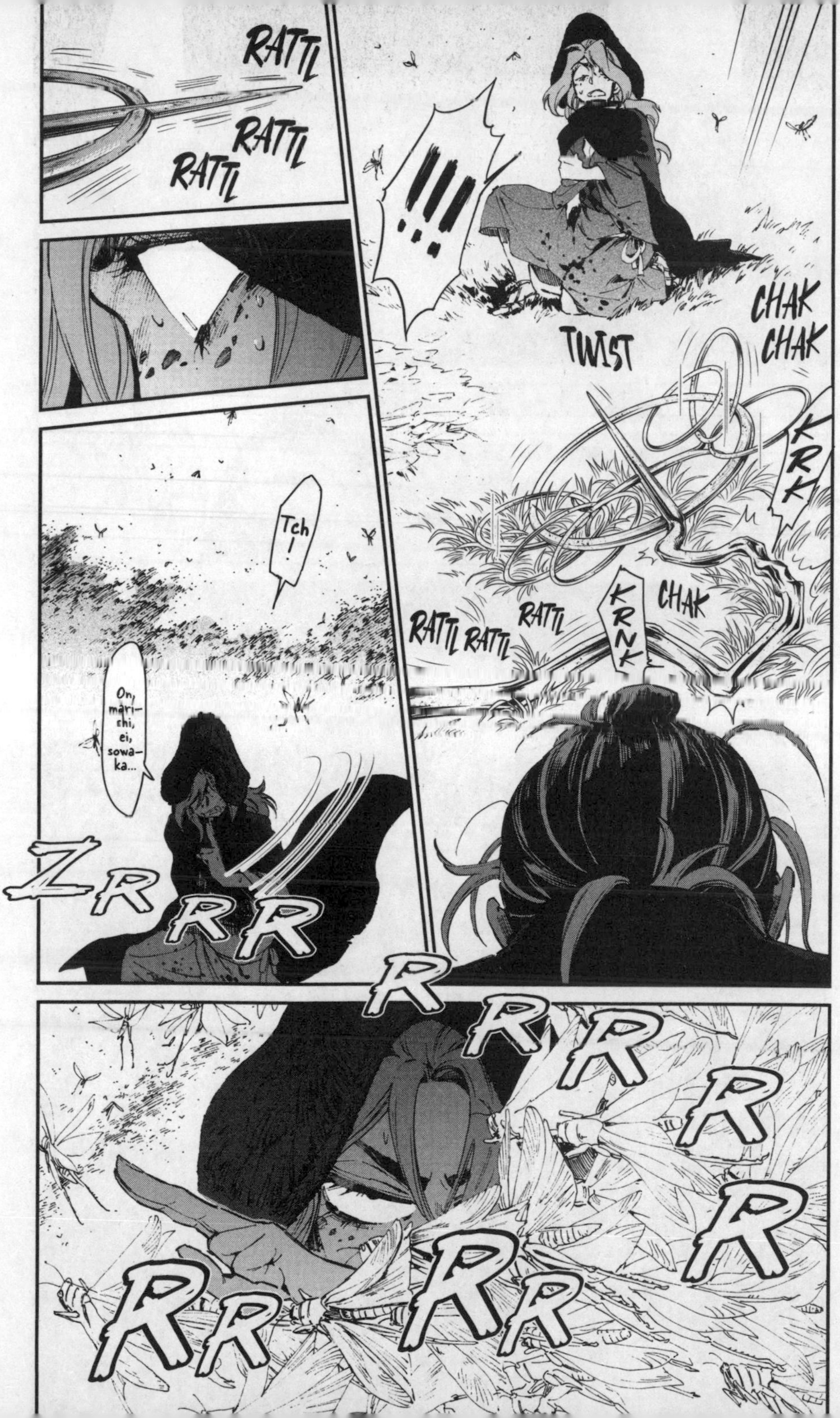
!!!
TWIST
CHAK CHAK
KRK
CHAK
KRNK
RATTL
RATTL RATTL
RATTL
RATTL
RATTL
Tch!
On, marishi, ei, sowaka...
ZRRR
RRRRRRRRR

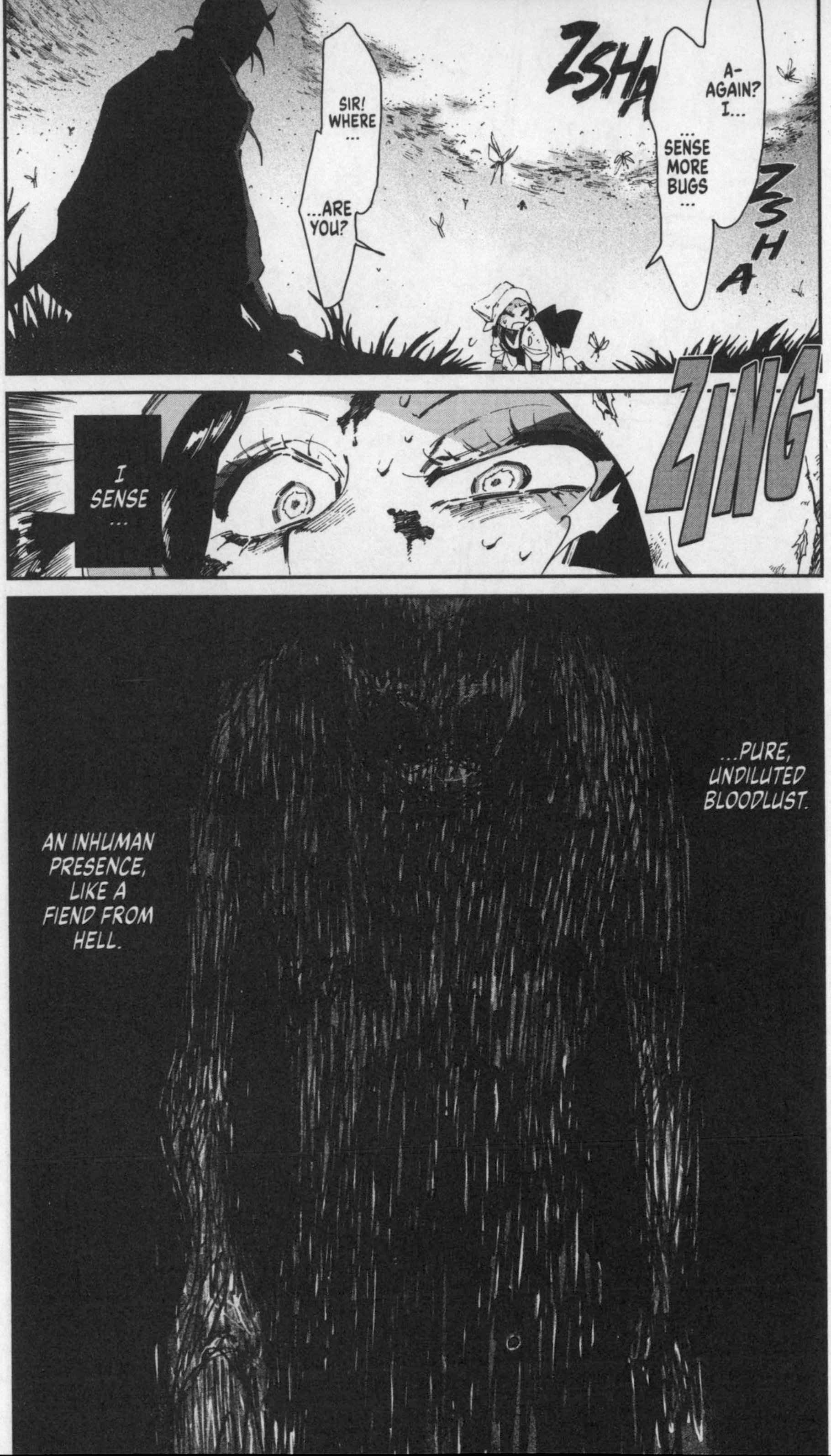
A- AGAIN? I... ...SENSE MORE BUGS...
ZSHA
ZSHA
ZSHA
SIR! WHERE... ...ARE YOU?
ZING
I SENSE...
...PURE, UNDILUTED BLOODLUST.
AN INHUMAN PRESENCE, LIKE A FIEND FROM HELL.

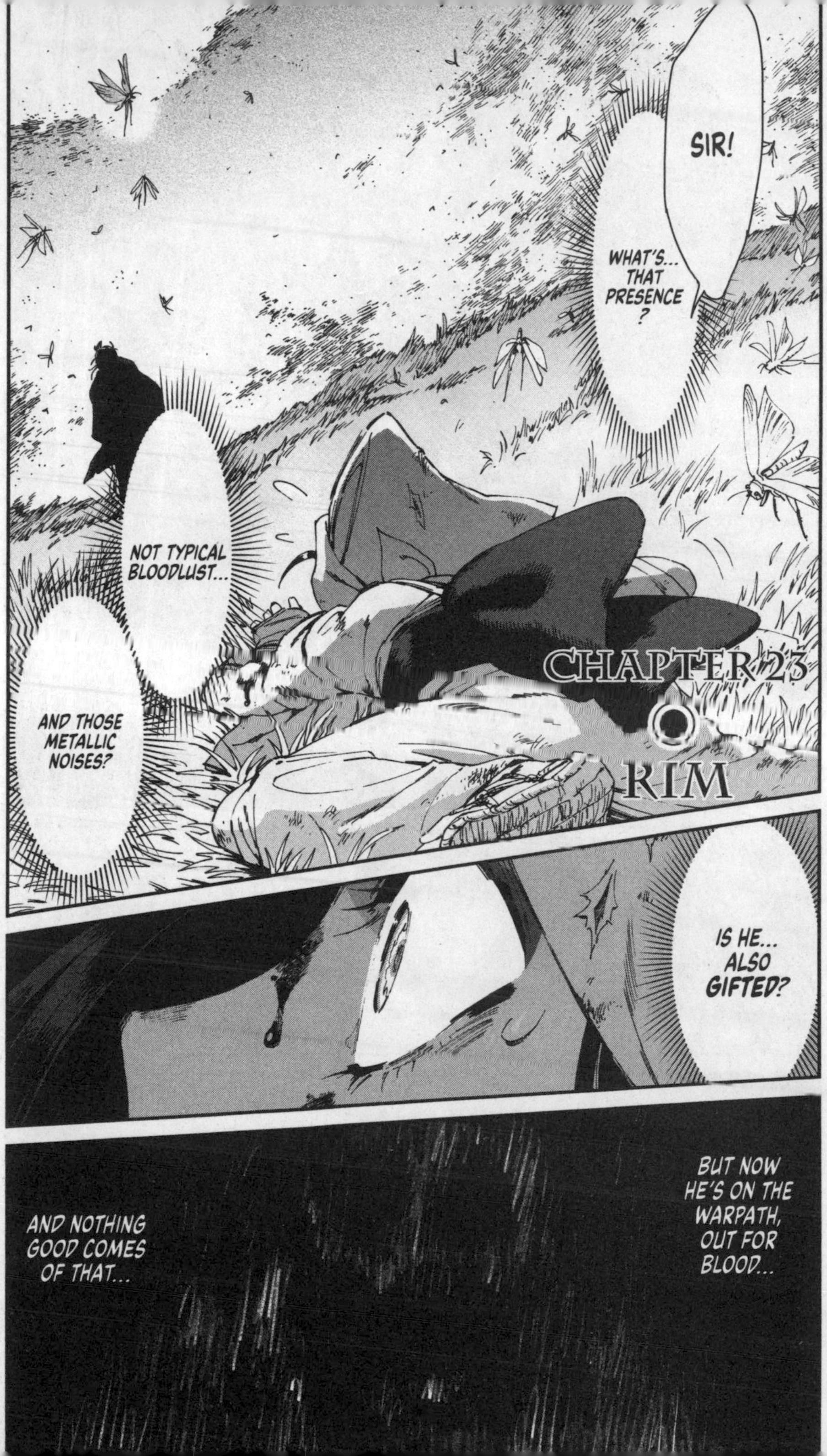
SIR!
WHAT'S... THAT PRESENCE?
NOT TYPICAL BLOODLUST...
AND THOSE METALLIC NOISES?
CHAPTER 23
RIM
IS HE... ALSO GIFTED?
BUT NOW HE'S ON THE WARPATH, OUT FOR BLOOD...
AND NOTHING GOOD COMES OF THAT...

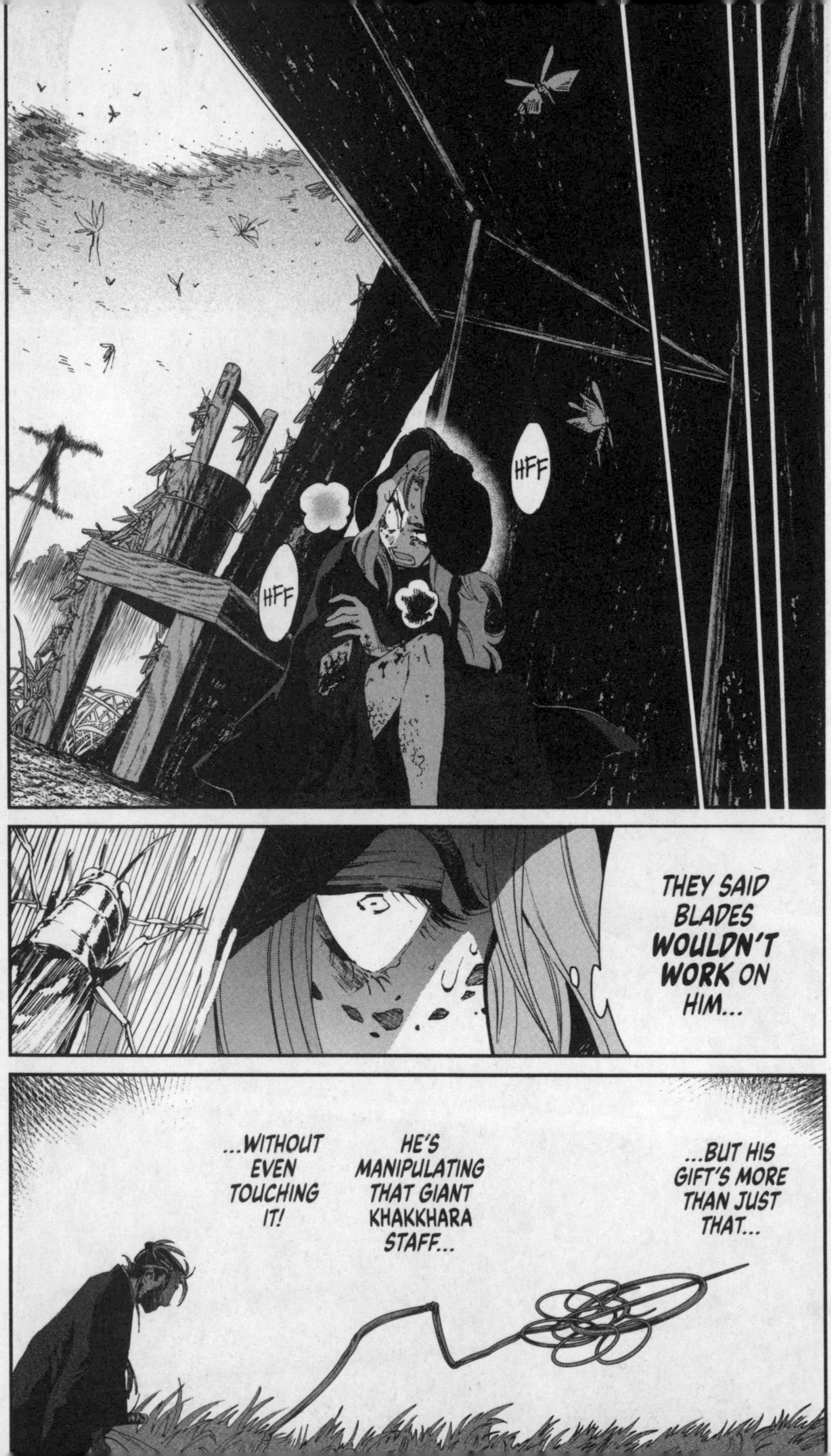
HFF
HFF
THEY SAID BLADES WOULDN'T WORK ON HIM...
...BUT HIS GIFT'S MORE THAN JUST THAT...
HE'S MANIPULATING THAT GIANT KHAKKHARA STAFF...
...WITHOUT EVEN TOUCHING IT!

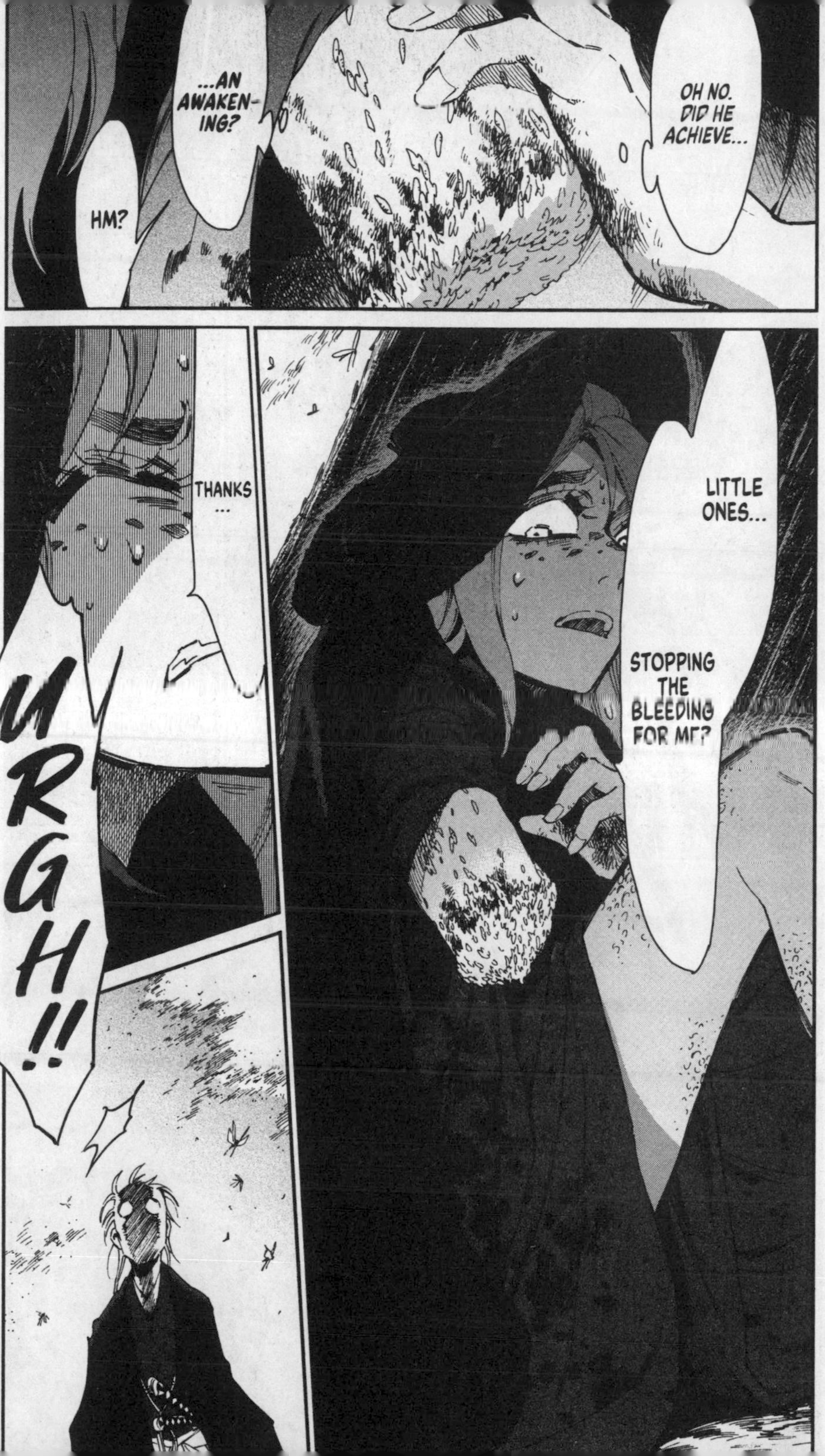
OH NO. DID HE ACHIEVE...
...AN AWAKENING?
HM?
LITTLE ONES...
STOPPING THE BLEEDING FOR ME?
THANKS...
URGH!!

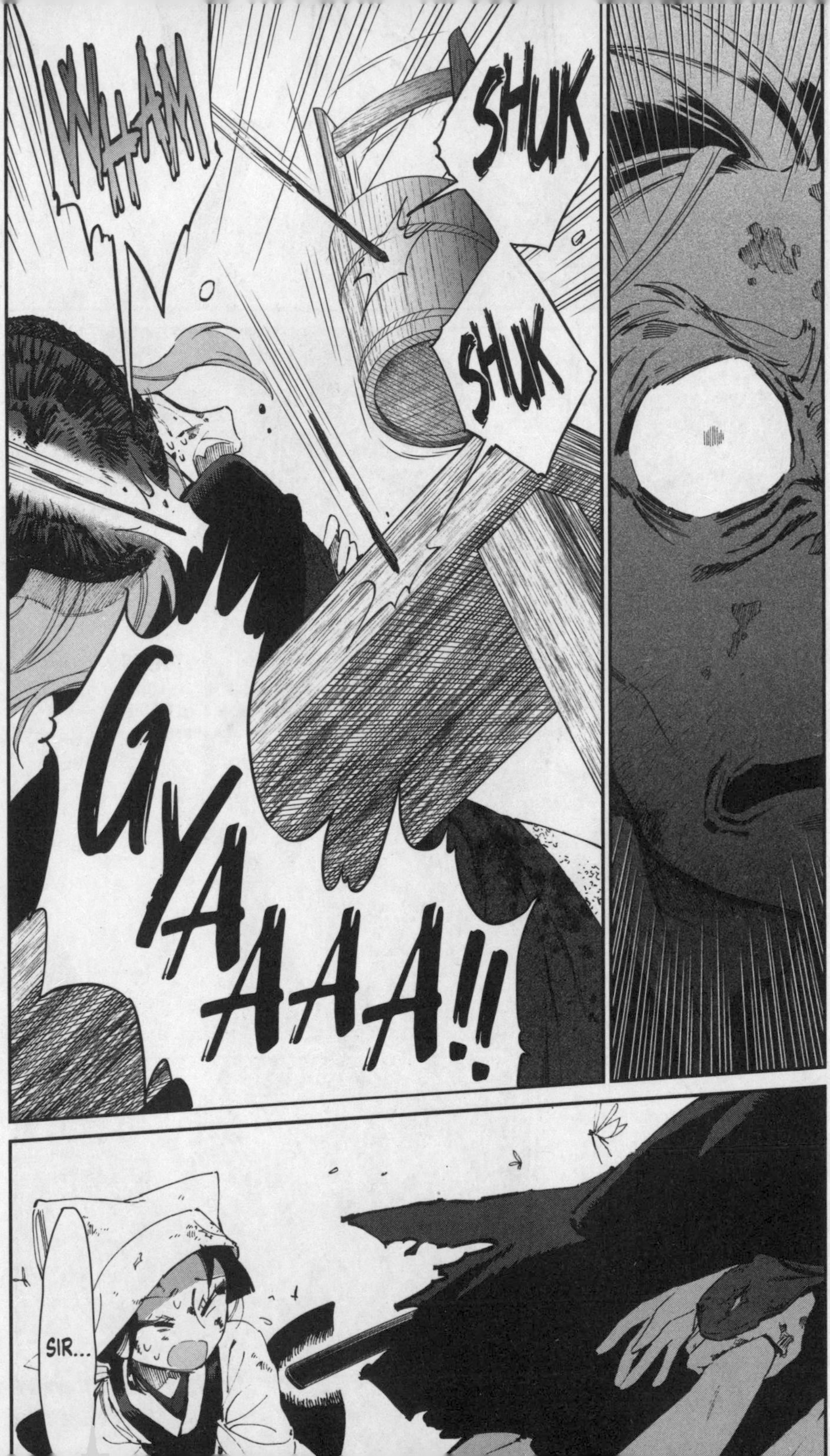
SHUK
SHUK
WHAM
GYAAAAA!!
SIR...

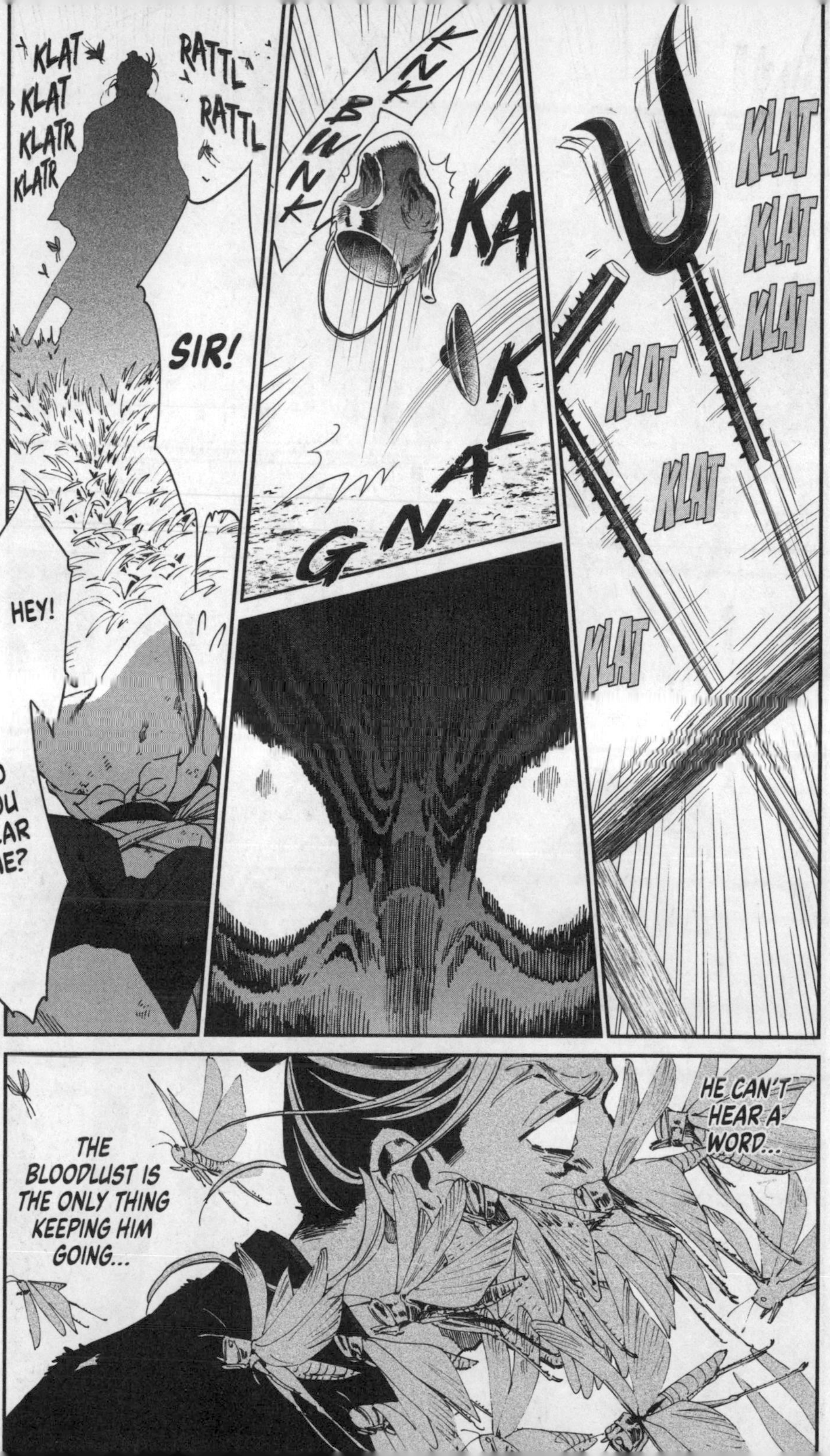
KLAT
KLAT
KLAT
KLAT
KLAT
KLAT
KNK
BWNK
KA
KLANG
KLAT
KLAT
KLATR
KLATR
RATTL
RATTL
SIR!
HEY!
DO YOU HEAR ME?
HE CAN'T HEAR A WORD...
THE BLOODLUST IS THE ONLY THING KEEPING HIM GOING...

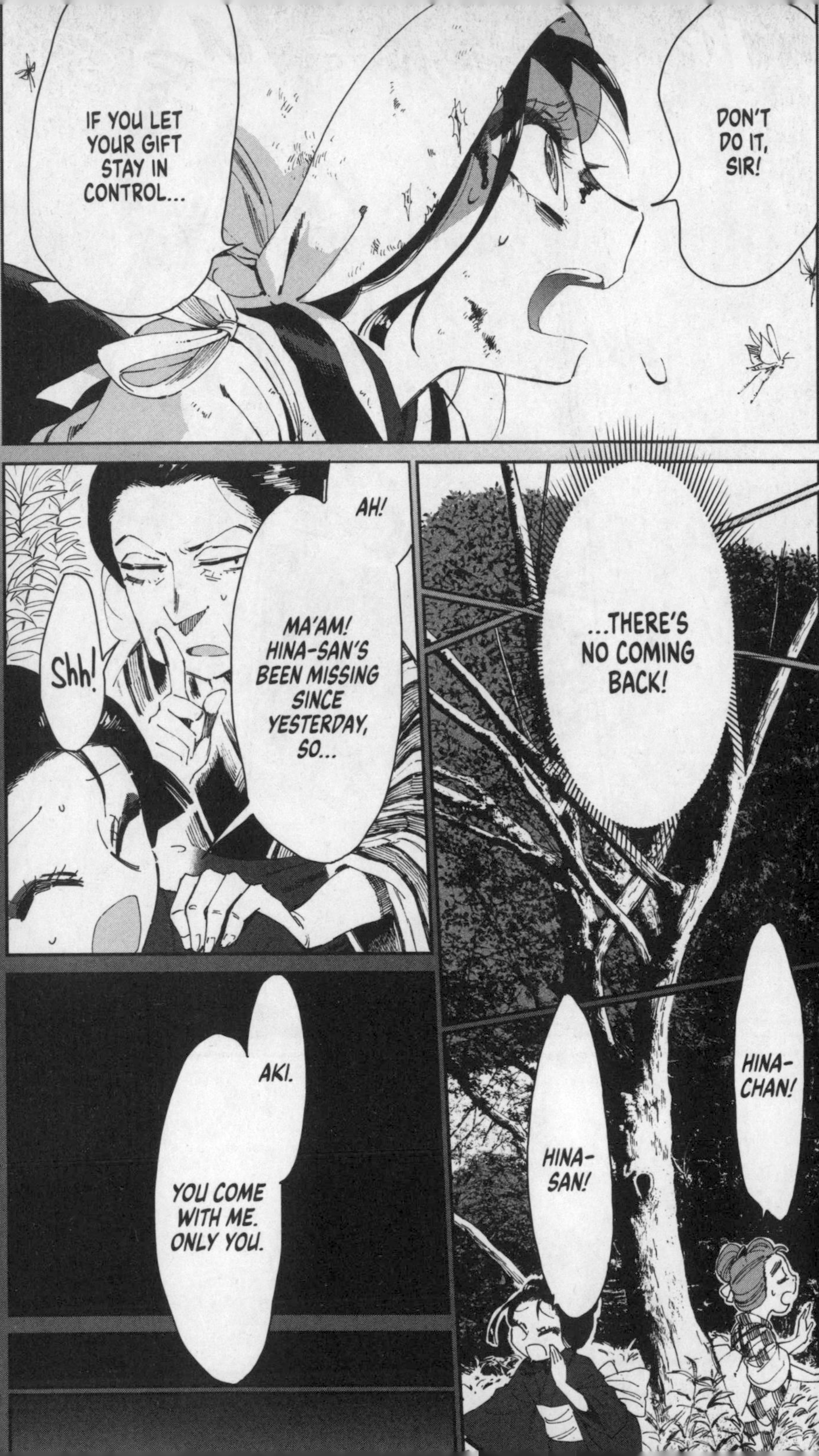
DON'T DO IT, SIR!
IF YOU LET YOUR GIFT STAY IN CONTROL...
...THERE'S NO COMING BACK!
HINA-CHAN!
HINA-SAN!
AH!
MA'AM! HINA-SAN'S BEEN MISSING SINCE YESTERDAY, SO...
Shh!
AKI.
YOU COME WITH ME. ONLY YOU.

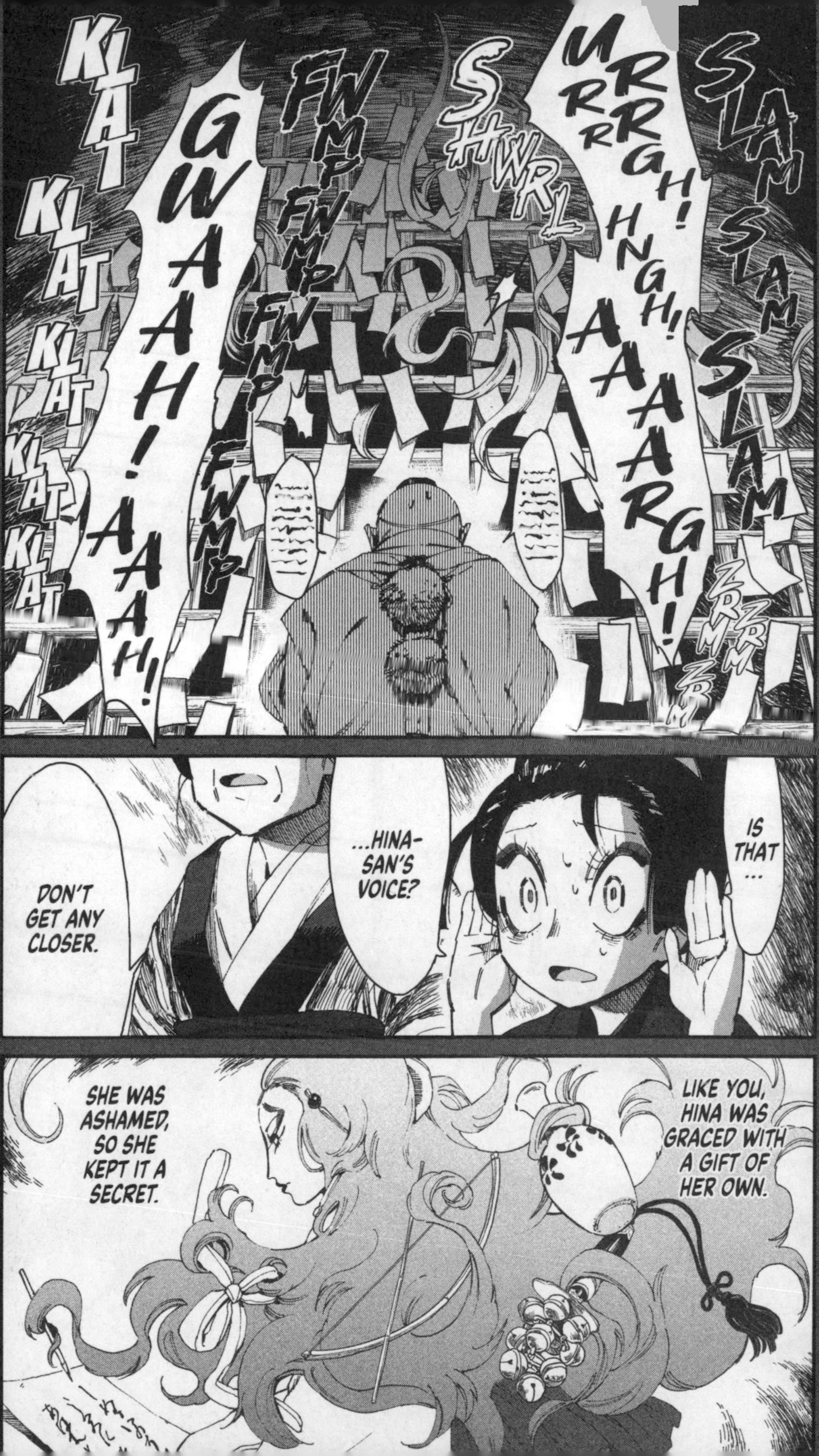
SLAM SLAM SLAM SLAM
URRRRRGH! HNGH HNGH! AAAARGH!
ZRMM ZRMM ZRMM
SHWRL
FWMP FWMP FWMP FWMP
GWAAH! AAAH!
KLAT KLAT KLAT KLAT KLAT
IS THAT ...
...HINA-SAN'S VOICE?
DON'T GET ANY CLOSER.
LIKE YOU, HINA WAS GRACED WITH A GIFT OF HER OWN.
SHE WAS ASHAMED, SO SHE KEPT IT A SECRET.

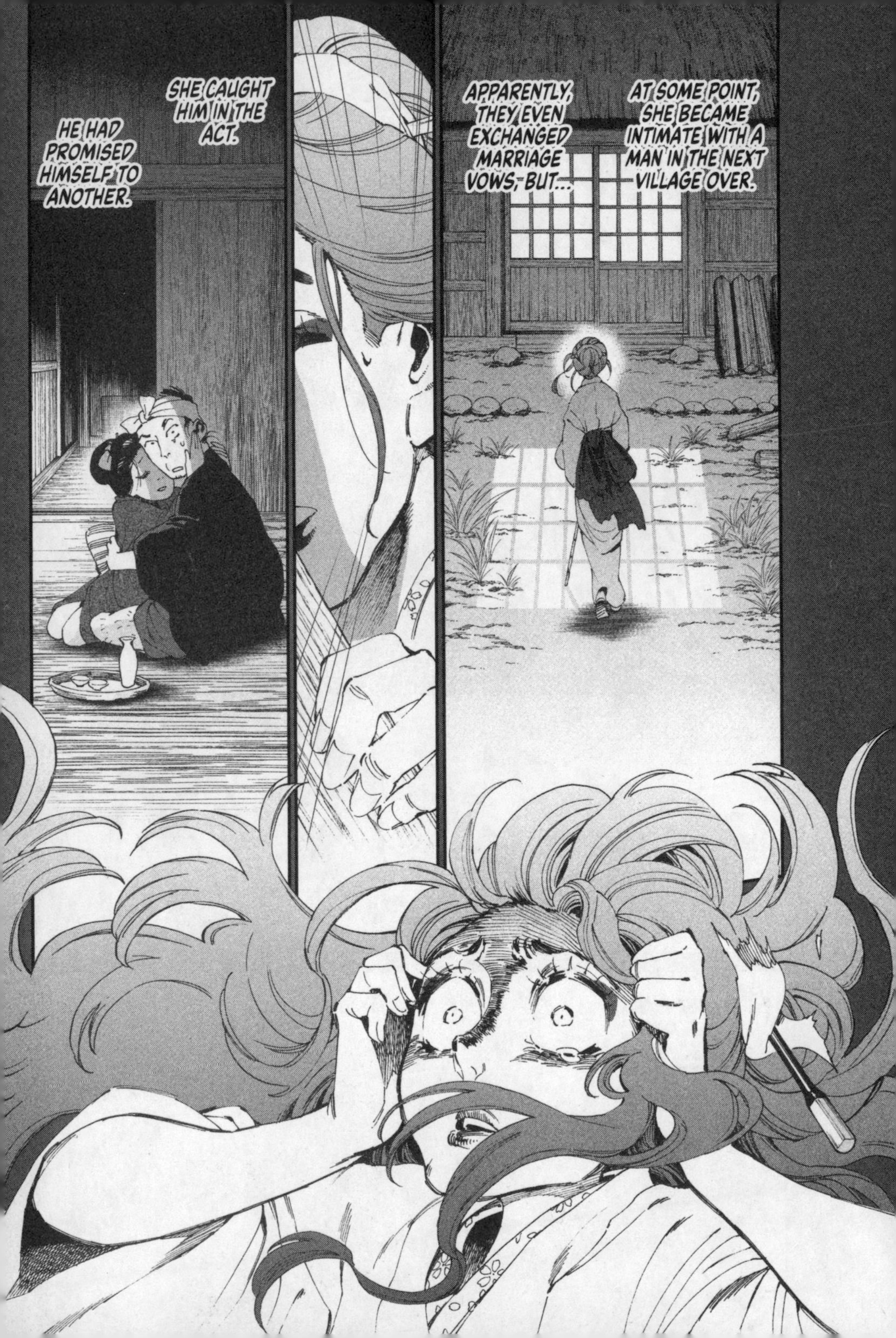
AT SOME POINT, SHE BECAME INTIMATE WITH A MAN IN THE NEXT VILLAGE OVER.
APPARENTLY, THEY EVEN EXCHANGED MARRIAGE VOWS, BUT...
SHE CAUGHT HIM IN THE ACT.
HE HAD PROMISED HIMSELF TO ANOTHER.

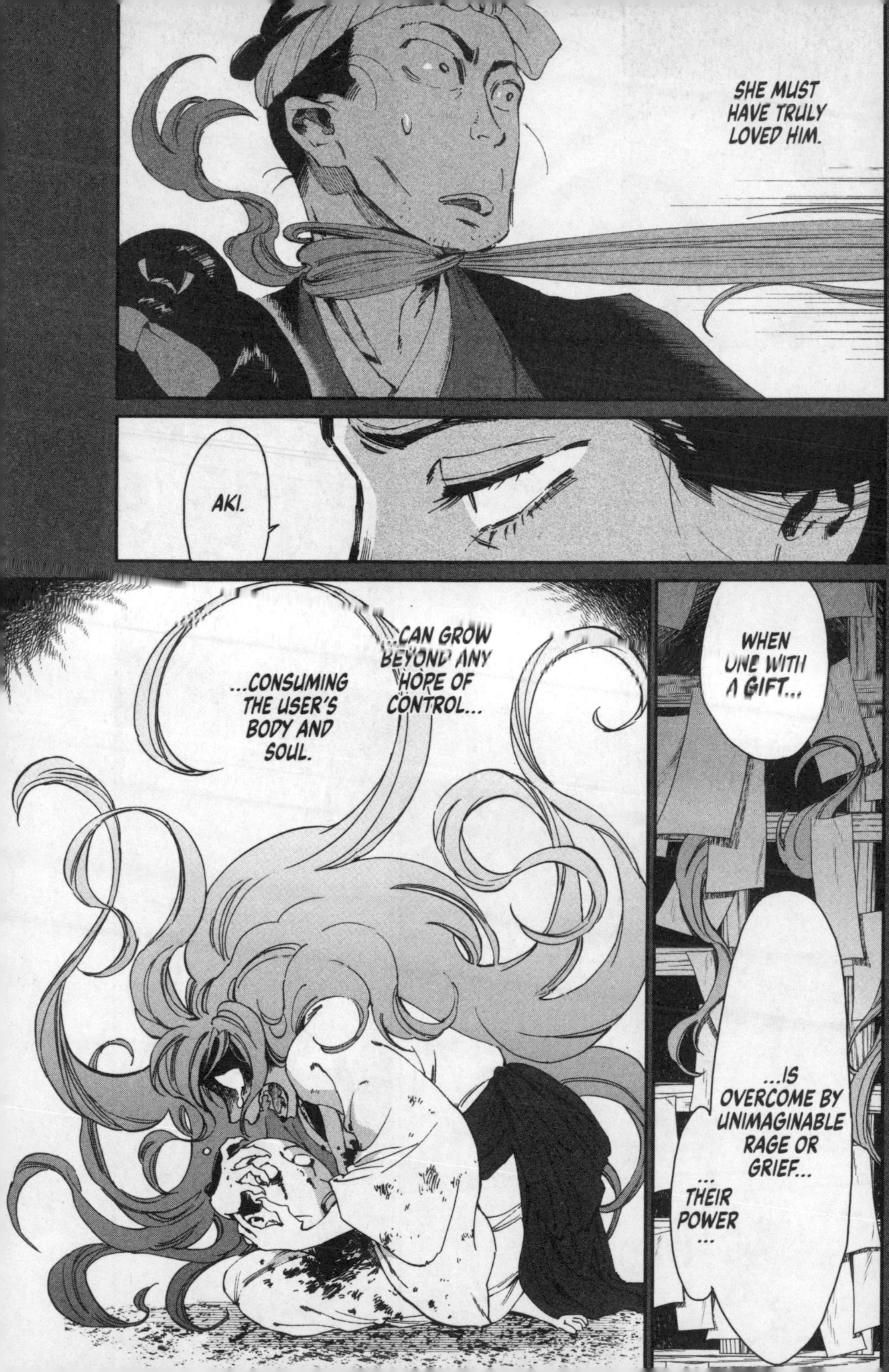
SHE MUST HAVE TRULY LOVED HIM.
AKI.
WHEN ONE WITH A GIFT...
...IS OVERCOME BY UNIMAGINABLE RAGE OR GRIEF...
...THEIR POWER...
...CAN GROW BEYOND ANY HOPE OF CONTROL...
...CONSUMING THE USER'S BODY AND SOUL.

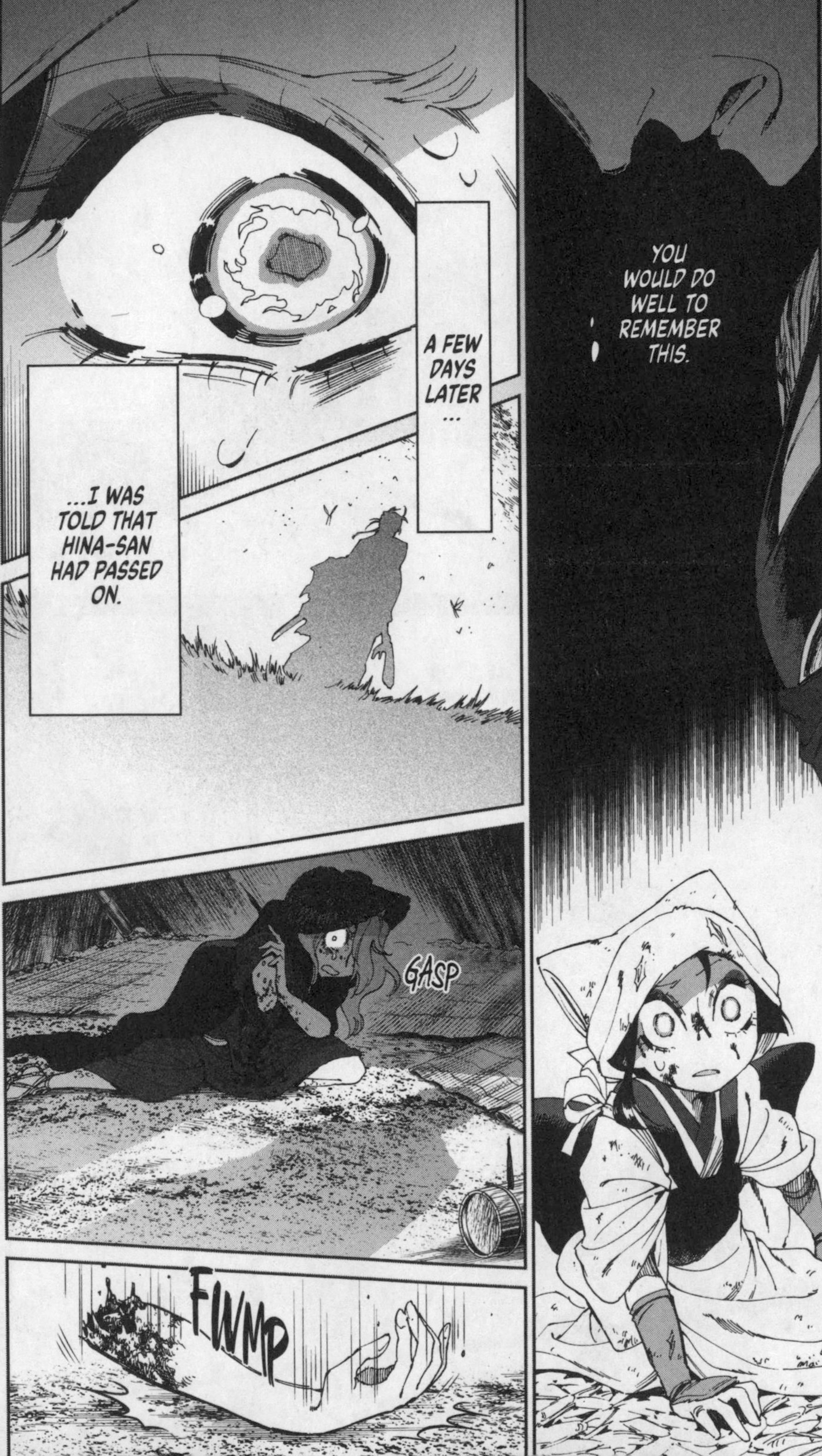
YOU WOULD DO WELL TO REMEMBER THIS.
A FEW DAYS LATER ...
...I WAS TOLD THAT HINA-SAN HAD PASSED ON.
GASP
FWMP

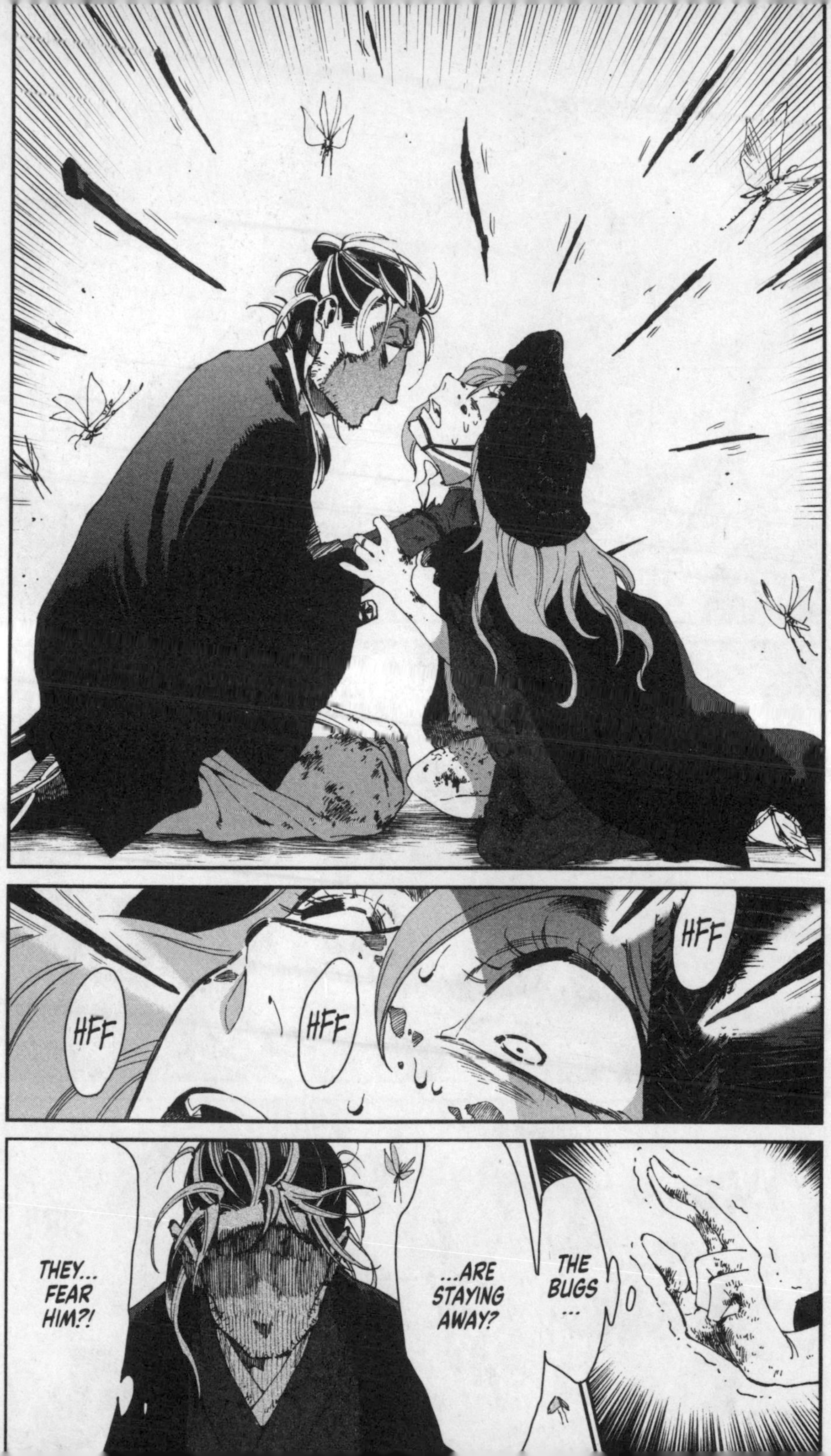
HFF
HFF
HFF
THE BUGS...
...ARE STAYING AWAY?
THEY... FEAR HIM?!

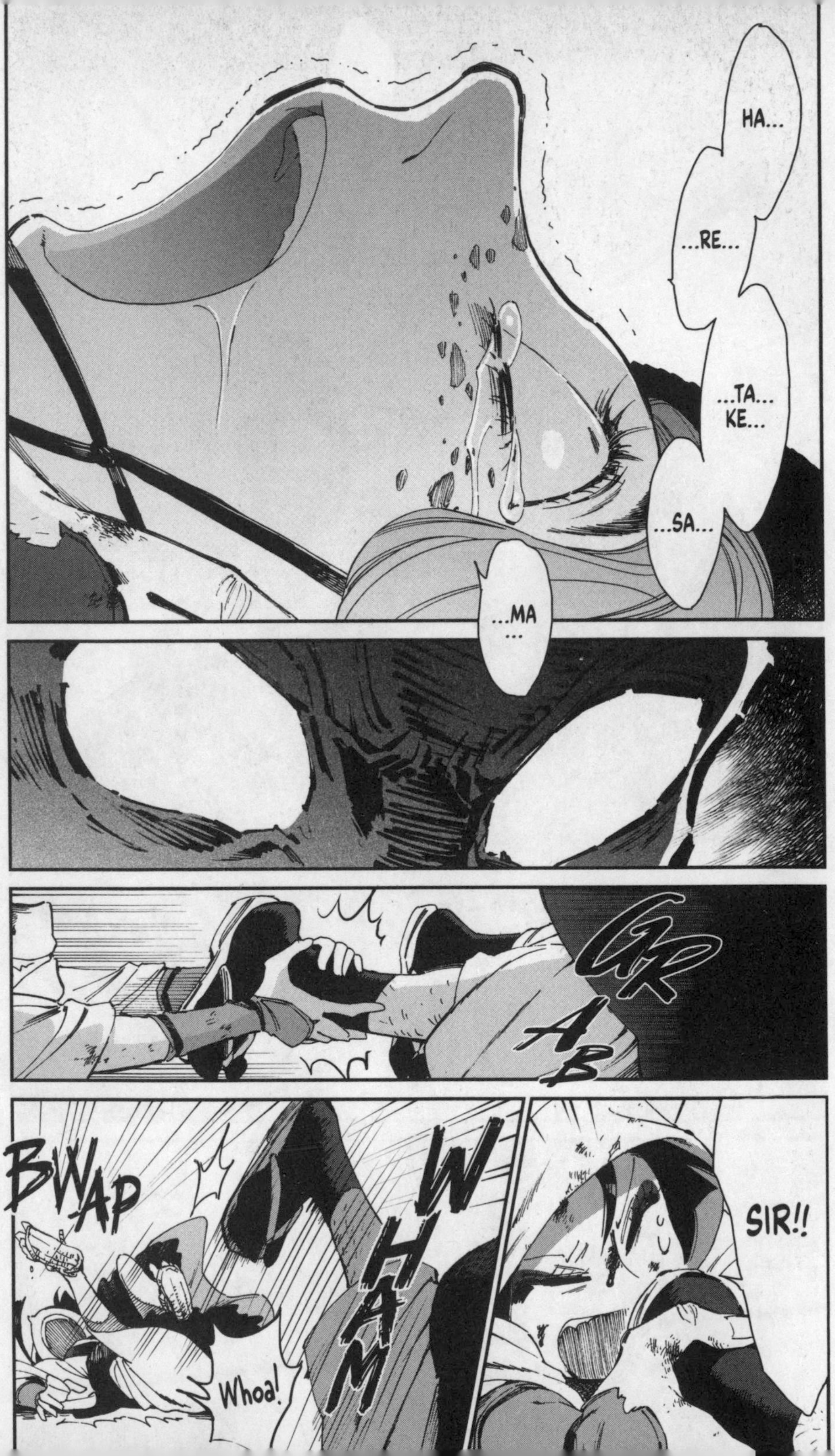
HA...
...RE...
...TA...
KE...
...SA...
...MA
...
GRAB
SIR!!
WHAM
BWAP
Whoa!

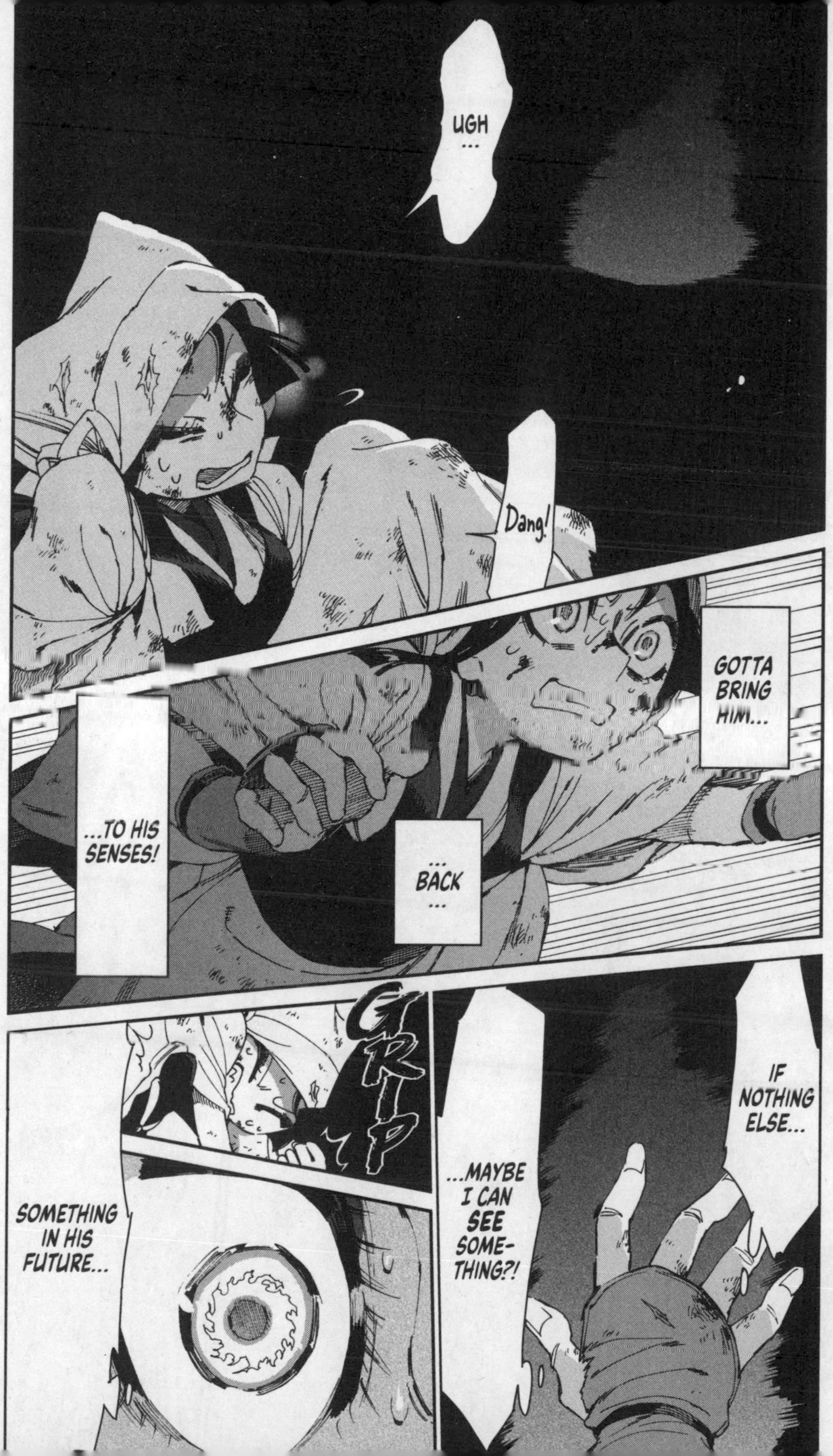
UGH...
Dang!
GOTTA BRING HIM...
...BACK...
...TO HIS SENSES!
IF NOTHING ELSE...
...MAYBE I CAN SEE SOME-THING?!
GRIP
SOMETHING IN HIS FUTURE...

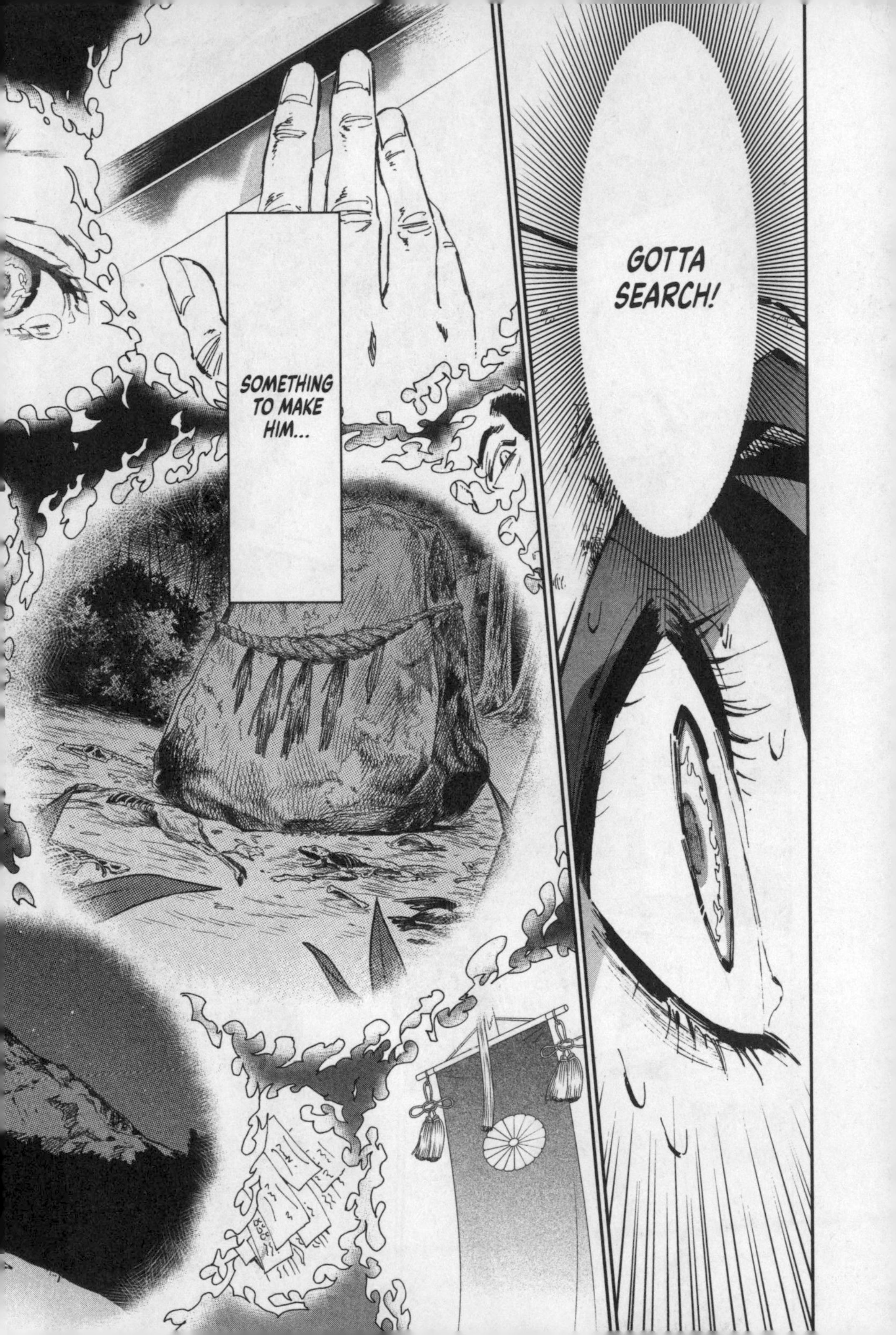
GOTTA SEARCH!
SOMETHING TO MAKE HIM...

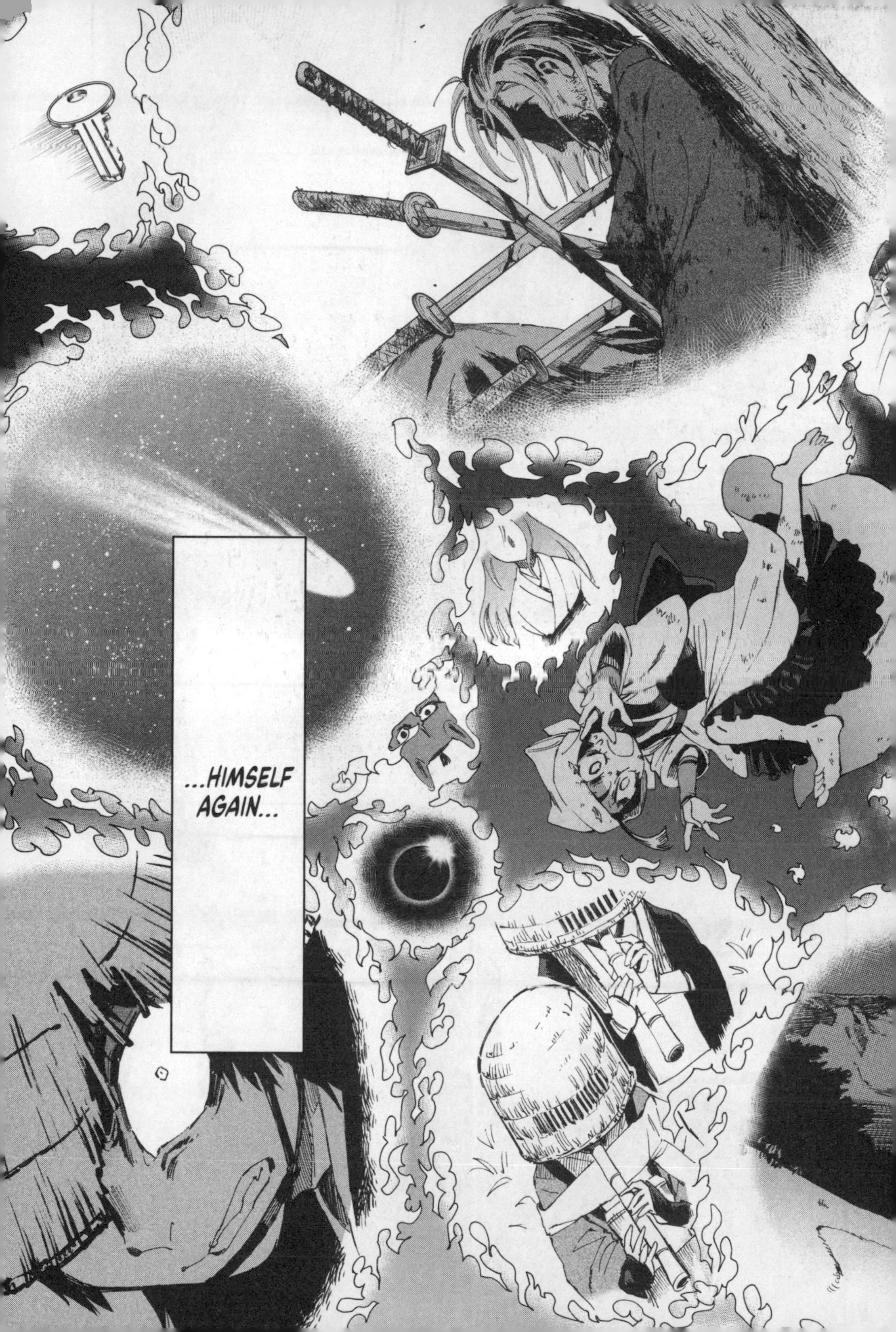
...HIMSELF AGAIN...

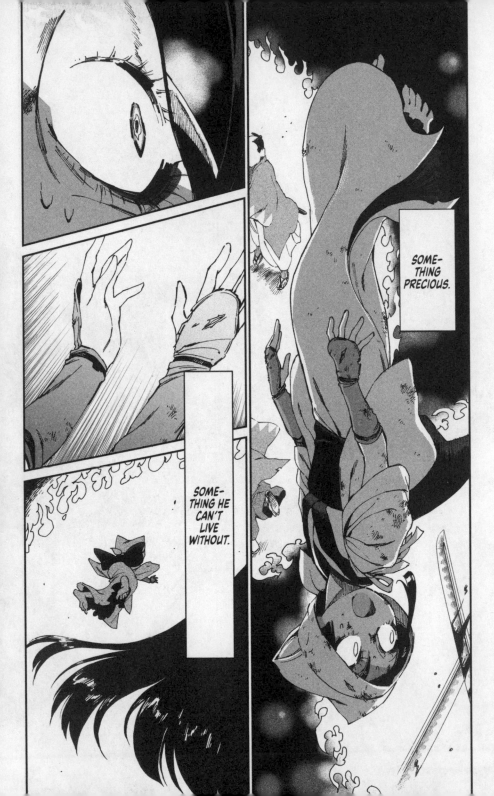

SOME-
THING
PRECIOUS.

SOME-
THING HE
CAN'T
LIVE
WITHOUT.

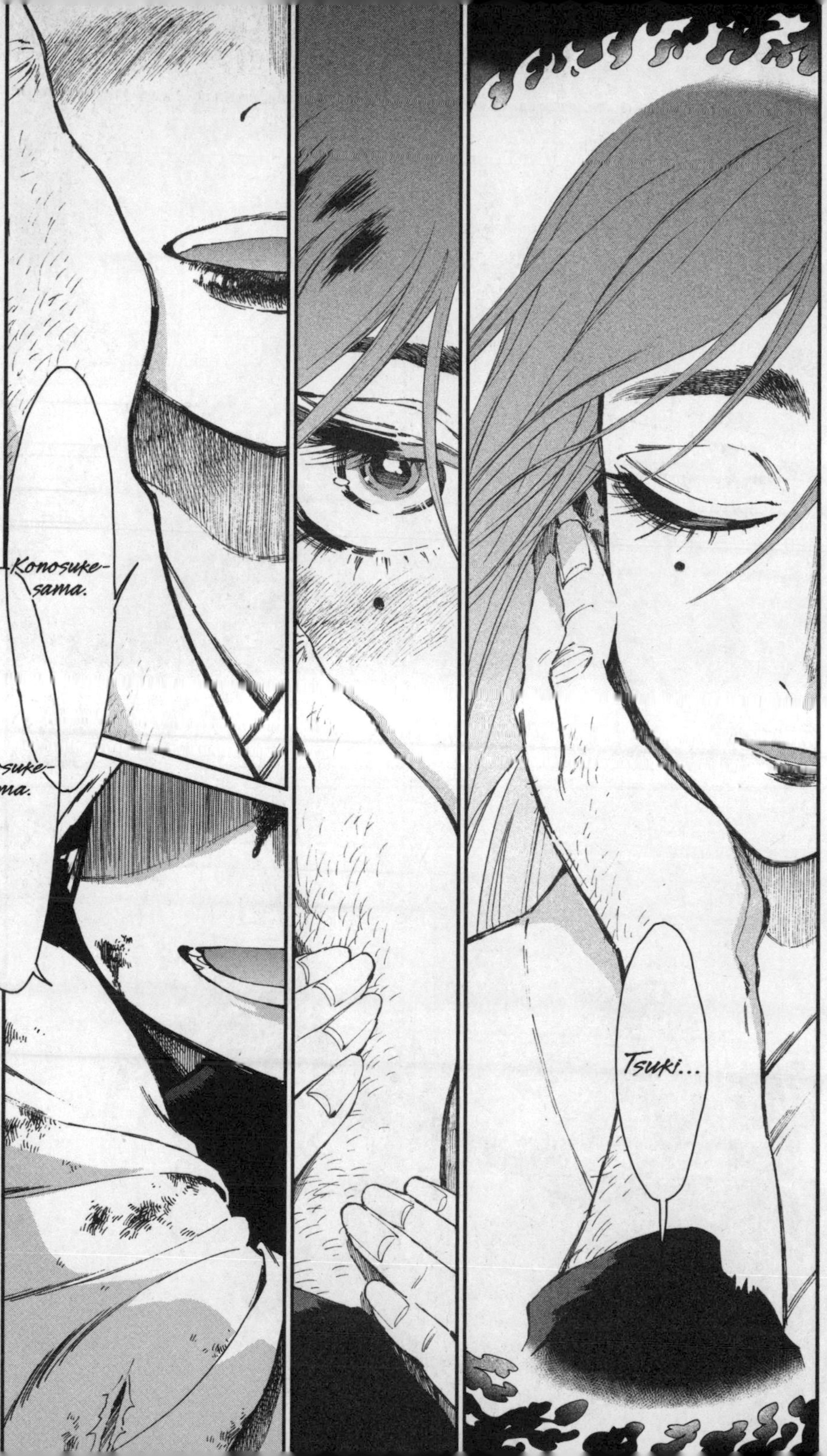
Tsuki...
Konosuke-sama.
Konosuke-sama.

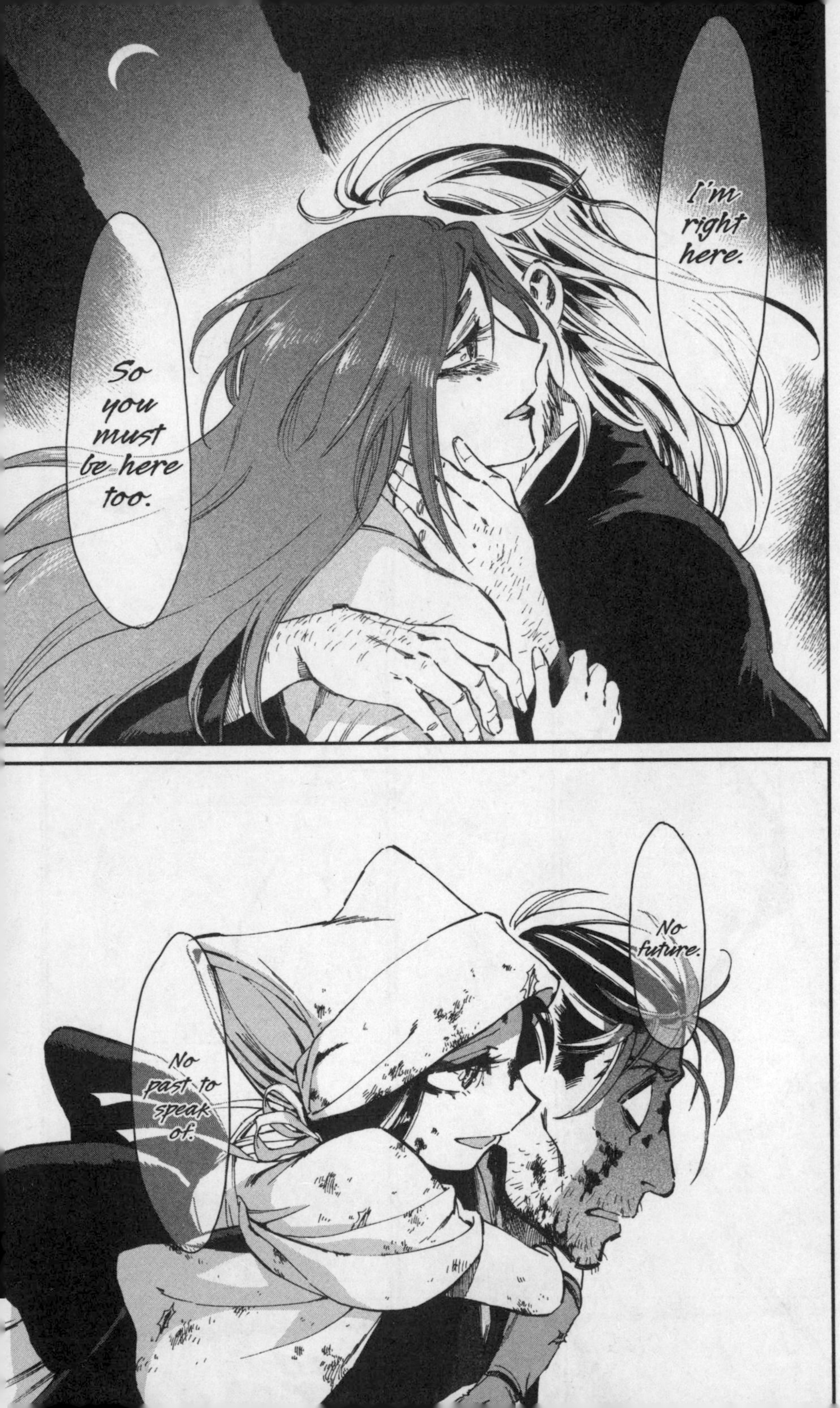
I'm right here.
So you must be here too.
No future.
No past to speak of.

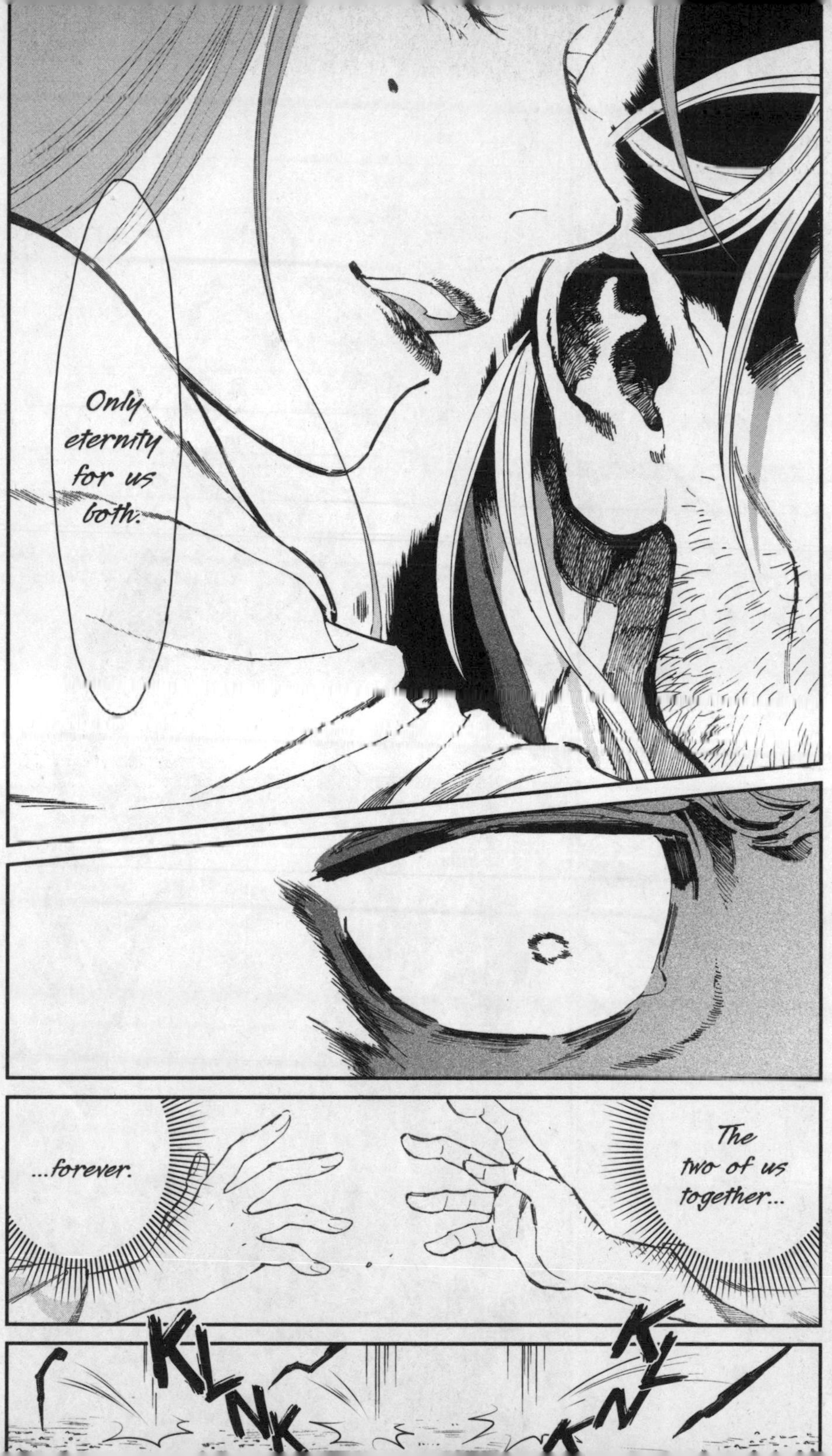
Only eternity for us both.
The two of us together...
...forever.
KLNK
KLNK

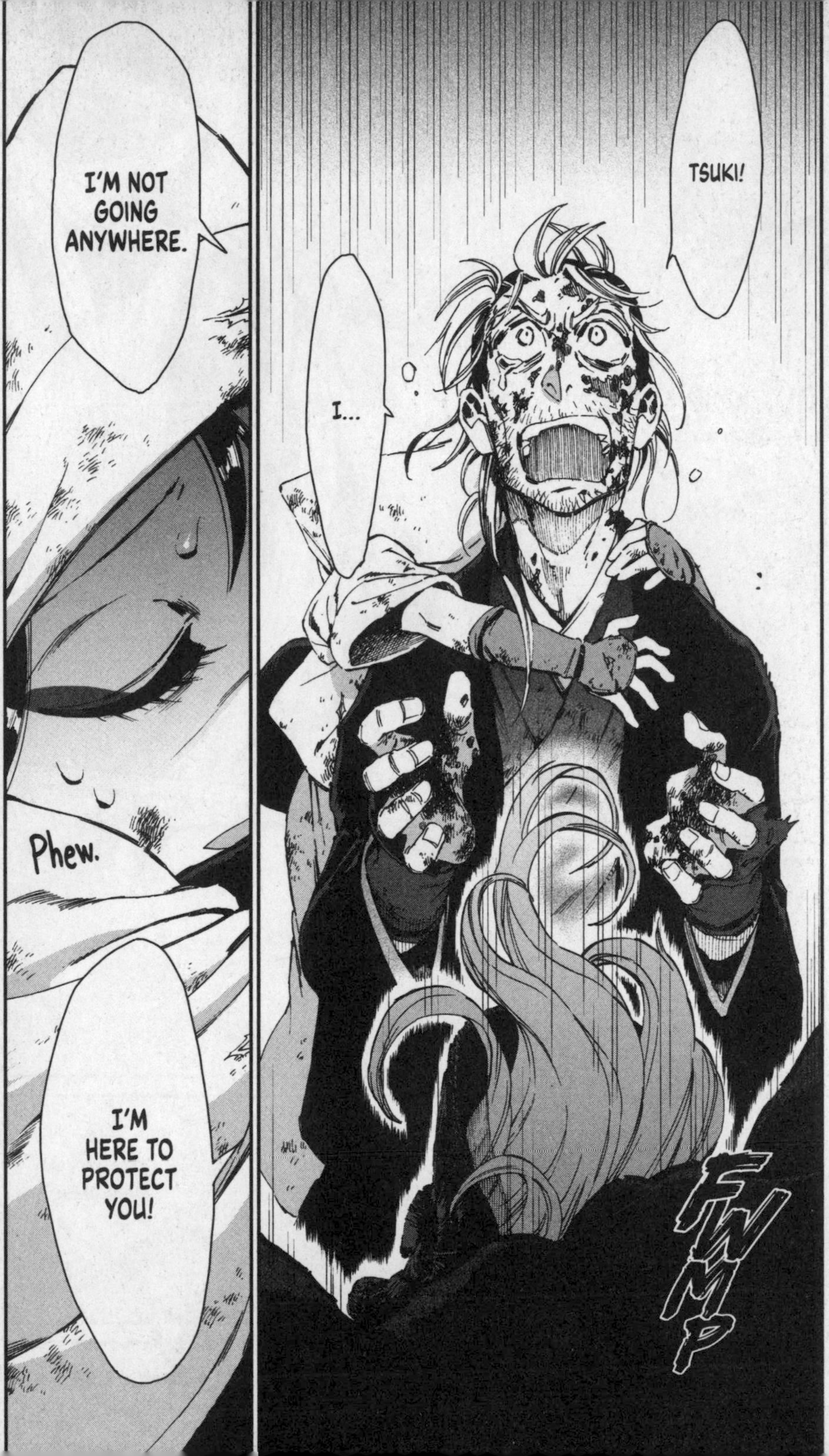
TSUKI!
I...
FWMP
I'M NOT GOING ANYWHERE.
Phew.
I'M HERE TO PROTECT YOU!

STEEL *of the*
CELESTIAL
SHADOWS

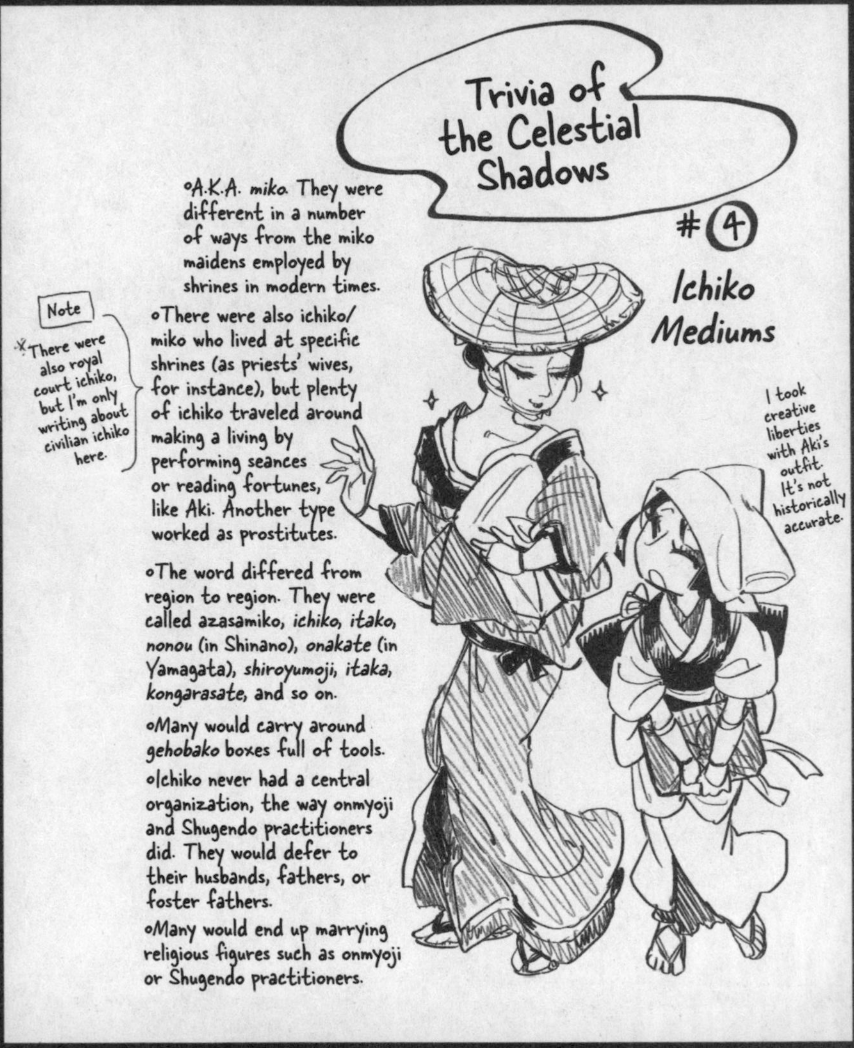
Trivia of the Celestial Shadows
#4
Ichiko Mediums
∘A.K.A. miko. They were different in a number of ways from the miko maidens employed by shrines in modern times.
∘There were also ichiko/miko who lived at specific shrines (as priests' wives, for instance), but plenty of ichiko traveled around making a living by performing seances or reading fortunes, like Aki. Another type worked as prostitutes.
Note
※There were also royal court ichiko, but I'm only writing about civilian ichiko here.
∘The word differed from region to region. They were called azasamiko, ichiko, itako, nonou (in Shinano), onakate (in Yamagata), shiroyumoji, itaka, kongarasate, and so on.
∘Many would carry around gehobako boxes full of tools.
∘Ichiko never had a central organization, the way onmyoji and Shugendo practitioners did. They would defer to their husbands, fathers, or foster fathers.
∘Many would end up marrying religious figures such as onmyoji or Shugendo practitioners.
I took creative liberties with Aki's outfit. It's not historically accurate.

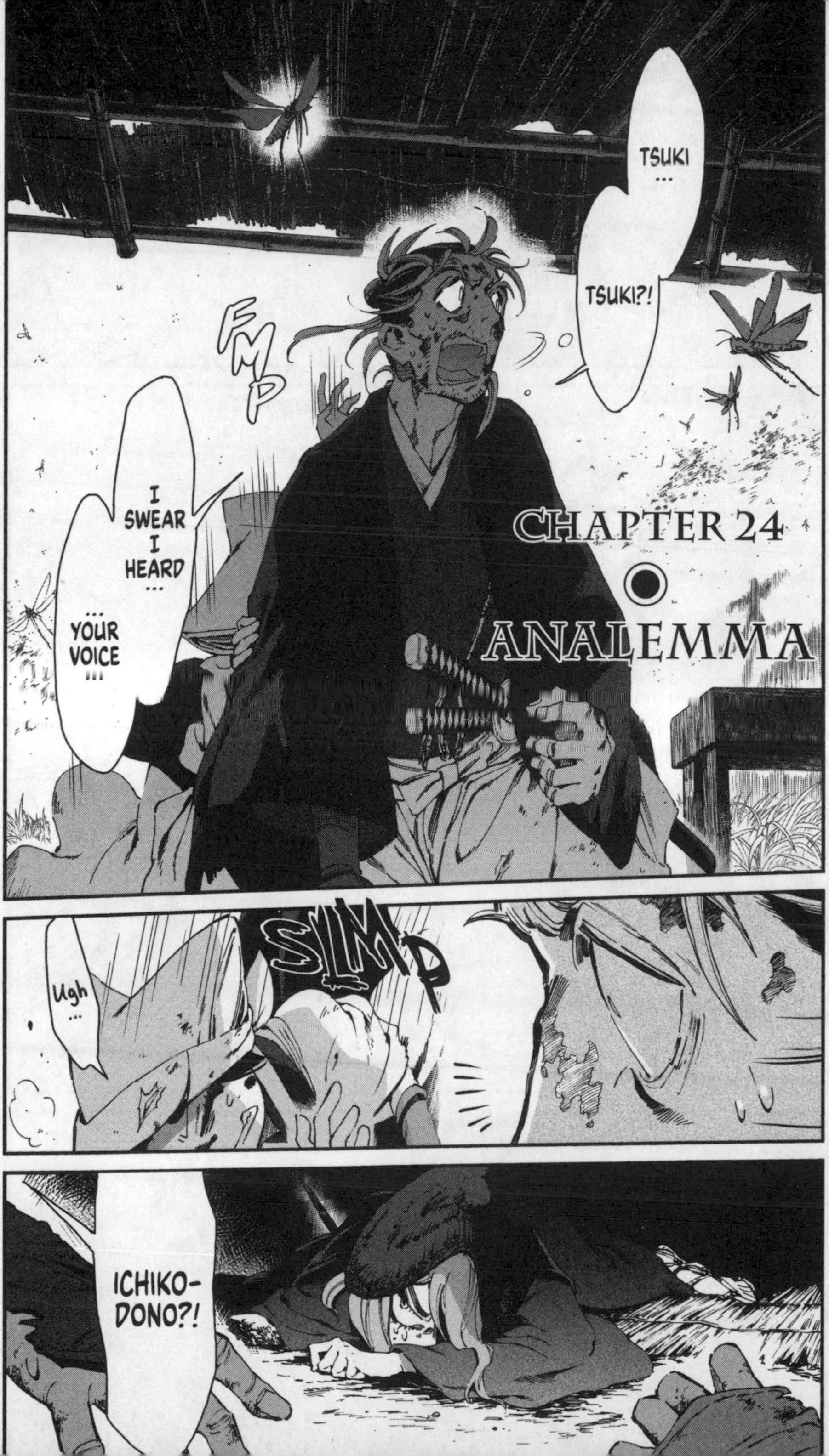
TSUKI...
TSUKI?!
FMP
I SWEAR I HEARD... ...YOUR VOICE!!!
CHAPTER 24
ANALEMMA
SLMP
Ugh...
ICHIKO-DONO?!

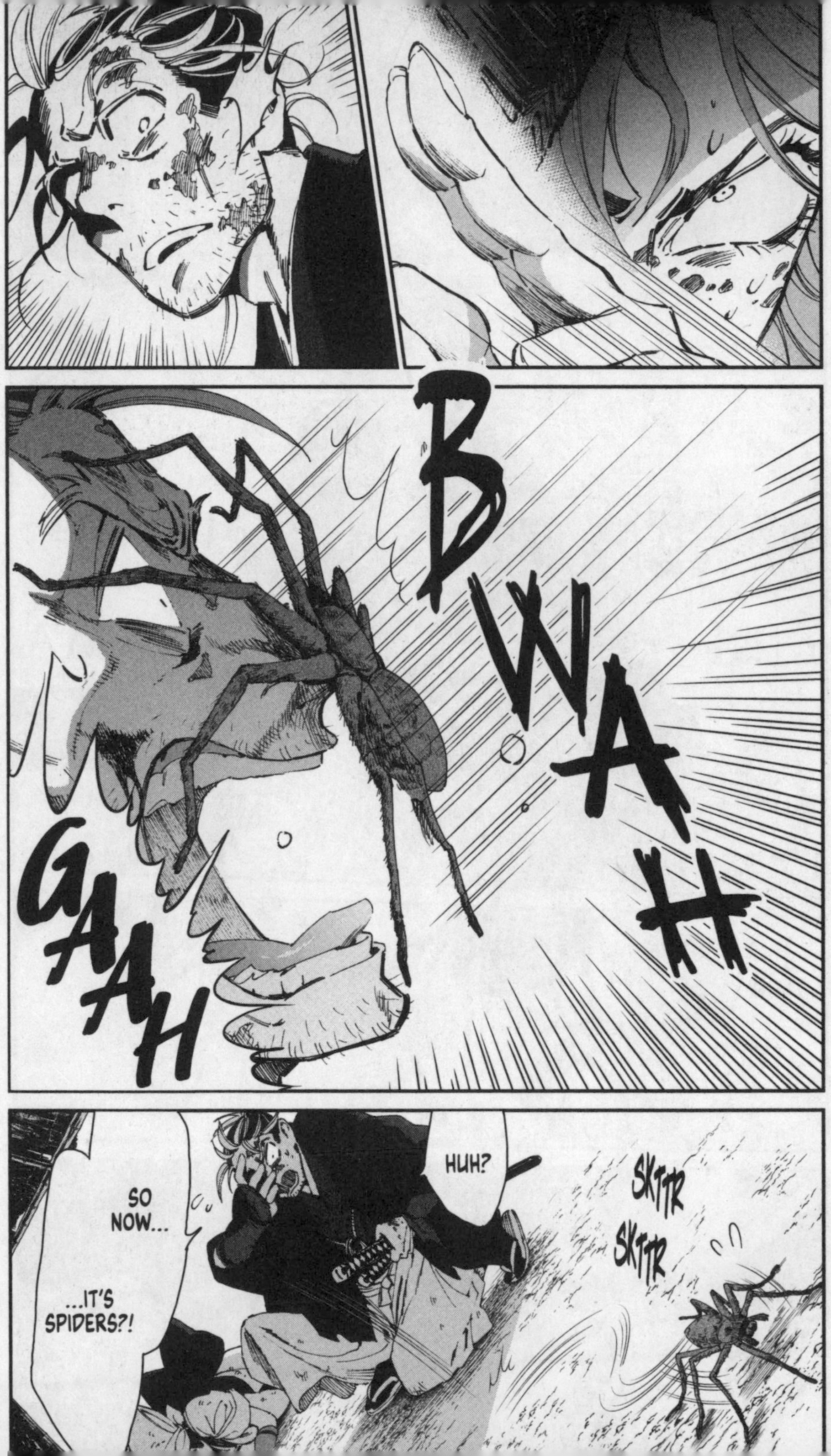
BWAH
GAAAH
HUH?
SO NOW...
...IT'S SPIDERS?!
SKTTR SKTTR

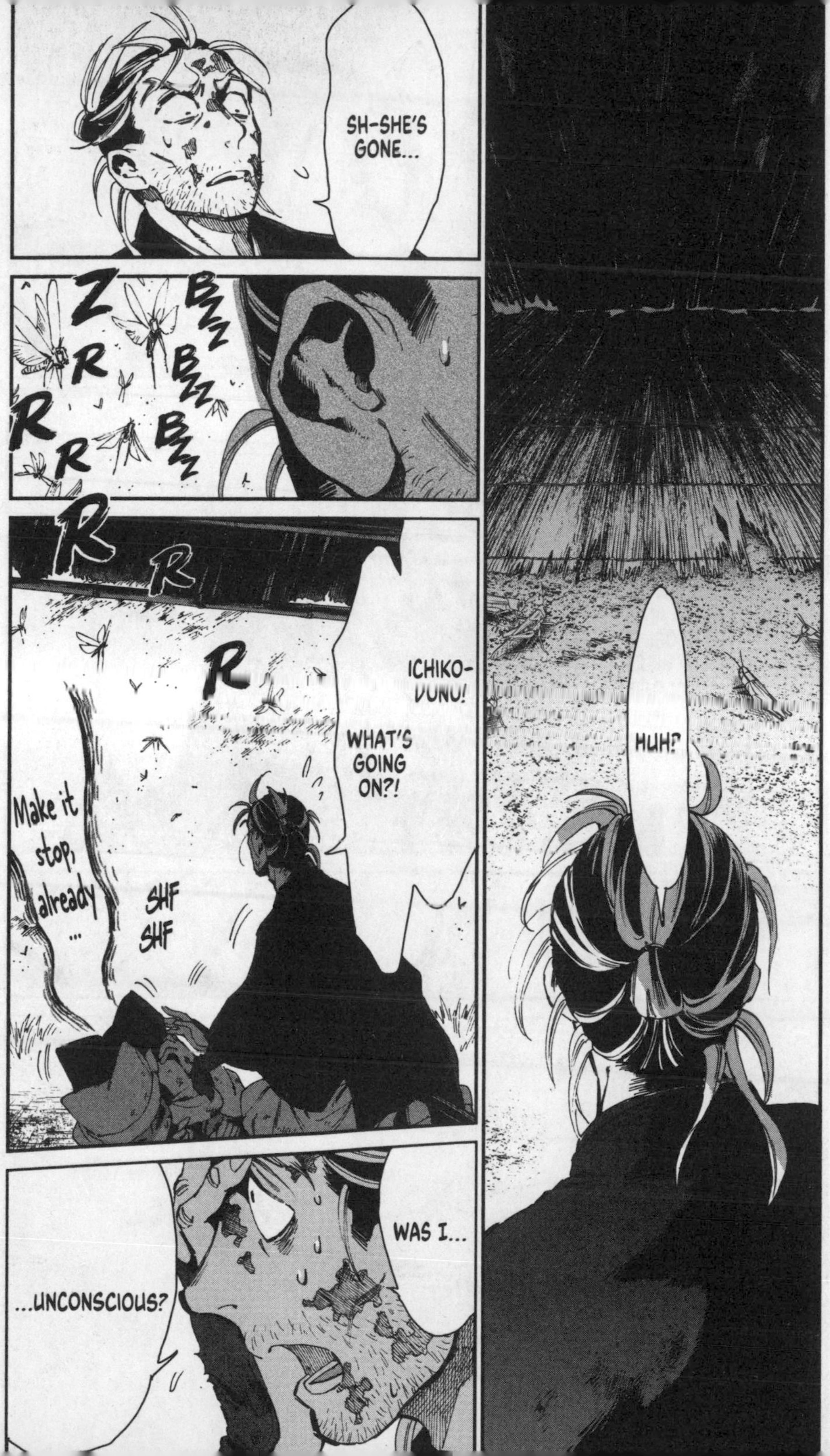
HUH?
SH-SHE'S GONE...
ZRRRR
BZZ BZZ BZZ
RRR
ICHIKO-DUNU!
WHAT'S GOING ON?!
Make it stop, already ...
SHF SHF
WAS I...
...UNCONSCIOUS?

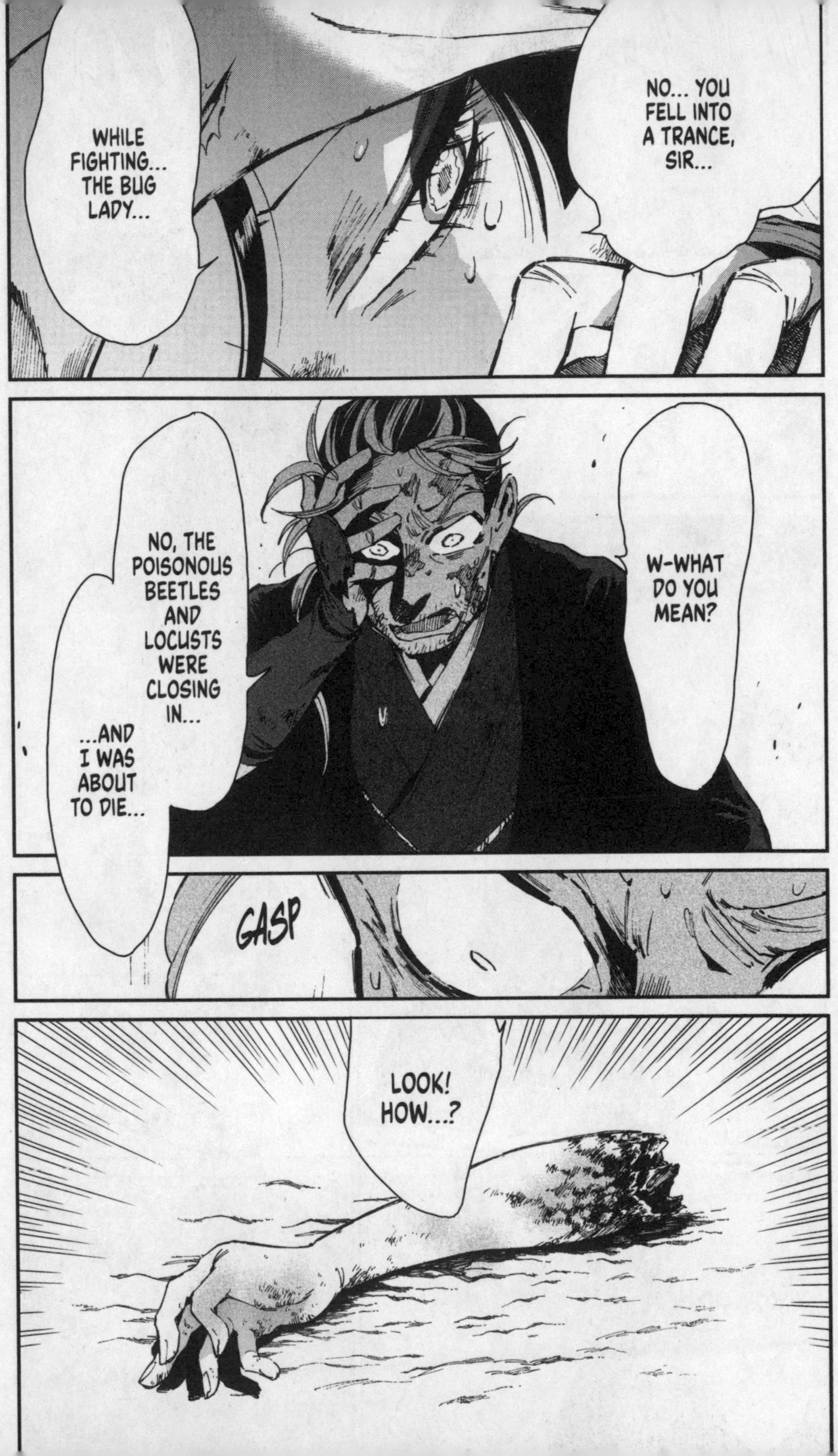
NO... YOU FELL INTO A TRANCE, SIR...
WHILE FIGHTING... THE BUG LADY...
W-WHAT DO YOU MEAN?
NO, THE POISONOUS BEETLES AND LOCUSTS WERE CLOSING IN...
...AND I WAS ABOUT TO DIE...
GASP
LOOK! HOW...?

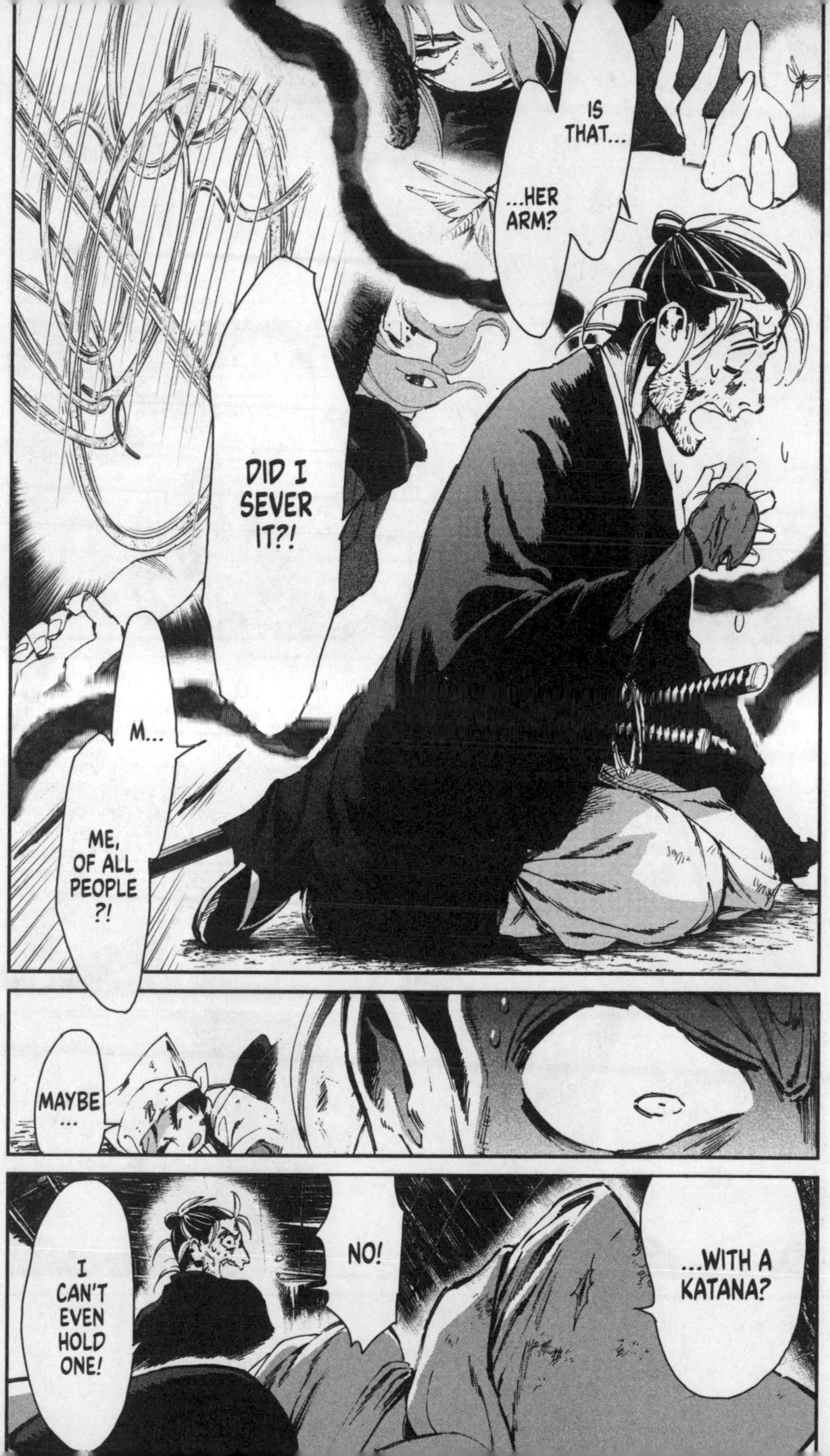
IS THAT...
...HER ARM?
DID I SEVER IT?!
M...
ME, OF ALL PEOPLE?!
MAYBE...
...WITH A KATANA?
NO!
I CAN'T EVEN HOLD ONE!

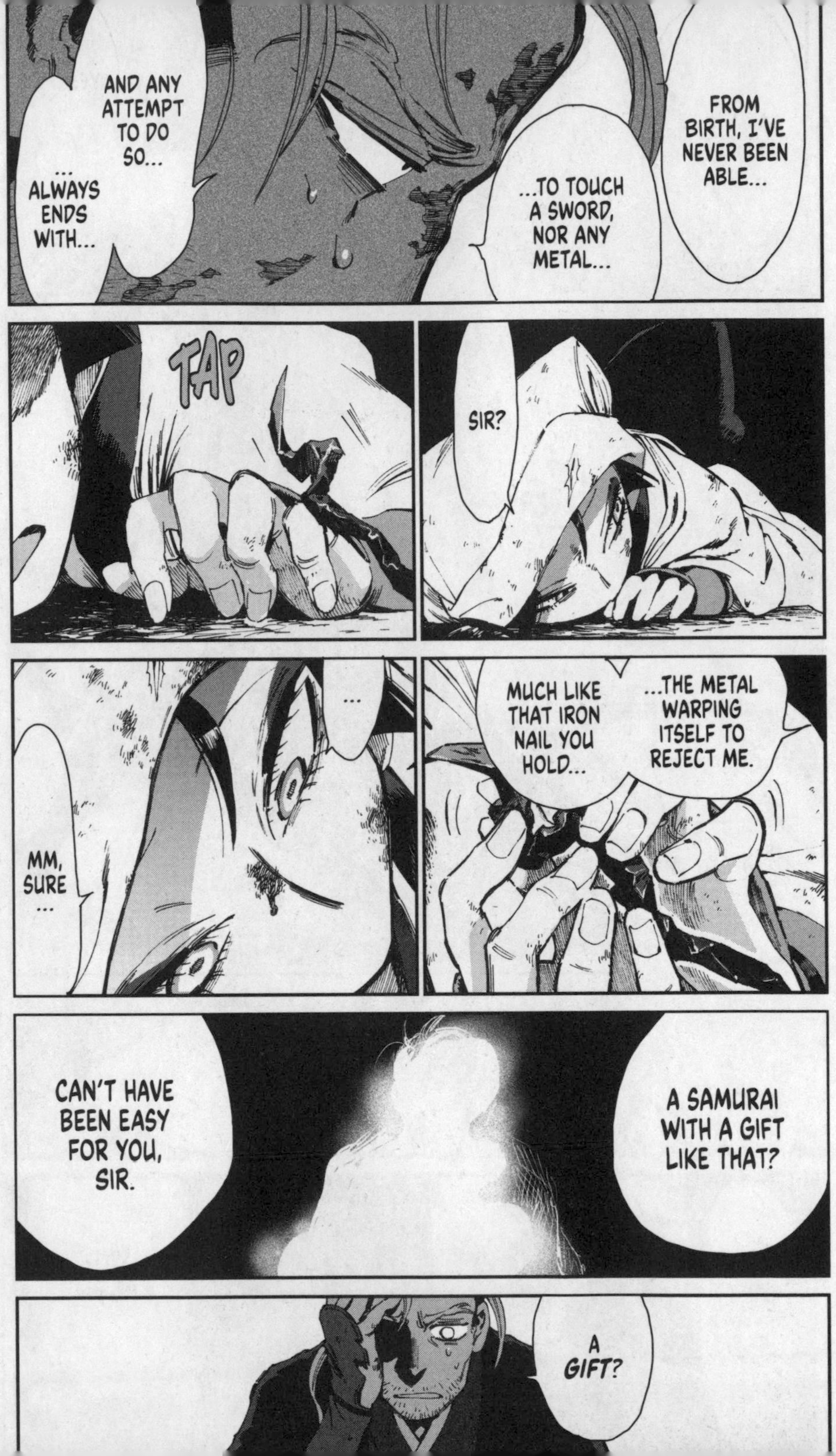
FROM BIRTH, I'VE NEVER BEEN ABLE...
...TO TOUCH A SWORD, NOR ANY METAL...
AND ANY ATTEMPT TO DO SO...
...ALWAYS ENDS WITH...
SIR?
TAP
...THE METAL WARPING ITSELF TO REJECT ME.
MUCH LIKE THAT IRON NAIL YOU HOLD...
...
MM, SURE ...
A SAMURAI WITH A GIFT LIKE THAT?
CAN'T HAVE BEEN EASY FOR YOU, SIR.
A GIFT?

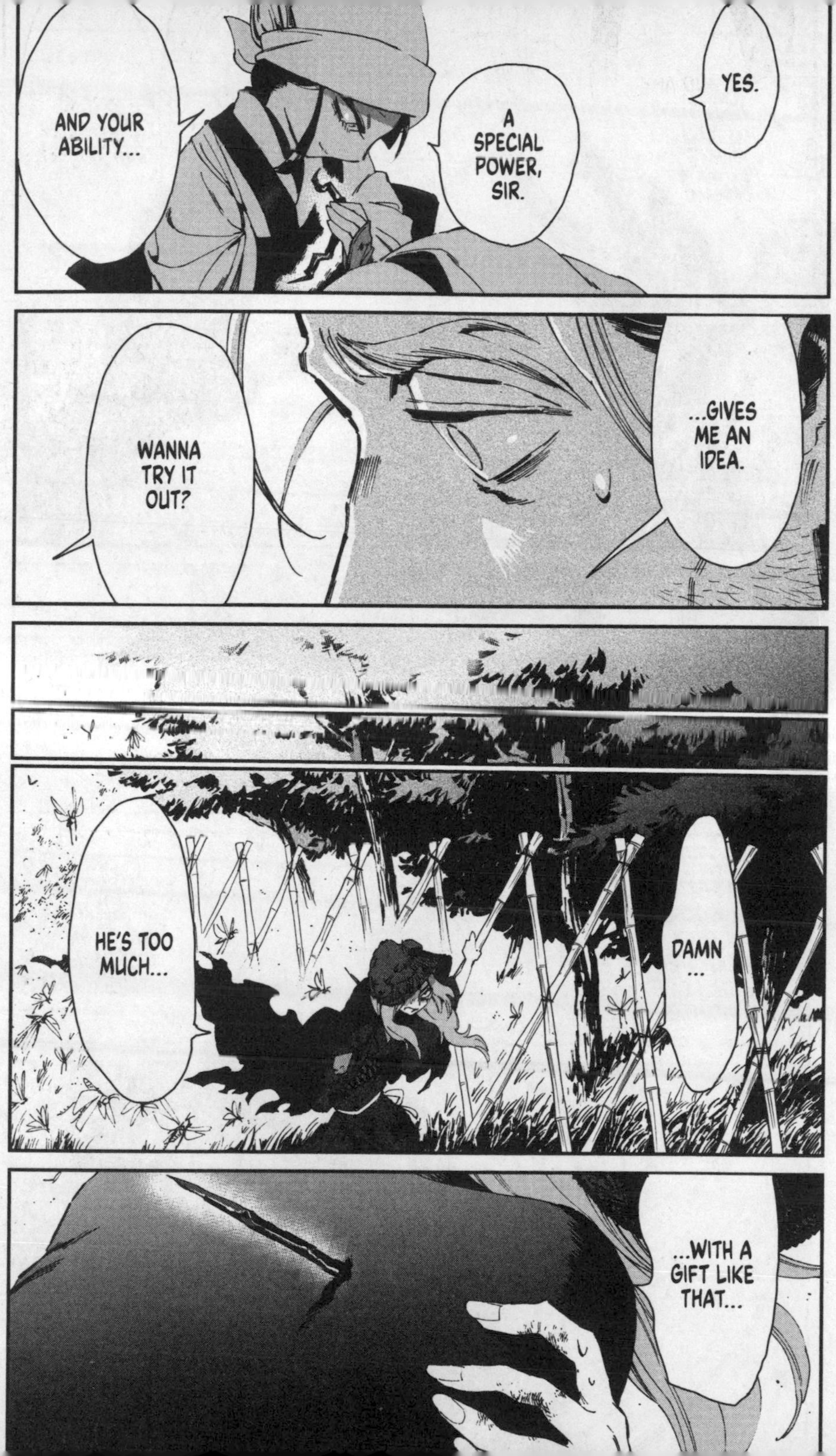
YES.
A SPECIAL POWER, SIR.
AND YOUR ABILITY...
...GIVES ME AN IDEA.
WANNA TRY IT OUT?
DAMN...
HE'S TOO MUCH...
...WITH A GIFT LIKE THAT...

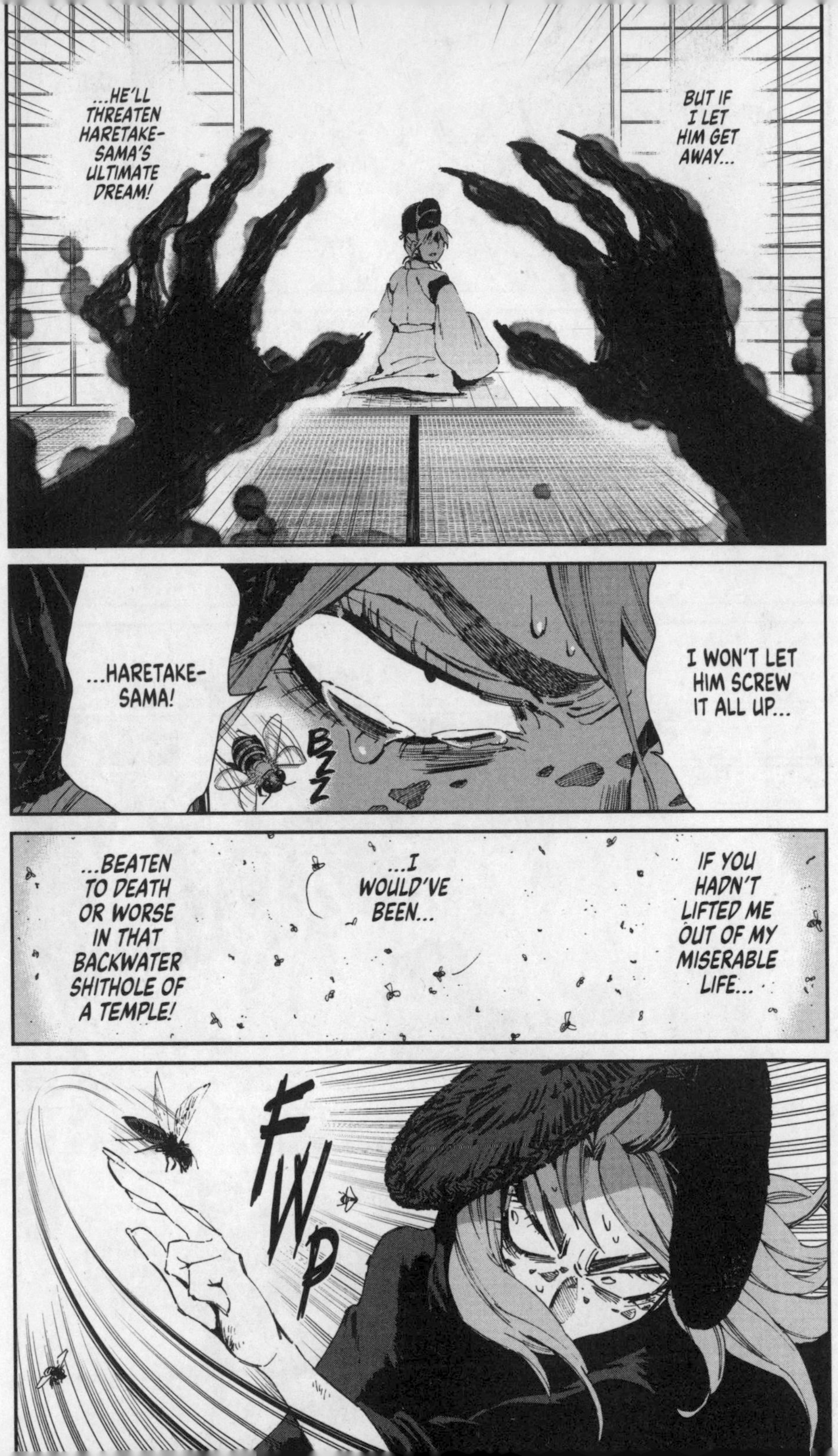
BUT IF I LET HIM GET AWAY...
...HE'LL THREATEN HARETAKE-SAMA'S ULTIMATE DREAM!
I WON'T LET HIM SCREW IT ALL UP...
...HARETAKE-SAMA!
BZZ
IF YOU HADN'T LIFTED ME OUT OF MY MISERABLE LIFE...
...I WOULD'VE BEEN...
...BEATEN TO DEATH OR WORSE IN THAT BACKWATER SHITHOLE OF A TEMPLE!
FWP

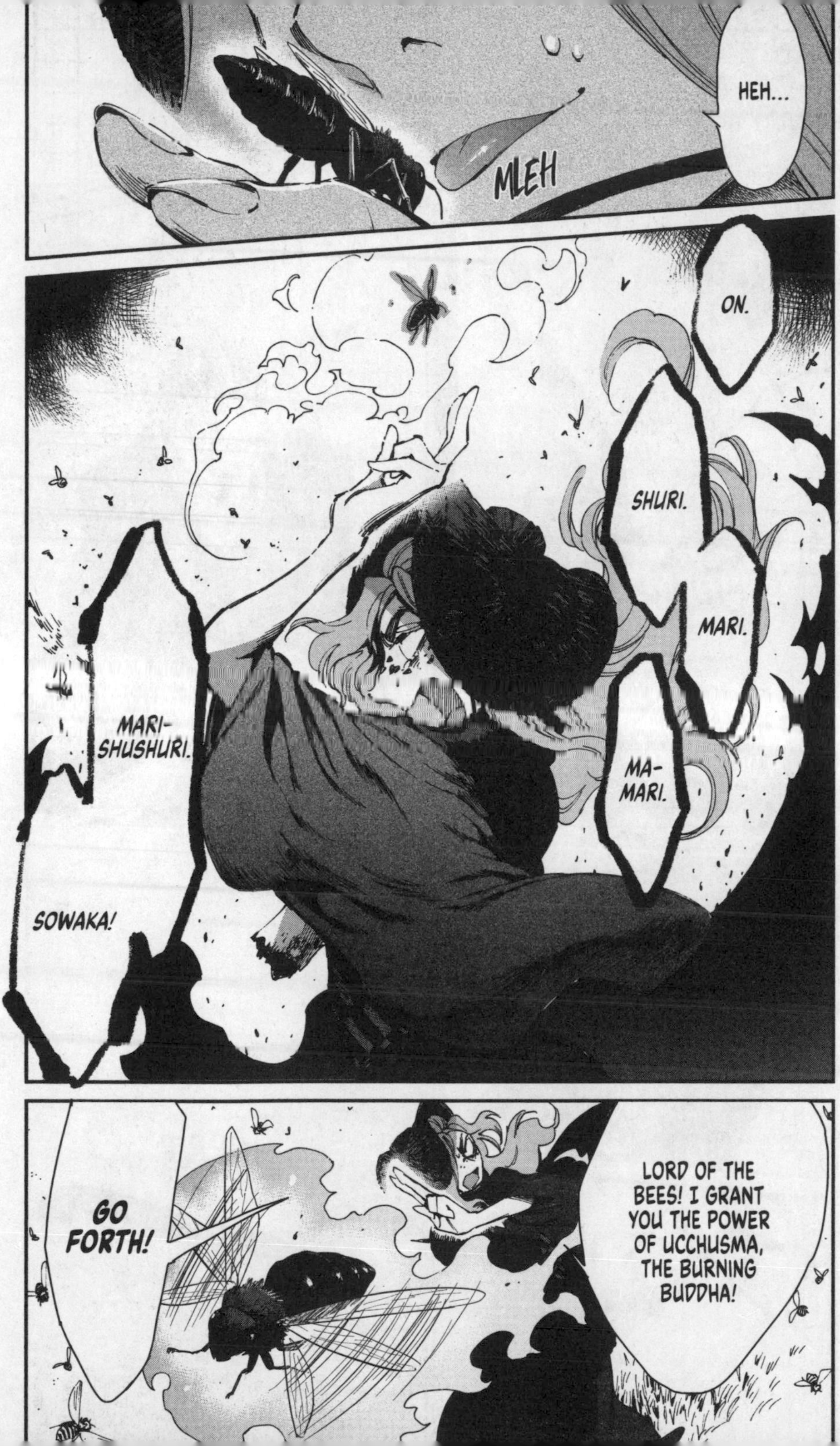
HEH...
MLEH
ON.
SHURI.
MARI.
MA-MARI.
MARI-SHUSHURI.
SOWAKA!
LORD OF THE BEES! I GRANT YOU THE POWER OF UCCHUSMA, THE BURNING BUDDHA!
GO FORTH!

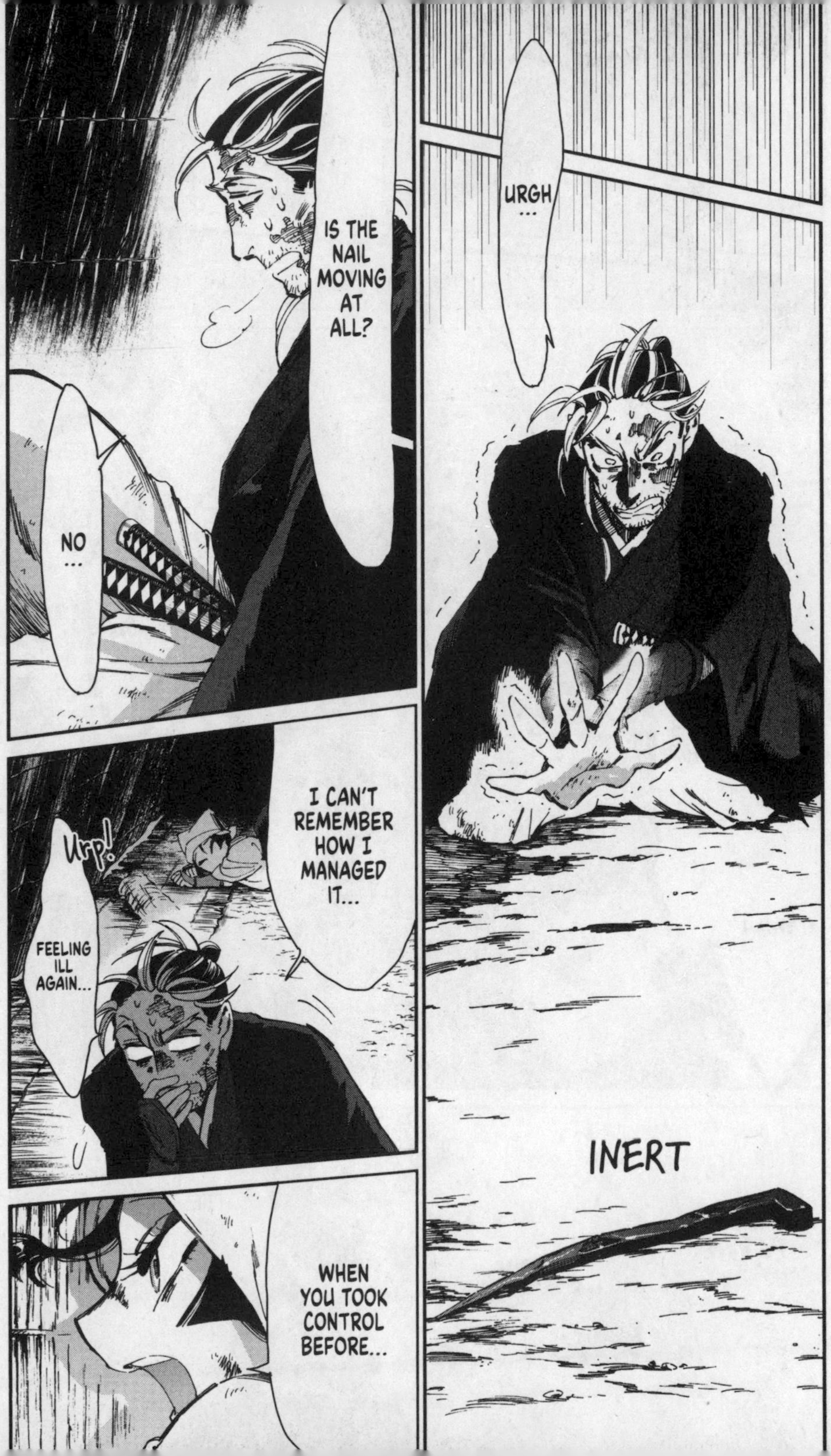
URGH...
INERT
IS THE NAIL MOVING AT ALL?
NO...
I CAN'T REMEMBER HOW I MANAGED IT...
Urp!
FEELING ILL AGAIN...
WHEN YOU TOOK CONTROL BEFORE...

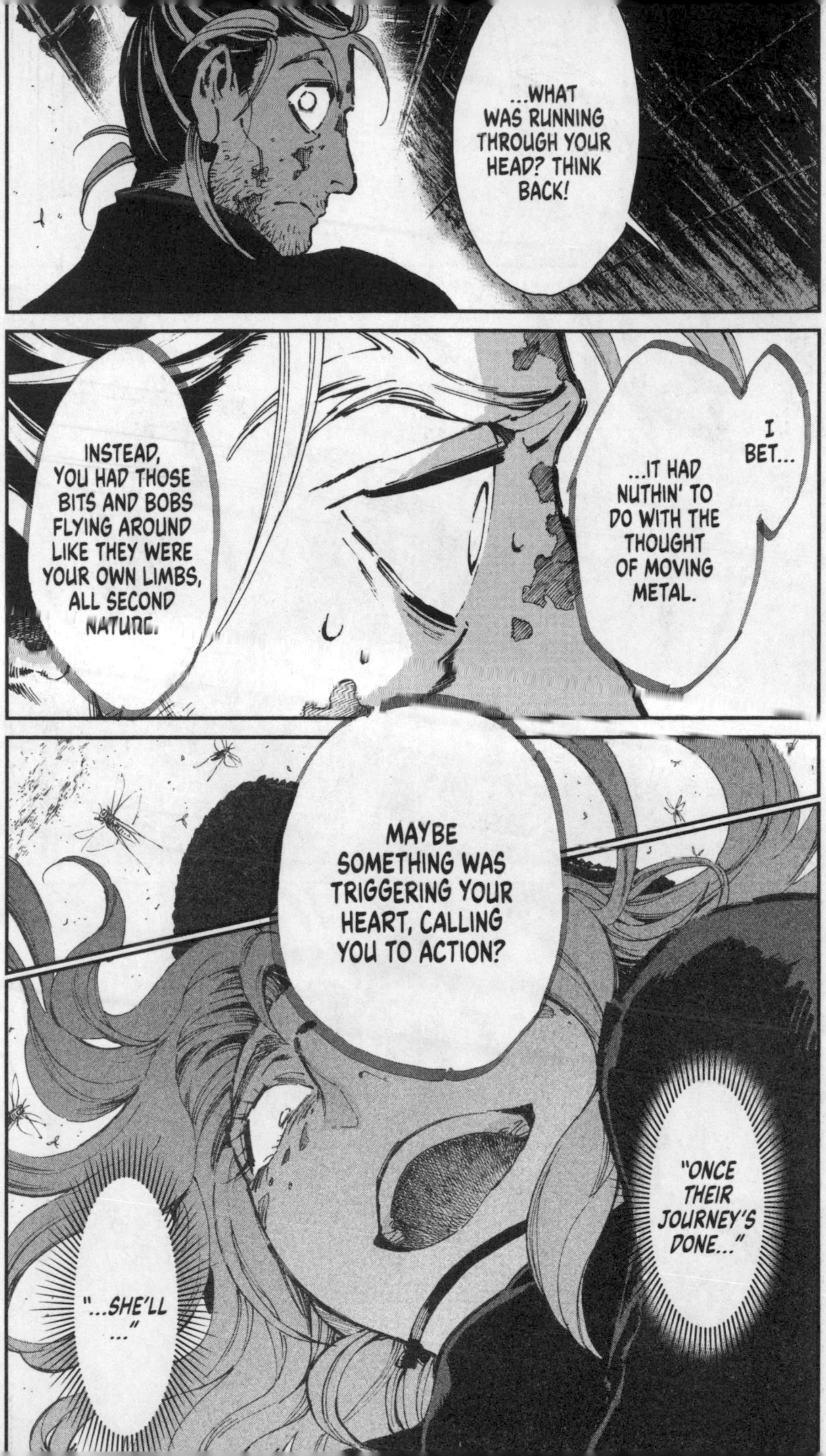
...WHAT WAS RUNNING THROUGH YOUR HEAD? THINK BACK!
I BET...
...IT HAD NUTHIN' TO DO WITH THE THOUGHT OF MOVING METAL.
INSTEAD, YOU HAD THOSE BITS AND BOBS FLYING AROUND LIKE THEY WERE YOUR OWN LIMBS, ALL SECOND NATURE.
MAYBE SOMETHING WAS TRIGGERING YOUR HEART, CALLING YOU TO ACTION?
"ONCE THEIR JOURNEY'S DONE..."
"...SHE'LL ..."

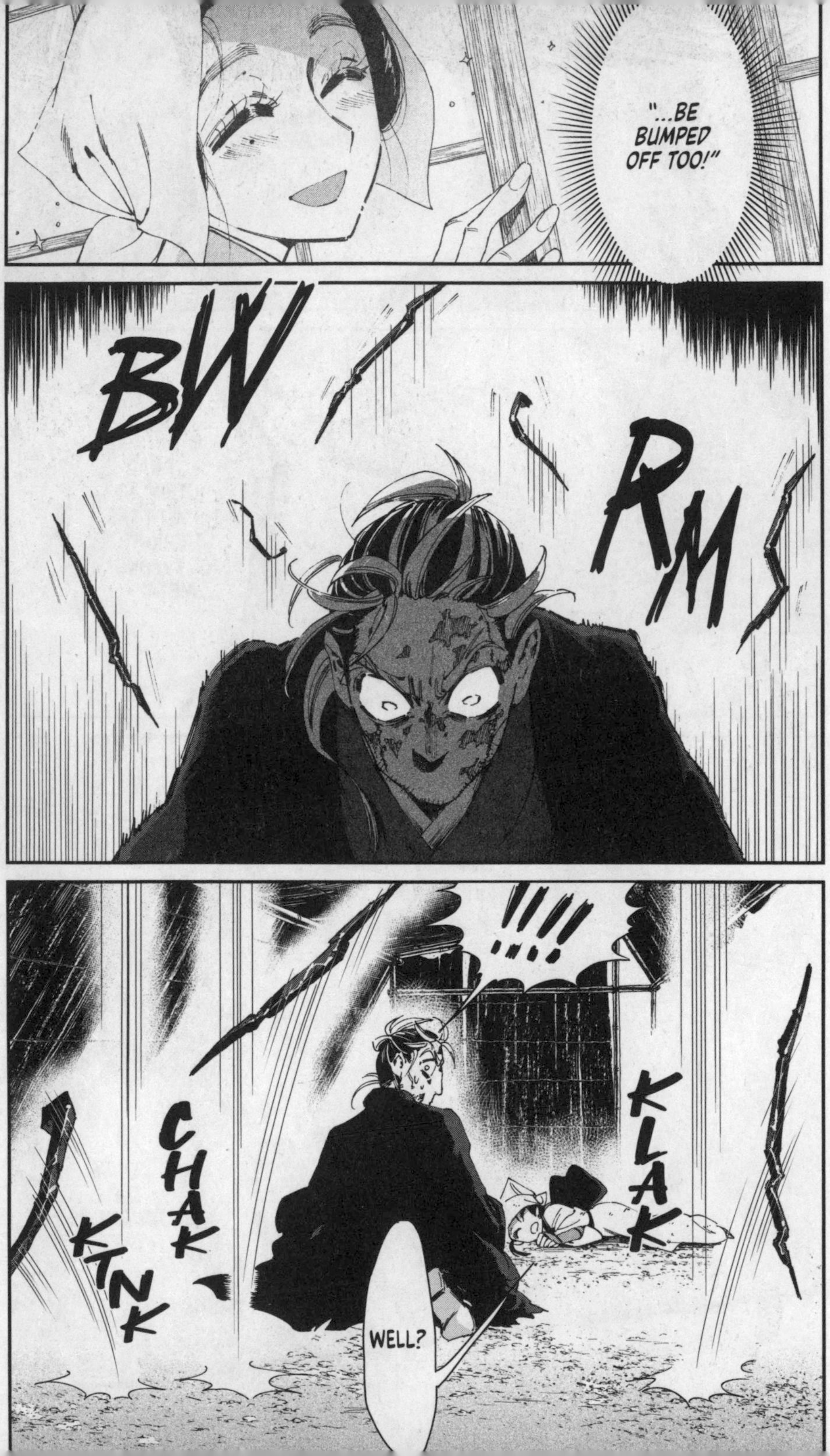
"...BE BUMPED OFF TOO!"
BWRMS
!!!!
KLAK
CHAK
KTNK
WELL?

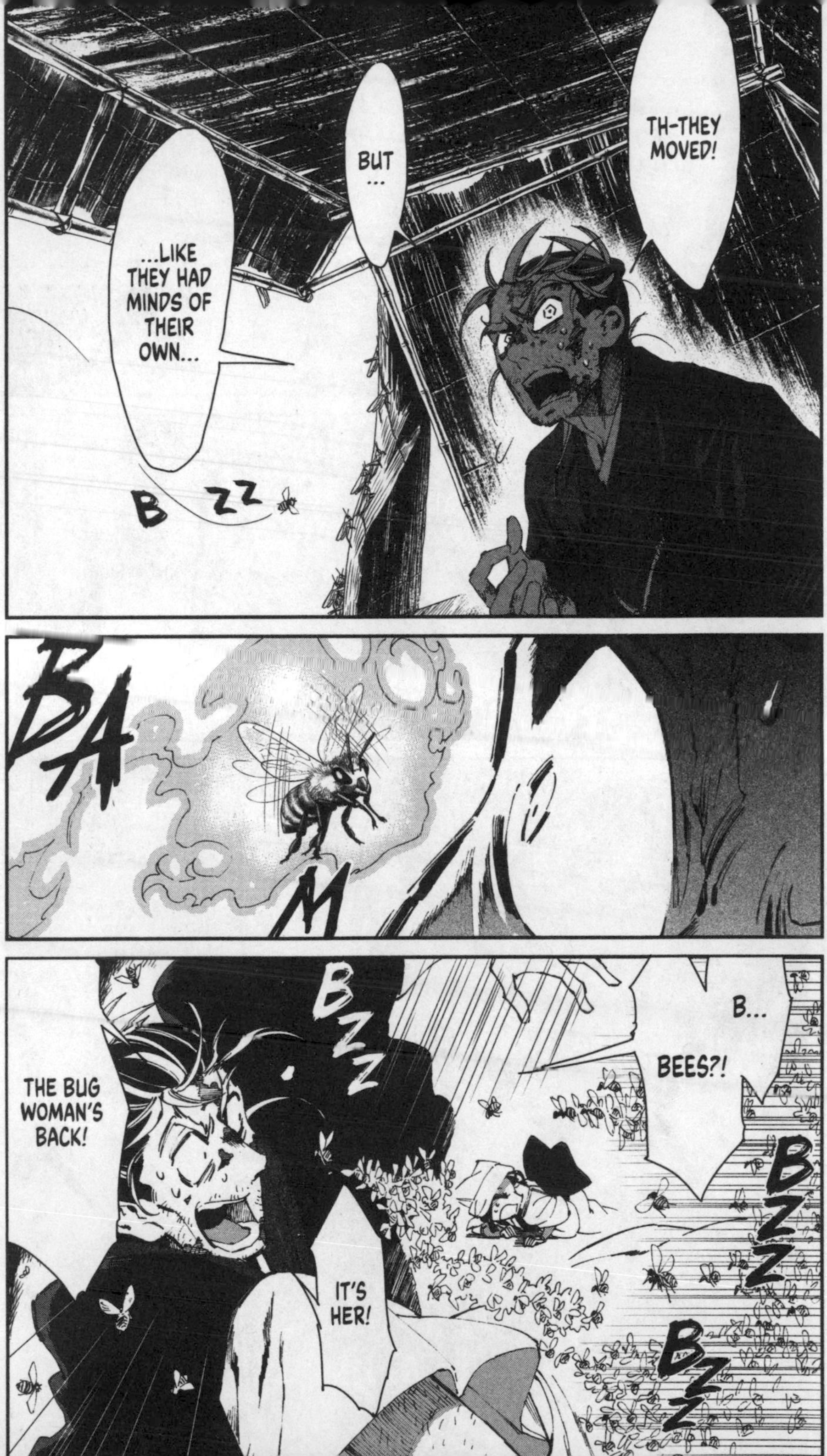
TH-THEY MOVED!
BUT ...
...LIKE THEY HAD MINDS OF THEIR OWN...
B ZZ
BAM
B...
BEES?!
BZZ
BZZ
BZZ
THE BUG WOMAN'S BACK!
IT'S HER!

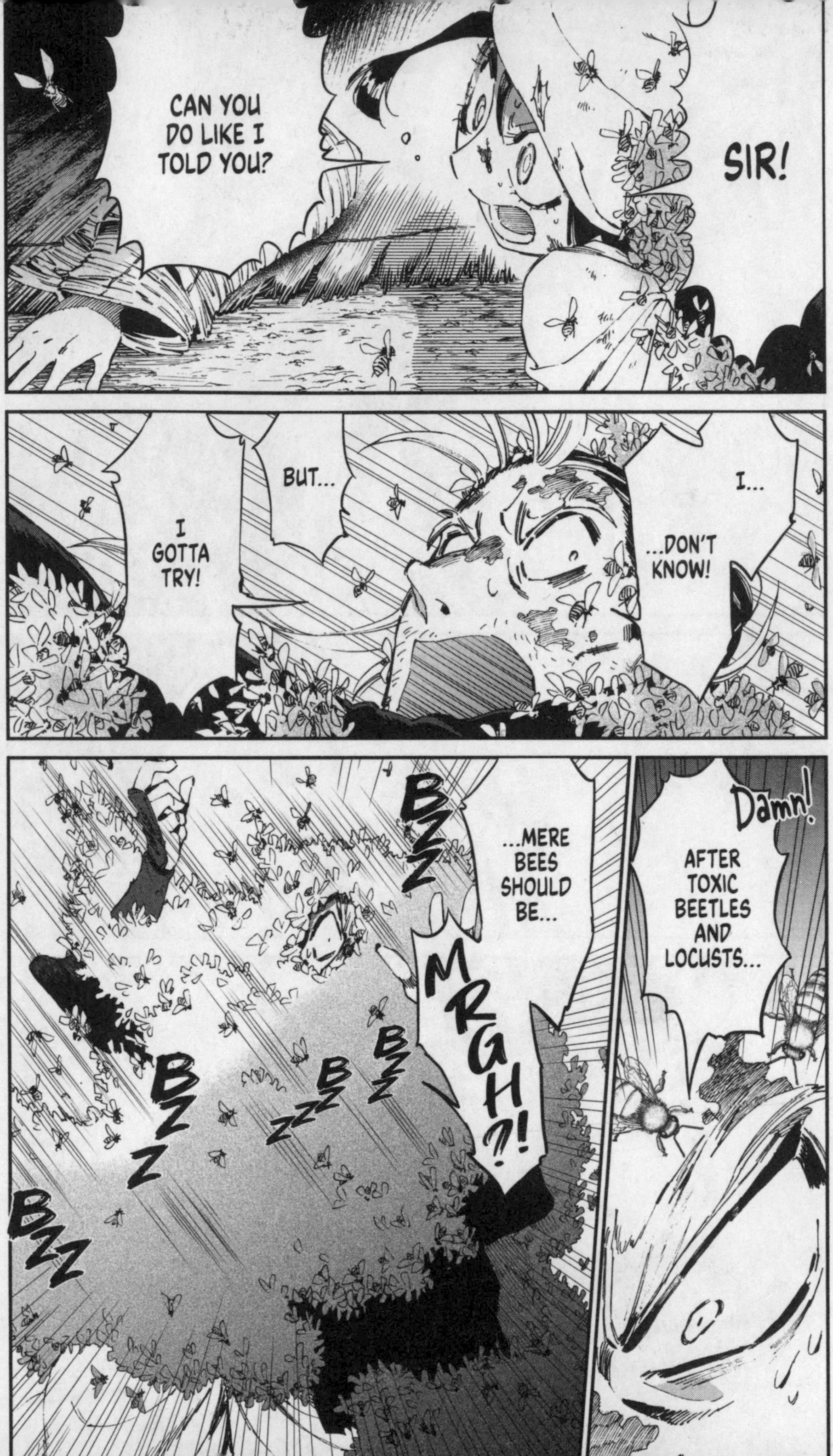
SIR!
CAN YOU DO LIKE I TOLD YOU?
I...
...DON'T KNOW!
BUT...
I GOTTA TRY!
Damn!
AFTER TOXIC BEETLES AND LOCUSTS...
...MERE BEES SHOULD BE...
BZZ
MRGH?!
BZZ
BZZZ
BZZ
BZZ

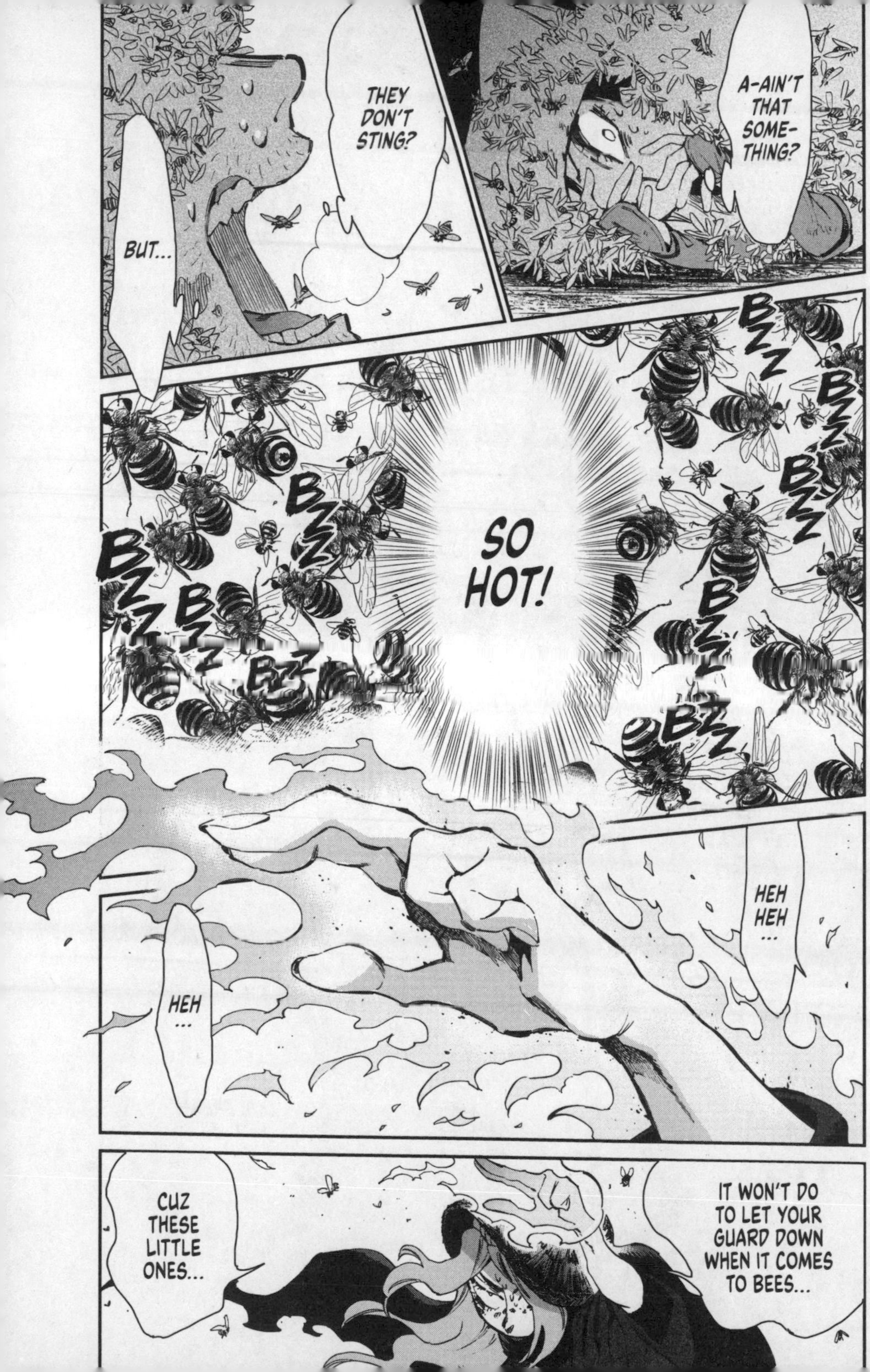
A-AIN'T THAT SOME-THING?
THEY DON'T STING?
BUT...
BZZ
BZZ
BZZ
SO HOT!
BZZ
BZZ
BZZ
HEH HEH...
HEH...
IT WON'T DO TO LET YOUR GUARD DOWN WHEN IT COMES TO BEES...
CUZ THESE LITTLE ONES...

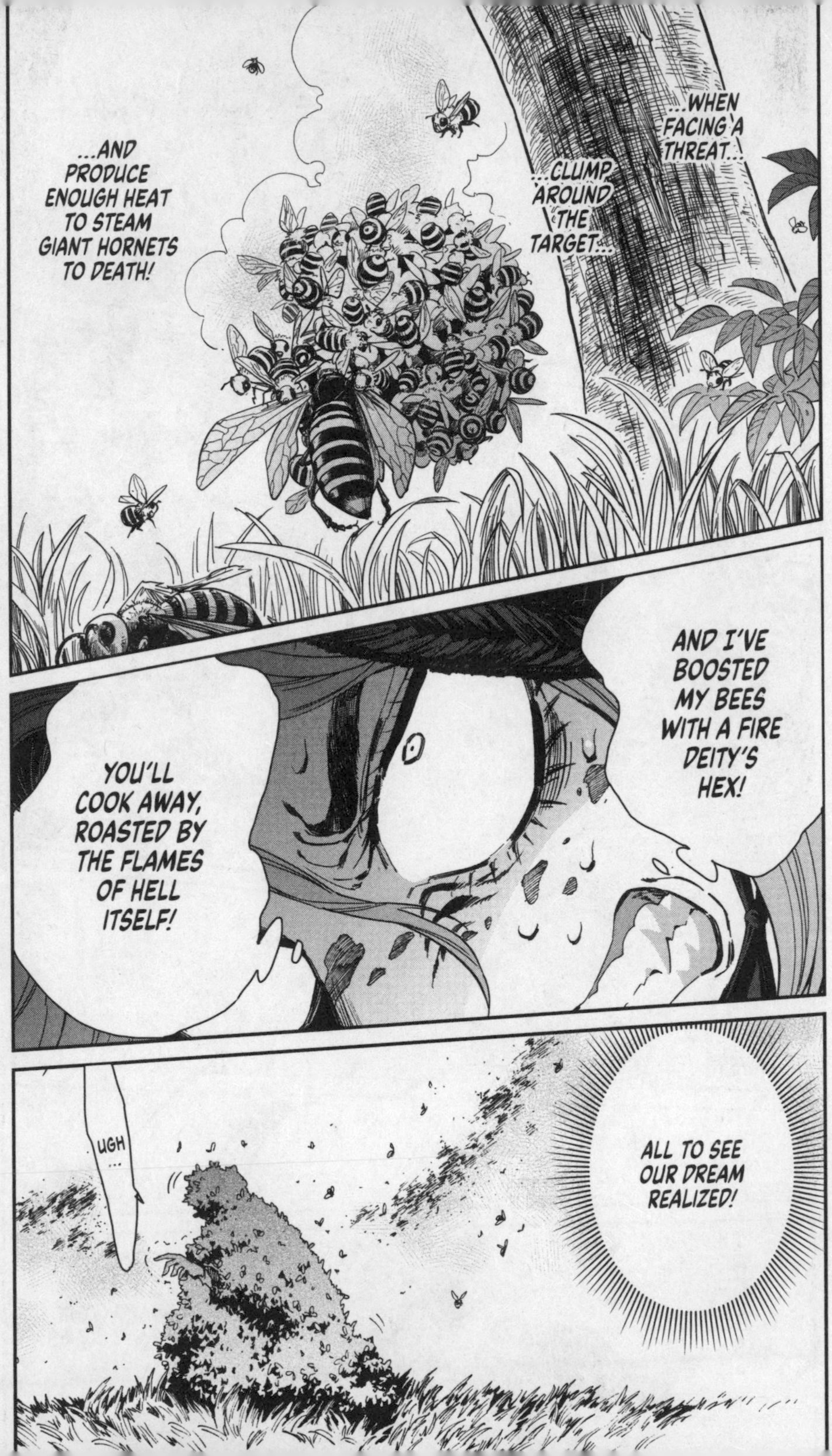
...WHEN FACING A THREAT...
...CLUMP AROUND THE TARGET...
...AND PRODUCE ENOUGH HEAT TO STEAM GIANT HORNETS TO DEATH!
AND I'VE BOOSTED MY BEES WITH A FIRE DEITY'S HEX!
YOU'LL COOK AWAY, ROASTED BY THE FLAMES OF HELL ITSELF!
ALL TO SEE OUR DREAM REALIZED!
UGH...

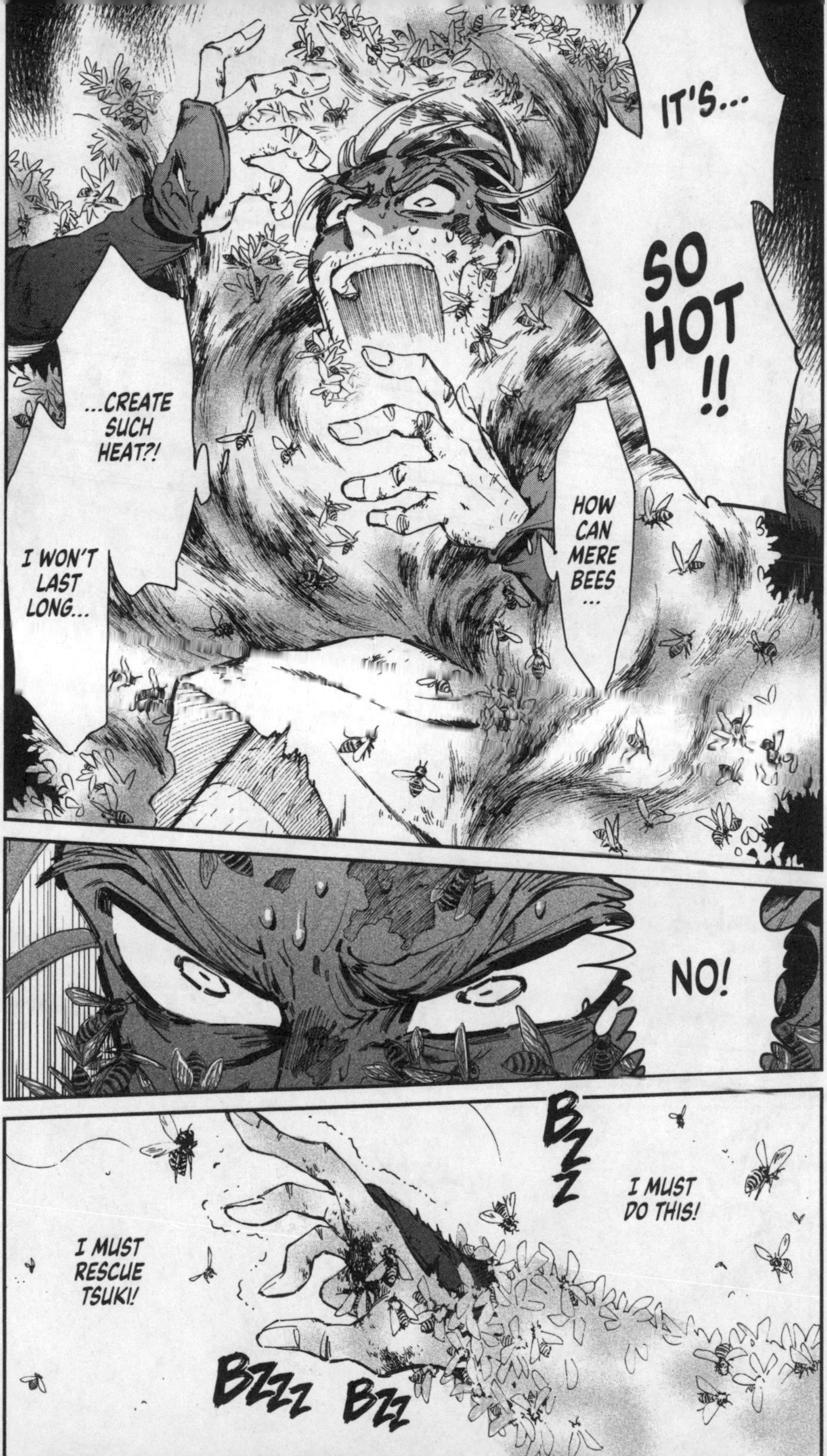
IT'S... SO HOT!!
HOW CAN MERE BEES...
...CREATE SUCH HEAT?!
I WON'T LAST LONG...
NO!
BZZ
I MUST DO THIS!
I MUST RESCUE TSUKI!
BZZZZ BZZ

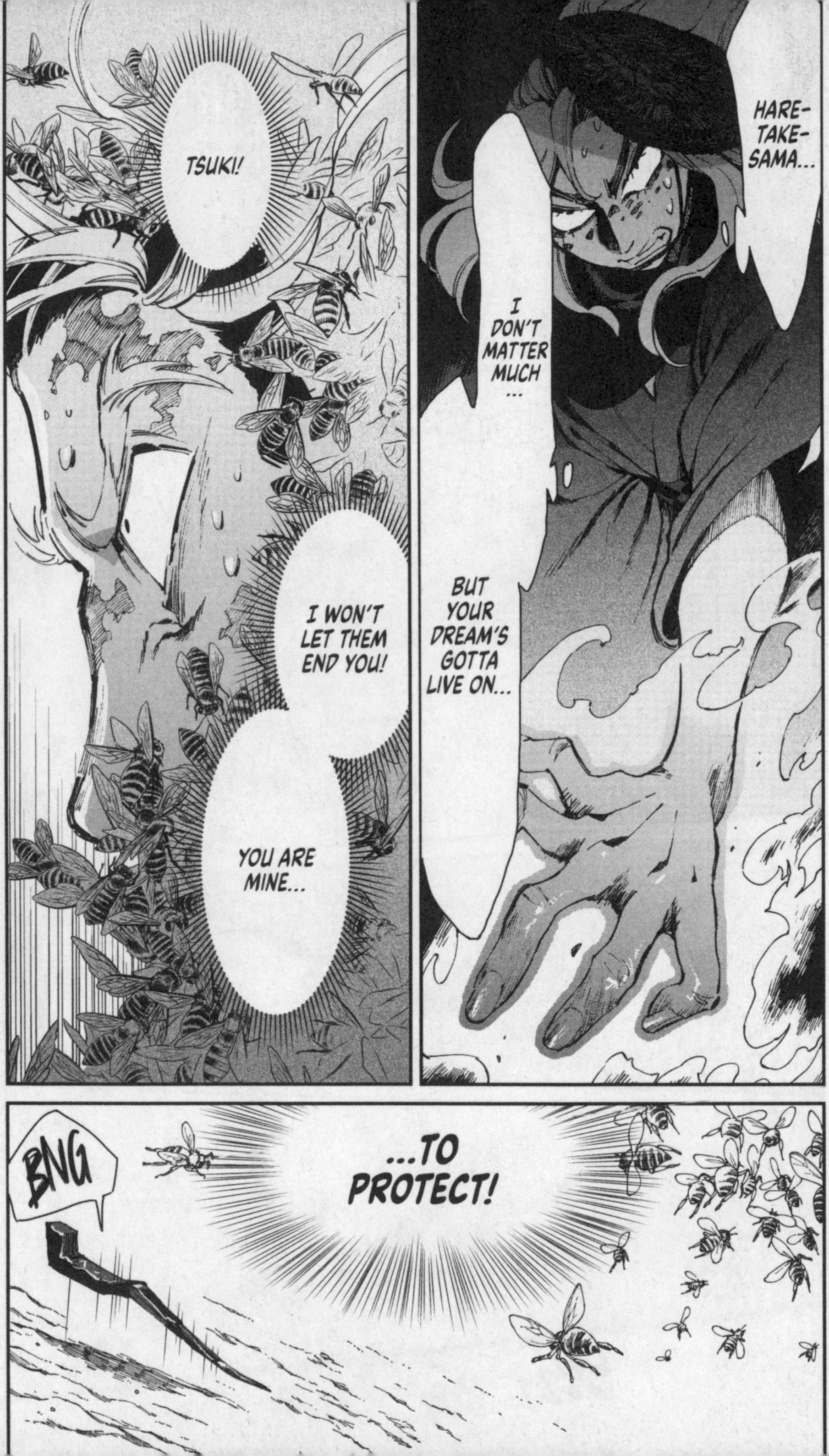
HARE-TAKE-SAMA...
I DON'T MATTER MUCH...
BUT YOUR DREAM'S GOTTA LIVE ON...
TSUKI!
I WON'T LET THEM END YOU!
YOU ARE MINE...
...TO PROTECT!
BNG

STEEL of the
CELESTIAL
SHADOWS

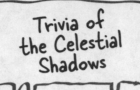

Trivia of the Celestial Shadows #5

Kozukappara Execution Grounds

Even at night, it's a bright, clean train station area (I took a stroll)

- Located near Minami-Senju Station these days.
- Travelers entering Edo via Senju would have to pass by. This was intentional; they ***had*** to bear witness.
- In the Bakumatsu period, samurai would casually suggest a visit to the execution grounds, as if on a dare.
- There was apparently a red-light district nearby. I'd expect there to be some spooky songs about the execution grounds from that period, but nothing turned up in my research. Maybe you'll have more luck searching?

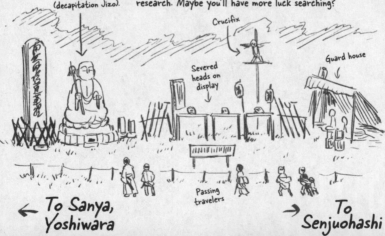

An *Enmei Jizo* statue was built here in memoriam of the condemned and executed. It still exists today, though it's known as the *Kubikiri Jizo* (decapitation Jizo).

Crucifix
Guard house
Severed heads on display
Passing travelers
← To Sanya, Yoshiwara
→ To Senjuohashi

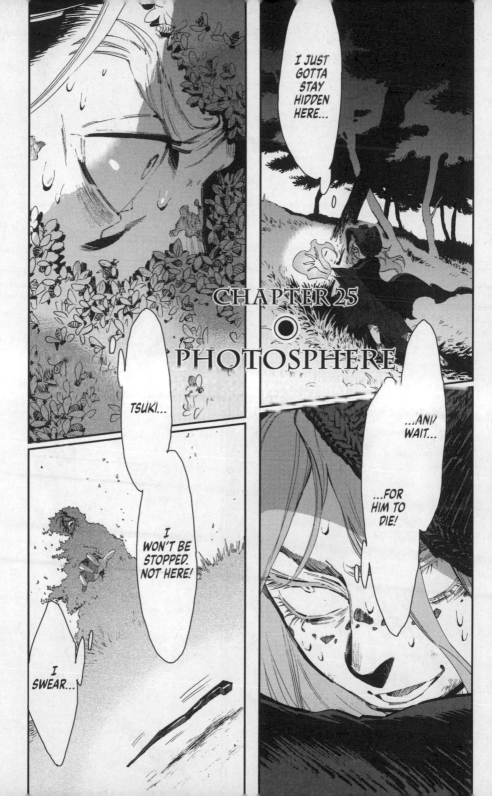

I JUST GOTTA STAY HIDDEN HERE...

CHAPTER 25
● PHOTOSPHERE

...AND WAIT...

...FOR HIM TO DIE!

TSUKI...

I WON'T BE STOPPED. NOT HERE!

I SWEAR...

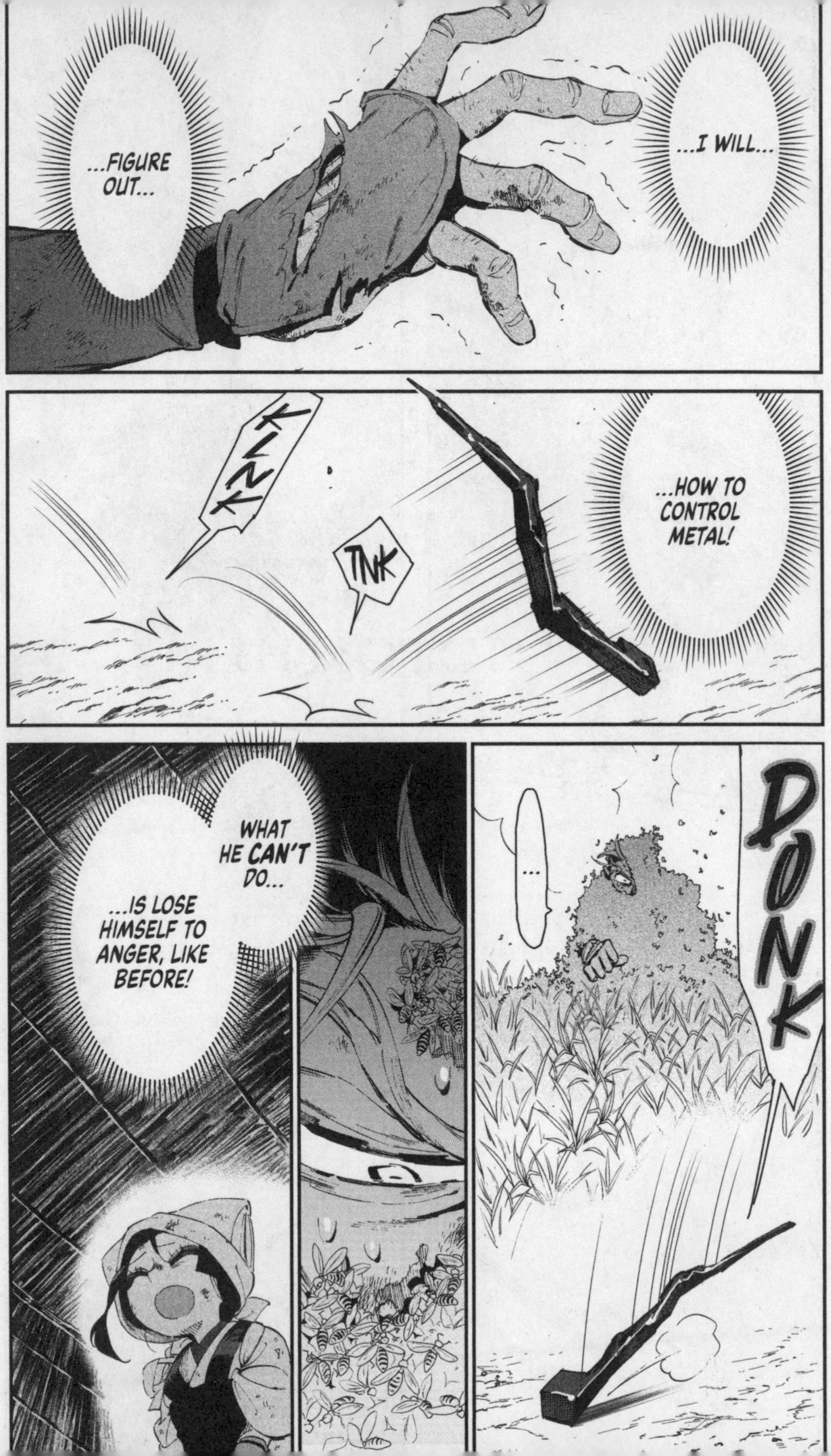
...I WILL...
...FIGURE OUT...
...HOW TO CONTROL METAL!
KLINK
TNK
DONK
...
WHAT HE CAN'T DO...
...IS LOSE HIMSELF TO ANGER, LIKE BEFORE!

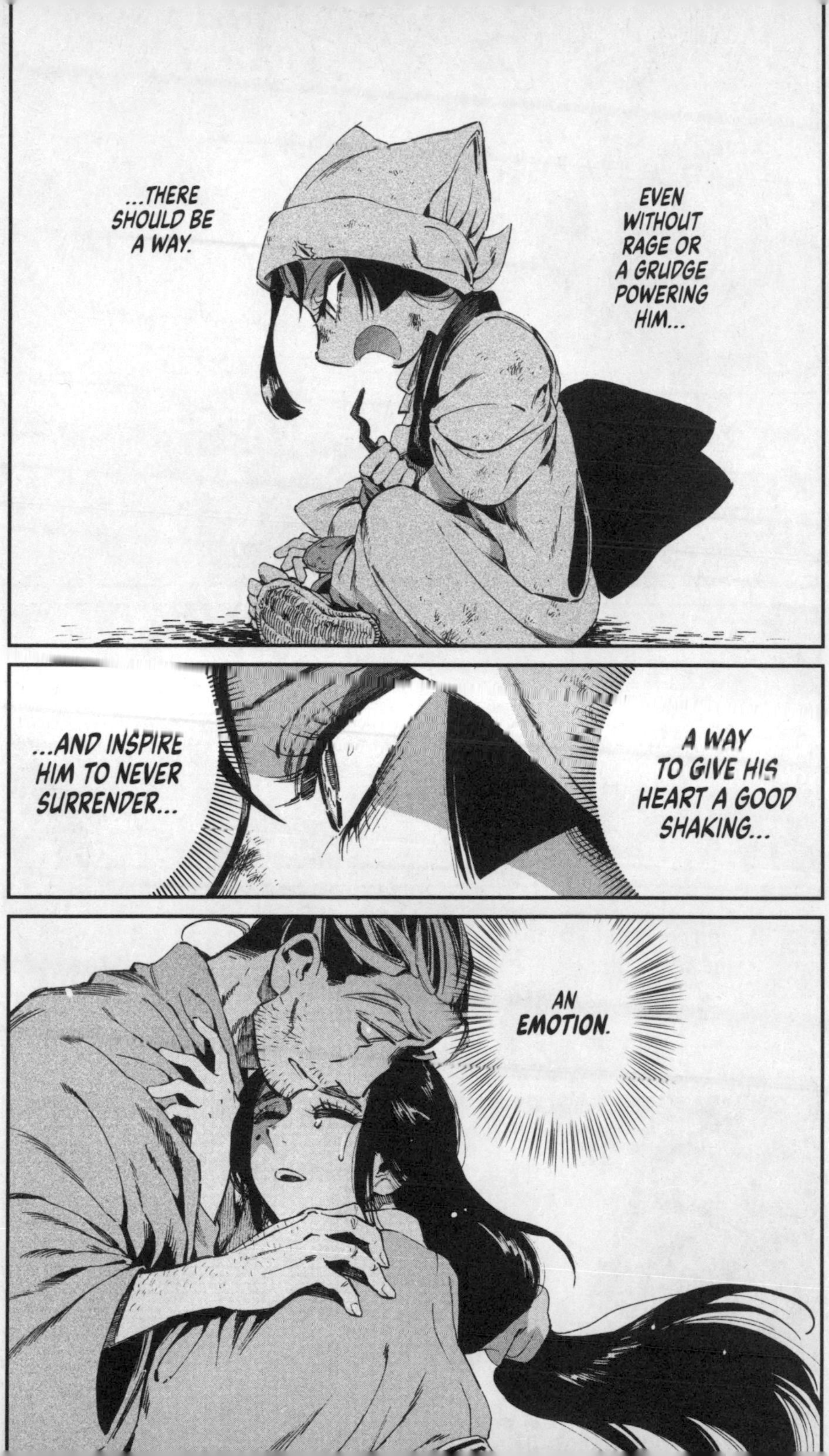
EVEN WITHOUT RAGE OR A GRUDGE POWERING HIM...
...THERE SHOULD BE A WAY.
A WAY TO GIVE HIS HEART A GOOD SHAKING...
...AND INSPIRE HIM TO NEVER SURRENDER...
AN EMOTION.

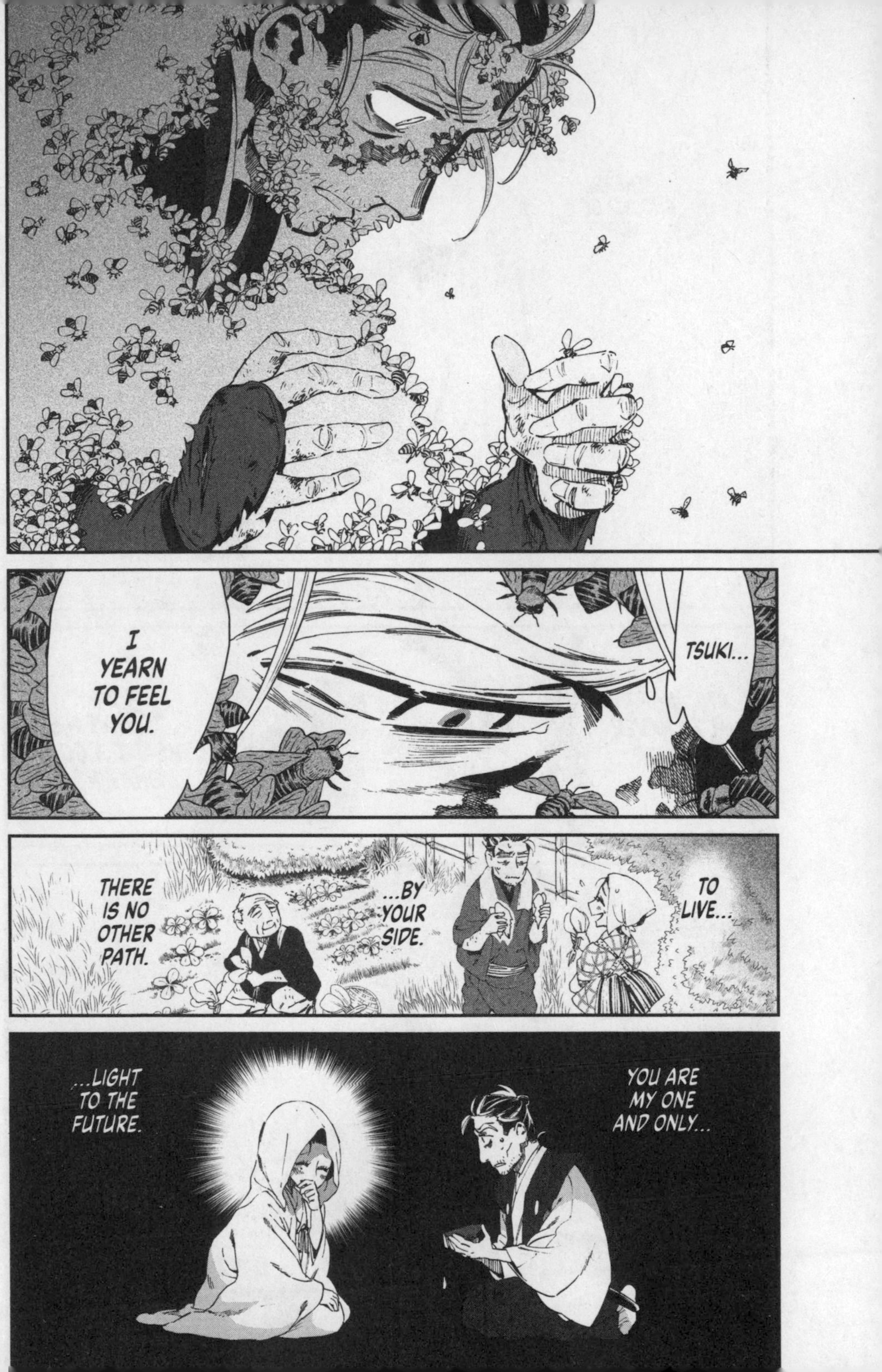
TSUKI...
I YEARN TO FEEL YOU.
TO LIVE...
...BY YOUR SIDE.
THERE IS NO OTHER PATH.
YOU ARE MY ONE AND ONLY...
...LIGHT TO THE FUTURE.

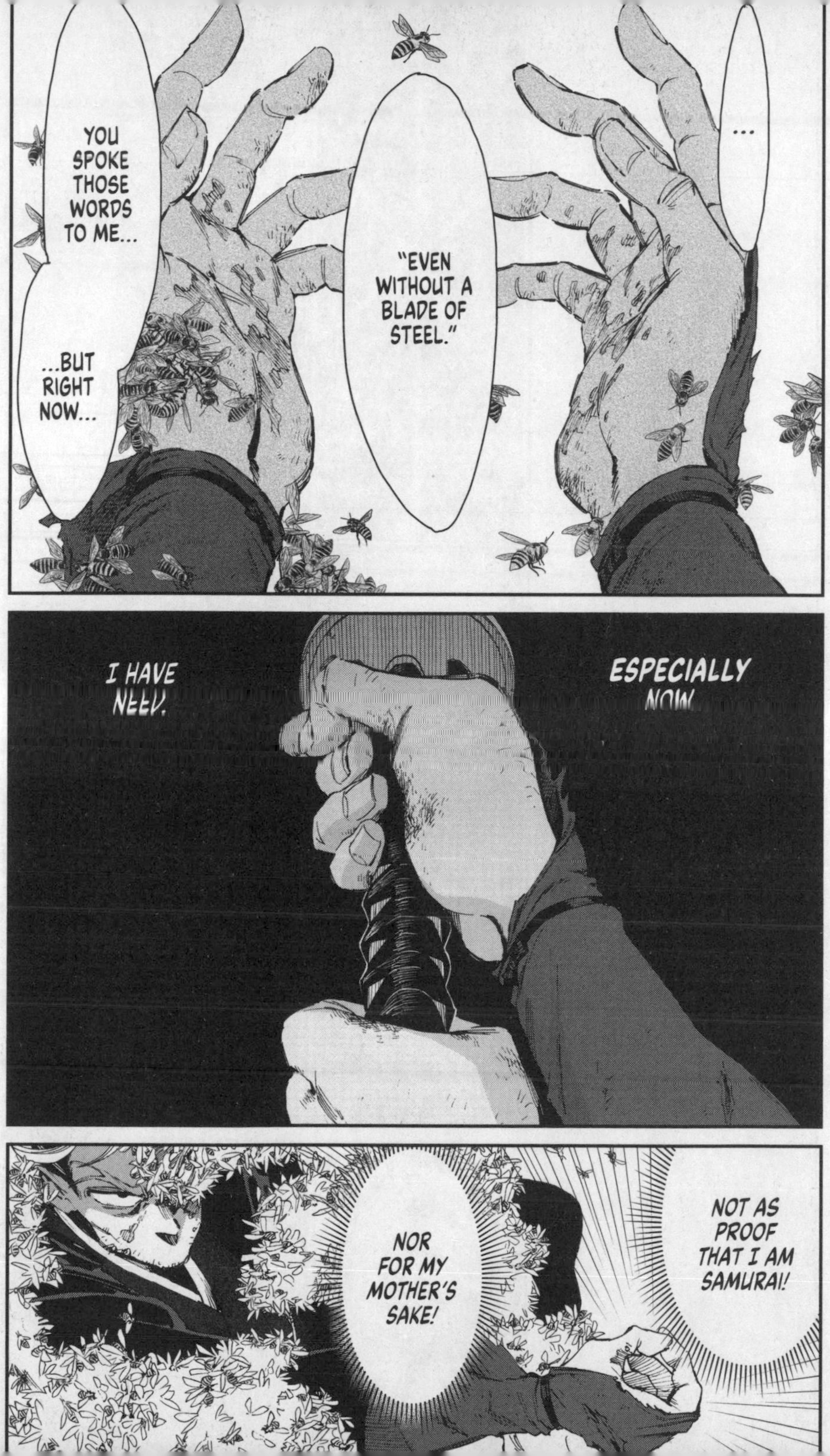
...
"EVEN WITHOUT A BLADE OF STEEL."
YOU SPOKE THOSE WORDS TO ME...
...BUT RIGHT NOW...
ESPECIALLY NOW.
I HAVE NEED.
NOT AS PROOF THAT I AM SAMURAI!
NOR FOR MY MOTHER'S SAKE!

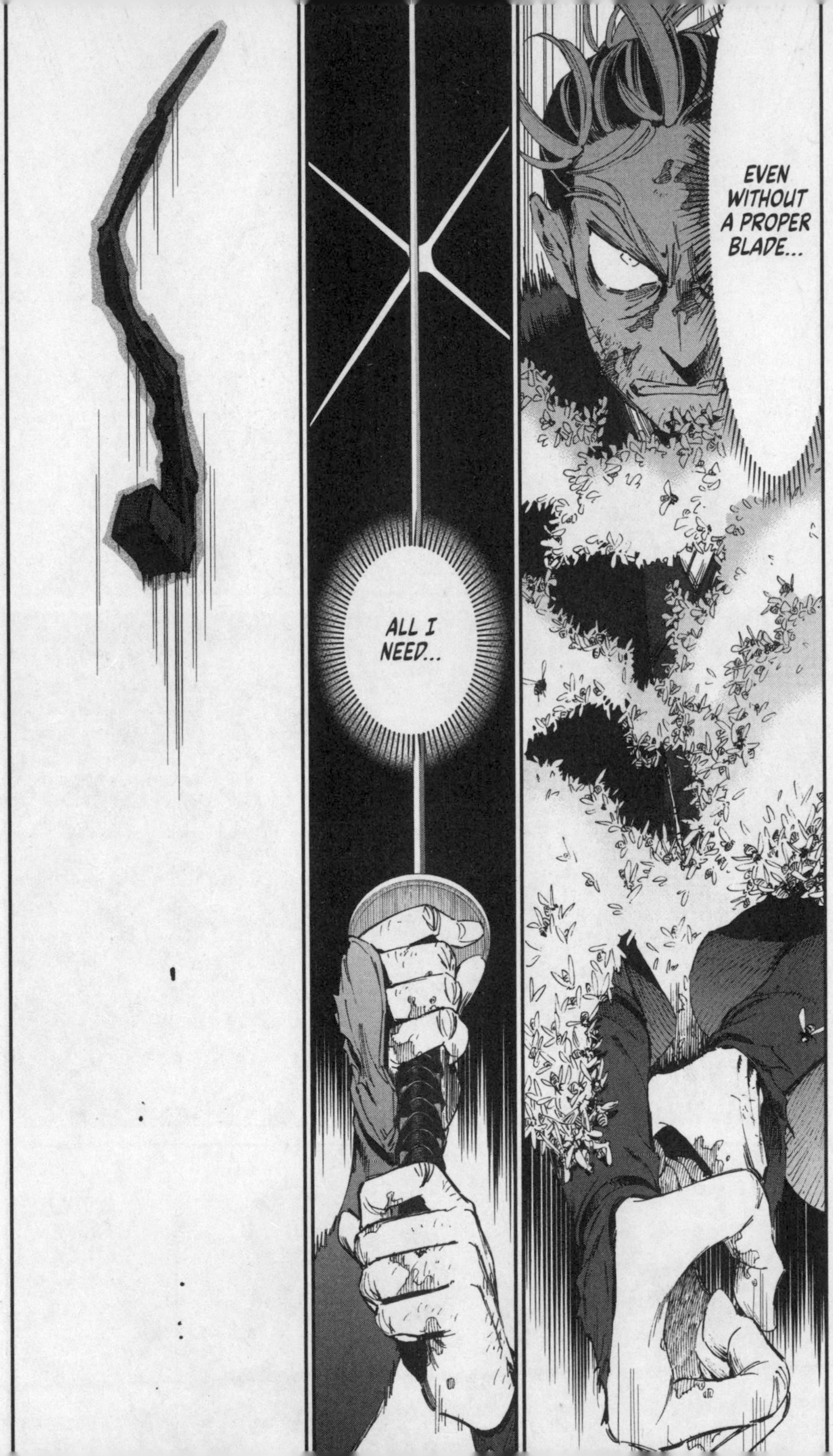
EVEN WITHOUT A PROPER BLADE...
ALL I NEED...

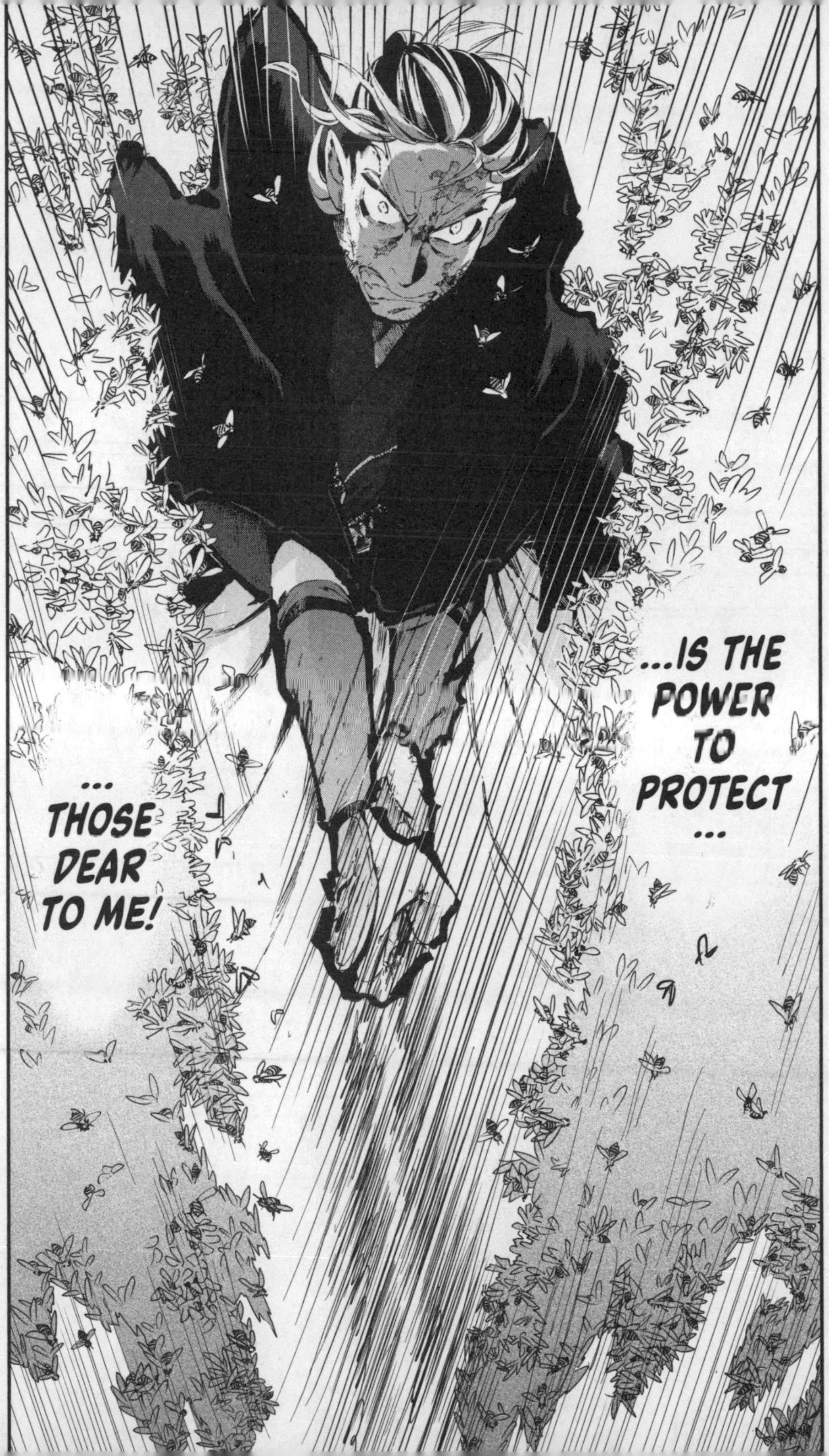
...IS THE POWER TO PROTECT ...
... THOSE DEAR TO ME!

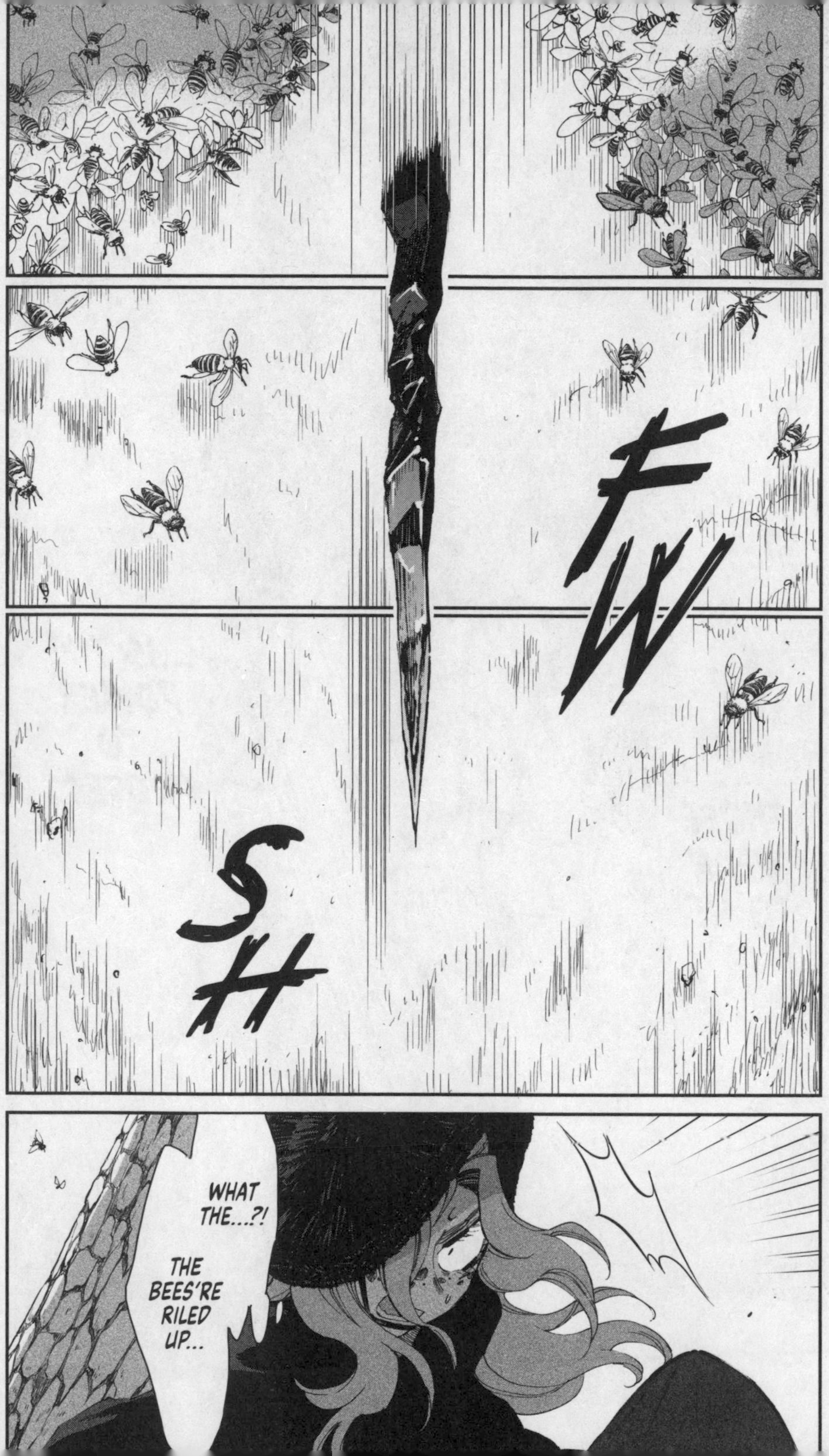
FW
SH
WHAT THE...?!
THE BEES'RE RILED UP...

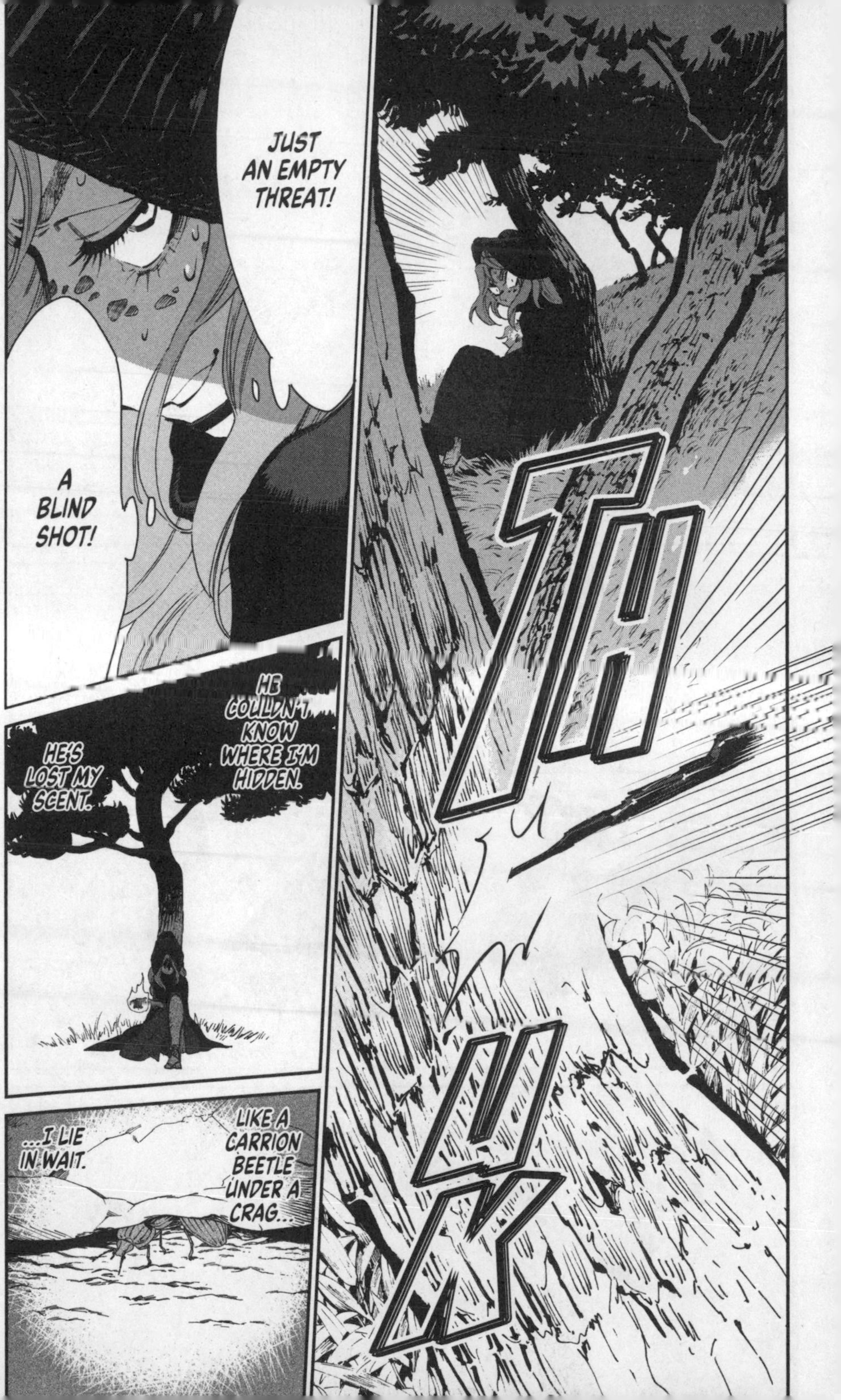
THUK
JUST AN EMPTY THREAT!
A BLIND SHOT!
HE COULDN'T KNOW WHERE I'M HIDDEN.
HE'S LOST MY SCENT.
LIKE A CARRION BEETLE UNDER A CRAG...
...I LIE IN WAIT.

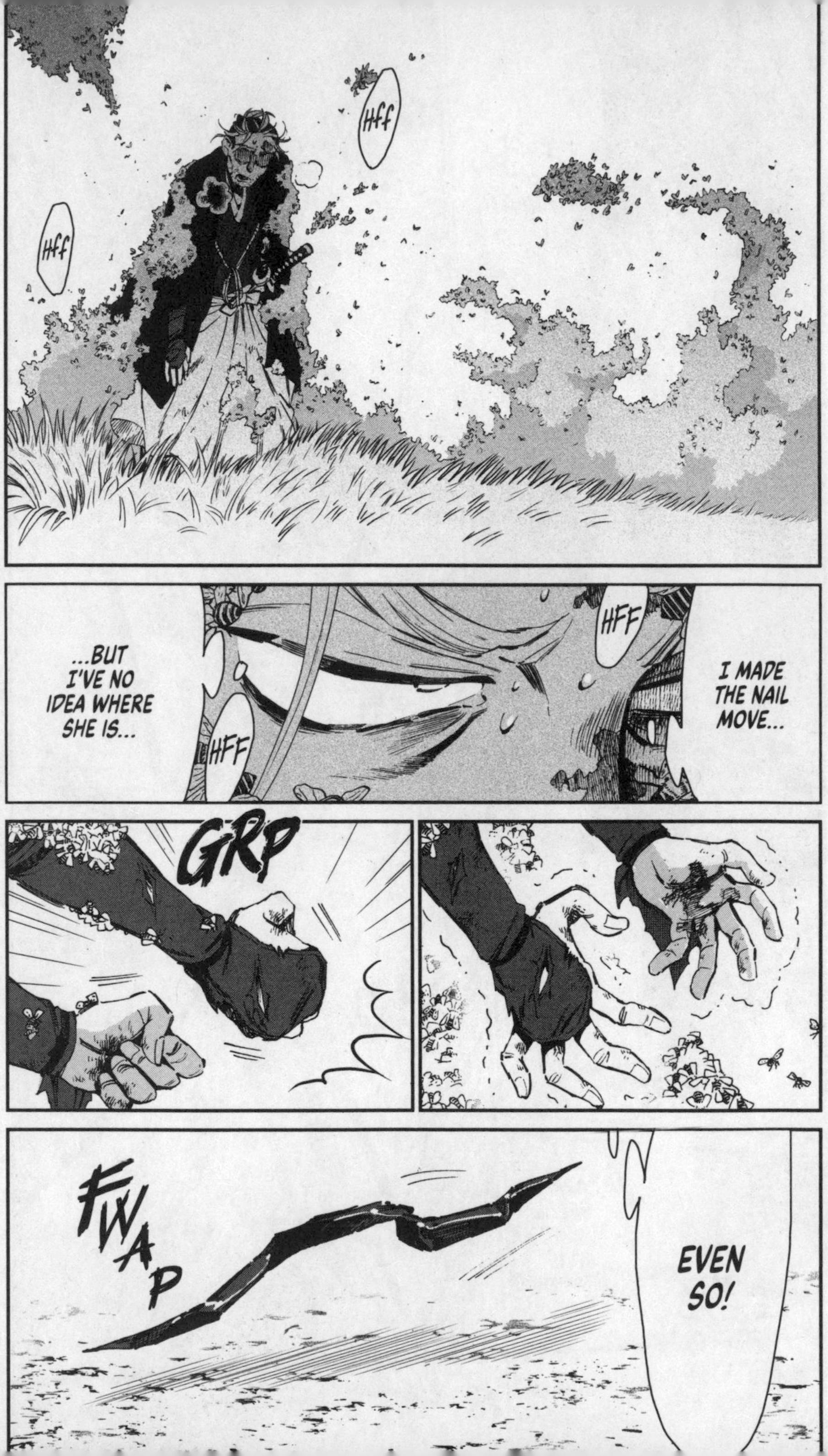
Hff
Hff
HFF
I MADE THE NAIL MOVE...
HFF
...BUT I'VE NO IDEA WHERE SHE IS...
GRP
EVEN SO!
FWAP

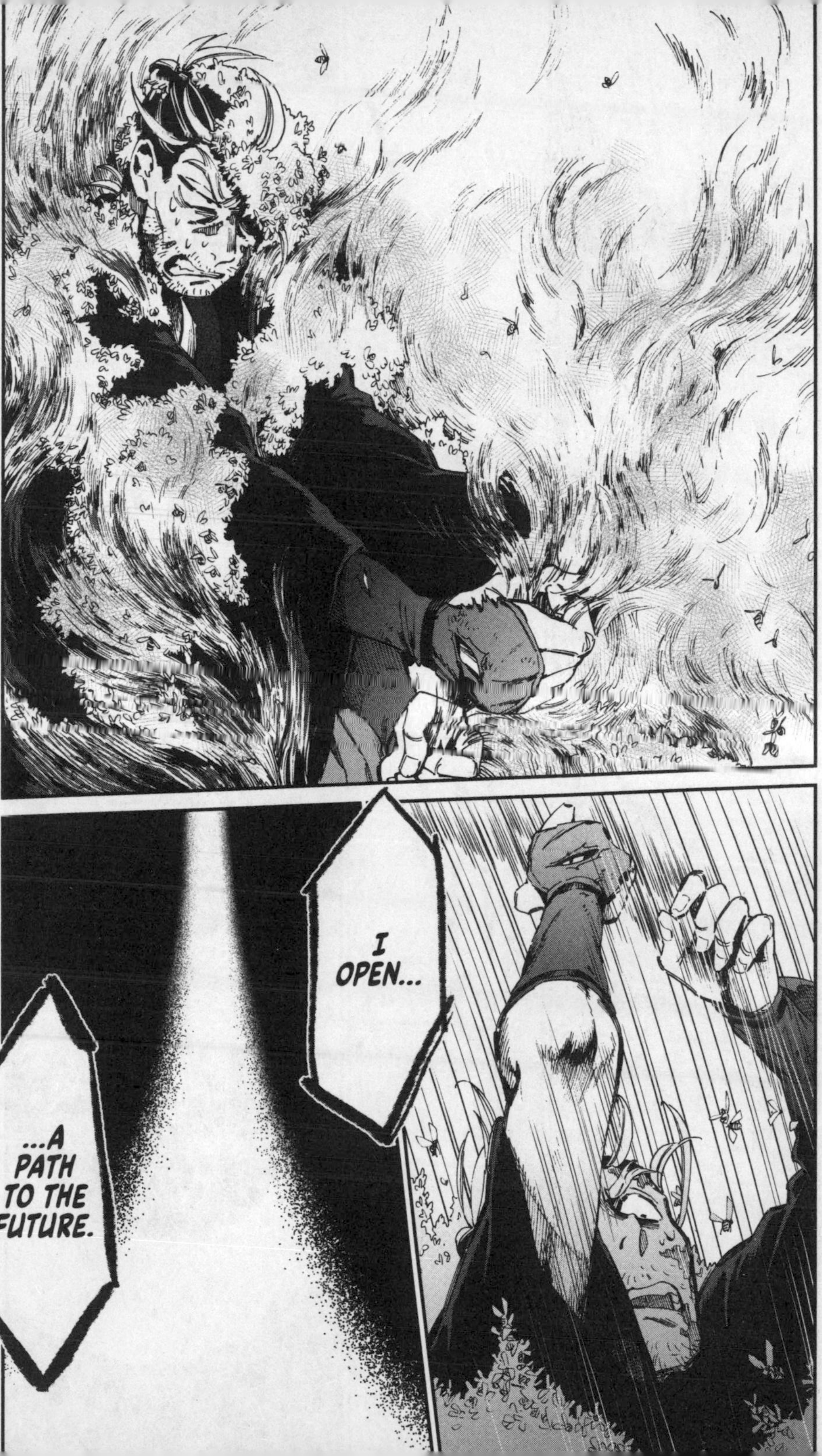
I OPEN...
...A PATH TO THE FUTURE.

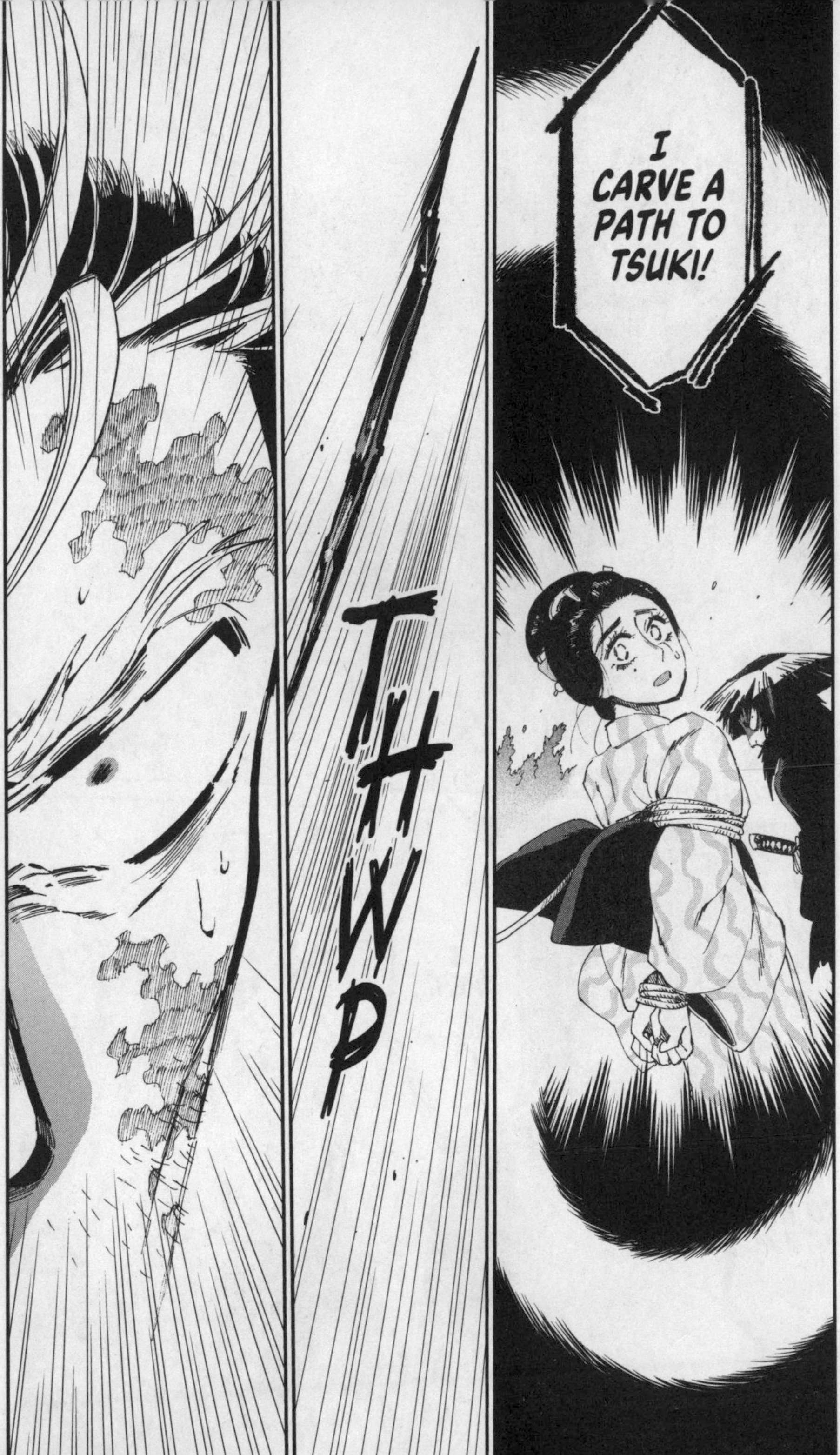
I CARVE A PATH TO TSUKI!
THWP

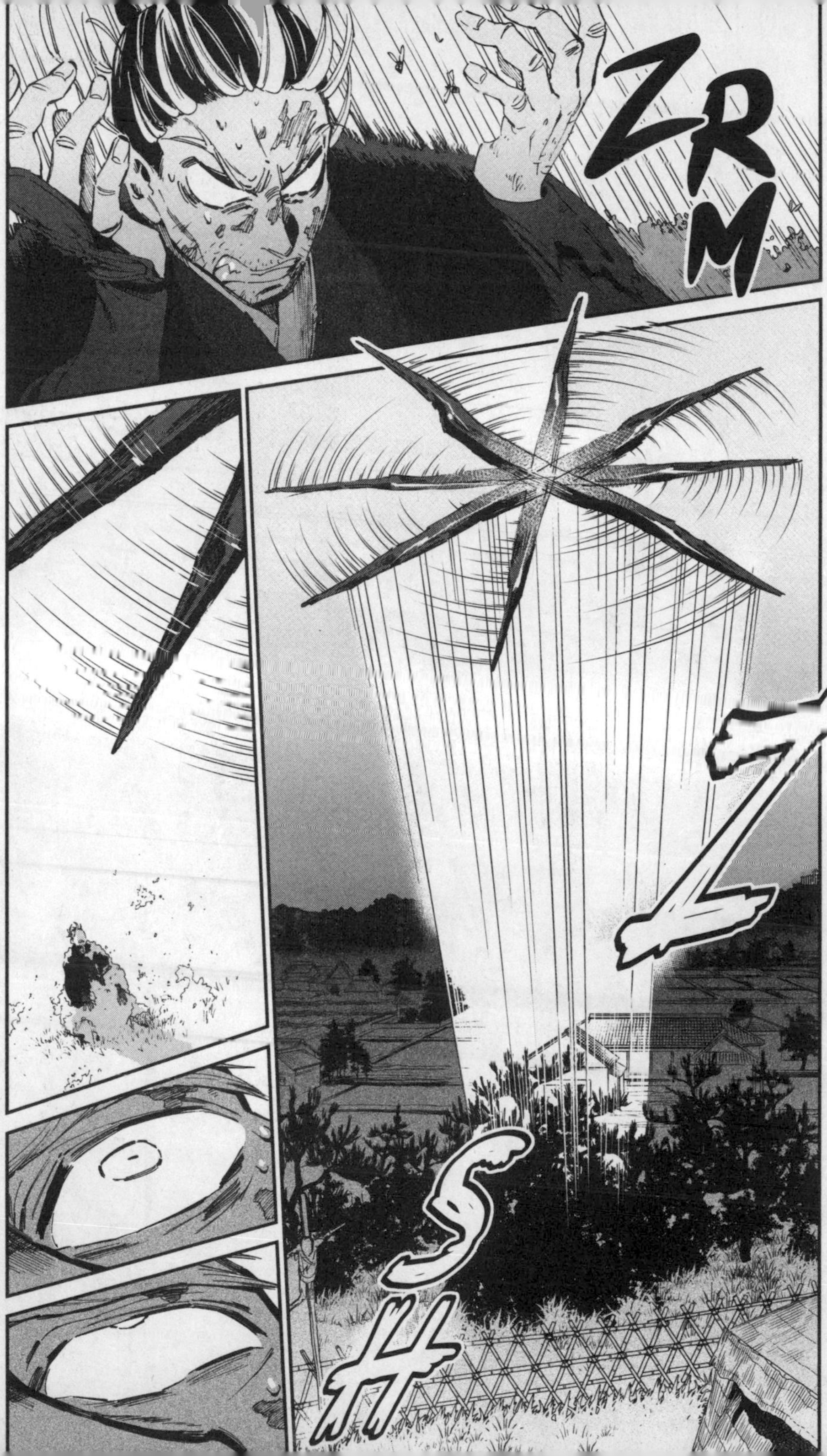
ZRM
ZSH

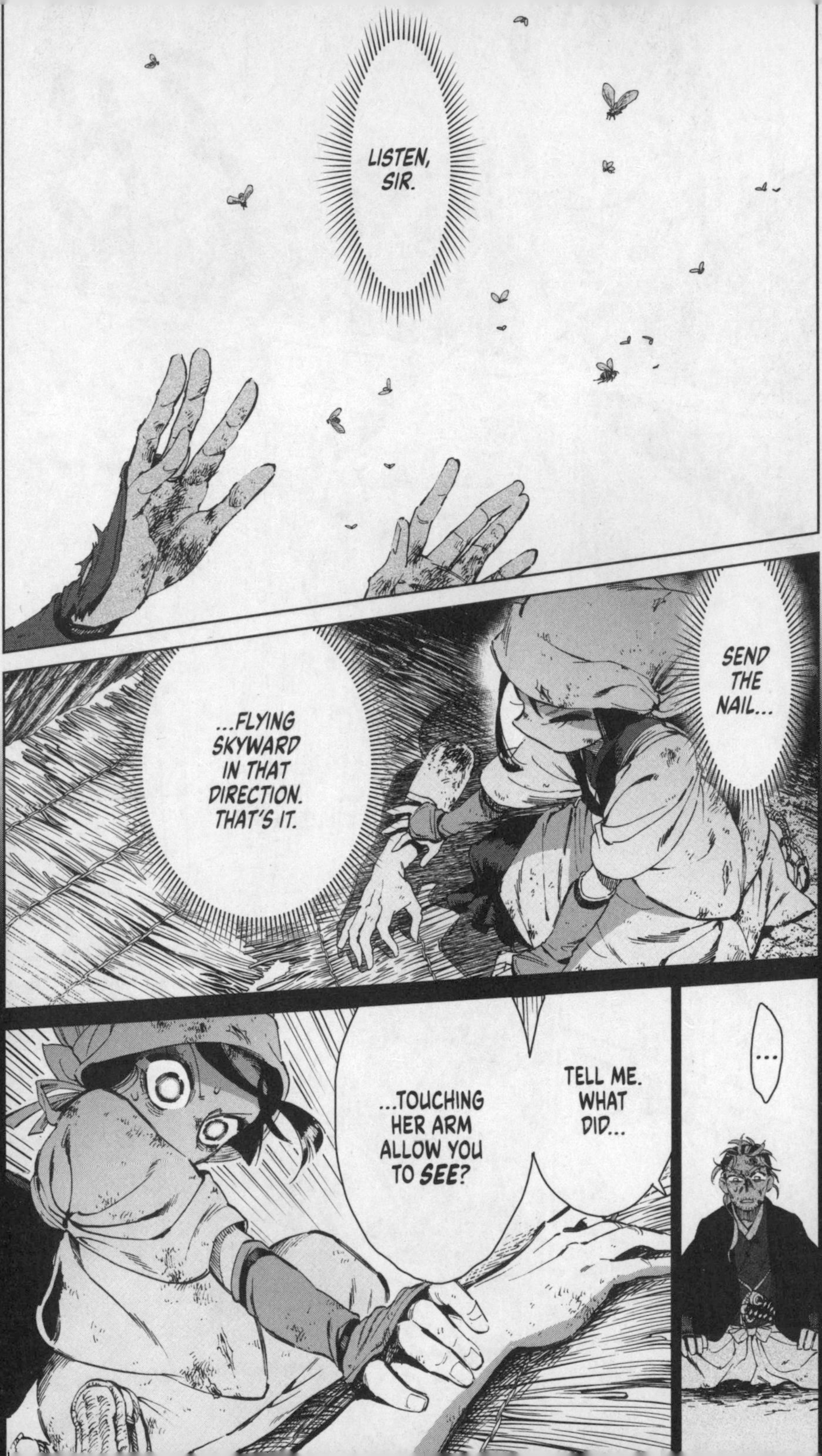
LISTEN, SIR.
SEND THE NAIL...
...FLYING SKYWARD IN THAT DIRECTION. THAT'S IT.
...
TELL ME. WHAT DID...
...TOUCHING HER ARM ALLOW YOU TO *SEE*?

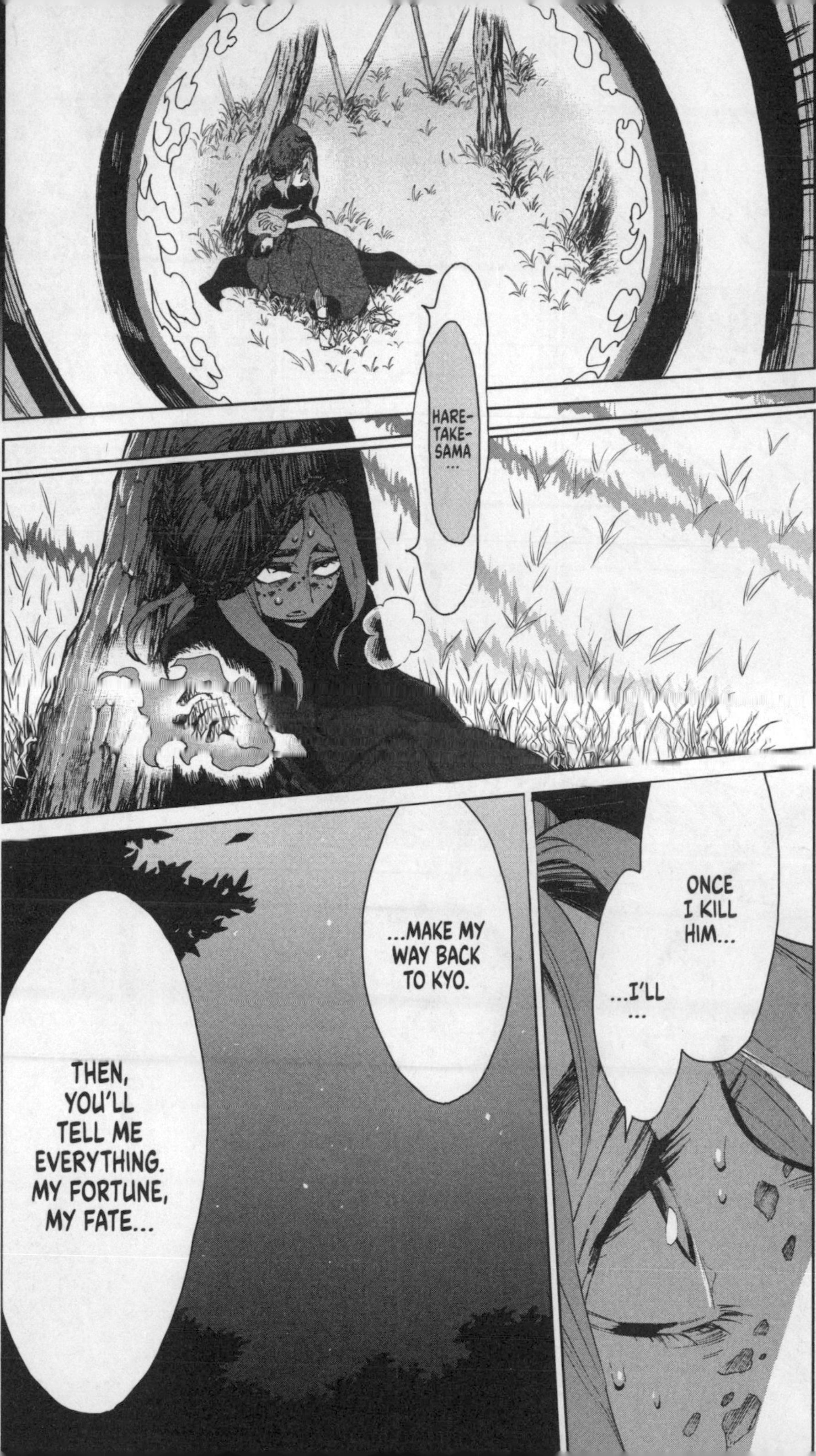
HARE-TAKE-SAMA...
ONCE I KILL HIM...
...I'LL...
...MAKE MY WAY BACK TO KYO.
THEN, YOU'LL TELL ME EVERYTHING. MY FORTUNE, MY FATE...

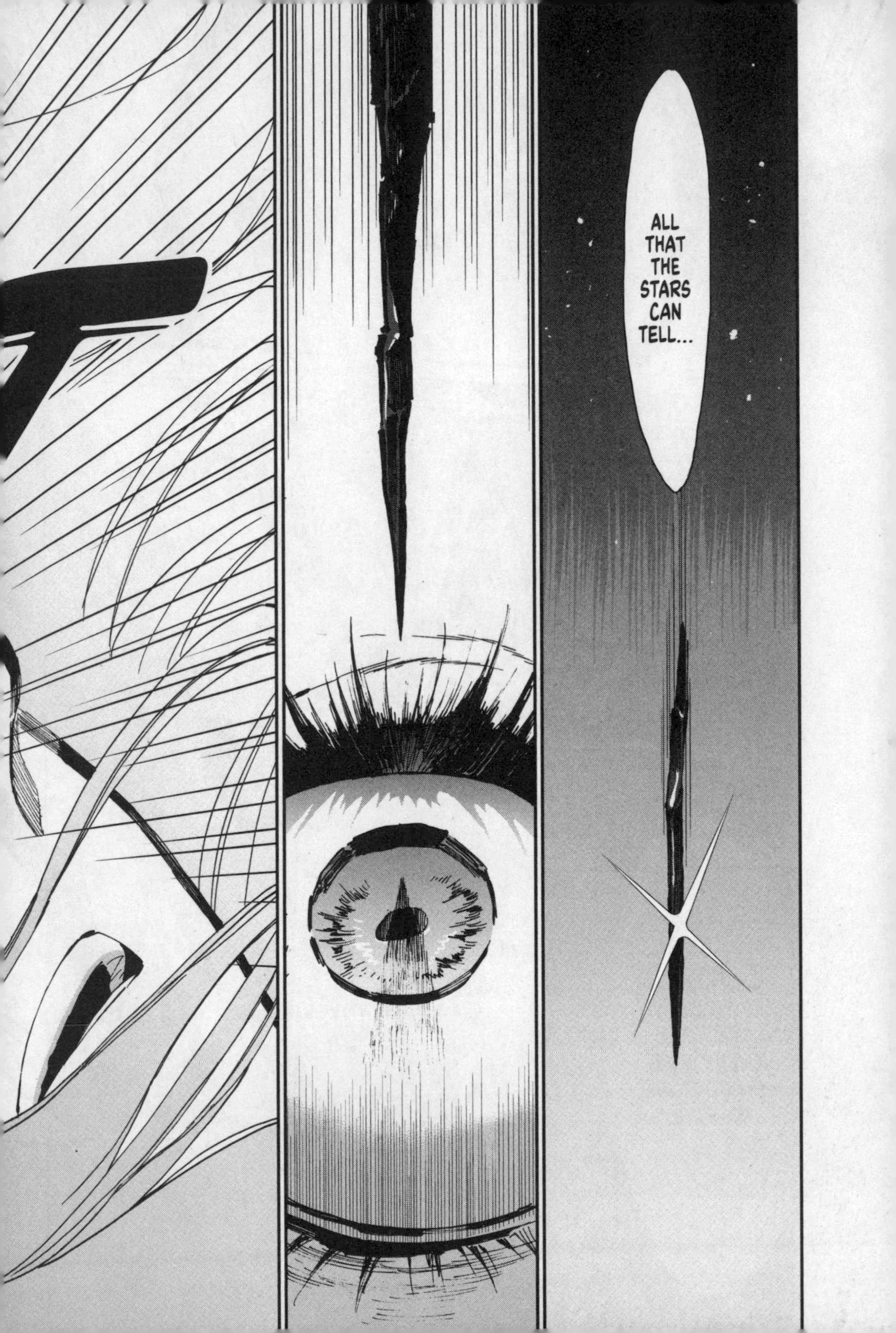
ALL THAT THE STARS CAN TELL...

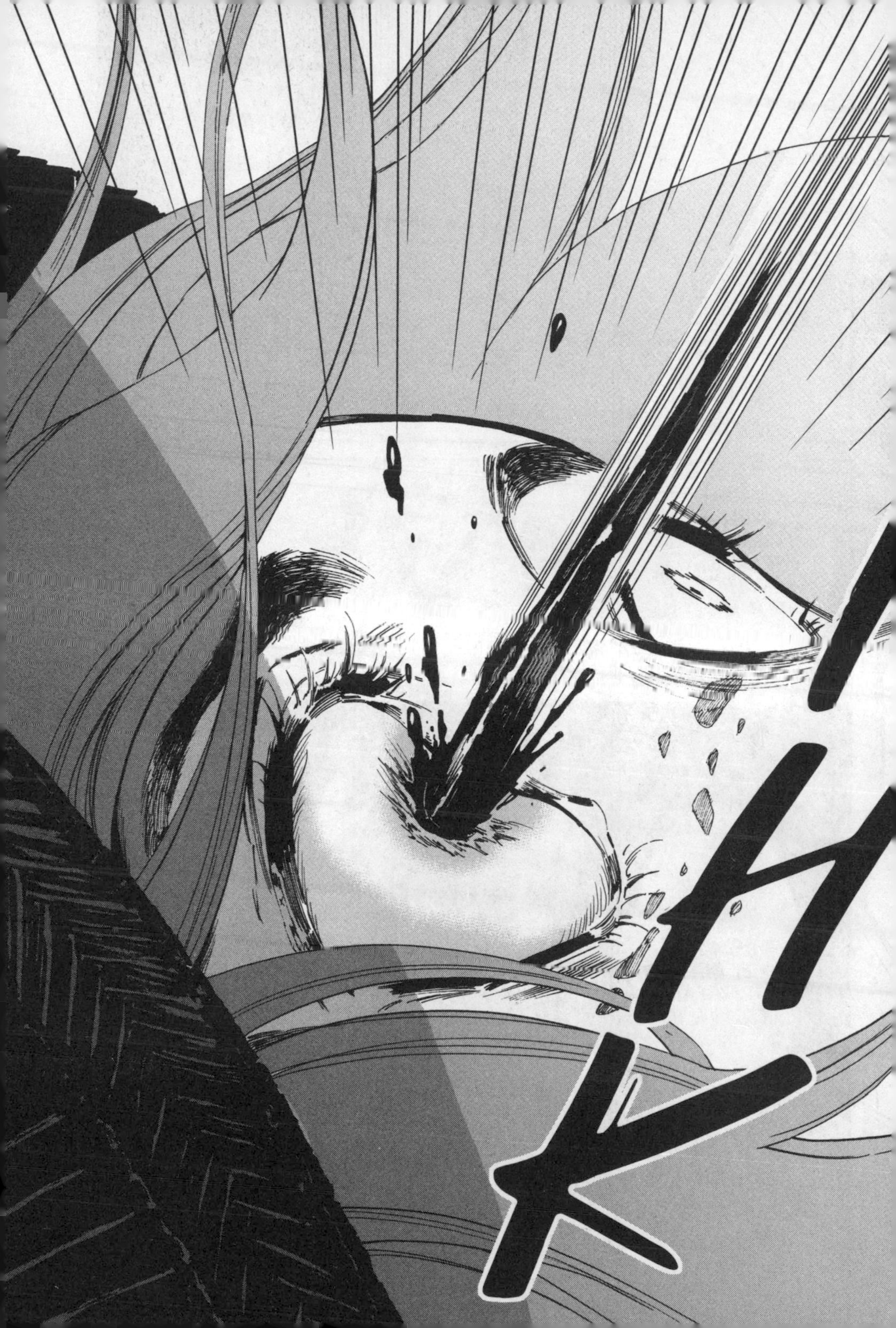
KHH

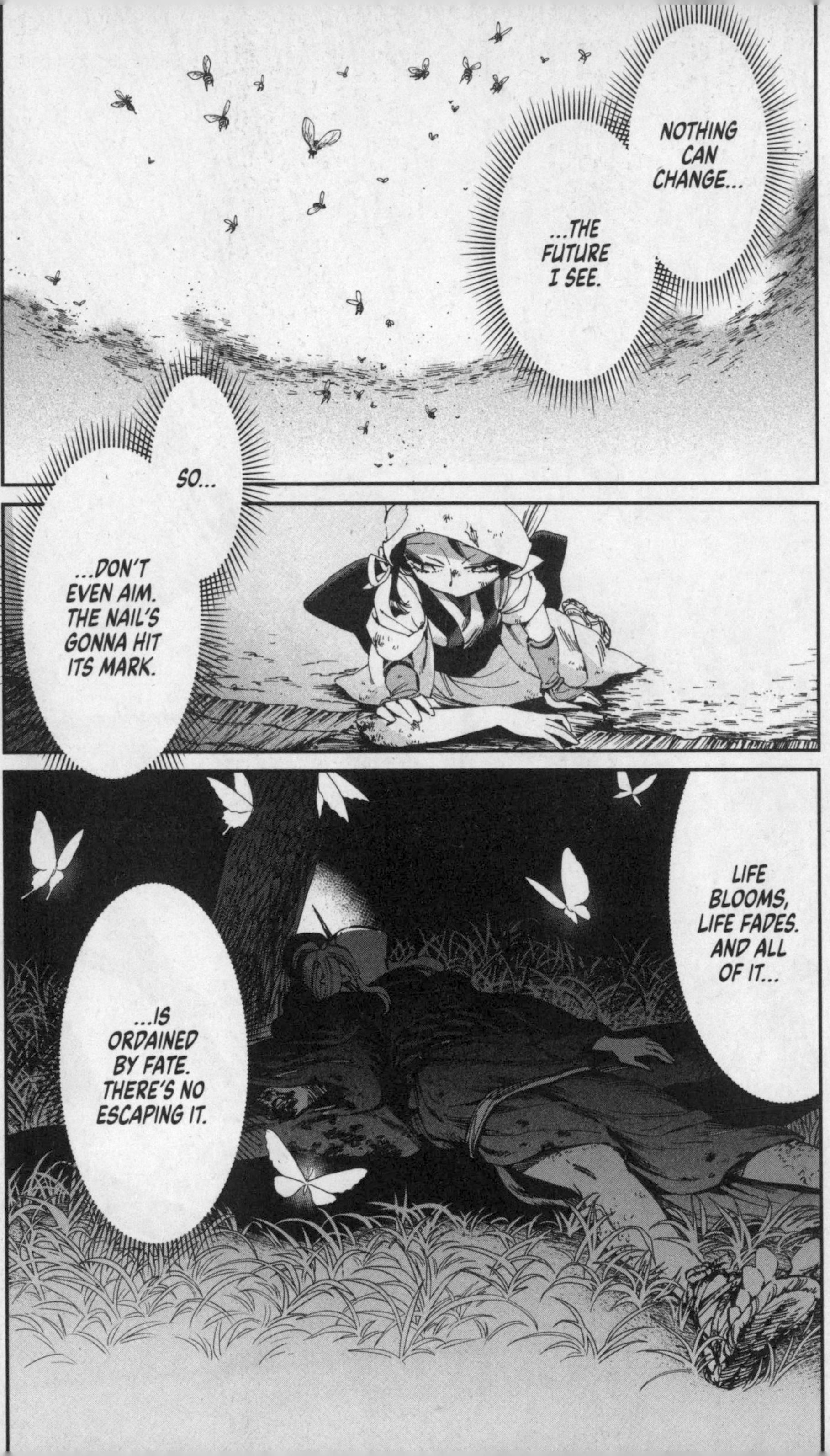
NOTHING CAN CHANGE...
...THE FUTURE I SEE.
SO...
...DON'T EVEN AIM. THE NAIL'S GONNA HIT ITS MARK.
LIFE BLOOMS, LIFE FADES. AND ALL OF IT...
...IS ORDAINED BY FATE. THERE'S NO ESCAPING IT.

STEEL of the
CELESTIAL
SHADOWS

Madara Concept Art

Madara

Wields bugs. Strictly speaking, she summons them from else-where.

Views herself and the bugs as one and the same.

Born in a rural community, she emerged from her mother covered in insects. Later, a poor harvest (caused by leafhopper bugs) was blamed on her. The townsfolk decided to burn her, in the fashion of the traditional torch procession to purge crop-eating bugs. After barely escaping with her life, she was taken in by a temple. While assisting grave diggers on the temple grounds, she could avoid prying eyes.

Haretake made her aware of the value of her own life, and of the lives of bugs. She came to believe that bugs, humans, and all of nature are essential elements of the world. Because Haretake is such an absolute figure to her, she's more than willing to kill those who might threaten him. By viewing all life as being equally valuable (to an extreme extent), she doesn't think highly of any given individual life.

Insect aficionado Shiba Kōkan once said, "I feel that humans and insects are not so fundamentally different."

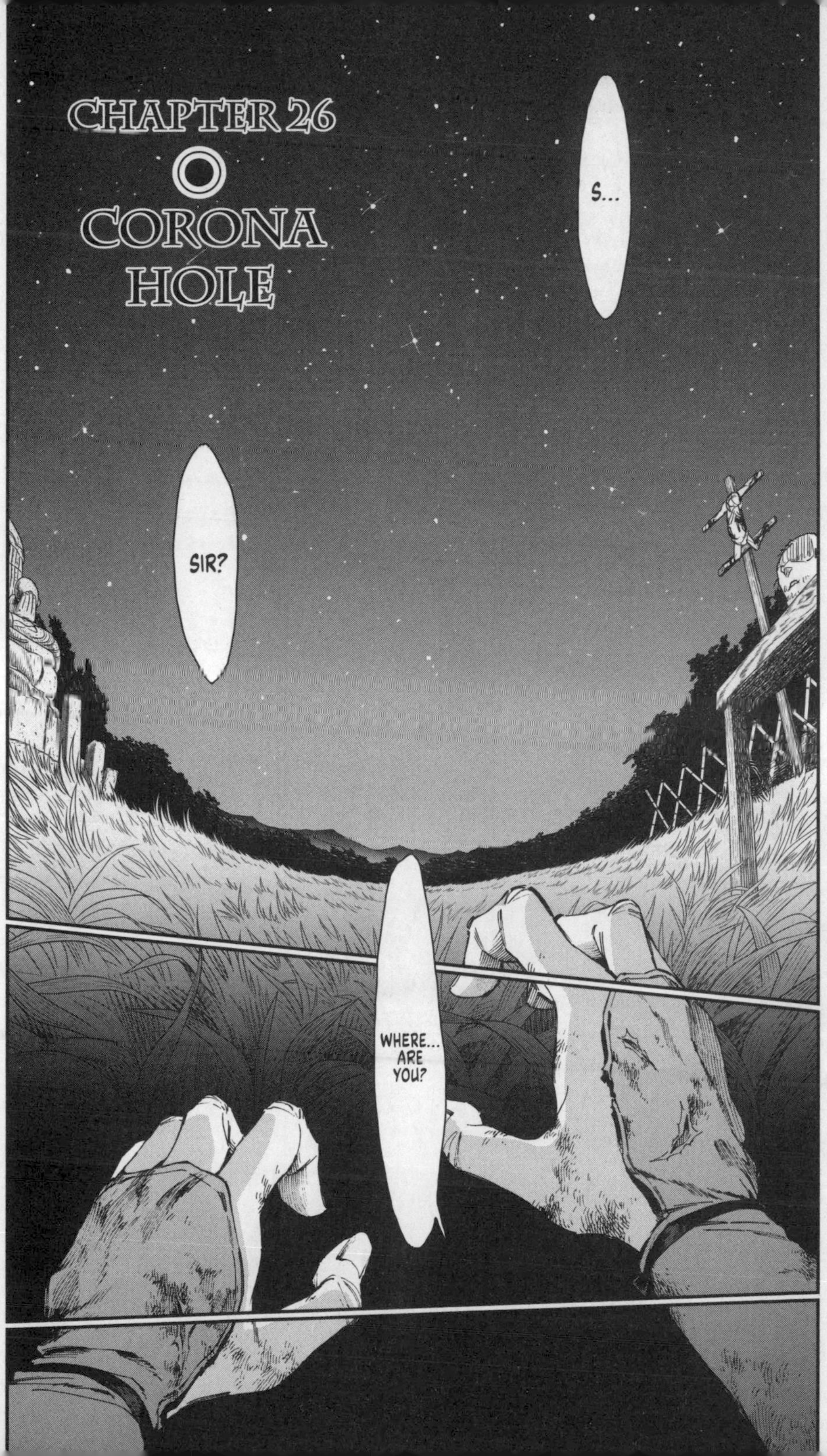
CHAPTER 26
CORONA HOLE
S...
SIR?
WHERE... ARE YOU?

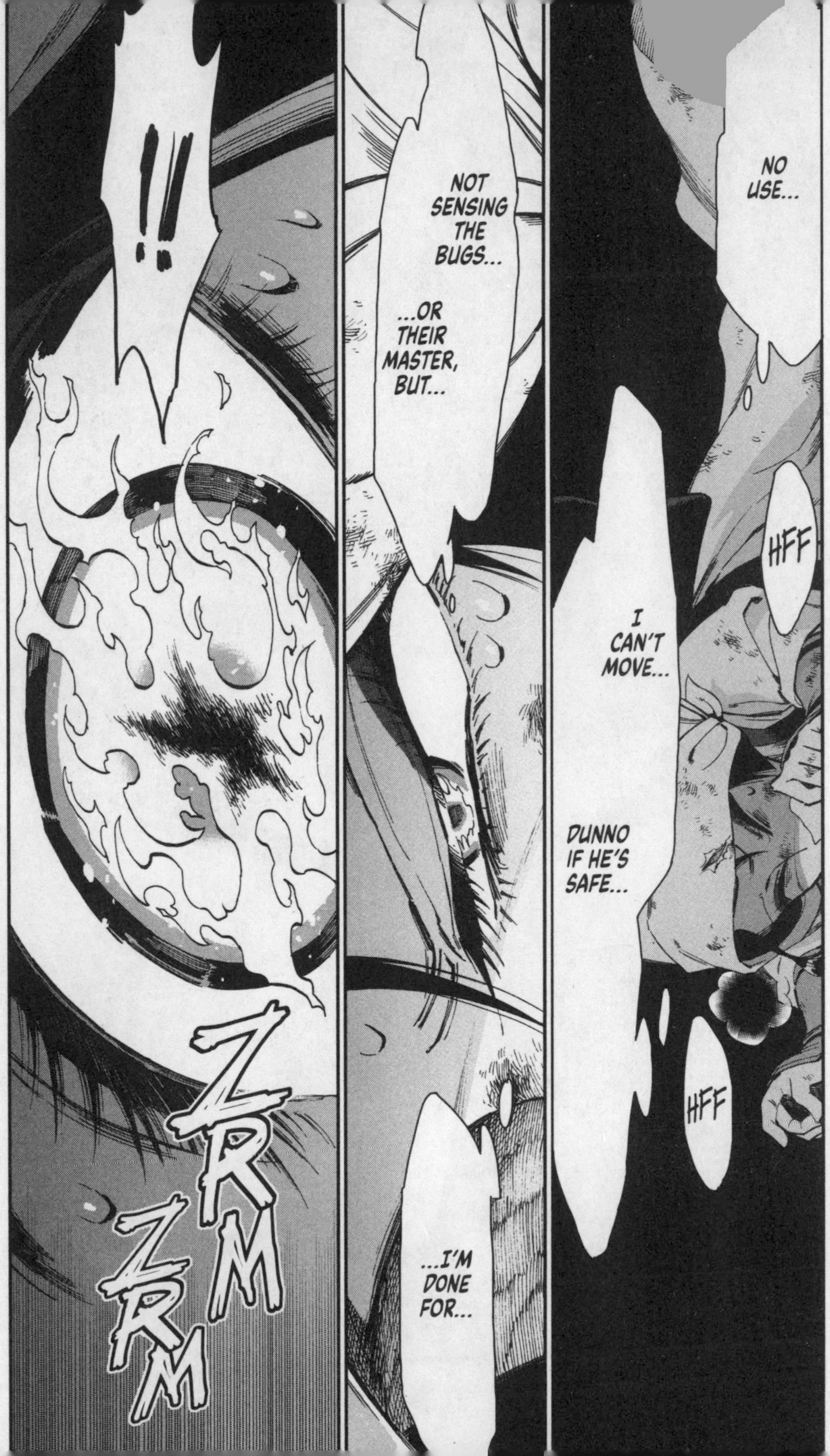
NO USE...
HFF
I CAN'T MOVE...
DUNNO IF HE'S SAFE...
HFF
NOT SENSING THE BUGS...
...OR THEIR MASTER, BUT...
...I'M DONE FOR...
!!
ZRM ZRM

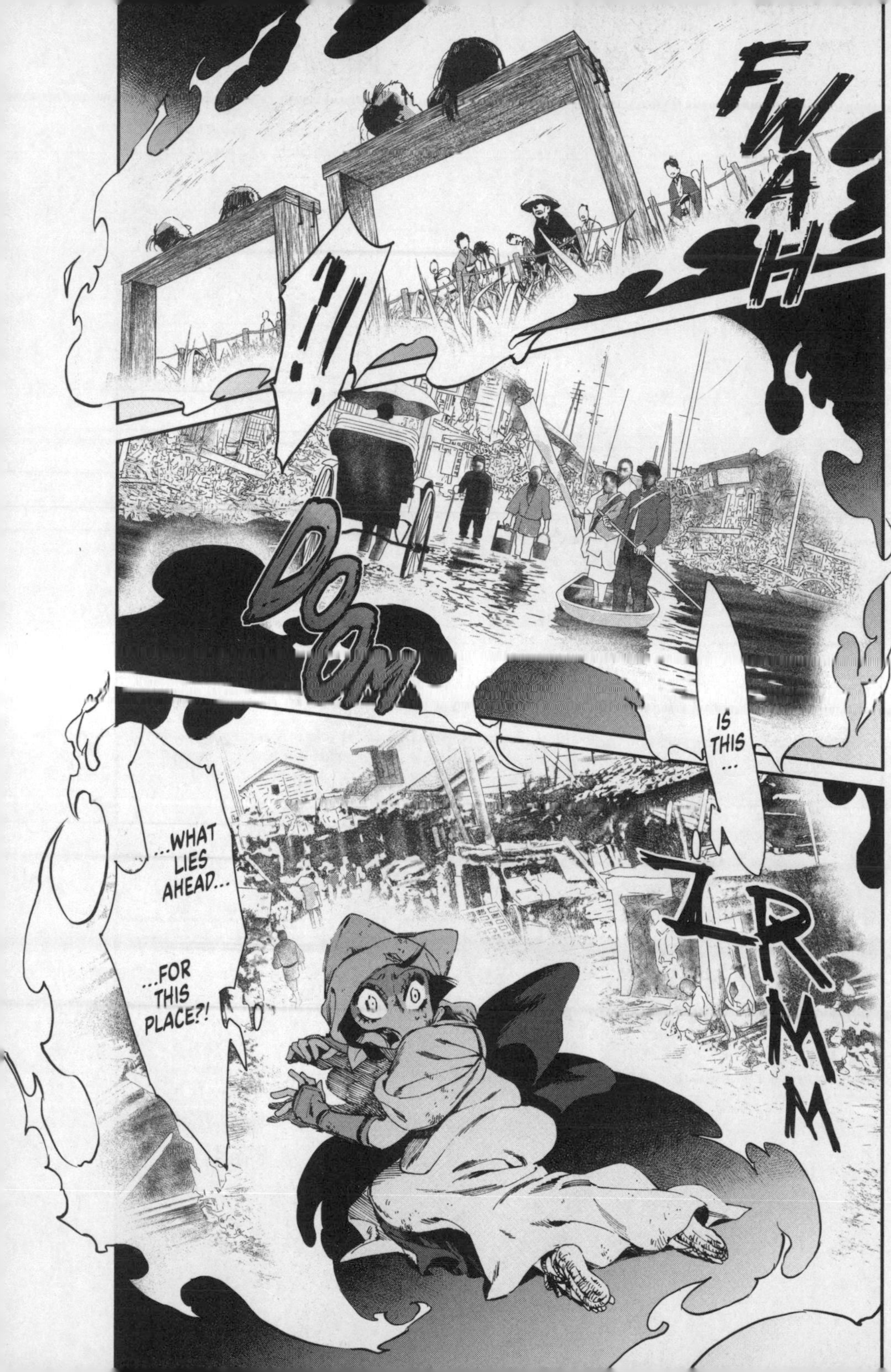
FWAH
?!
DOOM
IS THIS...
ZRMM
...WHAT LIES AHEAD...
...FOR THIS PLACE?!

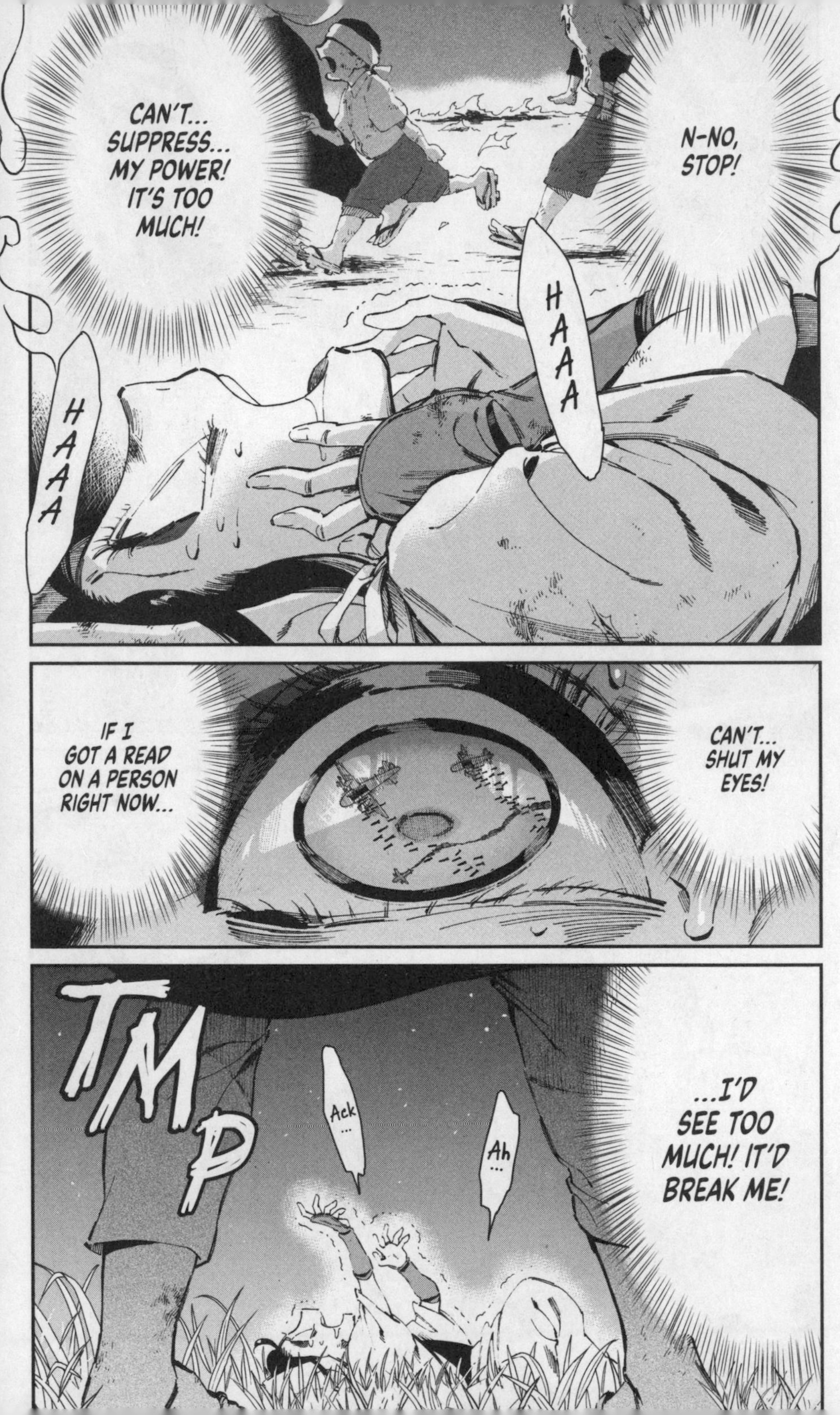
N-NO, STOP!
CAN'T... SUPPRESS... MY POWER! IT'S TOO MUCH!
HAAAA
HAAAA
CAN'T... SHUT MY EYES!
IF I GOT A READ ON A PERSON RIGHT NOW...
...I'D SEE TOO MUCH! IT'D BREAK ME!
Ah...
Ack...
TMP

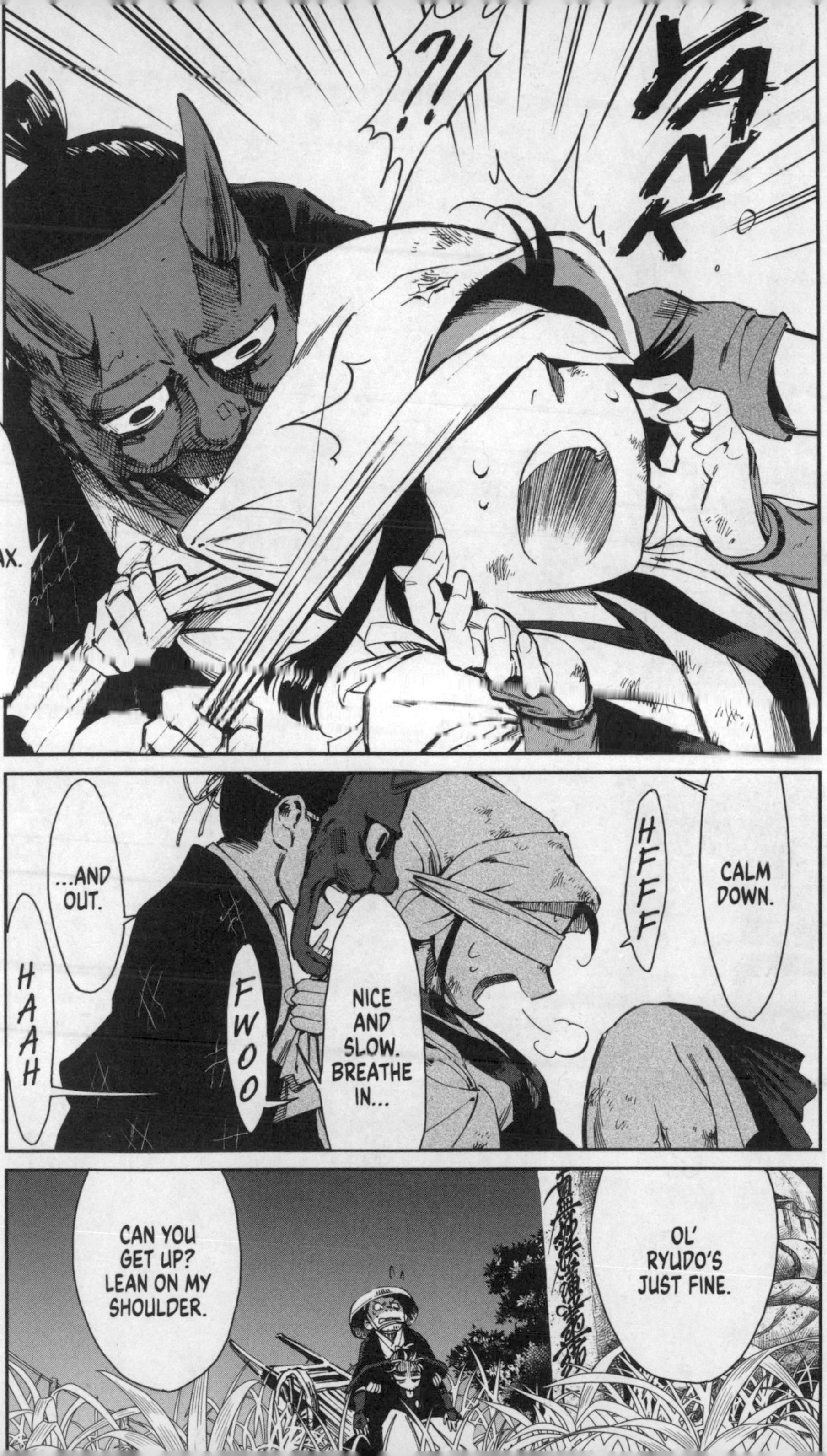
YANK
?!
RELAX.
CALM DOWN.
HFFF
NICE AND SLOW. BREATHE IN...
FWOO
...AND OUT.
HAAH
OL' RYUDO'S JUST FINE.
CAN YOU GET UP? LEAN ON MY SHOULDER.

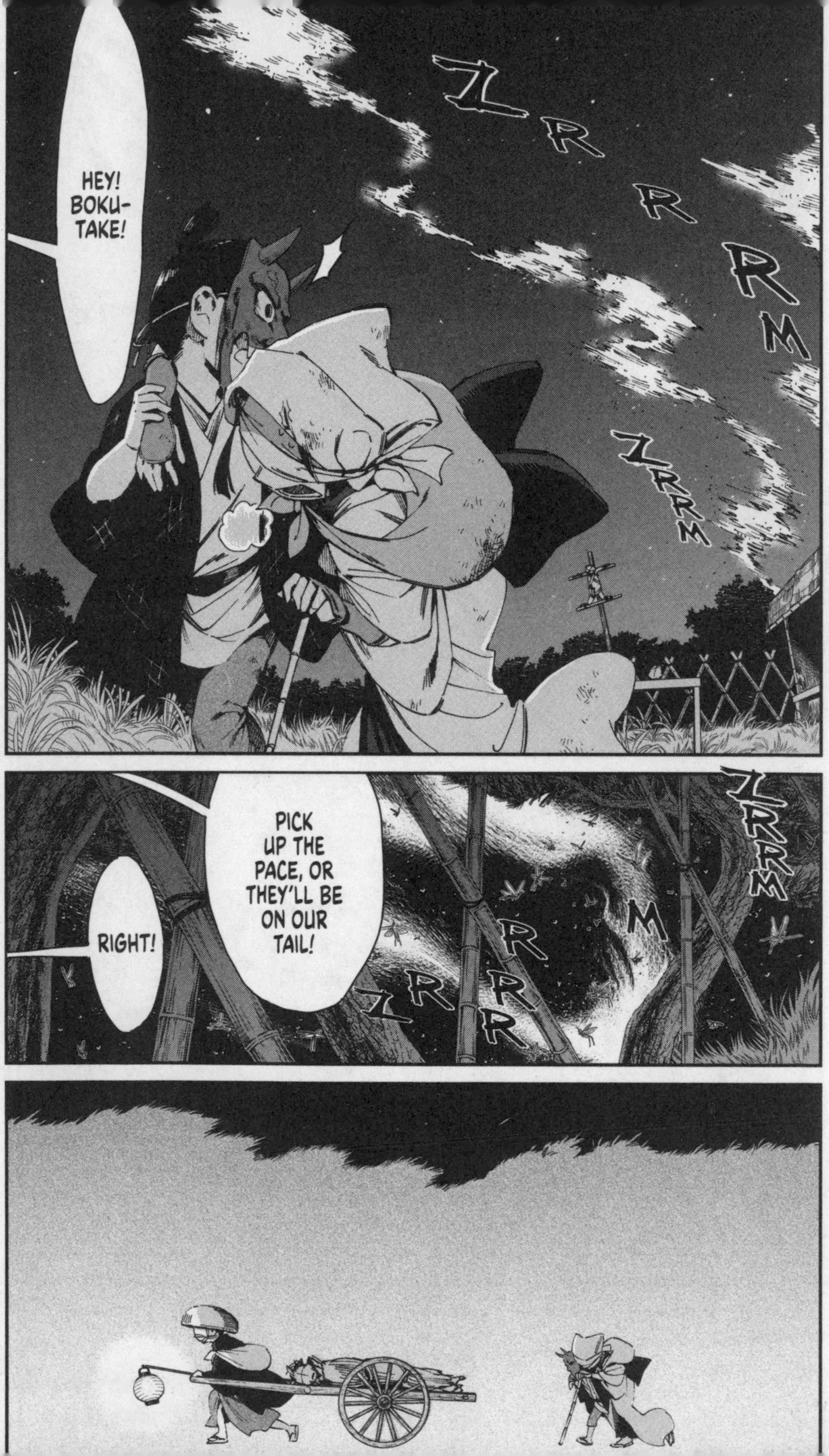
HEY! BOKU-TAKE!
ZRRRRM
ZRRRM
ZRRRM
PICK UP THE PACE, OR THEY'LL BE ON OUR TAIL!
ZRRRRM
RIGHT!

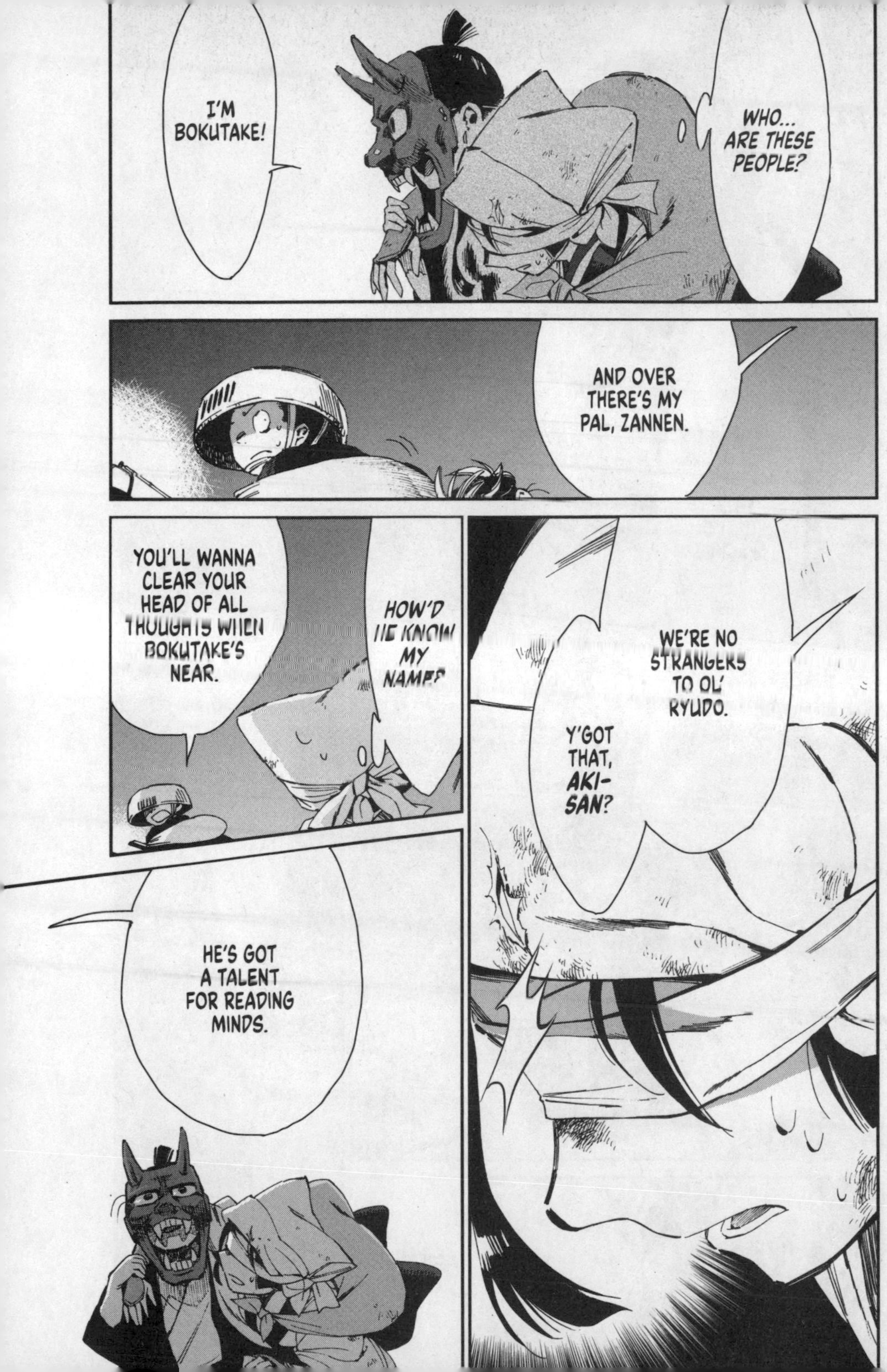
WHO... ARE THESE PEOPLE?
I'M BOKUTAKE!
AND OVER THERE'S MY PAL, ZANNEN.
WE'RE NO STRANGERS TO OL' RYUDO.
Y'GOT THAT, AKI-SAN?
HOW'D HE KNOW MY NAME?
YOU'LL WANNA CLEAR YOUR HEAD OF ALL THOUGHTS WHEN BOKUTAKE'S NEAR.
HE'S GOT A TALENT FOR READING MINDS.

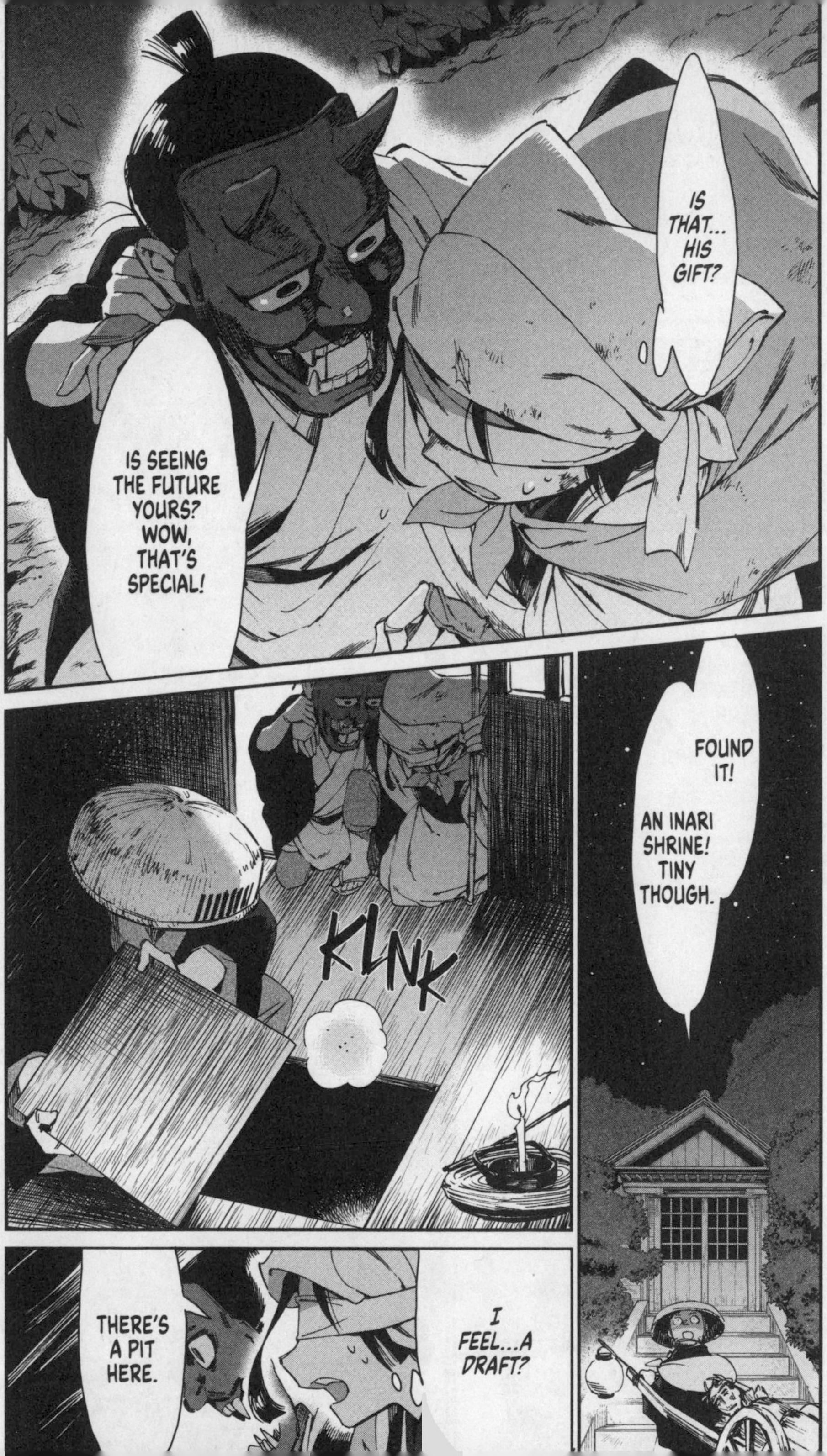
IS THAT... HIS GIFT?
IS SEEING THE FUTURE YOURS? WOW, THAT'S SPECIAL!
FOUND IT!
AN INARI SHRINE! TINY THOUGH.
KLNK
I FEEL...A DRAFT?
THERE'S A PIT HERE.

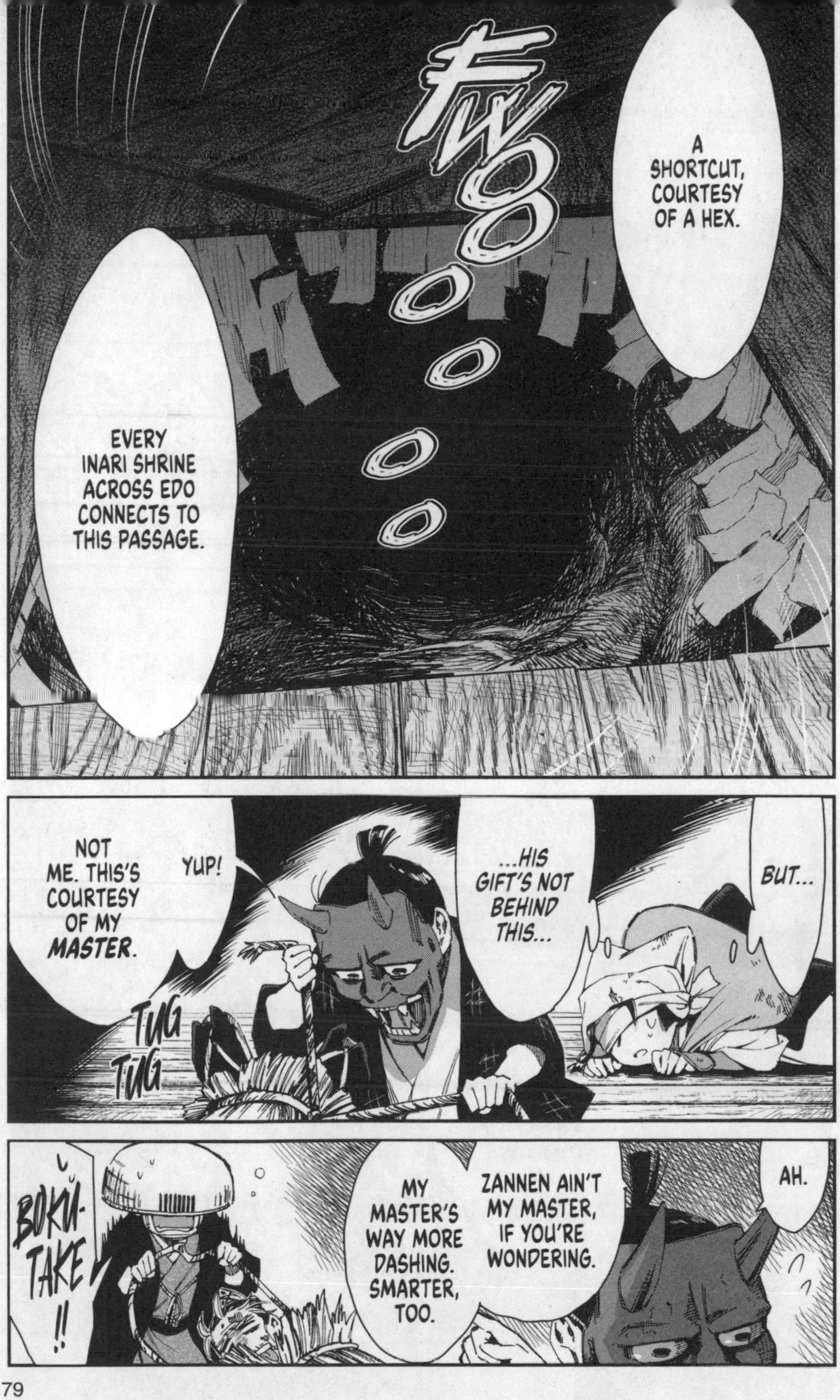
A SHORTCUT, COURTESY OF A HEX.
FWOOOOO
EVERY INARI SHRINE ACROSS EDO CONNECTS TO THIS PASSAGE.
BUT...
...HIS GIFT'S NOT BEHIND THIS...
YUP!
NOT ME. THIS'S COURTESY OF MY *MASTER*.
TUG TUG
AH.
ZANNEN AIN'T MY MASTER, IF YOU'RE WONDERING.
MY MASTER'S WAY MORE DASHING. SMARTER, TOO.
BOKU-TAKE!!

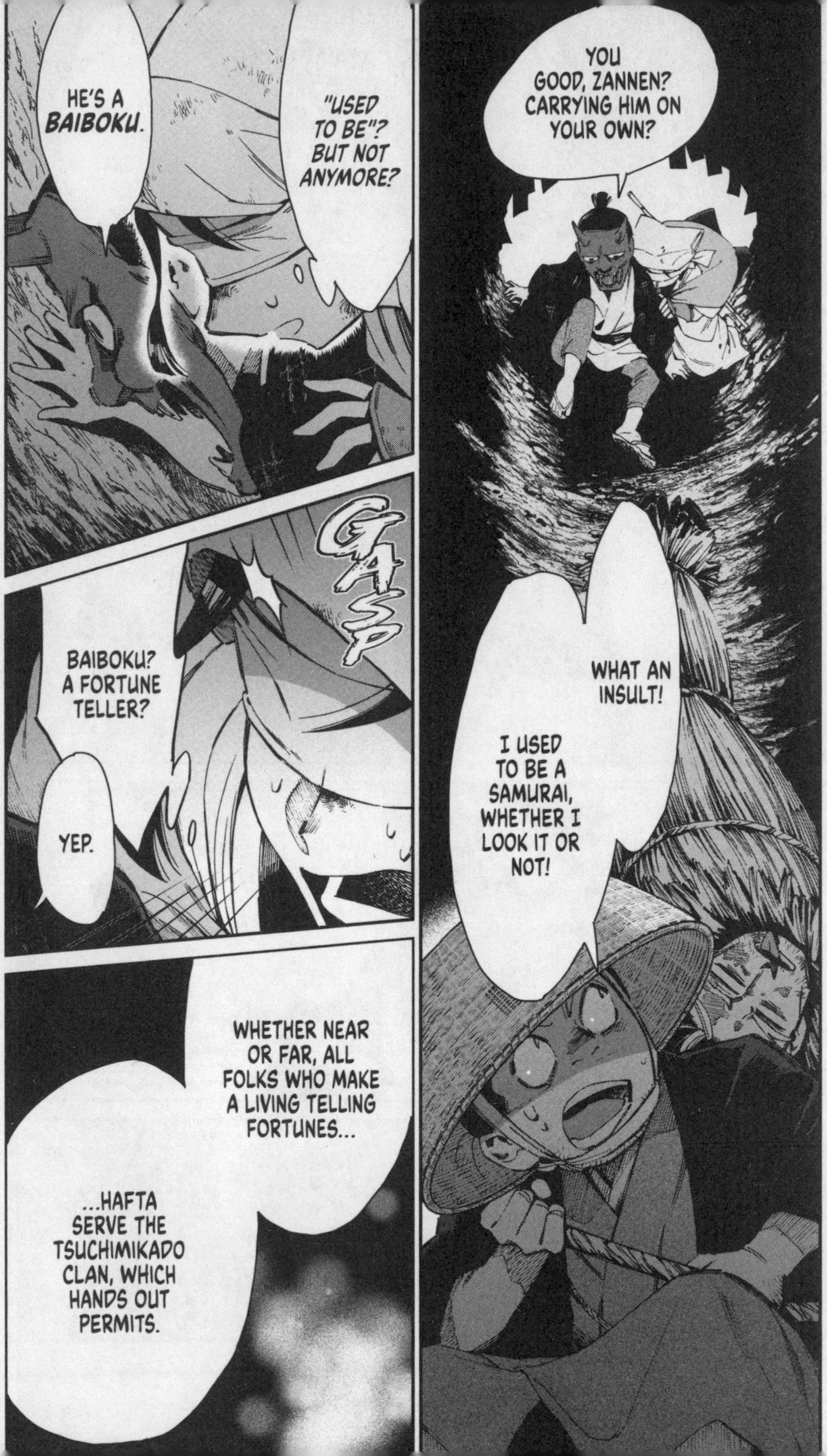
YOU GOOD, ZANNEN? CARRYING HIM ON YOUR OWN?
WHAT AN INSULT!
I USED TO BE A SAMURAI, WHETHER I LOOK IT OR NOT!
"USED TO BE"? BUT NOT ANYMORE?
HE'S A BAIBOKU.
GASP
BAIBOKU? A FORTUNE TELLER?
YEP.
WHETHER NEAR OR FAR, ALL FOLKS WHO MAKE A LIVING TELLING FORTUNES...
...HAFTA SERVE THE TSUCHIMIKADO CLAN, WHICH HANDS OUT PERMITS.

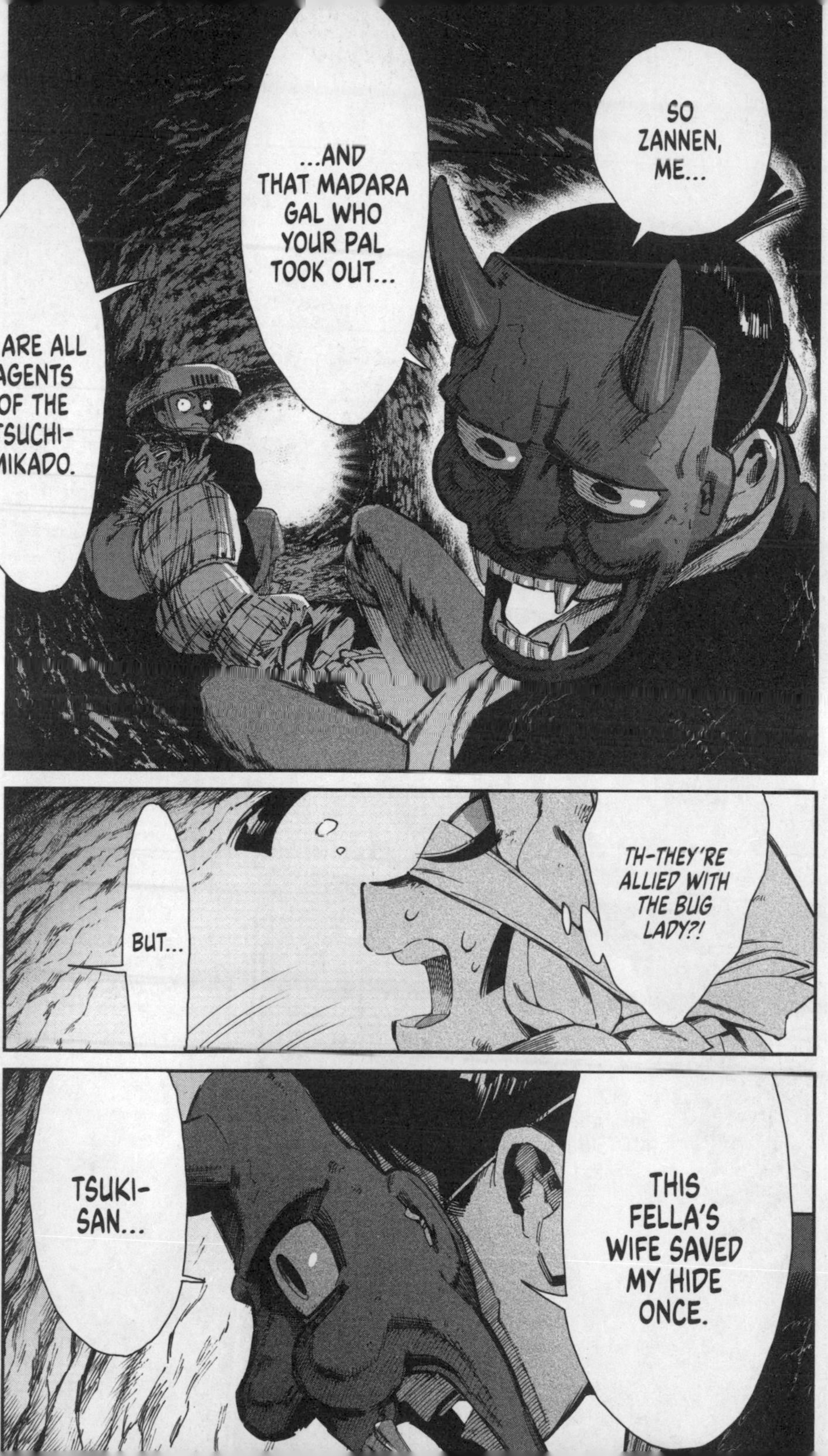
SO ZANNEN, ME...
...AND THAT MADARA GAL WHO YOUR PAL TOOK OUT...
...ARE ALL AGENTS OF THE TSUCHI-MIKADO.
TH-THEY'RE ALLIED WITH THE BUG LADY?!
BUT...
THIS FELLA'S WIFE SAVED MY HIDE ONCE.
TSUKI-SAN...

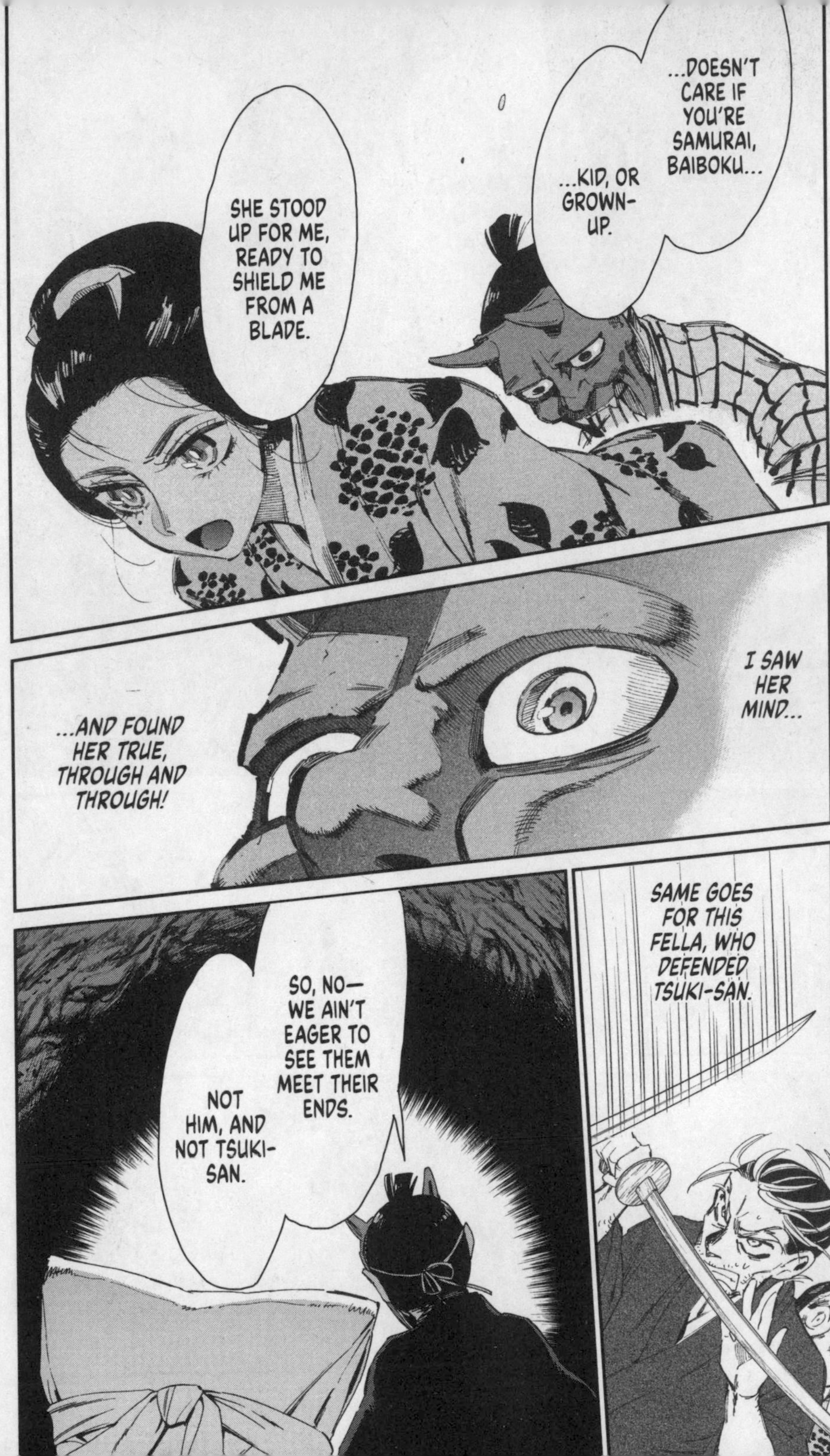
...DOESN'T CARE IF YOU'RE SAMURAI, BAIBOKU...
...KID, OR GROWN-UP.
SHE STOOD UP FOR ME, READY TO SHIELD ME FROM A BLADE.
I SAW HER MIND...
...AND FOUND HER TRUE, THROUGH AND THROUGH!
SAME GOES FOR THIS FELLA, WHO DEFENDED TSUKI-SAN.
SO, NO— WE AIN'T EAGER TO SEE THEM MEET THEIR ENDS.
NOT HIM, AND NOT TSUKI-SAN.

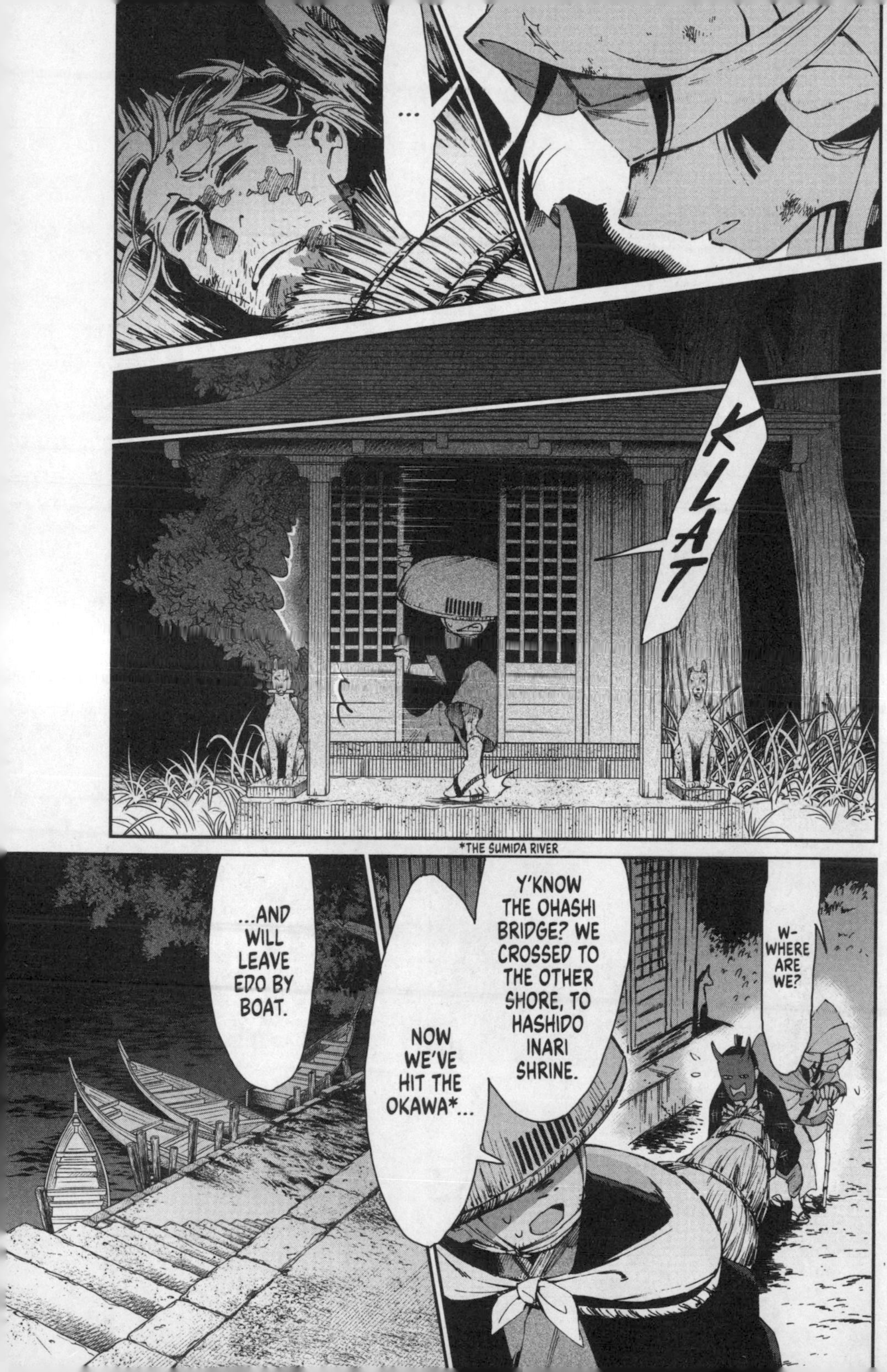
...
KLAT
W-WHERE ARE WE?
Y'KNOW THE OHASHI BRIDGE? WE CROSSED TO THE OTHER SHORE, TO HASHIDO INARI SHRINE.
NOW WE'VE HIT THE OKAWA*...
...AND WILL LEAVE EDO BY BOAT.
*THE SUMIDA RIVER

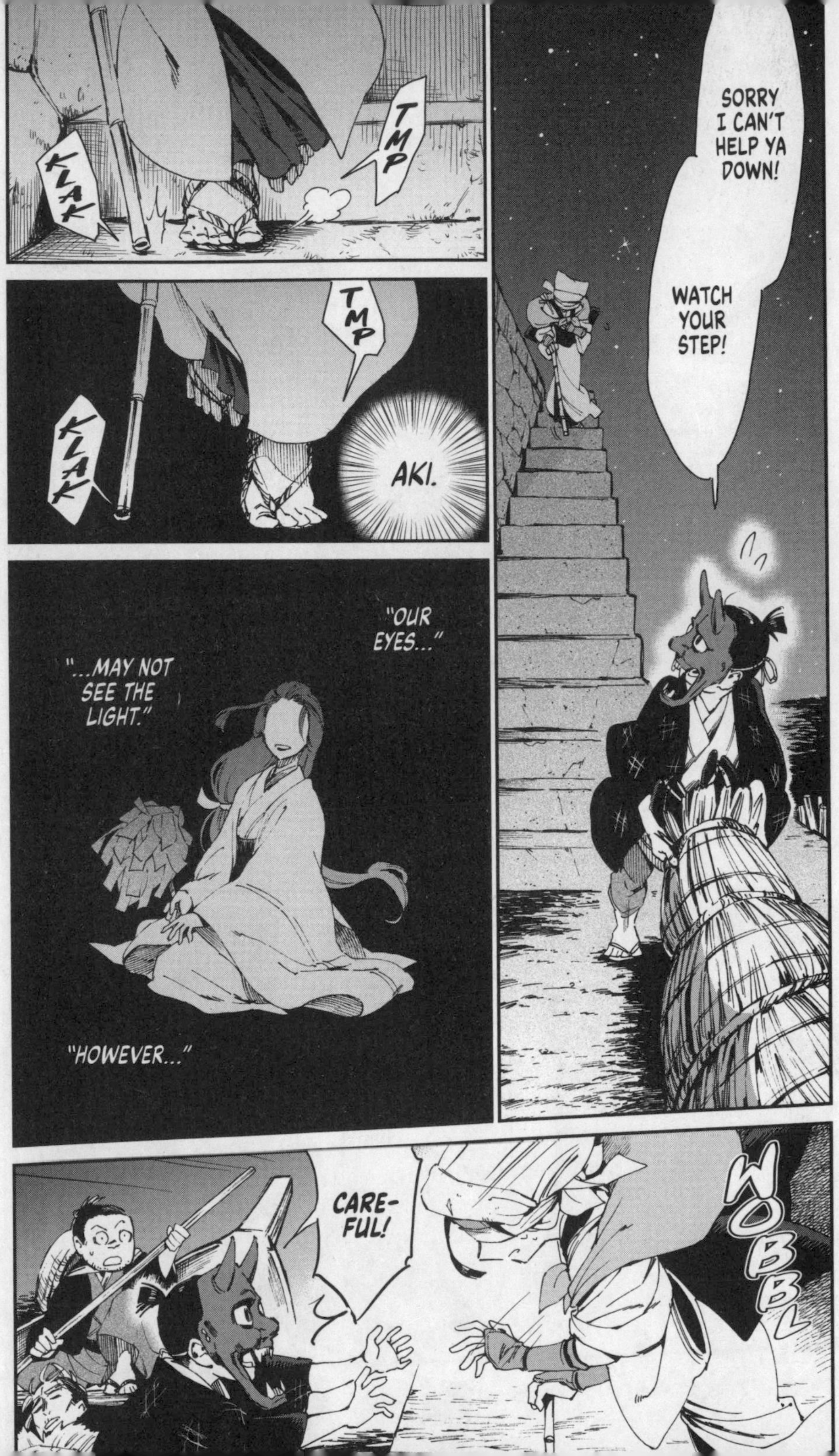
SORRY I CAN'T HELP YA DOWN!
WATCH YOUR STEP!
TMP
KLAK
TMP
KLAK
AKI.
"OUR EYES..."
"...MAY NOT SEE THE LIGHT."
"HOWEVER..."
WOBBL
CARE-FUL!

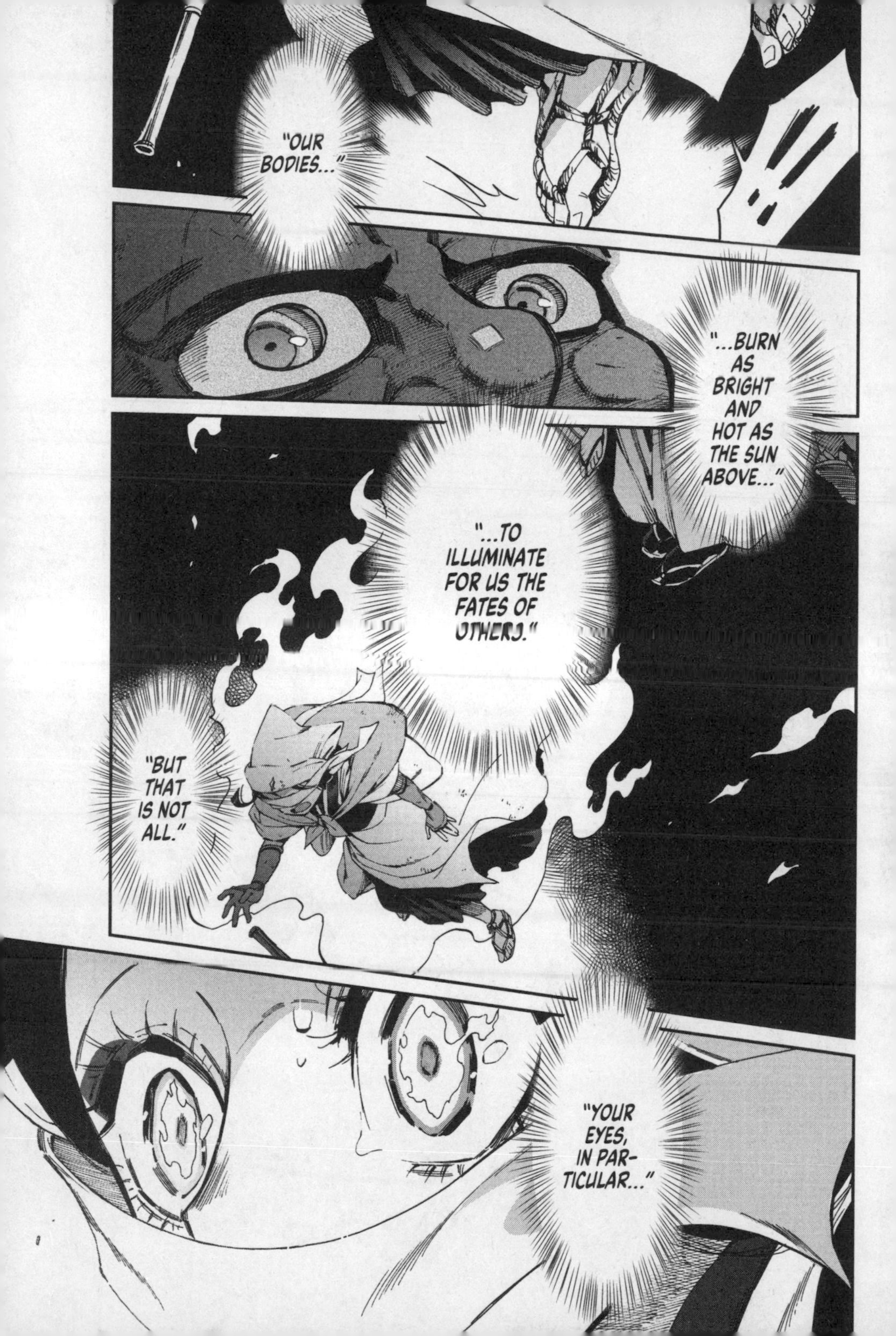
"OUR BODIES..."
"...BURN AS BRIGHT AND HOT AS THE SUN ABOVE..."
"...TO ILLUMINATE FOR US THE FATES OF OTHERS."
"BUT THAT IS NOT ALL."
"YOUR EYES, IN PAR-TICULAR..."

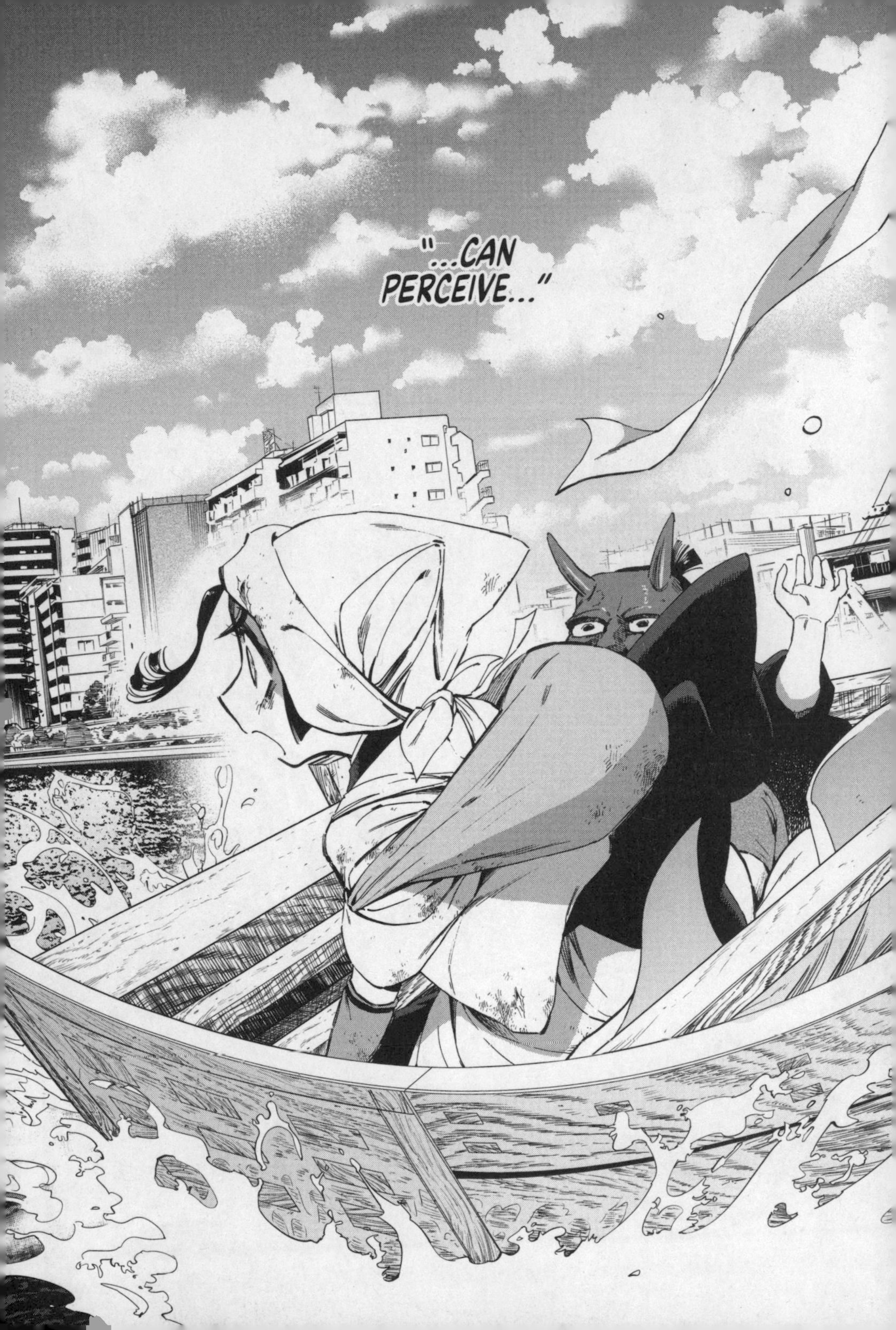
"...CAN PERCEIVE..."

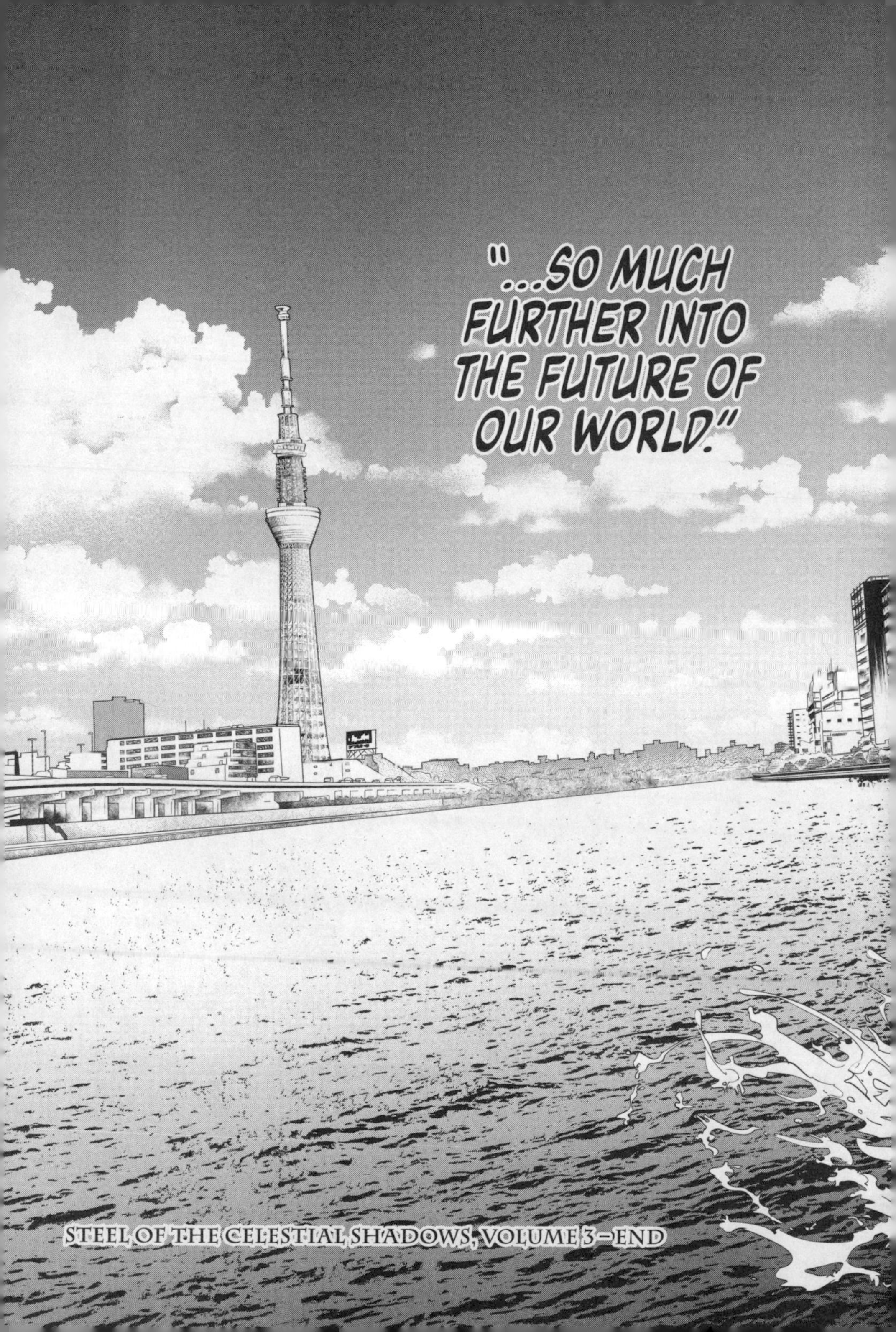
"...SO MUCH FURTHER INTO THE FUTURE OF OUR WORLD."
STEEL OF THE CELESTIAL SHADOWS, VOLUME 3—END

WITH HELP FROM

(in no particular order,
and with titles omitted)

My Staff

Saburo Kirigakure

Doom Kobayashi

Masashi Motegi (Tadashi Sato)

Satoko Matsumoto

Hiroto Yokoyama

Subaru Niina

Takanashi

Fuki Hinohara

Saki Toda

Daichi Kawada

CONSULTANTS

Noboru Hisayama

Toshiki Mizutani

ORIGINAL DESIGN

Kohei Nawata Design Office

RESEARCH ASSISTANCE

Kazuya Namiki
[Jikishinkage-ryu Kuunkai]

Akira Takemoto

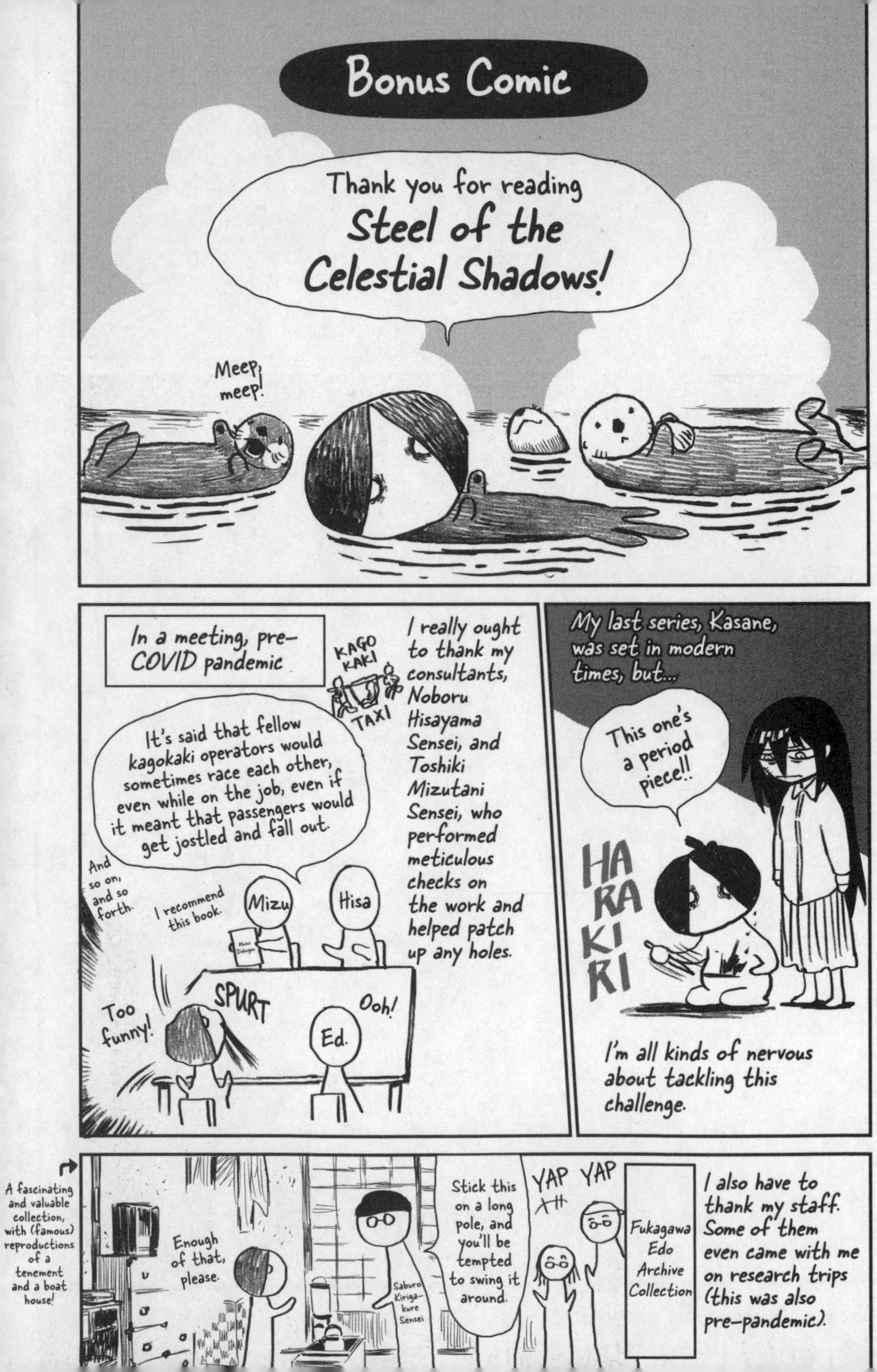

Bonus Comic
Thank you for reading Steel of the Celestial Shadows!
Meep, meep!
My last series, Kasane, was set in modern times, but...
This one's a period piece!!
HARAKIRI
I'm all kinds of nervous about tackling this challenge.
I really ought to thank my consultants, Noboru Hisayama Sensei, and Toshiki Mizutani Sensei, who performed meticulous checks on the work and helped patch up any holes.
In a meeting, pre-COVID pandemic
KAGO KAKI
TAXI
It's said that fellow kagokaki operators would sometimes race each other, even while on the job, even if it meant that passengers would get jostled and fall out.
Hisa
Mizu
I recommend this book.
And so on, and so forth.
Ooh!
SPURT
Too funny!
Ed.
I also have to thank my staff. Some of them even came with me on research trips (this was also pre-pandemic).
Fukagawa Edo Archive Collection
YAP YAP
Stick this on a long pole, and you'll be tempted to swing it around.
Saburo Kirigakure Sensei
Enough of that, please.
A fascinating and valuable collection, with (famous) reproductions of a tenement and a boat house!

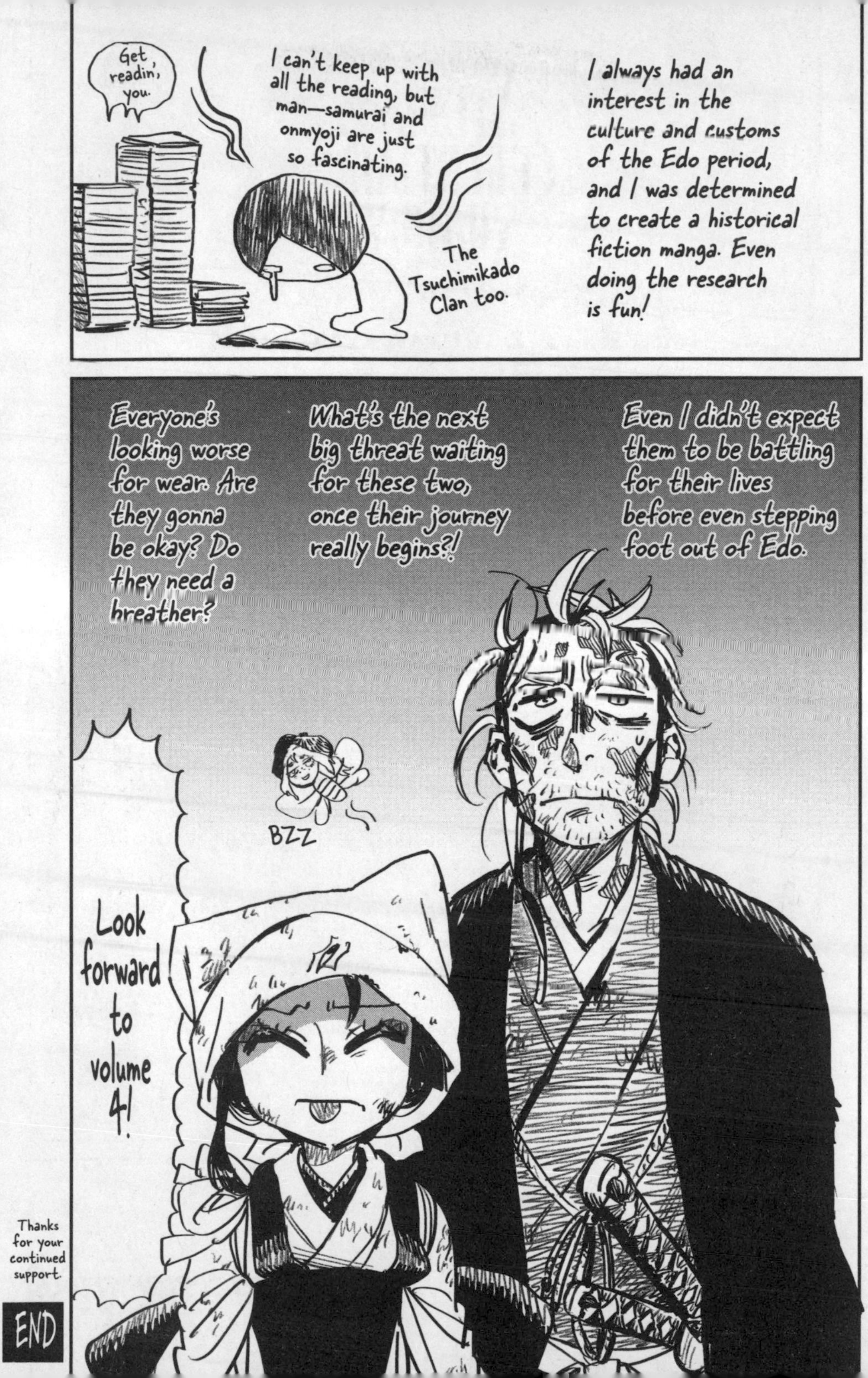
I always had an interest in the culture and customs of the Edo period, and I was determined to create a historical fiction manga. Even doing the research is fun!
I can't keep up with all the reading, but man—samurai and onmyoji are just so fascinating.
The Tsuchimikado Clan too.
Get readin', you.
Even I didn't expect them to be battling for their lives before even stepping foot out of Edo.
What's the next big threat waiting for these two, once their journey really begins?!
Everyone's looking worse for wear. Are they gonna be okay? Do they need a breather?
BZZ
Look forward to volume 4!
Thanks for your continued support.
END

STEEL of the CELESTIAL SHADOWS

Volume 3 • VIZ Signature Edition

Story & Art by DARUMA MATSUURA

Daruma Matsuura was born in 1984 in Kanagawa prefecture.
Her debut series, *Kasane*, was serialized in 2013 and made into a live-action film in 2018. Other works include *Imakako* and *Utakata to Tomoshibi*. *Steel of the Celestial Shadows* is currently serialized in *Big Comic Superior* from Shogakukan. Her favorite sushi is uni.

TRANSLATION Caleb Cook
TOUCH-UP ART & LETTERING Steve Dutro
DESIGN Shawn Carrico
EDITOR Mike Montesa

TAIYO TO TSUKI NO HAGANE Vol. 3
by Daruma MATSUURA
© 2020 Daruma MATSUURA
All rights reserved.
Original Japanese edition published by SHOGAKUKAN. English translation rights
in the United States of America, Canada, the United Kingdom, Ireland, Australia,
and New Zealand arranged with SHOGAKUKAN.

SUPERVISION BY Toshiki MIZUTANI/Noboru HISAYAMA
ORIGINAL COVER DESIGN Kohei Nawata Design Office

The stories, characters, and incidents mentioned in this publication are entirely fictional.

Printed in Canada

Published by VIZ Media, LLC
P.O. Box 77010
San Francisco, CA 94107

10 9 8 7 6 5 4 3 2 1
First printing, July 2024

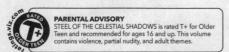

PARENTAL ADVISORY
STEEL OF THE CELESTIAL SHADOWS is rated T+ for Older
Teen and recommended for ages 16 and up. This volume
contains violence, partial nudity, and adult themes.

VIZ SIGNATURE
vizsignature.com